The Philosopher's Voice

SUNY series in Philosophy
George R. Lucas Jr., editor

The Philosopher's Voice

Philosophy, Politics, and Language in the Nineteenth Century

Andrew Fiala

STATE UNIVERSITY OF NEW YORK PRESS

Published by
State University of New York Press, Albany

Printed in the United States of America

For information, address State University of New York Press,
90 State Street, Suite 700, Albany, NY 12207

Production by Diane Ganeles
Marketing by Fran Keneston

Library of Congress Cataloging-in-Publication Data

Fiala, Andrew G. (Andrew Gordon), 1966–
The philosopher's voice: philosophy, politics, and language in the nineteenth century/ Andrew Fiala.
p. cm. — (SUNY series in philosophy)
Includes bibliographical references and index.
ISBN 0-7914-5483-5 (alk. paper) — ISBN 0-7914-5484-3 (pbk. : alk. paper)
1. Philosophy—History—19th century. 2. Political science—History—19th century. I. Title. II. Series.

B65 .F5 2002
190'.9'034—dc21 2002021818

10 9 8 7 6 5 4 3 2 1

Contents

Acknowledgments

Many people have contributed to the completion of this project. My thinking about this topic began with my dissertation on Hegel's *Philosophy of Right* at Vanderbilt University. I would like to thank my advisors for that project, John Sallis, John Lachs, David Wood, Gregg Horowitz, Idit Dobbs-Weinstein, and Victor Anderson. Further thanks goes to John Lachs who offered suggestions on early drafts of my outline of the present project and who provided moral support and inspiration as I continued to work on it. I would also like to thank Scott Zeman who criticized the chapters on Marx; Robert Metcalf who critiqued the chapters on Fichte; Jere Surber who offered me insight into Fichte's philosophy of language and the metacritique of Kant; and Sarah Cunningham who critiqued an early version of what became the chapters on Kant. Finally, I would like to thank my family for their support and patience as I completed this project: Julaine, Gordon, Don, Peggy, Bodhi, Tahoe, and Valerie.

CHAPTER 1

Introduction: The Philosopher's Voice

Voice and Philosophy

> Besides colors, it is especially *sounds* (*die Töne*) which evoke in us a corresponding mood (*Stimmung*). This is chiefly true of the human *voice* (*Stimme*); for this is the principal way in which a person shows forth his inner nature; what he is, that he puts into his voice.
>
> —Hegel, *Encyclopedia*[1]

Voice is the origin of philosophy, politics, and poetry. Voice is the medium in which persons commune with one another by communicating their thoughts. It is the conjunction of body, mind, and community. It is the material medium by which we expose ourselves to one another, by which we persuade one another, by which we pursue together the truth, and by which we create and share ideas and emotions. Voice is the mechanism by which the inner becomes outer. It is the source of dialectic and inspiration as well as the source of manipulation and coercion. Voice joins the universal and necessary laws of logic to a particular and contingent locus in space and time. All voices are embodied: they speak in concrete historically defined languages; they speak from a definite social and political position; and they address a concrete politically located audience. A voice is philosophical insofar as it is the active appearance of thinking, which aims beyond these historical contingencies toward the universal. The voice of philosophy is a mutual communication aimed at provoking thought in order to call forth truth. A voice is poetic insofar as it is actively creative. The voice of poetry sings, rejoices, mourns, and inspires. Such poetic vocalization aims at evoking a mood, feeling, or idea. Voice is political insofar as it is the mechanism for distributing social goods, for persuading others about legitimate distributions, or for invoking authority.

A continual problem for philosophy is to distinguish itself from poetic and political voices. This is a problem because philosophers cannot guarantee that their voices will be heard properly amid the cacophony of political life. As Aristotle noted, there are many other species of social animals, but only humans speak about justice. However, speaking about justice is not a simple task. Political life includes a complex web of interconnected voices. It resounds with the voices of the oppressed and the oppressors, the silenced and the silencers. Lately we have learned that political life is—and perhaps should be—polyphonic. It is both the raucous din and the harmonious symphony of a plurality of voices. Amid this polyphony, while political voices use poetic rhetoric to attain political ends at the expense of philosophical truth, the philosopher's voice struggles to articulate the question of justice that is the heart of political philosophy.

Despite the fact that philosophical thinking is expressed by particular, contingent, historically and politically located voices, the philosopher's voice is somehow different from the other voices of political life. Most notably, the philosophical goal of critical self-consciousness demands that philosophy account for the sound of its own voice. The philosopher must locate his/her own voice within the multiple voices of political life in order to differentiate his/her voice from those others with which it is often confused. The most difficult problem for political philosophy is to speak to a political audience while also speaking differently than the political voices, which also address that audience. Political philosophers who seek the truth about justice and political life must speak of politics while not speaking politically. They must deliberately revoke the poetic flourishes of political rhetoric in order to make sure that truth is revealed. Of course this is not a simple task because philosophers are political and poetic beings who speak in a historical language to an embodied audience. Like these other voices, the voice of philosophy also seeks to inspire and persuade. However, the norms of philosophical inspiration and persuasion are different from the norms of political and poetic speech.

Philosophy has struggled to defend these norms for millennia. This struggle has required philosophy to use its voice to defend itself against the voices of political interrogators. Socrates, for example, initiated his apology with the following words: "how you, men of Athens, have been affected by my accusers, I do not know."[2] His voice cried out to the crowd, addressing his audience by name, initiating and enacting the dialectic between philosophy and politics. Socrates' apology provides us with a vivid example of the dilemma of political philosophy: it is an attempt to comprehend political life within a broader purview that always remains tied to the partisan squabbles of political life. Socrates asked the members of his audience to look beyond their immediate interests in order to properly hear his voice, a voice that sought a higher good, which includes and reinterprets political life. He appealed to the philosophical imagination of the men of Athens and sought to encourage them in the pursuit of virtue by asking them to consider a truth about justice that transcends partisan politics and personal bias.

The problem for Socrates, and indeed for all philosophers, is that the philosophical imagination is often not yet active in the political audience. Moreover, philosophers are constrained by a normative conception of the philosopher's voice. While philosophers must use their voices to teach the political audience to hear differently, they ought not use their voices to persuade the political audience by way of rhetorical tricks because such persuasion no longer conforms to the norms established for the philosopher's voice.[3] The voice of the philosopher is thus at risk when it addresses a political audience because the political audience may not believe that the philosopher's voice initiates a disinterested pursuit of the good and that it is constrained by norms which run contrary to the standard practice of political persuasion. Nonetheless, philosophy must address a political audience. The philosopher's voice is, at least in part, an embodied, political voice: it is a voice that occurs within a given particular moment of history that is also directed toward a given particular political audience. The political nature of the philosopher's voice often leads to tragedy—as in the case of Socrates—because the political audience does not believe that the philosopher pursues a disinterested *elenchos*, a method of teaching devoted to disclosing truth. Rather, the political audience hears the philosopher's voice—including its own claims about its normative commitment to the truth—as merely another political voice dedicated to the political art of persuasion. The political audience cannot yet properly hear the philosophical voice, which would teach it how to hear differently. Rather, the political audience hears the philosopher's voice echoing through the agonistics of political life, where voice is used to manipulate and coerce but not to disclose truth.

This tragedy continues to repeat itself throughout the history of philosophy. Indeed, the continual repetition of this conflict would almost be comical, if it were not for its deadly seriousness. This tragicomedy seems to require a resolution in both philosophy and politics. One way of approaching such a resolution is to properly understand the nature of the philosopher's voice and the way in which its disclosive function differs from the persuasive function of a truly political voice. Socrates and Plato began this endeavor over two millennia ago. We continue to struggle with it today. A crucial moment of clarity about this struggle occurred in the nineteenth century, in the self-consciousness of voice that occurred in the development of thought from Kant to Hegel. Ironically, the very attempt to clarify the difference between the voices of philosophy and politics led to the repoliticization of the philosopher's voice by thinkers such as Fichte and Marx, who rejected the Kantian and Hegelian attempts to distinguish philosophy from politics. The present book attempts to consider the problem of the relation between philosophy, politics, and language, as it was instantiated in the thought and lives of Kant, Fichte, Hegel, and Marx.[4]

The Philosopher's Voice and the Problem of Enlightenment

> The articulate sound is torn from the breast, to awaken in another individual an echo returning to the ear. Man thereby at once discovers that around him there are beings having the same inner needs, and thus capable of meeting the manifold longing that resides in his feelings.
>
> —Humboldt, *On the Diversity of Human Language Construction and its Influence on the Mental Development of the Human Species*[5]

The focal point of the conflict between philosophy and politics is the philosopher's voice. A full consideration of the philosopher's voice must include an understanding of its quality as physical reverberation emanating from the real body of the philosopher in space and time. It must also include a consideration of the origins of language and its evolution from the emotional outbursts of our animal bodies to the abstract discourse of philosophical systems. Finally, it must consider the social and historical constraints imposed by the fact of linguistic diversity. These topics became explicit matters for philosophical concern in the nineteenth century, as can be seen, for example, in the writings of Wilhelm von Humboldt. Indeed, this concern with language grows out of the work of Leibniz in the late seventeenth century and Rousseau, Herder, and Hamman in the eighteenth.[6] By the nineteenth century, it was not remarkable that language should be a focus of philosophical concern. This was especially true given the historical context of the late eighteenth and early nineteenth centuries. European intellectuals, as a result of colonialism and imperialism, were beginning to comprehend the true nature of the diversity of languages. Moreover, this era was a time of rapid expansion of literacy, literature in vernacular languages, and political rights. European understanding of language was developing, just as the nature of political justice was expanding to recognize the bourgeoisie and eventually the proletariat. This historical situation resulted in a critical self-examination of the role that philosophy should have in leading the project of enlightenment.

The present book looks at this development by examining conceptions of philosophical method, rhetoric, philosophy of language, and political philosophy found in the development from Kant to Fichte, Hegel, and Marx. I focus on these thinkers, not because of the depth of their philosophies of language—indeed, their philosophies of language are often not explicit—but rather because of the importance of their political philosophies. One of my goals is to make explicit the philosophy of language that is implicit in these thinkers and to connect it with their political philosophies. Each of these thinkers represents a unique approach to the question of the proper relation between philosophy and politics. Although none of them offers a complete philosophy of voice, they each have something important to say about the link between philosophy, politics, and language.

Hegel says, for example, as quoted at the outset of the present chapter, that the voice (*die Stimme*) "is the principal way in which a person shows forth his inner nature."[7] The voice of the philosopher would be, according to this account, the point at which the "inner" spirit of philosophy enters the real material world of political life. In this transition of inner to outer, the conflict between philosophy and politics arises. For the most part, a political audience is persuaded by the *sound* of a voice: its intonations, inflections, location, and direction—as Hegel says, its "power to evoke in us a corresponding mood."[8] Despite the fact that the philosopher always has a voice in this sense—he or she inevitably vocalizes and externalizes the inner spiritual content of his/her thought—i.e., despite the material basis of philosophy in the embodied human voice, philosophers tend to use their voices to point beyond the material power of sound toward the "higher" more spiritual content of what Hegel calls "language [*Sprache*]": "the sound [*Ton*] which articulates itself further for determinate representations—speech [*die Rede*] and its system, language [*die Sprache*]—gives to sensations, intuitions, conceptions, a second and higher existence than their immediate existence—it gives them an existence which is valid in the realm of representation [*im Reiche des Vorstellens*]."[9] The spiritual content transmitted (sent across space in speech and time in writing) by the material medium of sound, when interpreted philosophically, is *logos* or reason: the universal idea that transcends the particularity of the voice which speaks it. Hegel's analysis leads us to the general problem of communication. How can material sound communicate the "higher" inner stuff of spirit without corrupting this spiritual content? The difference between language and voice indicates a problem in distinguishing that which is to be sent (language, *logos*, reason) from the medium in which it is sent (voice, sound, and written language). I should note at this point that I will for the most part ignore the difference between spoken and written language. Both of these are instances of voice. As we shall see, however, Hegel at least, does attempt to distinguish spoken language from written.

The problem of communication lies at the heart of the problem of philosophy and its political integument. This problem might seem to be exacerbated by the fact of diversity of languages: can a universal idea be expressed in a variety of languages? Or is there a properly philosophical language? This question has obvious political overtones and was considered variously by Leibniz, Herder, Fichte, Hegel, and Humboldt. The question of German nationalism thus lies just below the surface of much of this discussion. The history of the twentieth century gives us sufficient reason to be concerned with the way in which linguistic and philosophical nationalism can be tied to political tyranny. As we move into the cosmopolitan and multicultural world of the twenty-first century, the relation between language, rhetoric, philosophy, and politics continues to be a problem linked to questions of diversity, identity, and universality. The basic problem of cultural relativism can be understood as a problem of the relation between the diversity of linguistic expressions and ways of life and the supposed unity of the moral law and the universality of human rights.

Kant, the philosopher most closely associated with the idea of universal human rights and the cosmopolitan League of Nations, was not unaware of these problems. Although he was ultimately interested in pushing beyond the question of voice toward the universal truth of reason and the moral law, he did recognize the importance of style and form. In the *Anthropology,* in a consideration of good taste with regard to politeness and manners, Kant considers the way in which language helps us to communicate and participate in the goods of sociability. Kant goes so far as to claim that good manners have a tendency toward "the external advancement of morality."[10] This is so because the tendency to try to please others in speech and action is a rudimentary moral tendency. In other words, acting well and speaking properly are external "appearances" of inner morality: "morality in external appearance (*äußeren Erscheinung*)."[11] Kant states this, even though he admits that, strictly speaking, there is a contradiction implied in speaking of morality's outward appearance: morality is, for Kant, a matter of the good will in itself and not a matter of external action. Nonetheless, Kant concludes by claiming that poetry (*Dichtkunst*) and rhetoric (*Beredsamkeit*) are both examples of "the discursive way of imagining (*die discursive Vorstellungsart*) through the spoken or written word (*durch laute Sprache oder durch Schrift*)."[12] Speaking well (*Beredsamkeit*) might thus seem to be a way in which the inner truth of morality can make its appearance, a way of stimulating the imagination so as to be able to properly hear the philosophical content of speech, despite the fact that philosophy and morality are not supposed to be dependent upon concerns such as eloquence and politeness.

The problem of rhetoric, which Kant confronts in the *Anthropology,* is a reiteration of the basic problem with which he struggled in his transcendental idealism: how is one to distinguish the in-itself from the appearance? Kant is aware that we tend to be confused by the difference between form and content, appearance, and reality. In another section of the *Anthropology,* Kant condemns rhetorical skill for its tendency to deceive its audience and confuse the distinction between form and content. "The art, or rather the skill, of speaking in the socially proper tone, and appearing to be up-to-date, especially when the conversation is about science, is falsely called popularity, but should rather be called polished superficiality (*Seichtigkeit*) because it frequently cloaks the paltriness of a narrow-minded person. Only children can be fooled by this."[13] There are clear links here between Kant's understanding of critical enlightenment and his disapprobation of rhetorical skill. While Kant says in the *Anthropology* that only children can be fooled by rhetorical skill, in his response to the question "What is Enlightenment?" he says that "enlightenment is man's emergence from his self-incurred immaturity."[14] Critical rationality, then, involves the ability to see through rhetorical skill to the content that lies behind the form of its appearance. In other words, enlightenment is the ability to hear the *language* which is conveyed by the *sounds* of human speech; it is the ability to listen to the truth beyond rhetoric.

Unfortunately, we are not born with this ability. For the most part we only hear the surface of voice. We are susceptible to political manipulation because we are unable to penetrate beyond hearing to listening. As we shall see, Kant's disciple, Fichte, despaired of being properly listened to. He recognized the fundamental difficulty which his audience had in attending to the truths of transcendental idealism. He blamed this inability upon a deficient educational system and a degenerate political life. Fichte then took up the task of engaging political life on its own terms, by speaking its own language. Unlike Socrates, however, Fichte fully appropriated the rhetoric of political persuasion in order to prepare his audience to listen to his philosophical voice. Nonetheless, Fichte remained committed to the cosmopolitan moral vision of the Kantian project. Thus, unlike Marx who took up political rhetoric in earnest and viewed claims about the integrity of the philosopher's voice as a rhetorical strategy within political life, Fichte remained committed to an idealized conception of the philosopher's voice. The problem with this approach, however, is that it reaffirms the political audience's suspicions that the philosopher's voice is no different from the politician's. Indeed this is Marx's conclusion, as he finally rejects the Kantian and Hegelian attempts to differentiate philosophy from politics.

As Kant notes in "What is Enlightenment?" enlightenment requires the public use of reason, it requires speech addressed to others. However, the voice of enlightenment risks being misheard and confused with the superficiality of the rhetoric that conveys it. There are two iterations of this problem: a problem of reception and a problem of transmission. The problem of reception stems from the fact that there are always two ways in which we can "receive" the human voice. We can *hear* the physical, tonal quality of the voice or we can *listen to* the meaning conveyed through the voice. The first of these focuses on the rhetorical, persuasive, poetic, and indeed political mode of speech: *hearing* is a mode of reception that focuses upon the visceral quality of sound, its power to evoke vivid representations without invoking judgment about these representations, its power to compel reaction without reflection. This mode is primarily passive and reactive. The second focuses upon the philosophical, logical mode of speech: *listening to* is a mode of reception that focuses upon the logos transmitted by sound and thus invokes reflection and judgment about the representations evoked by the sound.[15] This mode of reception is active and is thus not merely receptive. It actively searches for meanings and reasons that lie beyond the sounds which were "passively" received. The problem of transmission stems from the fact that there are two analogous ways in which we can "speak." We can speak so as to persuade and sway our audience without provoking them actively to judge the content of our speech; such is the voice of poetry and politics. Or we can speak so as to transmit language and provoke active judgment about the content of our speech; such is the voice of philosophy.

Since both of the iterations of the problem involve the proper relation between judgment and voice, activity and passivity, this problem is not merely a philosophical problem, it is also a political problem. Given the fact that philosophical speech always occurs within the context of a given form of political life, the challenge for the philosopher is to synthesize both of these modes within his/her own voice so as to teach the political audience to listen properly, i.e., to *teach* the members of the political audience to exercise their active judgment upon the content of what is spoken without succumbing to the temptation to use the persuasive techniques of rhetoric. This was the problem of the Socratic *elenchos* and is also the ongoing problem of enlightenment: how to exercise public reason in such a way as to stimulate judgment in others without succumbing to the temptation to force one's own judgment upon those others by way of rhetorical tricks. The problem is that any synthesis of philosophical reflection and rhetorical skill such as must occur when the philosopher addresses the public always risks being misunderstood as merely another political ploy that uses persuasive rhetoric to stimulate passive/reactive judgment, rather than being an effort to stimulate active, enlightened judgment. In this way, the conflict between philosophy and politics is centered on the problem of voice.

Can the philosopher speak such that his or her voice will contribute to enlightenment without being misheard as merely another voice in the rhetorical cacophony of the political realm with "enlightenment" itself being misunderstood as code for some sort of hidden political agenda? Since there is no way to guarantee that his/her voice will be received properly, that it will be *listened to* as well as *heard*, the philosopher is always subject to political misunderstanding. Moreover, since the audience has no guarantee that the voice of a so-called philosopher is not merely another political voice, they have no guarantee that the "philosopher's" admonitions about enlightened judgment are not merely part of a very clever rhetorical ploy. Such was Marx's criticism of Hegel and his followers. Marx viewed the Hegelians as bourgeois apologists. Their rhetoric of "reason," "spirit," and "the absolute" was merely an attempt to sanctify the ideas of the ruling class. Thus Marx famously concludes in the *Manifesto* that "the ruling ideas of each age have ever been the ideas of its ruling class."

It is clear that "enlightened" philosophers require a sophisticated self-consciousness of the status of their own voices. Recent scholarship has begun to recognize the self-conscious style of Kant, the philosopher most closely associated with the concept of enlightenment. Hans Saner pioneered this approach to Kant with an analysis of the relation between Kant's transcendental and political philosophy, with an explication of Kant's polemical style, and an account of Kant's use of metaphor.[16] Dieter Henrich has also argued that Kant was a self-conscious stylist and that the political metaphors which haunt his critical philosophy are not accidental.[17] Willi Goetschel extends this account of Kant's rhetoric even further and argues implicitly throughout his *Constituting Critique* that Kant's recognition of the dilemmas imposed upon philosophical writing by the problem of addressing one's audience in the proper voice is a core issue in Kant's writing. Goetschel claims that Kant's awareness of the dialectical nature of the public-private distinction informs all of Kant's writings. He concludes by claiming that Kant was aware that his own philosophical activity was itself produced by the demands of the public realm.[18] Recent scholarship thus indicates that Kant was explicitly aware of the nature of his own activity as produced by a certain historically determinate form of political life, addressed back to political life, and even subject to misinterpretation within this form of political life. It is this self-consciousness of the sound of his own voice that leads to Kant and his follower's characteristically turgid style: they are trying to articulate their own self-consciousness of the limits of their language from within this very language.

Goetschel's intriguing analysis of Kant's use of literary devices indicates that it is Kant's republican ideal of justification that leads him to develop an explicit concern for his readers. However, Goetschel does not believe that this concern for the philosophical audience remains a concern in the subsequent development of German idealism. He states with regard to Kant that "such concern for his readers on the part of the philosopher is rather rare—for Hegel, for instance, who seems to address the absolute Spirit as his reader, it would be unthinkable."[19] This claim, which Goetschel leaves undeveloped, is one I argue against in what follows. I will argue that the self-conscious use of rhetoric that Goetschel demonstrates in Kant is also present in Fichte, Hegel, and Marx. While Goetschel is correct, for example, to state that Hegel addresses absolute spirit, this does not mean that Hegel is unaware of the presence of his readers and of the need for an adequate mode of presentation of his system. Indeed the systematic tendencies of Kant, Fichte, Hegel, and Marx—their need to account for the origin of their own process of thinking—leads them to be acutely aware of the use and abuse of rhetoric in philosophy. Moreover, their recognition of the historical and political situatedness of philosophical thought leads them to make the dilemma posed by the rhetorical and political nature of philosophy a central focal point of their political theory and practice. The philosophers of the nineteenth century attempted to resolve the dilemma of the philosopher's voice exposed by Kant's concept of enlightenment by thinking about the following question: how can a philosopher use his/her voice to enlighten his/her compatriots when this political audience will inevitably hear the philosopher's voice as merely another political voice resounding with the persuasive techniques of rhetoric? Although their answers differ radically, they were each aware of the importance of the question.

Situating the Dilemma

> The reform of consciousness consists *only* in making the world aware of its own consciousness, in awakening it out of its dream about itself, in *explaining* to it the meaning of its own actions.
>
> —Marx, "For a Ruthless Criticism of Everything Existing"[20]

Critical philosophy occurs in the space opened by the dilemma of the philosopher's voice as an attempt to clarify the difference between philosophy and politics. The need for critical clarification of this difference develops out of political life's lack of self-consciousness, its lack of enlightenment. This lack of self-consciousness makes it necessary for philosophy to continually defend itself against political misinterpretation. Political life cannot properly comprehend philosophy because it lacks philosophical enlightenment and cannot hear the subtle differences between the voice of the philosopher and the voice of the politician. Thus, the philosopher must continually defend, explain, and clarify the peculiar sound of his/her voice. Marx indicates that this is the nature of critical philosophy and of the age of enlightenment: "self-clarification (critical philosophy) to be gained by the present time of its struggles and desires. This is a work for the world and for us."[21] The ambiguity of Marx's claim is important. The struggle for enlightenment is a struggle situated in time and space. It is a work of our time in the sense that philosophy is itself a product of our time that focuses its critical activity back upon our time. Enlightenment would be self-consciousness of the dilemma. Said otherwise, enlightenment would be self-consciousness of the difference between political and philosophical speech, even when this self-consciousness amounts to denying the difference as in Marx's critique of Hegel.

Of course this dilemma is not limited in time and space to the nineteenth century. We see this dilemma again and again throughout the history of philosophy. Socrates' voice, his words, his manner of speaking, his arguments, diatribes, and dialogues—all of this is the very subject matter of his indictment.

The material impact of his voice resounds doubly throughout his apology. On the one hand, his voice is the only resource that he can employ in his defense. On the other, it is the strangeness of his voice, a voice unaccustomed to political speech and yet intimately involved in the life of the polis, which led to his indictment. The Athenians indicted the specific quality of Socrates' voice: the voice of a peculiar citizen who is guided by the daemons of philosophy. Ironically, this is the very voice that came before the Athenian assembly in defense of itself, futilely asking its audience to hear it otherwise, to *listen to* and *judge* it according to its content and not merely according to its rhetorical power. Thus, in responding to the indictment of the political community with his philosophical voice, Socrates effectively seals his fate and condemns himself to death by renouncing persuasion and remaining committed to the process of teaching. Socrates' voice was judged by a political audience according to political criteria, i.e., it was judged according to its persuasive power. Since Socrates avoided deliberate use of persuasive rhetoric, he cannot persuade his audience to judge him according to other criteria. Nor can he teach them otherwise, for, as I noted earlier, his political audience lacked philosophical imagination.

Socrates' case could be interpreted as an example of mishearing, a failure on the part of his audience to properly receive his words. One might conclude that his audience failed to *listen to* the language, in Hegel's sense (i.e., the *logos* or reason), behind his speech. However, what is significant about Socrates' case is that he is self-conscious of the fact that the failure of language and of reason is not merely a matter of mishearing but also of misspeaking. He speaks of the very issue of his own inability to speak in a properly political voice and is thus aware of the fact that his voice will be misheard. By misspeaking to the Athenian assembly, he effectively *teaches* us about the problem that lies at the heart of philosophy's political integument. The problem still remains, however: as long as the political audience lacks a developed philosophical imagination, the philosopher's admission of his inability to speak in a politically persuasive voice will still be heard as merely another rhetorical ploy.

The philosopher's voice has had to defend itself before courts of political judgment ever since Socrates asked his political audience to listen to the language conveyed by his voice. Moreover, philosophical audiences have heard, in the reverberations of the voices of philosophers silenced by political authority, a trenchant indictment of the injustice of political life. For centuries, from Socrates to Boethius, from Cicero to Russell, the voice of philosophy has addressed political life and has been addressed by political authority. Often, as in the above examples, this voice has been indicted by political power as a strange and treacherous threat to its authority. Often this voice indicts political life as biased, illogical, and ultimately unjust. And yet, throughout the history of the struggle between philosophy and politics, the philosopher's voice has also been embraced by power, from Aristotle's service to Alexander to Heidegger's service to the Nazi regime, from the American constitution's appropriation of Locke to Russian Communism's deification of Marx. One wonders about the differences in this odd dialectical history: why does one philosopher's voice antagonize power, while another's is accepted by it as an ally? Clearly the content of the philosopher's speech is important, as is the type of political power that confronts the philosopher's speech. Moreover, the philosopher's voice itself is important: the demeanor with which the philosopher addresses power, the geographical and historical location of the philosopher's utterance, the intended audience of the philosopher's speech, and the philosopher's stature within the political community.

Twenty-four hundred years after the death of Socrates, following in the wake of Kant, Fichte, Hegel, and Marx, the issue of the philosopher's voice has become an explicit matter of concern for political philosophers. A quite different voice, the voice of a woman, Iris Marion Young, makes this issue explicit in the introduction to her *Justice and the Politics of Difference:* "Philosophers acknowledge the partiality of the audience to which their arguments are addressed, it seems to me, often even less than they acknowledge the particularity of the voice of their writing."[22] Young claims that political philosophers must recognize the particularity of their own voices and refrain from trying to speak in the monological voice of an imperial reason. Our current fascination with the material reverberations of the voice of philosophy stems in part from the twentieth century's general obsession with language, itself a result of the growth of philosophy of language in the eighteenth and nineteenth centuries. Wittgenstein, for example, understood philosophy as clarification of language. "The results of philosophy are the uncovering of one or another piece of plain nonsense and of bumps that the understanding has got by running its head up against the limits of language."[23] It is the philosopher's task to expose these limits, as it were, from the inside. Gadamer made the same point from another perspective: "All human speaking is finite in such a way that there is laid up within it an infinity of meaning to be explicated and laid out."[24] Gadamerian hermeneutics amount to a continual circulation within the limits of language. The conclusion of both of these ways of thinking is that we cannot escape from our own linguistic context: philosophy is located at a certain point in space, time, language, and culture.

Moreover, multiculturalism and feminism have taught us that there are indeed different voices and that within this plurality of voices there is the continual possibility of misunderstanding. As Carol Gilligan concludes: "men and women may speak different languages that they assume are the same, using similar words to encode disparate experiences of self and social relationships."[25] Problems arise when we assume that there is some one voice that transcends the limits of these different voices, that each speaker means the same thing when he or she speaks, or that each listener hears the same words in the same way. The philosophy of the twentieth century has shown us that philosophy cannot attain the position of a disembodied transcendental subject who addresses the universal truths of the human being.

The bloody history of political life in the twentieth century has shown us that attempts to address finite human beings in a universal voice lead to perverse cruelties. The claims of the universal monological subject often become obsessed with homogeneity, purity, and unity at the expense of those others who do not fit the master narrative of monological reason. Young's politics of difference is a deliberate attempt to re-introduce into political philosophy the notion that the voice of the political philosopher is a spatially, temporally, and culturally located voice. I say "re-introduce" because this notion was already present in Socrates' address to the Athenians just as it was present, as we shall see, in the political philosophies of Kant, Fichte, Hegel, and Marx.

Accusations against the monological imperialism of philosophy are often aimed at the systematic philosophers of the nineteenth century specifically, Kant, Fichte, Hegel, and Marx. Ironically, these philosophers are also appealed to in attempts to break the hold of monological reason. These thinkers are often indicted for speaking in the monological voice of the transcendental ego, spirit, or the proletariat. At the same time, these thinkers are appealed to as progenitors of that type of critical dialectical reason that is offered as an antidote for monological reason. For instance, Seyla Benhabib claims that "Kantian ethics is monological, for it proceeds from the standpoint of the rational person, defined in such a way that differences among concrete selves become quite irrelevant."[26] Benhabib then appeals to Hegel and Marx—whom she admits inherited much from Kant—as forerunners of a more complete dialogical model of philosophical discourse. On the other hand, Karl Popper criticizes Hegel (and by implication Marx) for engaging in what he calls "oracular philosophy."[27] The problem is that, with Hegel, meaning becomes historically and culturally determined and thus, "a new kind of dogmatism becomes fashionable, in philosophy as well as in the social sciences. It confronts us with its dictum. And we can take it or leave it."[28] In other words, Popper accuses Hegel of consistently avoiding a dialogue with his readers in order to pronounce the truth from the oracular perspective of the famous owl of Minerva. Popper concludes his critique of Hegel and Marx's historicism by appealing to a historicism of his own: "Interpretations are important since they represent a point of view. But we have seen that a point of view is always inevitable . . ."[29] Popper does not recognize, however, that the issue of points of view is a crucial one for both Hegel and Marx. Indeed, each of the four philosophers we will discuss in what follows recognized the importance of understanding the location of one's voice.

The imperious, monological model of reason occasionally imputed to nineteenth century philosophers has been under attack for some time. After the critiques of thinkers such as Nietzsche, Freud, Adorno, Foucault, Lyotard, Derrida, James, Wittgenstein, and Rorty we can no longer believe that the voice of the philosopher is the voice of universal reason that can speak from everywhere and nowhere. As Habermas concludes: "master thinkers have fallen on hard times."[30] The problem for Habermas, however, is that "postmodern" critiques of philosophy themselves reiterate the problem of voice: "these discourses can and want to give no account of their own position."[31] Habermas calls for a return to Hegelian dialectics, albeit with a Kantian twist. Recent returns to Hegelian dialectics are themselves ironic, therefore, because Hegel was long considered to be one of those "master thinkers" who had fallen on hard times. Adorno's and Lyotard's critiques of Hegel themselves remain Hegelian, at least to the extent that they charge Hegel with not being enough of a dialectian himself to see the negativity that remains within the dialectic.

Does the tradition that includes Kant, Fichte, Hegel, and Marx represent the origin or the end of the monological tradition in philosophy? In what follows I argue that it is both. This tradition creates an awareness of the inevitable political sound of the philosopher's voice while also providing us with hope that we may become self-conscious enough of this to transcend it. It inspires us to pursue the norms of truth that govern the philosopher's voice while recognizing the inevitable politicization of these norms within the plurality of audiences to whom the philosopher must speak. The argument of the present text is that the issue of the location and embodiment of the philosopher's voice was a serious issue for these philosophers and that the roots of our contemporary realization of the importance of this issue can be found in these philosophers' thought, especially in their thought about political life and about the relation between philosophy and politics. Finally, I argue that in nineteenth century German philosophy, the importance of the political location of the philosopher's voice becomes a philosophical issue as philosophical judgment itself becomes defined in political terms. Kant, Fichte, Hegel, and Marx each explicitly recognize the political orientation of the philosopher's voice and its relation to power. They differ to the extent that each resolves the dilemma of the philosopher's voice differently; they agree to the extent that each recognizes the importance of situating and resolving this dilemma.

As we shall see, these philosophers address political life with their voices and offer theoretical accounts of the political importance of the philosopher's voice. They each occupied a similar position as Socrates in his address to the Athenian jury: they addressed the polis both as members of the polis but also as philosophers whose voices sought to transcend the finite perspectives of political life. Other philosophers have occupied this position before and after the era that stretched from the 1780s to the 1860s. What is of historical interest in the story of these four thinkers is (1) the way in which each recognizes that the sound of his own voice is of both political and philosophical significance and (2) the way in which this self-consciousness necessarily leads each to bring his voice to bear on political issues of the day, while self-consciously recognizing that this political intervention itself marks the limit of philosophical speech. In short, the story of the development from Kant to Marx is a story of the developing self-consciousness of the dilemma that persists between philosophy and politics.

This development occurs in a period of political turmoil. The period that stretched from the 1780s to the 1850s was a crucial period in the formation of German political and intellectual identity. The French Revolution had a strong impact on German liberals. Reaction against Napoleon's invasion of Germany acted as a catalyst for the formation of German identity. The revolutions of 1848 promised, if only for a moment, a new liberal era. And finally, in the 1860s and 70s the German empire was founded. It was a time that called for great philosophers as well as statesmen to reflect upon the issues of the day: the institution of a republican constitution, the identity of the German nation, and social justice during rapid industrialization. Kant, Fichte, Hegel, and Marx each responded to changing political conditions. I will try to indicate the importance of these changing conditions as we proceed.

Précis and Conclusion

> And yet they [philosophers] do not address their voices (*ihre Stimme an... gerichtet*) themselves in familiar tones to the people (who themselves take little or no notice of them and their writings), but in respectful tones to the state, which is thereby implored to take the rightful needs of the people to heart.
>
> —Kant, *The Contest of the Faculties*[32]

According to Kant, a proper understanding of the scope of our thought and the audiences to whom it is addressed ought to result in an increase of enlightenment. Unfortunately, as we have seen in the more than two hundred years since Kant responded to the question "What is Enlightenment?" enlightenment continues to be a problem. Kant envisioned the outcome of increased freedom in the public employment of reason as a benign result in which there would be a convergence of opinion toward truth and in which the moral politician would contribute toward a gradual reform of political institutions. However, it seems as if truth remains even more at a distance today than it did in Kant's time. The fractious nature of philosophical thinking at the end of the twentieth century, the "culture wars" that continue to rage, and indeed the whole of what has come to be known as "postmodernity" shows us that increased freedom for the public employment of reason results in an increase of disagreement, contention, and dispute. It is not too much to claim that philosophy itself (at least as it is practiced within the academy), which for over two thousand years had struggled to distance itself from cliquish factionalism and the irrational persuasive tactics of politics, has become thoroughly politicized. At the same time, philosophers find themselves more and more marginalized, unable to leave the ivory tower to have any real impact on political life.

This is true, in part, because with the proliferation of managed media sources, it is no longer possible freely to address the general reading public as it perhaps was in Kant's day.[33] Indeed it is no longer possible to assume that there is a unified public that could be addressed. This situation is not unique to political life in America at the end of the twentieth century, however. Even Kant was aware that the general public really did not care or understand the philosophical project of enlightenment. In part this is a problem of diversity, but more than this, it is a problem of the failure of the philosophical imagination. We can see the breakdown of the Kantian faith in a unified reading public as a concern for Fichte, Hegel, and Marx. Moreover, each of these philosophers was also aware of the inability of their intended audience to be able properly to listen to the philosopher's voice. Kant recognized that part of the problem was the state itself and its repression of free speech but also that another part of the problem was the timidity of philosophical speech and its reluctance to speak critically to power. For Fichte, the same problem obtains. The public is unable to comprehend philosophical thought because of the sorry state of political affairs. Fichte took it upon himself to address the political audience in order to create receptivity for his philosophical voice. Fichte thus recognized that philosophical reason is politically located and that there will always be different audiences with varying capacities for comprehension. Fichte's goal was to create a nation in which there would be individuals capable of knowing the truth of his philosophy, i.e., individuals capable of listening to the *logos* transmitted by his voice. Ironically, he endeavored to create this philosophical nation of listeners by addressing it with the manipulative, rhetorical speech that we would expect to hear from a politician. With Fichte, philosophy became political in order to create its own public audience.

Fichte's acknowledgment of the political role to be played by philosophy became institutionalized in Germany after Prussia obtained its independence from France. In post-Napoleonic Prussia, philosophy became a function of the state itself, a servant of the crown. Hegel's *Philosophy of Right* was delivered at a time when the nation already existed in the form of an independent Prussia. Although, like Fichte, Hegel acknowledges that individuals vary in their ability to comprehend philosophical thought according to their real historical conditions, he believes that there then (1820s) existed a class of people who had overcome the limitations of these conditions to such an extent that they were able to attain philosophical comprehension of themselves and their position within the state. Hegel's audience was an audience that Hegel, at least, seemed to believe was capable of properly listening to philosophical logos. This is why he did not address the members of his audience as individuals but, rather, as representatives of the spiritual or "universal class." This spiritual class is roughly equivalent to the general reading public that Kant claims the philosopher ought properly to address. While Fichte addressed the German nation in order to create this liberal public, Hegel addressed the universal class in order to help this "liberal" public understand itself.

With Hegel, however, the following problem arises: the truly universal aspect of the state, the sovereign, need not be conscious of itself. Philosophy was, thus, according to Hegel's own thought on the matter, an organ of the state, the state's consciousness of itself. Hegel, however, admitted that his own view was problematic. While the state demands that it be addressed by philosophy, the sovereign need not listen to the voice of philosophy. Despite the fact that his own political text explicitly addresses an audience that we would ordinarily think was political, the universal class of Prussia, Hegel's *Philosophy of Right* seems to contain the implication that philosophers cannot have an active impact upon the course of real political life. This is so, at least, because the sovereign need not comprehend the philosopher's voice. This is why Hegel's republican hopes trail off into vague spiritual politics. In addressing the state, Hegel claimed that he addressed everyone in general, no one in particular, and each of us as individuals. This is what Hegel means by spirit. This complex view, however, results in a vague account of the relation between theory and practice. On the one hand, Hegel argues for a radical connection between philosophical reflection and political action. He sees philosophical reflection as political action and understands political action as resulting in philosophical reflection. On the other hand, Hegel refuses to follow the implications of this conclusion beyond a mere statement of the case. He simply postulates this unity in the name of spirit without considering how recognition of this unity will transform both theory and practice. Hegel thus conservatively retreated to the ivory tower just as he discovered the fact that philosophy is inextricably tied to political life: the spirit whom Hegel addresses remains a political spectator who has yet to return to political action.

Marx rejected both Fichte's philosophical politics and Hegel's spiritual philosophy. For Marx, the nation, the universal class, the sovereign, and indeed spirit itself are ideological constructions which do not constitute the general public. Indeed for Marx, there is no "general public." For Marx, the proper address of philosophical thought is the proletariat, the "materially" universal class, which was itself marginalized and ignored by the Hegelian philosophy. Marx thus politicized his own philosophical activity in order to create the conditions under which the proletariat could become self-conscious. Like Fichte, Marx found that he could not address his audience directly because it did not yet exist as an audience: the proper audience of his address is incapable of listening to his voice because its ears have been muffled by the bourgeois ideology. Like Fichte, Marx attempts to create this audience in the very act of addressing it. However, Marx's goal is material freedom and not the abstract philosophical freedom of Fichtean and Hegelian philosophy. Moreover, Marx realizes that there will inevitably be unresolved contradictions within the material realm of politics. With Marx, then, philosophy becomes explicitly political to the extent that Marx recognizes the persistence of difference and the necessity of continued political struggle.[34]

Marx thus overturns Kant's view of the relation between philosophy and politics. One might claim, using Kant's terms, that Marx is more of a "political moralist" than a "moral politician": "one who fashions his morality to suit his own advantage as a statesman."[35] Indeed, many have criticized Marxism for the tendency of its leaders to be "opportunists." However, at his best, Marx resists the urge to demand a synthesis of philosophy and politics: he recognizes that the limits of present political life prevent us from clearly prognosticating the philosophy or morality of the future. The problem for Marx is that although he wanted to liberate both politics and philosophy from their bourgeois limitations, he found that he could only do so by engaging in politics. Marx thus recognized the problem of the philosopher's voice which this chapter has discussed: the philosopher's voice always reverberates within a certain form of social and political life and will be heard within that context, even when it endeavors either to point beyond it or embrace it. Finally, with Marx's recognition of the antagonisms that exist within the general human audience, Marx's voice becomes multiple. A different voice is required to speak to the different needs of the diverse members of the audience.

The history of thought from Kant to Marx thus shows us the roots of our own current struggle, a struggle in which philosophy has become politicized and in which political life proceeds heedless of philosophy. As we shall see in what follows, both the historical and rhetorical settings of seminal texts by Kant, Fichte, Hegel, and Marx indicate that their different approaches and conclusions depend upon the different audiences they address and the historical and political circumstances in which they speak. This history indicates a successive redefinition of the notion of the philosophical public and also indicates a redefinition of the distinction between philosophy and politics.

This story will be developed more fully in what follows. In Chapter 2, I will discuss historical antecedents in modern political philosophy by considering the issue of voice in Machiavelli, Hobbes, Locke, and Rousseau. I then look in detail at the issue of voice in the political philosophies of Kant (3 and 4), Fichte (5 and 6), Hegel (7 and 8), and Marx (9 and 10). In these chapters, I show that these philosophers were each aware of the problematic distinction between philosophy and politics. Each of these philosophers takes up a unique position within the struggle between philosophy and politics, and each builds upon the thought of his predecessors about the interconnections between philosophy, politics, and language. These chapters thus form a historical argument to the effect that Marx's turn away from philosophy represents the political culmination of the philosophical struggle to resolve the tension between philosophy and politics. I conclude in Chapter 11 by arguing that contemporary problems in political philosophy can be understood in terms of the ongoing struggle to resolve the dilemma of the philosopher's voice.

Note on Method

A final note on my own method and voice is apropos as I conclude this introduction. Some might see my focus on voice as a tangential issue focused on some obscure corners of the systematic edifices of these philosophers. However, I do not claim to have completed a systematic analysis of any of the philosophers I approach. Nor do I claim to have systematically resolved the question of what is political philosophy. I do not, for example, claim that these four philosophers can fit easily into a set of paradigms for political philosophy.[36] Indeed these four philosophers are fascinating precisely because they cannot easily be categorized. The complexity (and the contradictions) of their work develops out of the fact that they each audaciously attempted to bridge the gap between philosophy and politics while also acknowledging the paradoxical nature of the endeavor to build such a bridge. My modest goal is to weave together the threads of philosophy of language, political philosophy, and political activity found in these philosophers in order to gain clarity about the complexity of the conflict between philosophy and politics.

In order to achieve this goal, I focus extensively on places—occasionally obscure but never tangential—at which these philosophers provide us with indications of their own methodological self-consciousness. I interpret Kant's discussions of method in often-overlooked portions of the first *Critique* and compare these discussions to the spirit of his admittedly unsystematic political philosophy and his thoughts on progress as found in his book on religion. I look at Fichte's popular political works and his own explicit considerations of language and politics and compare these discussions to his account of imagination as articulated in the depths of the *Wissenschaftslehre*. I consider Hegel's systematic methodology and his brief but crucial philosophy of language in order to discuss its influence on his political voice as found in the *Philosophy of Right* and his other topical political articles. Finally, with Marx, I search for a philosophy of language scattered among his unsystematic writings and his collaborations with Engels in order to discover Marx's self-conscious appropriation of political rhetoric and his turn away from political philosophy. These reflections on language and philosophical methodology, which I have unearthed in the work of these philosophers, have been often overlooked. However, since the critical turn in philosophy, which begins with Kant, is a methodological turn, these considerations are essential for understanding the development of the critical project. Uniting this research agenda and the methodological considerations of these philosophers is the idea that philosophical self-consciousness demands that questions of language and method be made explicit, especially by philosophers who would speak to a larger political audience.

As part of this project I attempt to situate the political and philosophical activity of the philosophers in question. To this end I have provided some historical details about their lives and careers. These details are interesting for what they tell us about these men and about this era. I hope that these details can help us to conceive the concrete historical events with which these philosophers were concerned. However, since my chief task was to interpret the texts left to us by these thinkers—to listen to their voices—I have left out a narrative account of many of the details that would be found in a straightforward historical or biographical text. Moreover, the way I have organized the material into discrete chapters on each of the philosophers tends to disrupt the continuity that exists in this era. To remedy this and to make the biographical, bibliographical, and political history of this period more perspicuous, I have included as an appendix a detailed chronology of the lives, works, and events, which I am discussing. The reader will hopefully find this useful as a schematic synopsis of the story that I develop in the text.

Finally, I hope that this book is a book of philosophy and not merely a book of history or intellectual biography. What I mean by this is that the problem of the philosopher's voice that I address here is a philosophical problem, one with which we are still struggling. I hope that the reader will share with me a concern for this problem and that the reader will be familiar enough with the basic outlines of the history of philosophy to follow me through the development of this problem. It is still not clear to me what the solution to this problem is, although after having thought about it for several years now, it is clear to me that some solutions are not valid. Indeed, the resolutions of the conflict between philosophy and politics offered by Kant, Fichte, Hegel, and Marx each are inadequate in different ways, even if they are understandable given the historical and political contexts in which these solutions were enacted. I spell out these inadequacies in the chapters that follow. My hope is that by considering these inadequacies, we might begin to contemplate further solutions in the continual effort to bring reason to bear on political life.

CHAPTER 2

Voicc in Machiavelli, Locke, and Rousseau

> The tradition of all the dead generations weighs like a nightmare on the brain of the living.
>
> —Marx, *Eighteenth Brumaire of Louis Bonaparte*[1]

Concern with the philosopher's voice did not originate *ex nihilo* with the dawning of the nineteenth century. Rather, the issue of voice was already a pressing one for Machiavelli, Hobbes, Locke, Rousseau, and others for whom the question of how to address political life was important. The German philosophers of the early nineteenth century were aware of these historical antecedents. Kant, Fichte, Hegel, and Marx located their own thinking within a historical context created by their predecessors. They were also careful to attend to the proper context in which to understand these predecessors. Awareness of the history of political philosophy included an awareness of the problem of the philosopher's voice. In the present chapter I will discuss the history of the question of voice and will discuss the way in which Kant, Fichte, Hegel, and Marx critiqued and responded to this history.

Machiavelli and the Dangers of Political Speech

> Machiavelli calls out (*aufrufen*) to Lorenzo de Medici and speaks of the present as a favorable moment for the conquest of Italy.
>
> —Hegel, "The Constitution of Germany"[2]

It is obvious that Machiavelli is aware of the issue of voice. He is quite aware of whom he is addressing in his political philosophy. In *The Prince*, Machiavelli addresses himself explicitly to the prince. The opening line of *The Prince* states "Niccolo Machiavelli to Lorenzo the Magnificent son of Piero di Medici." The meaning of the text is found in this address: Machiavelli wants to explain princely power *to the prince* in order to inspire the prince to act. Moreover, Machiavelli is acutely aware of the limitations of his own situated position as a political observer who is not himself any longer an active participant in political life. He likens his own position vis-à-vis the prince to a landscape painter who views great mountains from a lowly vantage point within a valley. He concludes, however, that his own location provides him with better insight into the nature of princely power than a prince himself could attain: "so it is necessary to be a prince to know thoroughly the nature of the people, and one of the populace to know the nature of princes."[3] It may be true that Machiavelli was merely making traditional obeisance to the political authorities; however, it is also true that the necessity of paying homage to the prince in a political treatise indicates a certain awareness that political philosophy is located within political space.[4] In writing a treatise on politics one must beware of the political impact of the treatise. Clearly, as Hegel indicates, one of Machiavelli's aims in addressing *The Prince* to Lorenzo the Great was to inspire this prince to step forward as the liberator of Italy. In other words, Machiavelli explicitly addressed a political agent, the prince, in order to help this political agent better understand himself and thus take up his historic task. Given the fact that Italian politics consisted of petty monarchs at war with one another, it is not surprising that Machiavelli addressed his hopes to a monarch who would free Italy from anarchy and dissolution. Machiavelli addresses the house of Medici directly: "it is no marvel that none of the before-mentioned Italians have done that which is to be hoped your illustrious house may do . . ."[5] This indicates that, for Machiavelli, political philosophy is not just a passive theoretical activity aiming at comprehending political affairs. On the contrary, for Machiavelli, philosophical reflection on political affairs is always colored by a specific political agenda. It is natural then, that Machiavelli would address his reflections in *The Prince* explicitly to that prince who had the best chance of realizing Machiavelli's hoped for political end.

Unfortunately, as often happens when theorists attempt to influence political life, Machiavelli's attempts to inspire fell upon deaf ears. Hegel recognized this adverse outcome and concluded that "Machiavelli's voice (*Stimme*) died away without effect."[6] This is the problem of actualizing the thought of the philosopher by way of a politically active voice: there is no guarantee that the philosopher's voice will be properly heard by the political audience it addresses. Machiavelli was aware of the vicissitudes of political life: in 1512, he lost his political standing in Florence and was arrested and tortured by the new authorities swept in with the defeat of France in Italy. Machiavelli even devotes a whole chapter of his *Discourses* to a discussion of "The danger of being prominent in counseling any enterprise and how that danger increases with the importance of such enterprise."[7] Here, under the rubric of the general relation between political power and those who would speak to power, Machiavelli lays out the dangers of political philosophy quite nicely.

> Certainly those who counsel princes and republics are placed between two dangers. If they do not advise what seems to them for the good of the republic or the prince, regardless of the consequences to themselves, then they fail of their duty; and if they do advise it, then it is at the risk of their position and their lives; for all men are blind in this, that they judge of good or evil counsels only by the result.[8]

Machiavelli thus acknowledges that advice-giving is a dangerous affair, one which should be undertaken "calmly and modestly."[9] This is a problem of the proper way of speaking for one who would address power in the way that Machiavelli himself does in the *Prince*. Finally, Machiavelli concludes that even to remain silent is no recourse, "for to advise men to be silent and to withhold the expression of any opinion would render them useless to a republic, as well as to a prince, without avoiding danger."[10] To remain silent is still to be involved in political affairs, as Socrates and Aristotle both knew: there is no escaping the political location of language because silence within a political context is still a form of speech. Machiavelli makes this clear in his parable of the advisor who was killed "for having been silent when he should have spoken and for having spoken when he should have been silent."[11] Political life is a life of speech. There is no escape from the consequences of speaking if one wants to remain an active part of political life. The best that we can do is exercise calm judgment and moderation in our speech.

What then are the implications for philosophy of this way of locating speech in general within a politically charged atmosphere? The philosopher is perhaps the one who has the most difficult time remaining silent because the philosopher knows what ought to be and this normative vision impels him to act, to speak, to give advice. And yet, as Machiavelli would warn, the philosopher must recognize the danger that lies in speaking. That Kant was aware of this problem, even if he was not aware of Machiavelli's formulation of it, can be seen in his attempt to defuse political speech in "What is Enlightenment?": "Argue as much as you like about whatever you like, but obey."[12] Kant, naively perhaps, tries to keep theory and practice, political speech and political activity, separated in a way that Machiavelli and his later German pupils, Fichte, Hegel, and Marx, would be skeptical of. However, Fichte and Marx, and to a lesser extent Hegel, seem to have ignored Machiavelli's advice about calmness and moderation in advice-giving. Indeed, in the German nineteenth century we see philosophy turn to political life in a manner modeled on Machiavelli's *Prince* but without proper regard for Machiavelli's call for moderation in the *Discourses*. This vehemence in political speech is what leads Cassirer to claim that "the idealistic thinkers of the nineteenth century, Fichte and Hegel, became the advocates of Machiavelli and the defenders of Machiavellism."[13] This conclusion is too strong, as we shall see, because Kant, Fichte, and Hegel were also each concerned with the enlightenment ideal of universal morality.[14] Nonetheless, the problem of the relation between philosophy and politics embodied in Machiavelli continued to be a problem in the nineteenth century, culminating in Marx's deliberate rejection of those moral restraints on political action. Hegel, perhaps more than Fichte and Marx, was explicitly aware of the problems that occur when philosophers attempt to use their voices to affect political reality. For Hegel, Machiavelli was the modern embodiment of this problem. Nonetheless, even in Hegel's supposed "silence," his reticence about issuing instructions on how the world ought to be, his method in the *Philosophy of Right* reflects Machiavelli's method in the *Prince,* i.e., the idea that the theorist ought to use his insight to help the prince understand his own activity.[15]

It is important to acknowledge that this interpretation of Machiavelli—one that understands Machiavelli as directing *The Prince* to a particular audience in the form of Lorenzo de Medici for a very specific political purpose—is a contentious interpretation and one that first gained prominence under the new historicist approach of the Enlightenment. Machiavelli's notorious *realpolitik* had been the subject of numerous anti-Machiavellian polemics, most notably Frederick the Great's *Anti-Machiavelli,* written in 1740. Even Frederick's critique is acutely aware of the address of the text. He recognizes that Machiavelli addresses those in power. Indeed it is the nature of this address that leads Frederick to condemn Machiavelli.

> But he speaks to all men, for an author who comes out in print communicates with the entire world, and he addresses himself primarily to those who should be the most virtuous since they are destined to govern others. What then is more infamous or insolent than to teach them treachery, perfidy, murder, and all the crimes?[16]

Frederick condemns Machiavelli because he was not sensitive to the task which he had undertaken, i.e., to educate princes about the proper exercise of power is a task of universal moral import. Frederick subscribes to the view that sees *The Prince* as a treatise arguing in favor of the prince's immoral lust for power. This is why Frederick begins his work with the condemnation that "Machiavelli's *The Prince* is one of the most dangerous works ever to be disseminated in the world."[17] Frederick does not read *The Prince* ironically as a satire on political power as someone like Diderot did. Rather, Frederick takes it as a deadly serious piece of immorality, the product of a "misanthropic," "hypochondriac," "drunken" mind that "portrays the world as hell and men as demons."[18] Moreover, Frederick claims that Machiavelli's theory is irrelevant because of crucial historical differences between the sixteenth and the eighteenth centuries. Frederick thus rejects Machiavelli as both immoral and irrelevant.

Following upon Frederick's condemnation of Machiavelli, Herder resurrected serious interest in Machiavelli by recontextualizing *The Prince* and by listening even more carefully to the specific address of Machiavelli's voice. In 1795, the same year as Kant published *Perpetual Peace,* just five years before Hegel's discussion of Machiavelli in the "German Constitution" and twelve years before Fichte published his article "*Ueber Machiavelli,*" Herder wrote that *The Prince* was "neither a satire, nor a manual of morals, nor an intermediary between these two; it is a work of politics, written for the Italian princes of its epoch, according to their taste, according to their principles, and to the goal which Machiavelli indicates in the last chapter, to liberate Italy from the barbarians . . ."[19] It is significant that Herder admits the possibility that a work of politics could have a unique genre as something other than moral, for this is the very possibility that Kant tries to reject in *Perpetual Peace.* At issue in Kant's rejection of a division between morality and politics is Machiavellism, although Kant does not indicate it by this name. Kant concludes that "A true system of politics cannot therefore take a single step without first paying tribute to morality. And although politics in itself is a difficult art, no art is required to combine it with morality. For as soon as the two come into conflict, morality can cut through the knot which politics cannot unite... for all politics must bend the knee before right . . ."[20] Although Kant makes this argument in the name of his philosophical theory of morality and justice, this same argument was made by Frederick in the name of prudence. Frederick argued that the prince should pursue justice because only justice is able to prevent revolutionary sentiment from growing in the masses. We can see, then, that the question of Machiavelli is a question of the proper relationship between philosophy and politics. Should there be political theory that does not include philosophical reflection about justice, or should philosophy criticize such amoral political activity? Finally, one wonders whether such criticism is itself a matter of justice or a matter of prudence, i.e., a matter of theory or of practice.

In the nineteenth century, Hegel and Fichte both endeavored to rehabilitate Machiavelli, following Herder's historicist approach, by recognizing the importance of locating *The Prince* precisely in terms of its address. They each flirted with the idea, contra Kant, that expedient political activity was sometimes historically necessary. In 1801, in his essay on the "Constitution of Germany," Hegel wrote:

> You must come to the reading of the *Prince* immediately after being impressed by the history of the centuries before Machiavelli and the history of his own times. Then indeed it will appear as not merely justified but as an extremely great and true conception produced by a genuinely political head endowed with an intellect of the highest and noblest kind.[21]

In his 1807 essay "On Machiavelli," Fichte tried to defend Machiavelli's political insight against those who saw him as a moral devil. Fichte's defense of Machiavelli is based upon his recognition of the different criteria that one must apply to different theorists, depending upon their differing intentions. Fichte states, for example, quite adamantly that Machiavelli must not be judged according to the criteria one would use to judge a transcendental philosopher:

> By no means ought one to judge him according to concepts that he did not have and according to a language (*Sprache*) that he did not speak (*redet*). But the most wrong-headed approach would be if one were to judge him as if he had wanted to write a transcendental political constitution and to force him, centuries after his death, into a school which he would have had no opportunity to go.[22]

Both Fichte and Hegel asked for a more nuanced response to Machiavelli, one which recognized the peculiarities of Machiavelli's historical task and the type of voice and language with which he spoke. In their reflections upon Machiavelli, they ask the historian of philosophy to be aware of the real historical quality of the philosopher's voice and to locate it historically as a form of address. Moreover, they stressed the similarities between the historical situation in Italy in the sixteenth century and Germany in the nineteenth century, i.e., a nation in disarray that needed a strong hand to bring about national unity. Fichte and Hegel both seemed to realize the need for a German Machiavelli—a philosopher who would address political affairs in order to inspire action. Fichte completed this thought in his 1807 *Addresses to the German Nation,* which can be read as a nationalistic version of Machiavelli's *The Prince*. These *Addresses* were composed at around the same time that Fichte completed his essay on Machiavelli. Taking this into consideration when we turn directly to the *Addresses,* it will be important to keep in mind Fichte's recognition of the difference between trying to compose a *transcendental constitution* (as Fichte endeavored to do in his more transcendental works, *System der Sittlichkeit* and *Geschlossene Handelsstaat*) and trying to influence political life (as he did in the *Addresses*). Hegel, to his credit, moves away from such a use of theory to defend nationalistic politics, despite the fact that he still recognizes in his *Philosophy of Right* that the expedient political use of power is sometimes justified in war and that heroic individuals may have the right to utilize seemingly immoral political expedients.[23]

We have thus exposed in Fichte's and Hegel's interpretation of Machiavelli the fact that they both thought that the voice of the political philosopher must be understood in terms of its address. Of course, there are those for whom Machiavelli represents a pernicious influence on the subsequent history of political philosophy. Leo Strauss, for example, condemns the whole tradition of political philosophy that stretches from Machiavelli, through Hobbes, Rousseau, Kant and on to Hegel and Marx. Strauss writes:

> The right order may have been as loftily conceived by Hegel as it was by Plato, which one may doubt. It certainly was thought by Hegel to be established in the Machiavellian way, not in the Platonic way: it was thought to be established in a manner which contradicts the right order itself. The delusions of communism are already the delusions of Hegel and even of Kant.[24]

The problem Strauss sees in the tradition that stems from Machiavelli is that, when philosophers address their voices to political life, they become susceptible to the injustice of political life. A philosopher, according to Strauss, ought not lower himself to address the often-immoral disputes of political life.[25] On the other hand, in defense of Machiavelli, it is important to remember that *The Prince* self-consciously avows its intentions by making its address—to Lorenzo the Great—explicit at the outset. As Cassirer states, in defense of Machiavelli: "The Prince is neither a moral nor an immoral book: it is simply a technical book."[26] In addressing power in an attempt to elucidate the techniques of power, Machiavelli indicates the contradictory nature of political philosophy: philosophy, when it attempts to have an impact upon political life, ceases to be philosophical and becomes political. Machiavelli is thus the first modern philosopher to broach this problem, and his model of political philosophy had a significant impact on the nineteenth century.[27]

The philosophers of the nineteenth century took this problem up as an explicit matter for philosophical contemplation. Indeed, it may be the case, as Otto Pöggeler notes, that Hegel overcame his early fascination with Machiavelli precisely because of the problem indicated in the Straussian critique of Machiavelli. Although Hegel never adopted the Kantian hope, as articulated in *Perpetual Peace,* that there could be a final synthesis of morality and politics, he did distance himself from his early interest in Machiavelli. Pöggeler writes,

> Hegel doesn't name Machiavelli in the *Philosophy of Right* and, in his *Lectures on the History of Philosophy,* he does not take the trouble to explain the fundamental concepts of Machiavelli. This shows that Machiavelli interested Hegel more as a patriotic writer (*écrivain patriotique*) than as a theoretician of politics (*théoricien de la politique*).[28]

In subsequent chapters we shall consider whether Hegel was able to maintain this distinction.

The question opened by Machiavelli, a question of which our German philosophers were aware, is thus whether a philosopher could address his voice directly to political life without ceasing to be a philosopher.[29] The question of the possibility that philosophy could change the world and could import its theoretical innovations into the political realm is of the utmost concern for Kant and his followers. The homage that both Fichte and Hegel pay to Machiavelli shows that they were aware, prior to Marx's "Theses on Feuerbach," that philosophy can and should become practical. Although they both admired the manner in which Machiavelli used his voice to speak to his political audience, they each developed the lessons taught by his example in a different way. Unfortunately, neither Fichte nor Marx took Machiavelli's recommendation for "calm and moderation" seriously enough, although perhaps Hegel did so in his more mature (and un-Machiavellian) works. Such moderation was especially Kant's virtue, although Kant's reluctance to take the plunge into Machiavellian political practice makes his political voice equally problematic, for it remains hidden, as we shall see, behind his fear of political revolution.

Hobbes, Locke, and the Problem of Political Liberalism

> [Hobbes' books] contain sounder reflections on the nature of society and government than many now in circulation. Society, the state, is to Hobbes absolutely preeminent.
>
> —Hegel, *History of Philosophy*[30]

The central problem of Hobbes's *Leviathan,* although it is usually taken to be the question of the *justification* of sovereignty, or the civil power, is really the question of *education.* Indeed, the aim of the book is to educate people who inhabit the commonwealth about the nature of the commonwealth and its power over them. This is the same project which Kant, Fichte, Hegel, and Marx each took up in their own way. For Hobbes, this educational task is a problem, as it was for Kant, Fichte, Hegel, and Marx. The problem is that those who need education most are debased to such an extent that their education may well be impossible. This problem can be seen in the middle of *Leviathan,* as Hobbes begins the transition from the first two parts of the text and moves from a consideration "Of Man" and "Of Common-Wealth" to a consideration "Of a Christian Common-Wealth" and "Of the Kingdome of Darkness." Hobbes writes that he realizes that a profound understanding was necessary to follow his arguments ("how much depth of Morall Philosophy") and concludes that "I am at the point of believing this my labour, as uselesse, as the Common-wealth of Plato."[31] Hobbes goes on to explain that this despair results from the fact that it seems that Plato was right to claim that there would be no justice until philosophers were kings. Since this is absurd, Hobbes despairs. Nonetheless, Hobbes remains hopeful because he claims that his sovereign need not be a mathematical or philosophical genius as Plato demanded. Rather, Hobbes claims that the sovereign only needs to understand the "Science of Naturall Justice." He concludes the first part of his book with the following:

> I recover some hope, that one time or other, this writing of mine, may fall into the hands of a Soveraign, who will consider it himselfe, (for it is short, and I think clear), without the help of any interested or envious Interpreter; and by the exercise of entire Soveraignty, in protecting the public teaching of it, convert this Truth of Speculation, into the Utility of Practice.[32]

Hobbes thus indicates both the importance of philosophical understanding for the commonwealth and the difficulty of this. Moreover, Hobbes makes it clear that this educational activity is not to be limited to the education of the sovereign but is to be a "public teaching." Thus the Hobbesian project is a step beyond the Machiavellian project in that it is not merely addressed to the sovereign. Moreover, Hobbes anticipates the enlightenment project of moral education by claiming that education ought to be addressed through the sovereign back to a public which is itself to be enlightened by the enlightened sovereign. We can see that Hobbes is thus thoroughly immersed in the problem of the proper relation between philosophy and politics. One recent interpreter of Hobbes has argued that the entire second half of *Leviathan* is dedicated to the problem of preparing the commonwealth for the task of understanding the philosophical reflections contained in the first half of the text and that the rhetorical flair of *Leviathan* is a deliberate affect of Hobbes's "new ambition to appeal to a large, public audience and thus shape popular opinion directly . . ."[33] At the same time, it is to Hobbes's credit that he is aware of the difficulties of this task. However, it is important to note that Hobbes's task was still significantly easier than the task of later philosophers who had to deal with the problems that arose out of the very content of modern political philosophy after Locke, i.e., the problems that occur when liberalism attempts to divorce political and philosophical activity in the name of toleration.

Before we turn to Locke, let us note, in advance, that subsequent (post-Kantian) solutions to the problem of liberalism tend to return us to the Hobbesian Leviathan. Fichte's strong coercive educational state is a sort of Leviathan. Marx's attempt to construct a life beyond liberal politics ends up calling for the creation of a state-apparatus that would overcome state-apparatuses. Hegel is perhaps the clearest follower of Hobbes in both systematically undertaking the educational task and in thus justifying a strong state. However, Hegel's appropriation of the Hobbesian educational task tends to result in the same problem that Hobbes encountered: the system of truth about the state ends up being incomprehensible to those who live within the state—both the sovereign whom Hegel eventually leaves blithely dotting the "i's" of state policy and the rabble and women who are excluded from state education. The further problem encountered by Hegel, a problem that Hobbes did not feel the need to confront, was the very question of the place of the philosopher within the Leviathan.[34] Thus, although the post-Kantian philosophers rejected Lockean liberalism and returned to Hobbes, they did so with much more self-consciousness about the way in which the philosophical account and/or critique of the state was itself located within political life.

We thus turn to Locke's liberalism with a recognition that Locke's theory was offered as an antidote to the strong state of Hobbes. Locke's *Second Treatise of Government* is structured according to its motto, *salus populi suprema lex esto,* "the welfare of the people is the supreme law." As we shall see, the meaning of "the people" is, however, ambiguous for Locke: Locke's theory is predicated upon a recognition of class differences in political life. Thus while Locke addresses his text to a general reader who is a member of the citizenry, i.e., to the people whose welfare is the supreme law, the meaning of this address is ambiguous: it is both all of the people and only those educated, rational, property owners who make up the ruling class. Locke's text announces itself as an attempt to justify *to the people* of England the right of William III to the throne. It also announces itself as addressed to the world.[35] Locke locates his remarks in time and space and addresses them to a specific historical audience. He does not address the prince, as Machiavelli does, but he does address his remarks to the sovereign. In Locke's case, however, it is the people themselves who are sovereign and not the prince, for the power of the prince to rule over the people is based upon the consent of the people.

Locke's notion of sovereignty and of majority rule is not as straightforward as it might seem. While Locke claims that sovereignty is found in the hands of the majority, the majority is conceived on a class-basis. Those who are able to pay, from out of their estates, taxes which are used to support the common-wealth are those who ought to have a say about taxation and the uses of tax revenue.[36] The nonpropertied classes have a reduced participatory role. Locke's work is thus addressed to the people in a double sense. On the one hand, he addresses all of the people in order to justify the class structure in which the nonpropertied classes lack political power. On the other hand, he addresses the propertied classes in order to explain the origins and limitations of their power within the system of natural rights. Locke tends to resolve this ambiguity in favor of the propertied classes because he tends to think that the nonpropertied classes are somewhat limited, if not incapable of being addressed by the philosophical discourse of justification.[37] As we shall see, this was a problem that haunted the nineteenth century: can philosophy address those who are the subjects of political power but who, because they are excluded from the educational advantages that come with political power, are incapable of understanding the philosophical theory of society? The tendency of Locke's voice to direct itself, as a class-oriented voice, toward the ruling class, opens the problem of the moronization of the masses who are excluded from the address of political philosophy.[38] This was a problem with which the philosophers of the nineteenth century struggled.

The implicit ambiguity of Locke's address may help to explain the interesting rhetorical form of Locke's "Letter Concerning Toleration." Locke begins the "Letter" as a letter, addressing it to an unnamed "Honored Sir." In the letter itself it is not clear to whom Locke addressed his famous "Letter," nor was it clear, at the time the "Letter" was published anonymously in Amsterdam in Latin in 1689, that Locke was its author. The vagueness of the "Letter's" rhetorical context is understandable, however, given the nature of its content. Both the "Letter" and the *Second Treatise or Government,* which was also published anonymously in 1689, were inflammatory political tracts. The *Second Treatise* argues for the right to revolution, and the "Letter" argues for a radical extension of liberty. Indeed, the year in which they were both first published, 1689, was a crucial year politically in England: the protestant William and Mary had just acceded to the throne in the "Glorious Revolution." Both of these essays are thus practical political interventions, addressed to the English people, the ruling class, and the throne, in a deliberate attempt to bring philosophical reflection to bear on the vicissitudes of political life.

Most importantly, Locke used his voice to educate the people about the fact that they are themselves the sovereign power behind the legislative and executive powers. His *Second Treatise* is thus written to clarify this fact for the people. However, as mentioned above, this project occurs in the context of a class-structured view of society. Thus Locke writes to educate the bourgeois class about the proper limitations of the legislative and executive powers before the welfare of the commonwealth. Locke's defense of revolution must be read in this light. It is addressed to the ruling class in order to encourage them to endure trifling troubles, which do not undermine their own sovereignty or the welfare of the commonwealth. It is also seemingly addressed to the legislative and executive bodies as a warning to indicate that the people, i.e., the ruling class, will only endure a limited amount of abuse.

The "Letter" is, likewise, addressed to the "civil magistrates" in order to delineate the limits of civil power in its difference from ecclesiastical power. This distinction pushes Locke toward a decisive claim about the apolitical nature of truth. He says:

> But the business of laws is not to provide for the truth of opinions, but for the safety and security of the commonwealth, and of every particular man's

> goods and person. And so it ought to be. For the truth certainly would do well enough if she were once left to shift for herself. She seldom has received, and I fear never will receive, much assistance from the power of great men, to whom she is but rarely known and more rarely welcome. She is not taught by laws, nor has she any need of force to procure her entrance into the minds of men. Errors indeed prevail by the assistance of foreign and borrowed succors. But if truth makes not her way into the understanding by her own light, she will be but the weaker for any borrowed force violence can add to her.[39]

Here Locke divorces political life from the pursuit of truth. This claim is momentous in that it removes not only religion but also philosophical activity to the private sphere. Locke's intention is not to divorce philosophy and politics, as is clear from the fact that he, a philosopher, writes political essays. However, such claims, combined with his suspicions about the limited rationality of the masses, make it clear that Locke was anxious about the relation between philosophy and politics. Moreover, Locke articulates this anxiety in terms of the relation between truth and force: the political method of using force cannot cohere with the religious and philosophical methods of discovering truth. While Locke's goal is to keep force and violence from infecting the pursuit of truth, it also has the added effect of distancing philosophy and religion from political life. The tendency of those of us who have inherited Lockean liberal ideals is thus to understand tolerance as meaning both that philosophy and religion ought not to be concerned with public life and that political life can legitimately ignore philosophical and religious issues. This divorce between public and private is articulated by Kant, as seen above, in "What is Enlightenment?" and *Perpetual Peace.* This divorce, furthermore, forms the basis of the attempts by Fichte, Hegel, and Marx, to heal the gap between philosophy and politics.

Despite his anxiety, Locke's philosophical activity was political. The *Second Treatise* was not a disinterested work of philosophical reflection. Indeed, the work itself was formed in a crucible of political foment and rebellion. This is quite clear in Locke's defense of property and in his defense of revolution. Locke asks his readers to question who is to blame for political upheaval and revolution: "But whether the mischief hath oftener begun in the people's wantonness, and a desire to cast off the lawful authority of their rulers, or in the ruler's insolence, and endeavours to get and exercise an arbitrary power over their people; whether oppression or disobedience, gave the first rise to the disorder, I leave it to impartial history to determine."[40] Locke clearly understood the incendiary force of his discussion of rebellion and recognizes, in part, that history would judge the outcome of the Glorious Revolution. By addressing himself to those readers who were taking part in the Glorious Revolution (during the time Locke wrote it in the 1680s) and to those readers who were evaluating the results of that revolution (i.e., the "reader" he addressed directly in his preface), Locke locates his project within the context of his own view of critical political judgment. It is the people and their welfare who form the basis of critical judgements about political life. Indeed, it is the people who will ultimately judge whether what he says is true or false, patriotic or treasonous. Locke thus transforms the address of political philosophy from the prince to the people and leaves open the realm of political contestation about political "truths."

Locke's attempt to bring philosophy to bear on real political action has been the subject of much criticism. Strauss sees Locke as a follower of Machiavelli and locates Locke's immoralism in his defense of property. According to Strauss, "economism is Machiavellianism come of age."[41] What is at issue in this critique of Locke is what Strauss sees as a generally degraded conception of man and a corresponding degradation in political philosophy. According to Strauss, when political philosophy understands human beings as merely power hungry acquisitive creatures and when it addresses itself specifically to human beings in these terms—power in Machiavelli's case, the need for property in Locke's—political philosophy ceases to be "philosophical." When it engages in the factional disputes of political life, political philosophy degenerates and becomes political rhetoric. This problem stems from the view that the public (i.e., the masses and not just the bourgeoisie) is so debased and irrational that it cannot properly be addressed by the philosopher's voice. The idea of toleration for competing religious and philosophical theories leads to the antiphilosophical and irreligious notion that there is no truth to the matter of politics.[42]

Kant's difficulties with the public use of reason and his defense of republicanism owe much to Locke. Hegel and Marx each react to Locke's defense of private property. Most significantly, Locke's personal figure, his role as a political philosopher whose words form the focal point of revolutionary theory and practice prefigures both Fichte's and Marx's revolutionary theory and practice. With Locke, philosophers acquire the courage to address political life with the voice of critical philosophy, even to the point of risking revolution. However, in the name of toleration, Locke opens the schism between politics and philosophy that Kant, Fichte, Hegel, and Marx each sought to cure. Although Marx does not mention Locke by name in "On the Jewish Question," this text can be read as a reaction both against the Lockean notion of toleration and against the ambiguous, dualistic class-based notion of "the people" that Locke utilizes in the *Second Treatise*. Marx states, for example, that "where the political state has attained to its full development, man leads, not only in thought, in consciousness, but in reality, in life, a double existence—celestial and terrestrial. He lives in the political community, and in civil society where he acts simply as a private individual, treats other men as means, degrades himself to the role of mere means, and becomes the plaything of alien powers."[43] Marx traces this dualism back to the very nature of bourgeois politics. Religious liberation as advocated by Locke did not, Marx claims, truly liberate us; it merely succeeded in further divorcing theory and practice. "The political (i.e., liberal) revolution dissolves civil society into its elements without revolutionizing these elements themselves or subjecting them to criticism."[44] This is the decisive factor for Marx, as it was for Kant, and to a lesser degree, Fichte and Hegel: liberal reforms and revolutions have served to distance philosophical criticism from political life rather than making political life more open to critique.

Despite the fact that Locke opens the door to the problem of uncritical politics, he was dedicated to the project of bringing critical reason to bear upon political life. In this he preceded the German philosophers of the nineteenth century. Although Kant does not address Locke by name, his argument against Hobbes in "Theory and Practice" is inspired in part by the Lockean concept of "inalienable rights." The most basic of these inalienable rights is, for Kant, "the freedom of the pen." Kant rejects Hobbes's claim that the sovereign "can do no injustice to a citizen, but may act towards him as he pleases."[45] In fact, Kant concludes that Hobbes's claim is itself "quite terrifying."[46] As an antidote to the coercive power of the sovereign, Kant requires that citizens ought to be able to address the public power, i.e., the sovereign, directly with their grievances. The freedom of the pen that Kant advocates is a freedom of thought that Kant claims lies at the heart of the commonwealth. To deny freedom of thought and, especially, to deny citizens the capacity to address their concerns to the sovereign, would be to deny to the sovereign, his right to have knowledge of the interests of his subjects. Kant claims that this would be to put the sovereign in a "self-stultifying position."[47] Kant concludes with Locke, contra Hobbes, that "the citizen must, with the approval of the ruler, be entitled to make public his opinion on whatever of the ruler's measures seem to him to constitute an injustice against the commonwealth."[48]

Nonetheless, Kant, in opposition to Locke, claims that citizens do not have the right to rebel. Although the second part of "Theory and Practice" is entitled as a polemic, "Against Hobbes," the specter of Locke's revolutionary doctrine haunts its pages. Kant writes that revolutionaries deserve to be executed as "great political criminals."[49] He further refers to the English constitution of 1688 and concludes that there could be no mention in such a constitution of an entitlement to stage further revolutions. This begs to be compared with Locke's claim in 1689 that tyranny may be resisted and that governments may be dissolved from within. Kant's objection is that a constitutional entitlement to revolution would have to decree a second head of state, a second publicly constituted power, to justify revolution and prevent it from slipping into anarchy.[50] This would itself already undermine the concept of sovereignty and thus cannot logically be part of the constitution. Locke, however, avoids this problem by postulating the distinction between civil society and government that will be taken up in earnest by Hegel. Locke maintains that the people (which at this point must mean, the bourgeoisie and not the masses) possess the right and the power to judge, to dissolve, and to reconstitute the government.[51] Kant is reluctant to admit such devolution of sovereignty to the people because he lacks insight into the fact that the bourgeoisie are, as Locke claims, inherently conservative. Nonetheless Kant recognizes that the people (i.e., the masses) often lack judgment. Locke also noted that the masses were ignorant and lacked rationality, however, his recognition of a "rational" class, the bourgeoisie, allowed him to claim that "the people shall be judge."[52] Locke's optimism is thus only justified within his own class-structured view of rationality. Kant's fear, coming after the French Revolution, a popular revolution in which the excesses of both the uneducated masses and the educated liberals were apparent, goes to the heart of the dilemma between philosophy and politics. Kant fears that in a revolution more democratic than the type envisioned by Locke, a debased populace and its leaders would not be able to hear the voice of reason and restrain itself. This is so because in an exploitative political situation in which freedom of thought has been repressed, the people are not rational enough to hear the voice of the philosopher. Nonetheless, just as Locke decried the use of violence to impose truth, Kant recognizes that right cannot be imposed by force but must be the work of reason. Kant thus remains hopeful that the people can become rational. This is the task of the philosopher: to use his voice to educate the people: "But if both benevolence and right speak in loud tones, human nature will not prove too debased to listen to their voice with respect."[53]

Rousseau: Addressing the Problem of Language

> The first language of man, the most universal and most energetic of all languages, in short, the only language he needed, before there was a necessity of persuading assembled multitudes, was the cry of nature.
>
> — Rousseau, *First Discourse on the Origin of Inequality*[54]

Machiavelli used his voice to address princely power, and Locke used his voice to reassert the power of the bourgeoisie. Neither of these made voice a central concern of their political reflections. With Rousseau, however, the public nature of language became an explicit matter for political philosophy. Of course, Rousseau was not the first to consider the question of language. Indeed, epistemological discussions of the nature of universals, connected with the problem of nominalism in Hobbes and Locke, led to explicit considerations of language. This led to discussions of the public nature of language as the medium for communication of ideas and to conjectures about the conventional or arbitrary nature of our signs. This empiricist approach to language was a response to traditional discussions of the divinely ordained language of nature. Furthermore there was an interest, significant for our present endeavor, in the difference between philosophical language and common usage.[55] The question of language was not unrelated to political thought, as Locke indicates in his *Essay* when he says that language was "the great instrument and common tie of society."[56] In his *Thoughts Concerning Education,* Locke had emphasized the *political* need for a Young Gentleman to be able to express himself eloquently in his own language (as opposed to an exclusive emphasis on Latin, Greek, and other learned languages).[57]

Moreover, the question of the relation between language and thought opened up questions of social and historical relativity at the same time that Enlightenment reason was attempting to push forward toward universal moral progress. One should mention Condillac in conjunction with the French Encyclopedists in this regard. But the most important figure here is Leibniz, whose goal of political and religious harmony in Europe was linked to his dream of a universal *Lingua Philosophica*.[58] For Leibniz, a reformed symbolic structure would allow us to communicate with each other, to properly understand ourselves, and to complete a comprehensive encyclopedia of the universe. Leibniz responded to the diversity of languages, religions, and legal traditions in Europe at the time by looking for a unifying language. He also was active in promoting enlightenment in Germany, working together with Sophia Charlotte, the Queen of Prussia (and mother of Frederick the Great) to found the Academy of Science in Berlin in 1700.[59] The problem of unifying diversity and the question of language will return in earnest in Fichte and Hegel, who pick it up by way of Herder and Hamann. It is important to note, in passing, that Leibniz himself praised the German language for its concreteness—as Fichte was later to do.[60] Moreover, in all of these discussions we see the question of the proper style of philosophical speech, including the question of how to distinguish philosophy from rhetoric: a theme that becomes acute for Kant, Fichte, Hegel, and Marx.

Nonetheless, it is Rousseau who most clearly links language with politics and who most decisively influenced the development from Kant to Marx. In Rousseau's anthropology, property, society, and speech all develop concurrently. This is why Rousseau leaves unresolved the problem of "which was the more necessary, society already formed to invent languages or languages already invented to form society?"[61] In other words, Rousseau is aware that the social nature of human beings is intimately tied up with human linguistic ability. This is significant because it leads Rousseau to make the question of voice an explicit matter for philosophical consideration.

This development has profound effects on the subsequent development of philosophy in Germany, where language and its connection to both philosophy and politics became an ongoing matter of concern. That Rousseau was a crucial influence on the German philosophers who followed in his wake can be seen from a consideration of Kant's discussion of Rousseau in his "Conjectures on the Beginning of Human History":

> In his essays *On the Influence of the Sciences* and *On the Inequality of Man,* he [Rousseau] shows quite correctly that there is an inevitable conflict between culture and the nature of the human race as a physical species each of whose individual members is meant to fulfill his destiny [*Bestimmung*] completely. But in his *Emile,* his *Social Contract*, and other writings, he attempts in turn to solve the more difficult problem of what course culture should take [*wie die Cultur fortgehen müsse*] in order to ensure the proper development [*Entwicklung*], in keeping with their destiny, of man's capacities as a moral species, so that this destiny will no longer conflict with his character as a natural species.[62]

The problem, which Kant indicates here, is a variation of the problem of the philosopher's voice: how can we ensure the proper development of humanity by bringing philosophical reflection to bear upon political life? As Cassirer indicates, Kant admired Rousseau's interest in solving the problem of morality in practice and not just in theory.[63] Kant learned from Rousseau that philosophy had to be brought to bear on the question of the proper relation between philosophy and politics. Kant's claims about universal consent as the touchstone of both truth and justice—a claim I will unpack in the next two Chapters—can be traced back to Rousseau's claims, in *The Social Contract,* about the *volonté générale*. After Kant, there were further developments of Rousseauian themes. Fichte's explicit consideration of the problem of the origin of language finds its source in Rousseau's *Discourse on the Origin of Inequality*. Hegel's social ethics of *Sittlichkeit* is prefigured in Rousseau's discussion, in the *Discourse,* of the developmental progress of languages and mores from family life to local societies and on to nations. Finally, Marx's concern for the oppressed classes and his historical view of the development of oppression owes much to Rousseau's historical argument in the *Discourse*. Indeed, Marx's socialist/materialist understanding of language and consciousness can be traced back to Rousseau's discussion of the formation of speech in the context of the formation of society.

Rousseau is an acutely self-conscious rhetorical stylist. This self-consciousness stems from his awareness that speaking is a political act. The "cry of nature" mentioned in the quote with which we opened the present section was sufficient for the solitary lives of Rousseau's mythic presocial savages. However, speech and complex grammar developed so that language was able to "express all the sentiments of man, to assume an invariable form, to bear being spoken in public, and to influence society."[64] Rousseau's own speech is thus not only a solitary meditation, despite his reputation as a solitary hermit. Rather, Rousseau recognizes that speaking is a public activity addressed to a public audience with the intention of "influencing society." Indeed Rousseau's self-consciousness of the function of his voice is made explicit in the Prefaces and Introductions to both the *Discourse* and *The Social Contract.*

Rousseau mentions his own voice, for example, in the Introductory Note to *The Social Contract:* "Having been born a citizen of a free State, and a member of the sovereign body, however feeble an influence my voice may have in public affairs, the right to vote upon them is sufficient to impose on me the duty of informing myself about them; and I feel happy, whenever I meditate on governments, always to discover in my researches new reasons for loving that of my own country."[65] Rousseau recognizes that he speaks from a position within political life although he does not make it clear at this point who his audience is. Indeed, from the above statement it seems that his audience is himself—his goal is to inform himself and to satisfy himself, in his meditations, that his own country is the best country. Although he does mention specific political events and actors in *The Social Contract,* he does not explicitly acknowledge the role that his own text has within political life.

It is clear from what Rousseau says about the conformity of opinion to the general will and about the constitution of the body politic, that he is aware that even his own text is part of that body and an attempt to articulate that will. He states, for example, that he is aware of the necessity of undertaking an explicit consideration of "speaking, proposing, dividing, and discussing"; however, he further states that this would "require a separate treatise and I cannot say everything at once."[66] Nonetheless Rousseau notes two extreme types of public speech. The first extreme occurs where unanimity of the general will has declined or failed to occur. At this point, political discourse is characterized by "long discussions, dissensions, and uproar."[67] The second extreme type of public speech occurs under despotism when men speak under fear as, for example, in "the most disgraceful mode of speaking in the Senate under the Emperors."[68] Throughout *The Social Contract,* Rousseau recognizes that public speech is a problem and that useful public speech ought to occur somewhere between these two extremes as the expression of the genuine *volonté générale*. The problem is that successful public speech needs to be aware of the necessity of addressing the needs and expectations of the audience while not undermining the speaker's philosophical intentions. Rhetoric is a serious problem for the formation and expression of the general will. He states, for example, in a claim reminiscent of Socrates, that "Wise men who want to speak to the vulgar in their own language instead of in a popular way will not be understood. Now, there are a thousand kinds of ideas which it is impossible to translate into the language of the people."[69] This problem is similar to the one Rousseau discussed in the *Discourse:* it is not clear which comes first, social spirit or political government. In the *Discourse,* Rousseau saw this as the unresolved problem of the origin of language vs. the origin of society. In *The Social Contract,* Rousseau sees it as a problem of the legislators speaking properly to the public so as to guide it toward the formation of the *volonté générale.*

Not only do those in power have a problem in speaking to those who are ruled, but those who are ruled have a problem in speaking to those in power. Rousseau mentioned this problem in the Introduction to *The Social Contract.* Moreover, this problem is the focal point of the Introduction and Dedication of the *Discourse.* This treatise begins with an extended "Dedication" addressed "to the Republic of Geneva: Most Honorable, Magnificent, and Sovereign Lords" and signed "I am, with the most profound respect, most honorable, magnificent and sovereign lords, your most humble, and obedient servant and fellow-citizen, Jean-Jacques Rousseau, Chambéry, June 12, 1754." This address and return-address invites us to consider the time and place of the treatise as well as the difference in status and power that exists between the author and its intended audience. Rousseau speaks as a mere citizen addressing the magistrates and lords. The dedication is full of fawning praise for both the lords and the laws of Geneva, just the type of speech Rousseau would later warn us against in *The Social Contract.* Rousseau recognizes, however, that since Geneva is a republic, the way to gain the ear of power is by way of the people. In an ironic twist, within his explicit address to the sovereign lords of the republic in the dedication, Rousseau rhetorically addresses his fellow citizens: "Affected with a tender disinterested love for my distant fellow-citizens, I should have addressed them (*je leur aurais addressé*) from my heart in about the following terms."[70] The address that follows heaps more praise onto the laws and institutions of Geneva, still intended, it seems, to curry the favor of the magistrates, for the address to the citizens concludes with the following: "And you, most honorable and magnificent Lords, you, the worthy and respectable magistrates of a free people, permit me to offer you in particular my duty and homage."[71]

One wonders why Rousseau, the unsocial hermit, would adopt this fawning posture? Perhaps because he realizes that what he is about to say will not set well with the authorities. Indeed, this is a recurrent problem from the time of Socrates up until the nineteenth century and beyond. The philosopher who would speak truth to power must always be aware that power may not be prepared to hear the truth. Philosophers since the time of Socrates have thus been forced to dissemble before the censors, to speak duplicitously before the political authorities. As we shall see, the issue of necessary duplicity and dissemblance in political philosophy continues to be a problem in the nineteenth century.

If we look more closely at Rousseau's *Discourse,* beyond the official dedication, we find another address of the text. In the first real chapter of the text Rousseau addresses his words explicitly and directly to humankind and especially to the sages of mankind who would judge his words:

> It is of man I am to speak; and the question into which I am inquiring informs me that it is to men that I am going to speak; for to those alone, who are not afraid of honoring truth, it belongs to propose discussions of this kind. I shall therefore defend with confidence the cause of mankind before the sages, who invite me to stand up in its defense; and I shall think myself happy, if I can but behave in a manner not unworthy of my subject and of my judges.[72]

This is a theme to which we will return subsequently: the political philosopher speaks to human beings about human beings. In other words, the political philosopher offers to make the public self-conscious.

The difficulty here is that the public may not be ready to hear the truth about itself. Thus Rousseau's intended audience is mankind in general but, more specifically, that part of mankind which is interested in truth. Rousseau indicates that the political audience consists of both those who are interested in knowing truth and those who are not. This poses a problem for the political philosopher who attempts to change political life merely by articulating the truth of political life, for not all of the political audience will be interested in truth! Thus, political philosophers may have to use rhetoric to persuade their audience. This is an issue that, as we shall see, becomes explicit for Fichte and Marx: how to persuade those who are not prepared for truth.

The double address of Rousseau's text results in an interesting problem with regard to the efficacy of his political philosophy. Rousseau poses a problem for himself at the outset of his revolutionary text: the problem he seeks to resolve—the problem of inequality—cannot be resolved if the text is addressed only to the two audiences whom he explicitly mentions. On the one hand, those authorities and fellow citizens of Geneva whom he addresses in the dedication are themselves the cause of the problem which he addresses in the text. "Moral" inequality, according to Rousseau, did not exist in the state of nature and indeed, only exists within civilization, i.e., under the rule of those authorities he addresses. Rousseau's dedication is full of duplicitous praise for the authorities of Geneva, even while the whole of the text makes it clear that political authority lies at the heart of the problem. This same problem is reiterated in his more general address to humankind. In the opening lines of the *Discourse* quoted above, Rousseau makes a crucial distinction between those "who are not afraid of honoring truth" and those who remain committed to the general inequity of their social and political institutions. Rousseau's text is addressed to those who are already committed to truth and justice. This is a problem, however, because those who are already interested in the truth about inequality need not be convinced. To induce social and political change, what is needed is not a restatement of truth that, as it were, merely preaches to the choir. Rather, it is necessary to speak to and convince those others who are not interested in truth, justice, and equality. But this Rousseau's text cannot do because those who need convincing are themselves already beyond the reach of the persuasive power of truth. Rousseau's text thus ironically admits is own impotence at the outset in both its dedication to the civil authorities and its address to that part of humanity interested in truth. This problem becomes even more difficult if we recall that within the text itself, Rousseau equates the origin of moral inequality with the development of both language and political life. Marx will develop this problem into the issue of ideology: language itself develops in a context of oppression in which "truth" becomes defined by the oppressive regime.

Rousseau gives us a hint in his *Émile* as to what is needed to achieve the goal of social and political change: proper education. This is a tricky business, however, because education is easily confused with persuasive rhetoric. Although Rousseau realizes that rhetoric is a dangerous tool because it is mostly used to degrade human society and not to uplift it, he acknowledges in *The Social Contract,* for example, that in real political life, some form of rhetoric is needed that "can compel without violence and persuade without convincing."[73] Such rhetoric is necessary because the masses lack the education needed to fully comprehend the general will. In the *Discourse,* Rousseau indicates that the need for persuasive rhetoric developed only after the state of nature had been overcome. In the state of nature all that was needed for communication was the "cry of nature." The use of rhetoric, in its pernicious form, arises out of the rich master's desire to unite the multitude and convince the multitude to give up their liberty in order to work and die for him. In Rousseau's account, it is persuasive speech, not force alone that seduces people and convinces them to live in servitude.[74] Despite the necessity of persuasive speech indicated by Rousseau in the *the Social Contract,* rhetoric is a dangerous tool, which is why Rousseau is loath to teach the art of rhetoric to the young Emile.[75]

Rousseau's problem is the same problem that haunted Socrates. He wants to effect social and political change. However, what is needed for social and political change is rhetoric that will inspire change. The difficulty is that rhetoric is not a proper tool for the goals of truth, justice, and equality. As we shall see, the tension between political rhetoric and philosophical truth haunts the subsequent history of political philosophy in the nineteenth century. The philosophers of that time, drawing on the problem as found in both Plato and Rousseau, recognized the difference between political and philosophical speech. They struggled to resolve the same dilemma, which Rousseau articulated and embodied: how to use philosophical reflection about justice to change political life without also succumbing to the injustice that accompanies the use of political rhetoric.

In *Émile,* education is presented as the proper tool, which ought to be used to bring human beings to truth, justice, virtue, and equality. This is not a new claim and indeed hearkens back to Plato's own solution in the *Republic*. However, Rousseau, like Plato, realizes that his own proposals for proper education run contrary to the established views on education. And unlike Locke, he has a more general audience in mind than simply the Young Gentleman of Locke's *Thoughts Concerning Education*. Rousseau insists that education must begin from an early age, must occur at a slow pace, and must not allow itself to be corrupted by the injustice of social and political life. When it comes to education about social, political, and moral issues, Rousseau claims that this must be handled with a delicate touch. For example, proper education about the truth of society can only occur during a specific time in a person's life: during puberty, when the child becomes a man. This is the most important period for Rousseau's educational plan, the time of the so-called "second birth": "this period when education is usually finished is just the time to begin."[76] This is so because at this point of development, the youth develops an intellectual understanding of being human, morality, and politics without yet being corrupted by social intercourse: "before this time men would have been strangers to him; later on he would have been like them."[77] Rousseau's educational plan thus seeks to create a just society by beginning with the "raw material" of society and by forming this raw material anew, without the corrupting influence of past society. Despite Rousseau's claim in the preface to *Émile*, that his scheme of education can be easily carried out with minor variations for local circumstances, it remains an ideal that cannot easily be actualized. Again, Rousseau's goal of creating a just society finds itself in contradiction with the actuality of political life.

Rousseau's return to education as the crucial issue in political philosophy is an important one, which will be taken up in Germany by Lessing in the 1780s and subsequently by Fichte and Hegel. This educational approach can be understood as a response to the failure of the philosopher's voice to have an impact upon the present generation of political agents. When political philosophy addresses itself directly to its political audience, it is doomed to failure. The current generation is unable to hear political philosophy as philosophy because this generation has been corrupted by politics so that it always expects rhetoric and thus misinterprets political philosophy as a party to the biased arguments of political life. Moreover, political rhetoricians have the power to drown out the less persuasive voice of the philosopher. Rousseau's response to this difficulty is to refocus his address away from the current citizens and rulers, toward the next generation of political agents. This turn to education, however, results in a further difficulty because in order to address the children, the philosopher must address and convince the parents who are part of the social and political regime. Thus Rousseau appeals directly to parents in the preface to *Émile*: "Fathers and mothers, what you desire, that you can do. May I count on your goodwill?"[78] This reiterates the problem we found in the *Discourse on the Origin of Inequality:* if the parents were products of a corrupt education and if they are members of an unjust civil society, Rousseau ought not to count on their goodwill.

It is not clear whether Rousseau recognizes his difficulty, although he does admit that his plan for the education of Émile is something of a chimerical ideal. While Rousseau does not make the problems we have discovered in the *Discourse* and *Émile* an object of explicit reflection, those philosophers of the nineteenth century who follow him do. As we shall see, the problem of how the philosopher can properly address an uneducated and corrupt society becomes an explicit theme in the nineteenth century, especially for Fichte and Marx—each of whom proposes a scheme for transforming society via education and political action. Moreover, we shall see that Rousseau's recognition of the differences and connections between political speech and philosophical speech becomes an explicit theme, especially for Hegel who wants to draw a distinction between political and philosophical language, while holding on to the Leibnizian aspiration of a universal language and encyclopedia.

CHAPTER 3

The Politics of Pure Reason

> The field of philosophy, in this context of world citizenship, allows for the following questions to be brought: What can I know? What should I do? What may I hope? What is the human being?
>
> —Kant, *Logic*[1]

The title of this chapter appears to be an oxymoron. Pure reason should be that which transcends the political realm. It would thus seem that there could be no "politics of pure reason." However, philosophers are political beings. They are human beings who consider the essential questions of being human: knowledge, ethics, hope, and indeed the very definition of human being all within the context of the political question of world citizenship. The philosopher's voice is a human voice that speaks to other human beings. As such it is a form of political activity. Even Kant, the philosopher of pure reason, inevitably addressed a politically located audience. In the present chapter I will argue that self-consciousness of the political location of philosophical speech is built right into Kant's critical method. I will examine Kant's use of political metaphors in the *Critique of Pure Reason*. I will discuss the methodology of the *Critique* and Kant's republican ideal of free unanimity among his readers, an ideal that should produce the conditions for certainty about the truth of the *Critique*. I will consider Kant's encounters with the Prussian political authorities who controlled the publication of Kant's philosophical texts. Finally, I will consider the linguistic "metacritique" of Kant's critical project and will consider Kant's own recognition of the question of linguistic expression. My thesis in the present chapter is that Kant was aware of the political ground of his critical project: self-consciousness of the political location of philosophical speech is built right into the Kantian critical method.[2]

Human Reason and the Critical Project

> Reason must in all its undertakings subject itself to criticism; should it limit freedom of criticism by any prohibitions, it must harm itself, drawing upon itself a damaging suspicion. Nothing is

> so important through its usefulness, nothing so sacred, that it may be exempted from this searching examination, which knows no respect for persons. Reason depends on this freedom for its very existence. For reason has no dictatorial authority; its verdict is always simply the agreement of free citizens, of whom each one must be permitted to express, without let or hindrance, his objections or even his veto.
>
> —Kant, *Critique of Pure Reason*[3]

Reason is human activity. It is a ruthless practice of freedom that is itself only possible within a political life in which freedom of expression has been vouchsafed. It is the *human* capacity for law-governed freedom, the spontaneity of imagination brought under epistemological, moral, aesthetic, or political laws. While such a faculty is ours by nature, it can only flourish under certain forms of social and political life, i.e., those forms of life in which spontaneity can come to recognize that seemingly external laws are actually the result of self-legislation. Reason, Kant further explains, is the "faculty of principles"[4]: it is that ability of human beings to infer a unity, a principle, which grounds the rules of the understanding. The problem of human reason is that it seeks ultimate grounds—such as God, immortality, and freedom of the will—without recognizing its own limitations. Pre-Critical metaphysics results from a lack of self-consciousness about the limits of human reason. The *Critique of Pure Reason* is Kant's attempt to turn the faculty of reason upon itself in order to discover those limits and thus to infer those principles which necessarily ground the human quest for those ultimate grounds. It is not by accident that I use the adjective "human" in this discussion, for Kant repeatedly states that reason is a human faculty. Indeed, he speaks of human reason as being "impelled by an inward need (*durch eigenes Bedürfniß getrieben*)" that leads us "irresistably" to ask metaphysical questions.[5] The crucial question that Kant asks in the introduction to the *Critique* is "how is metaphysics, as natural disposition possible? That is, how from the nature of universal human reason do those questions arise which pure reason propounds to itself and which it is impelled by its own need to answer as best it can?"[6] In the *Critique,* Kant leaves this issue undeveloped in order to pursue the question of how metaphysics "as a science" is possible. Nonetheless, he implicitly answers the question of the metaphysical disposition or the metaphysical need by appealing to the nature of reason as a faculty universally shared by all human beings: reason is the universal human urge to seek unity in principles that ground the multiplicity of experience.

At this point one might ask what justifies Kant in claiming that reason, as he so defines it, is a natural and universal human disposition to seek unity? It seems that Kant here situates his critical endeavor by appealing to an empirical generalization that may or may not be true, i.e., that all human beings naturally ask metaphysical questions. Experience tells us that this is simply not true: there are human beings who are not driven by the "inward need" to ask these questions. Kant's response to this problem is to hold reason up as a regulative principle: human beings *ought* to be driven by the inward metaphysical need. This sort of argument will however seemingly spin us into a circle when we ask why ought we be driven by the metaphysical need? The answer to this seems to be that such is the essence of human being: *human* beings are those beings who ask these sorts of questions.[7] Thus Kant's reference to the "human" in his definition of reason brings in another empirical consideration: what we mean by "reason" will depend upon what we mean by "human." And again we see that normative ideals enter into this definition: reason is the faculty that makes it possible to ask the types of questions that human beings ought to ask.

The question-begging nature of this account is quite obvious to those who have tried to argue with students about the value of studying philosophy. At a certain point one is wont to argue that the questioning attitude is simply the proper or essential attitude for human beings. It should be obvious that the dogmatic nature of this response actually undermines the point argued. One seems entitled to ask: why ought I ask metaphysical questions? A further response to such a question can be found by reference to our form of social and political life. Indeed, this is Kant's response as well. The question can be understood as a moral and political question about who belongs as a member of the human community. We expect those who are members of our moral and political community to possess the faculty of reason which is that capacity to ask metaphysical questions, i.e., to be free in Kant's sense. Our understanding of moral and political freedom can thus help explain our understanding of reason. The idea of reason found in Kant's *Critique* can thus be explained by reference to the autonomy of the moral subject and eventually by reference to the political community. Reason is the faculty that ought to be present in all members of the moral community. It is also a prerequisite for membership in the political community.

One may object, at this point, that moral freedom alone is a sufficient criterion for determining who is a human being: human beings are those who have the capacity to will the categorical imperative. However, both moral freedom and intellectual freedom rely in part upon political freedom. The capacity for moral and intellectual freedom is developed within the context of real political freedom. While it might make sense to say that the capacity for reason exists without the possibility of instantiating itself in the empirical world, Kant recognizes that even moral freedom is a project to be completed in the empirical world.[8] This project of becoming free cannot be completed without a certain amount of real political freedom. While political freedom is not the condition for the *possibility* of intellectual and moral freedom, it is certainly the condition for the *actualization* of these. Thus, for Kant, the idea of freedom leads to a demand for transformation in political life as will be developed in the next chapter.

We can understand reason, then, by examining what members of the moral and political communities are supposed to be able to do. This will give us some insight into what actual freedom would look like if it were to be more than a mere possibility. A moral subject, i.e., one who is a member of the "kingdom of ends" is supposed to be able to "give universal laws in it while also [being] himself subject to these laws."[9] In other words, moral subjects are able to be autonomous. The problem is that moral beings who may be autonomous when considered in themselves are inevitably members of political communities whose external, historically contingent laws threaten to introduce an element of heteronomy into their empirical lives. The problem that arises here is that, if the system of pure reason appeals to empirical subjectivity together with all of the contingencies of psychology, history, and sociology as part of its attempt to define reason, then there seems to be a heteronomous element in the system itself. Kant precludes this explicitly in the Introduction to the *Critique of Pure Reason:*

> What has chiefly to be kept in view in the division of such a science, is that no concepts be allowed to enter which contain in themselves anything empirical, or, in other words, that it consist in knowledge wholly a priori. Accordingly, although the highest principles and fundamental concepts of morality are a priori knowledge, they have no place in transcendental philosophy . . .[10]

Here Kant goes so far as to preclude that morality could be used in support of the critique of pure reason. Unfortunately, given these restrictions, the critique itself would be impossible to complete because without some moral and political definition of reason, the object of the critique, reason itself, remains undefined. It is obvious that Kant violates his stricture by invoking the *human* quality of reason, as noted above. He does this because the very activity of critical philosophy is a human activity carried on as a dialogue between the words of the text and the actual reader of Kant's text. There can be no critique without empirical human beings who exercise their faculties of reason.

Since the critique is undertaken by real human beings, since it is articulated from a given place in space and time, and since it addresses a human audience with real moral concerns, Kant cannot completely divorce the critique from political life and its definition of human reason. Kant is explicitly aware of the political context of his critique. He repeatedly appeals to his real human readers as those who will help him complete the task of the *Critique.* For example, Kant says, as he begins to define the question of how synthetic a priori questions are possible: "For we not only lighten our own task, by defining it accurately, but make it easier for others, who would test our results (*jedem anderen, der es prüfen will*), to judge whether or not we have succeeded in what we had set out to do."[11] Kant's *Critique* does not occur in a vacuum; it is addressed to empirical human beings who will help to complete it when they themselves scrutinize it critically.

The problem faced by Kant is thus the relation between the transcendental aim of the critical philosophy and its empirical basis. This is why Kant states that the critique is a negative process that attempts to clarify and correct reason: it is a method used by empirical individuals in an attempt to transcend the contingencies of their own empirical existence in order to arrive at knowledge of the necessary conditions for the possibility of that empirical existence. Thus Kant cannot deny that the critique must make use of empirical language, that it must proceed by way of empirical analogies and/or metaphors, and that it is addressed to an empirical audience. It proceeds by negating that which is contingent within the experience of real human beings in order to determine what remains of necessity. This dialectical method is, at every turn in Kant's *Critique,* addressed to empirical individuals. This explains why Kant's critical method occurs in a voice that freely uses the metaphors of republican politics: such metaphors form the empirical background, which the critical dialectic seeks to purify.

The Task of Justification

> Jurists, when speaking of rights and claims, distinguish in a legal action the question of right (*quid juris*) from the question of fact (*quid facti*); and they demand that both be proved. Proof of the former, which has to state the right of the legal claim, they entitle the deduction.
>
> —Kant, *Critique of Pure Reason*[12]

Kant celebrated republican political principles and used metaphors borrowed from political life in order to develop his critique of reason. The question of justification that lies at the heart of the first *Critique* is itself best understood in terms of a metaphorical legal proceeding. Kant assumes that his legal metaphors would supply us with some insight into his methodology. The task of justifying reason to itself can be analogically related to the task of republican self-government. Throughout the first *Critique,* Kant appeals to republican principles of justice and justification. By "republican," I mean that type of political organization in which political subjects are considered as morally autonomous subjects capable of self-government: the members of the republic are the ultimate source of the authority of those who rule them.[13] Reason itself, then, can be understood in terms of what members of the political republic ought to be able to do: citizens of the political republic ought to be able to justify to themselves their own political laws; members of the republic of reason ought to be able to criticize and justify the laws of reason.[14] Kant's regulative methodological principle is that the critique of reason will be justified and complete when it is clear that all members of the community of rational beings freely consent to its conclusions. The system of reason operates, in principle, as a republic in which all rational beings have the right to question the legitimacy of any putative theory of reason. The system of reason is thus involved in the political process of building a consensus among rational beings about what it is to be a rational being. The political goal of republican self-government and the systematic goal of a self-grounded system stem from the same normative view that holds that all disputants ought to have the right to raise objections and have their voices heard. This normative view leads Kant to hover uneasily between the transcendental account of reason and its material, historical, and political basis.

There are at least four ways in which epistemological justification and political justification are linked. 1.) This is based upon a long tradition, beginning with Plato, in which the good, the just, and the true are seen as more or less the same thing. While skeptics like Hume undermine this linkage by understanding truth in terms of psychological justification and ethics in terms of custom or habit, the Kantian system attempts to rehabilitate the Platonic tradition's conception of the unity of truth, justice, and the good. While Plato realized that the philosopher's voice is also a political voice, he despaired of philosophy's ability to justify itself politically. Kant, on the other hand, remained hopeful that political and philosophical enlightenment could converge. 2.) The etymological linkage of moral and epistemological terms such as *Recht* (right, law, moral or epistemological correctness) and related terms like *Gerechtigkeit* (justice, fairness, legitimacy) and *Rechtfertigung* (moral and epistemological justification) led Kant to see conceptual connections between epistemology, ethics, and politics. Thus the consideration of the *Rechtfertigung* or justification of knowledge leads to a consideration of *Recht* in ethical and political contexts.[15] Most important in this context is the fact that the ideas of law and justification in both epistemology and politics are used as methodological principles that are opposed to authority and domination. 3.) Kant's demand for systematic completeness forced him to complement his epistemological considerations with an ethical and political "system." Just as Aristotle, for example, had written ethical and political treatises in addition to his *Physics* and *Metaphysics,* so too, Kant wanted a complete systematic account of the whole of reason. A system of the whole demanded a consideration of politics. Moreover, the demand for completeness is itself a political demand: justice and the good require the complete self-transparency of an explicit written constitution and freedom of speech to question anything and everything. 4.) A sense of the historical situatedness of philosophy required that philosophy deal with contemporary political life. The tumultuous political events of the end of the eighteenth century demanded a response from philosophy. Kant was profoundly influenced by liberalizing transformations in political life including the French Revolution. His political essays can be understood as responses to this turbulent time. This interest in practical politics spills back over into the epistemological system even when this political involvement seems antithetical to the supposedly apolitical interests of the critical philosophy.

While the preceding arguments are significant, they do not adequately explain how the norms of epistemological justification are linked to the norms of political legitimation. For Kant, epistemic justification and political legitimation both appeal to an ideal of free and equal universal self-legislation. The critical project shares the theory and practice of republican justification as the ground of its methodology. In historical terms (as in 4 above), the republican spirit of justice that finally erupted in the French Revolution forms the ground of the whole of the system. In the republican atmosphere at the end of the eighteenth century, reason was understood, following Rousseau, as the *volonté générale;* justification, both in politics and in epistemology, was understood as conformity to the universal and necessary principles which constitute that general will. While we may want to draw a distinction between legitimation (according to law) and justification (according to the idea of justice), Kant's republican ideal elides this distinction because the criterion of universality equates legitimation and justification in practice. Justice, according to the republican ideal, is the result of the free agreement of all. Just laws are universally agreed upon laws. There is some connection here between the universally necessary laws of the understanding and the universally agreed upon laws of political justice. Kant's moral theory clarifies this by defining autonomous moral action as actions whose maxims are universalizable. In the political sphere, Kant defines the "general legislative will" as that which makes possible "the conditions under which alone every man is able to enjoy his right."[16] In the epistemic sphere, Kant states that the critique of reason is based upon "the original right of human reason, which recognizes no other judge than that universal human reason in which everyone has his say."[17] In the *Critique of Judgment* we find further emphasis on universality in his idea of the subjective universality of the aesthetic judgment. Moreover, Kant elucidates his discussion of the *sensus communis* by postulating what he calls maxims of common human understanding: "1) to think for oneself; 2) to put ourselves in thought in the place of everyone else; 3) always to think consistently."[18] For

Kant, the political project of enlightenment and the critical philosophical project were one and the same process by which reason progressed toward autonomy and universality.

The Context of Political Enlightenment

> For enlightenment of this kind, all that is needed is freedom. And the freedom in question is the most innocuous form of all—freedom to make public use of one's reason in all matters.
>
> —Kant, "What is Enlightenment?"[19]

The *Critique of Pure Reason* assumes that its readers will share a certain form of political life. Its readers must understand Kant's political metaphors and his appeal to republican norms of justification. Most importantly, Kant's *Critique* assumes that its readers share that "most innocuous" form of freedom, i.e., "the freedom to make public use of one's reason in all matters" as Kant described it in "What is Enlightenment?" The *Critique* would be impossible to complete if its readers did not possess such political freedom since its readers constitute the jury that will decide if reason has been just in its adjudication of itself. Thus this form of freedom is hardly innocuous. Indeed it is the basis of the critical project. As Kant says in the *Critique,* freedom of thought is required in order for his readers "to test our results, to judge whether or not we have succeeded in what we had set out to do."[20] Such freedom of thought is itself only possible within a political republic in which judgment can be exercised freely.

In considering the historical and political location of Kant's critical philosophy, it is important to remember that philosophy itself, at the time Kant published his *Critiques,* was a political affair. In 1781, at the time of the publication of the first *Critique,* Kant was a professor at the University at Königsberg: he was a royal employee subject to the censorship of the Prussian government. In the 1770s and 1780s under the "enlightened despotism" of Frederick the Great, Kant had been supported in his endeavors. He dedicated the first *Critique* to Baron von Zedlitz, the minister of education and religion under Frederick, to whom he appeals as an "enlightened judge."[21] The essay "What is Enlightenment?" was published in 1784 during Frederick's regime, three years after the publication of the *Critique of Pure Reason.* In 1786 Frederick died, and his successor Frederick Wilhelm II imposed a more rigid religious orthodoxy on Prussia. Kant had to be careful not to offend the authorities and thus had to be aware of the limitations imposed upon his work by political life. Although it is not clear that this censorship had an effect on the content of the first *Critique* (the second edition was published in 1787), the importance of freedom of expression in these tumultuous times must have been obvious to Kant. If it were not obvious before, in 1788, Wöllner, the new minister of religion and education, imposed a strict censorship. In 1792 Kant ran into trouble with this censorship and had to publish his religion book without the state's official sanction. In 1794, in response to Kant's circumvention of the censors, Frederick Wilhelm II himself wrote to Kant admonishing him for his disobedience. For example, after the publication of his religion book, Kant was ordered not to publish anything further on religious matters and refrained from doing so until Frederick Wilhelm died in 1797.[22]

In the first *Critique,* Kant was obviously aware of the political context in which he wrote. Kant's conception of "enlightenment" as a political condition in which one can freely exercise one's reason in public is obviously already at play here, three years earlier than his explicit definition of enlightenment in "What is Enlightenment?" That conception calls for a political state that would permit free public dialogue. Indeed, throughout the text Kant repeatedly invites such a dialogue between himself and his reader. For example, in the preface to the A edition he states that he looks to his reader "for the patience and impartiality of a judge."[23] In other words, Kant opens the *Critique* up to the critical scrutiny of his readers; they are to be the ultimate judges of the work. In the prefatory material of the first *Critique* Kant thanks the political authorities who permit enlightened critique and asks his readers to continue the performance of such a critique. The critique of reason thus assumes that we already share a form of political life in which both the political authorities and the readers of the *Critique* already know what it means to judge impartially and to engage in the dialogical process of enlightened critique.

Within the first *Critique,* the political metaphors themselves are connected with the political idea of enlightenment. Such metaphors are used to describe the critical method itself, thus begging the question of what that critical method is, that is, unless we admit that the critical method itself has already been defined within political life. For example, Kant describes the task of the *Critique* with the following famous words:

> It is a call to reason to undertake anew the most difficult of all its tasks, namely, that of self-knowledge, and to institute a tribunal (*Gerichtshof*) which will assure to reason its lawful (*gerechten*) claims, and dismiss all groundless pretensions, not by despotic decrees (*Machtsprüche*) but in accordance with its own eternal and unalterable laws (*Gesetzen*). This tribunal is no other than the critique of pure reason.[24]

Here Kant explicitly speaks the language of politics to describe the critique of reason: a *tribunal* is required to justify knowledge; this tribunal will *base its judgments on law*; it will not be *despotic*. The conception of justification that Kant appeals to here takes it for granted that his readers will share his conception of political justice and will understand what it means to justify reason in a law-governed manner. What Kemp-Smith translates as "despotic decrees" in the above passage, i.e., *Machtsprüche*—the voice of power, is implicitly contrasted with a different way of speaking that is more dialogical. While the ultimate goal of the critique, self-knowledge, may seem to invoke a monological conception of reason, Kant's appeal to his readers as those who would judge his endeavor makes it clear that reason's self-knowledge only occurs by way of dialogue between different voices.

References to political justice return frequently in the *Critique*, especially in the section on the "Transcendental Doctrine of Method," where Kant distinguishes critique from skepticism and dogmatism. To cite but one example, Kant says: "Reason must, in all its undertakings, subject itself to critique . . . For Reason has no dictatorial authority (*kein dictatorisches Ansehen*); its verdict (*Ausspruch*) is always simply the agreement of free citizens (*die Einstimmung freier Bürger*), of whom each one must be permitted to express without let or hindrance, his objections or even his veto."[25] Here Kant invokes a conception of justice that sounds quite similar to the conception behind the republican constitutional state. Within the republic of reason, the orderly rule of law is supposed to supplant the capricious rule of the despot. In the republic of reason, the verdicts or pronouncements (*Aussprüche*) of reason are supposed to be nothing other than the uncoerced agreement of free citizens, the expression of the general will. Such pronouncements are not to occur as *Machtsprüche* or despotic decrees by the voices of power but as the *Einstimmung* (literally the one-voiced-ness) or agreement of free citizens each of whose voices must be heard. This claim is significant, for it points the critical method beyond Kant's text and invokes a public conception of reason that requires a specific form of political life. Indeed, this is the same criterion that Kant appeals to in the *Rechtslehre* with regard to the justification of legislative power. "Only the concurring (*übereinstimmende*) and united will of all—that is a general and united will of the people by which each decides the same for all and all decide the same for each—can legislate."[26] Not only are the principles of justification within the republic of reason the same as those within the political republic, but the republic of reason implicitly requires the presence of a political republic wherein the uncoerced agreement of free citizens would be possible. In short, Kant's ideal of the uncoerced agreement of free thinkers would itself only be possible within an enlightened republic in which these thinkers are actually free citizens: critique can only occur within an actual political republic where freedom of thought is allowed to flourish.[27]

Certainty and the Critical Method

> The touchstone whereby we decide whether our holding a thing to be true is conviction or mere persuasion is therefore external, namely, the possibility of communicating it and of finding it to be valid for all human reason.
>
> —Kant, *Critique of Pure Reason*[28]

The ironic conclusion that we reach at this point is that reason can only complete the system of itself when political life is such that reason can engage in unfettered self-critique. This conclusion is ironic because it brings seemingly external considerations into the supposedly pure critical method. These external considerations are political and historical: the critique can only be completed when the historical conditions are such that enlightened political life allows the dialogical method of the critique to occur.

In his political writings Kant explicitly discussed the constituents of republican politics. There are definite parallels between Kant's definition of republican politics and his definition of the critical method. In his article on "Perpetual Peace" Kant defines the three principles of the republican constitution as follows: "firstly, the principle of *freedom* for all members of a society (as men); secondly, the principle of *dependence* of everyone upon a single common legislation (as subjects); and thirdly, the principle of legal *equality* for everyone (as citizens)."[29] The constitutional republic respects the freedom and equality of individuals while also requiring dependence on and compliance to the universally agreed upon law. The key concept of the republican state is what Kant calls "rightful freedom," which he defines as the "warrant to obey no external laws except those to which I have been able to give my own consent."[30] As Postema explains the Kantian concept of legitimacy: "no law can lay claim to justice unless it can withstand full public scrutiny."[31] All citizens ought to be equally free to scrutinize and debate the laws. Equality is indeed further defined by Kant as a relationship "whereby no-one can put anyone else under a legal obligation without submitting simultaneously to a law which requires that he can himself be put under the same kind of obligation to the other person."[32] The universality of freedom mentioned here is reminiscent of the Categorical Imperative—freedom and equality are defined in terms of the universality of the moral law in which the will wills without contradiction. Moreover, this moral law is a "single common legislation" to which all wills that would be good must equally conform. We can see then that Kant's understanding of political legitimation is intimately tied to his theory of practical reason: both practical reason and political legitimacy are based upon a republican conception of a self-grounding, self-critical employment of reason.

This conception of practical reason can be extended to Kant's *Critique of Pure Reason* in the following way. Knowledge claims are justified insofar as these claims are adjudicated within a context in which knowers are equal, free, and subject to a single law. Each individual knower has the right to scrutinize and give his or her free consent to the knowledge claim in question. Freedom means that each individual ought to be able to agree or disagree with a knowledge claim. The equality of knowers makes acceptance of the knowledge claim a matter of universality of assent. The truth ought to be accepted by all rational knowers who have equal say in the matter. Finally, the truth is unique. The single common legislation which is the truth imposes itself upon everyone in the same way. Thus there ought not be a multiplicity of truths.

The ideal of the political republic seeks to legitimate laws that will govern multiple agents with diverse interests. This may appear to be a problem foreign to pure reason because the complete system of reason would appear to reject both a multiplicity of knowers and a diversity of interests: pure reason, one would think, ought to be a unity devoid of multiplicity or difference. However, it is clear that Kant realizes that the systematic project is a goal to be achieved. Kant explicitly states that the critique of pure reason is itself only a "propaedeutic to the system of pure reason" intended merely to clarify or prepare for the organon or canon of reason which will itself eventually complete the system.[33] Kant further states that the systematic project must appeal to what he calls in the first *Critique* "regulative" ideals or principles.[34] Kant states that these regulative principles are themselves justified by appeal to the multiplicity of knowers who will assent to them.

In his discussion of truth and knowledge in "The Canon of Reason," Kant explicitly appeals to the practical, republican dimension of truth described in the last paragraph:

> Truth depends upon agreement with the object, and in respect of it the judgments of each and every understanding must therefore be in agreement with each other. The touchstone whereby we decide whether our holding a thing to be true is conviction or mere persuasion is therefore external, namely, the possibility of communicating it and of finding it to be valid for all human reason (*ist also äußerlich die Möglichkeit, dasselbe mitzutheilen, und das Fürwahrhalten für jedes Menschen Vernunft gültig zu befinden*). For there is then at least a presumption that the ground of the agreement of all judgments with each other, notwithstanding the differing characters of individuals, rests upon the common ground, namely, upon the object, and that it is for this reason that they are all in agreement with the object.[35]

Even though truth is conceived as the agreement of a judgment with its object, Kant admits that this agreement can only be established by way of universal agreement of knowers. We are justified in believing that a judgment is "objectively" true, we can claim, in Kant's terms, to possess "certainty (*Gewißheit*)," when all other individuals agree with us about the veracity of that judgment (Kant says that certainty is "for everyone [*für jedermann*]").[36] The system of reason, the justification of human reason, will be complete then, when the regulative ideals that guide this system are assented to by all free and equal knowers. The construction of the organon of reason requires the agreement of all. This will only be possible when all knowers are actually able to raise objections and have their voices heard. In other words, the laws, which ensure the freedom of criticism that exists within the political republic, are themselves the necessary propaedeutic for critical philosophy. Epistemic justification can only be completed when political life has become enlightened, i.e., when one is free, as Kant says in "What is Enlightenment?" "to make public use of one's reason in all matters."[37]

One may object that the first *Critique* is an attempt at transcendental justification that seeks necessary laws for experience, not merely laws that we all happen to agree upon. The categories of reason are necessary because all rational beings *must* employ them. I am not denying this. Rather, I maintain that Kant characterizes the transcendental proof of this necessity as relying upon the free agreement of all rational beings. The categories are not necessary because we all agree to use them. However, we can only say that we *know* that they are necessary because we all agree that they are. This is the sense of "touchstone" or criteria to which Kant appeals above.

For Kant, the deduction of the categories is valid because all free and equal knowers will agree that it is. In the Transcendental Deduction, Kant explicitly invokes juridical and political categories of proof. Kant defines "deduction" in terms of the question of right (*quid juris*), the question being by what right we can establish the *a priori* necessity of this list of the categories of the understanding. Kant states that his conception of deduction is taken over from "jurists" (*Rechtslehrer*) among whom deduction means "to state the authority (*Befugniss*) or the legal claim (*Rechtsanspruch*)" to a judgment.[38] Kant's explicit reference to jurisprudence here indicates that the critique of reason relies upon the norms of republican political practice. Not only does transcendental proof appeal to the methodological practices of republican government, it also requires that political practices already be republican. The Transcendental Deduction occurs before the tribunal of reason, which consists of all free and equal members of the commonwealth of reason, those who can freely engage in the critical practice of publicly scrutinizing the laws of reason. Critique itself is thus only possible within republican political life because only in a real political republic will knowers be free to carry out the critique.

While Kant, in the Transcendental Deduction, merely hints at this in his use of juridical language, his methodological considerations throughout the first *Critique,* some of which were cited above, indicate that he is aware that the *Critique* itself takes part in the process of public scrutiny and deliberation. Kant says, to cite a few more examples, in his description of what he has accomplished in the section called the Transcendental Dialectic, that he has "thought it advisable, with a view to the prevention of errors in the future, to draw up in full detail what we may describe as being the records of this lawsuit [of reason against itself] and to deposit them in the archives of human reason."[39] Most significantly, at the beginning and end of the first *Critique,* Kant addresses the reader of the text directly, asking the reader to think for himself about the arguments put forward in the text. The reader of the *Critique* is described both as a free citizen and an impartial judge (A xxi; B 766–7), one who can listen rationally, who can freely bring objections before the bar, who can judge for himself (B 884), and who must in the end reach an agreement with Kant about the necessity of the categories. In short, the *Critique* is itself an experiment in republican self-government in which the arguments for the necessary rules of reason are open to public scrutiny and which will be viewed as conclusive when agreed to by all.

Expression and The Metacritique

> Despite the great wealth of our languages, the thinker often finds himself at a loss for the expression (*Ausdruck*) which exactly fits his concept, and for want of which he is unable to be really intelligible to others or even to himself.
>
> —Kant, *Critique of Pure Reason*[40]

Let us assume that Kant's use of political metaphors was deliberate. Indeed, as the above epigraph indicates, it is clear that Kant was aware of the importance of the problem of expression. This can be seen, moreover, in his efforts in the *Prolegomena* to present the content of the *Critique of Pure Reason* in a more "popular" fashion. Kant admits in the Introduction to the *Prolegomena* that his *Critique* had been misjudged and misunderstood in part because "the work is dry, obscure, opposed to all ordinary notions, and moreover long-winded."[41] Here Kant explicitly recognizes that the mode of presentation is an important factor to be considered. In the preface to the second edition of the *Critique,* Kant again admits that the mode of expression of the *Critique* may have been, in places, inadequate. He indicates here that the critical project is part of an ongoing dialogue within the community of philosophers and thanks his critics. Indeed one may argue that Kant's

Prolegomena and the subsequent edition of the *Critique* were written in response to his critics. One of the most famous of these critical reviews was the Garve-Feder review of 1782. This review itself had some political overtones, as Feder altered Garve's review in order to suit his own ends.[42] Kant's consternation with his critics shows that he was concerned with being understood and that he recognized that language and style—the issue of voice—was important. He concludes the preface to the second edition with the hope that some popular stylist would take up the critical philosophy so that it might "secure for itself the necessary elegance of statement."[43] This suffices to show that Kant was concerned with the linguistic mode of expression and desired to be understood by the philosophical public.

In bringing up the question of expression, Kant seems to foreshadow the metacritique of his system as articulated by his colleagues Hamann and Herder.[44] The metacritique focused upon two crucial facts about Kant's transcendental arguments: these arguments must be articulated in ordinary language, and this ordinary language is historically and politically located. There are two possible conclusions reached by the metacritical challenge to Kant: either the critique of reason is impossible because it exceeds the limits of language, or the critique of reason should become a critique of language. Both Hamann and Herder share the conclusion that language and reason are socially and historically located. Hamann's metacritique is aimed at the fact that the very language of the critical project is itself an empirical historical residue that cannot then attain its goal of purity. Herder expands this critique of Kant to include the claim that we can only ever understand the world from analogy with our own historically determined perspective. At issue here is the question of the autonomy of reason and the completeness of the critical project. The metacritique claimed that reason could not transcend its historical situatedness in order to arrive at an a priori comprehension of itself. The best that could be done was to undertake a historical reconstruction of the origin and development of language and reason. This project was taken up explicitly by Fichte, as we shall see subsequently.

It is important to note that Kant himself was aware of the metacritical question even within the first *Critique,* as indicated in the quote with which we began the present section. Language as the mode of expression is an important question, although it is not one that Kant takes up in earnest. Kant is aware of the fact that thinking requires an adequate mode of expression in which it can be communicated both to others and to the thinker himself. As early as 1784, three years before the appearance of the second edition of the first *Critique*, Kant speculated on language in response to Herder. This is evidenced in Kant's review of Herder's *Ideas on the Philosophy of the History of Mankind,* where Kant quotes Herder's statement that "Only in conjunction with his erect gait does true human language appear.—Both in theory and in practice, reason (*Vernunft*) is merely something acquired (*vernehmen*) and learned, a proportion and direction of man's ideas and faculties to which he was predetermined by his organization and way of life."[45] The issue here, indicated by Herder's pun upon the German word *Vernunft,* is whether reason is somehow dependent upon historical, social, and political antecedents. Indeed, Kant takes up the issue of history in an effort to show that reason, although it has unfolded historically, is not dependent upon this historical unfolding. In his ironic account of human history in his "Conjectures on the Beginning of Human History," Kant claims that we can only deduce the origins of human reason by using the imagination: such imaginative reconstructions are more fiction than philosophy. Within this account, Kant simply assumes that human beings developed language from natural sociability and "the urge to communicate."[46] And Kant goes no further into the question of language.

We might argue that Kant sidesteps the metacritique by simply assuming that logic transcends empirical language.[47] However, his own recognition of the importance of the mode of expression, his use of political metaphors, and his dialogical approach to critical philosophy indicate that the question of language was important for Kant. Kant's transcendental method, however, aims beyond language and politics to the conditions for the possibility of these even while language and politics are the condition for the possibility of completing the critical project. There is indeed a circle here. Although Kant does not take up this issue, he does not neglect language and politics. Indeed, these are essential for his project. Kant does recognize, as I've shown above, that the critical project is bound up with the political project of republicanism, and he does not sidestep the issue of the political context. This can be seen, for example, in "What is Enlightenment?" where enlightenment is defined as the public use of reason. Habermas interprets this by saying that Kant "conceived of the 'public sphere' at once as the principle of legal order and as the method of enlightenment."[48] Kant responds to the metacritique, not by taking up the question of language, but by making the public use of reason a matter of concern in the critical project. It is not language per se that is an issue for Kant. Rather, it is the public use of reason that includes speaking, writing, and especially thinking. In other words, Kant realizes that the critical project is dependent upon the political project of enlightenment.

The methodological problem that Kant confronts is that, although we think we know the meaning of concepts such as freedom of thought, self-government, autonomy, and reason, we cannot be sure that we have properly understood these concepts until we have completed the critical project by examining these concepts among ourselves, using our own language. We will not know that we are exercising our freedom until we complete the process of becoming critically aware of the nature of freedom and its relation to the laws of political life and epistemology. This is what makes the critique itself necessary: it is an attempt to clarify such concepts. However, if we do not yet have political autonomy, we cannot be sure that the critical project is fully justified. There are several problems here. If we are not free publicly to exercise reason, then how will we know whether we have properly tested the results of the critique under the scrutiny of free public judgment? If the self that undertakes the task of self-critique is not yet empirically free, how will this self ever know that its self-criticism reaches the purity it set out to establish?

These problems reiterate the conflict between rhetoric and philosophy. On the one hand, Kant's critical philosophy claims that it is philosophical in the sense that it freely brings us to self-knowledge. On the other hand, all of this talk of self-knowledge may be merely another rhetorical ploy that is in service to ideological structures of domination. Kant's project requires both intellectual and political autonomy and assumes that philosophical language can transcend the ploys of rhetorical oratory. The question of linguistic expression becomes explicit for Kant in the third *Critique*. Kant criticizes abuses of rhetoric, for example, by describing them as "the art of carrying on a serious business of the understanding as if it were a free play of the imagination."[49] The rhetorician uses images as substitutes for arguments. Although rhetoric may persuade people toward truth and justice, Kant's ideal demands that human reason be persuaded by proper reasons and not by beautiful images.[50] Thus although Kant is aware of the metacritical question of language, he believes that language, when properly used in the context of enlightenment, can lead to a genuine transformation of spirit. Kant searched for a mode of expression that did not beguile the spirit by way of beautiful rhetoric. Nonetheless, he recognized that analogies and metaphors (specifically those referring to political life) were necessary to communicate his purpose.

Conclusion

> We do admittedly say that whereas a higher authority may deprive us of freedom of speech or of writing, it cannot deprive us of freedom of thought. But how much and how accurately (*Richtigkeit*) would we think if we did not think, so to speak, in community with others to whom we communicate our thoughts and who communicate their thoughts to us (*wenn wir nicht gleichsam in Gemeinschaft mit andern, denen wir unsere und die uns ihre Gedanken mittheilen, dächten*)! We may therefore conclude that the same external constraint which deprives people of their freedom to communicate their thoughts in public also removes their freedom of thought . . .
>
> —Kant, "What is Orientation in Thinking?"[51]

Kant's most general project is a project of human enlightenment. His political and epistemological concerns implicate one another. This explains the earnestness with which Kant turns to political themes. His struggle to transform the political realm can be understood, in part, as a struggle to create the conditions under which the critical project could be completed. In all of Kant's political writings he uses his voice to speak in favor of that enlightened state in which freedom of thought is allowed to flourish. The above statement from "What is Orientation in Thinking?" was first published in October of 1786, just a few months before the second edition of the *Critique of Pure Reason* was published. Kant is clearly aware here that freedom of speech is a crucial prerequisite for freedom of thought. While Kant admits that some freedom of thought would be possible without freedom of speech, freedom of speech serves to guarantee the extent and the accuracy of our thought. A critical enquiry that would be complete and accurate could only occur within an enlightened political space that permitted free speech to flourish. It is thus, perhaps, not too much to conclude that Kant's political writings aim at *clarifying* the conditions for the possibility of completing the critique of reason. In the next chapter I will extend this conclusion further and consider the way in which Kant uses his voice actually to *create* the conditions for the possibility of completing the critique of reason.

Before we turn to this further conclusion, let us consider a significant problem with Kant's critical project. In real historical terms, experiments in self-government have occasionally lead from freedom to despotism. Once the traditional authorities had been done away with, as in France, for example, freedom devolved into terror. Kant is aware of this problem as he undertakes his critique of reason.[52] He warns us repeatedly that the *Critique* ought not be despotic. However, he seems to be aware that his revolutionary experiment in the republic of reason can have troubling consequences. Kant admits, for example, that the demand for justification that is taken up in the Transcendental Deduction "involves us in considerable perplexity, in that no clear legal reason (*Rechtsgrund*) can be produced through which the authority (*Befugniss*) of their [the concepts] use can be made clear, neither from experience nor from reason."[53] This problem amounts to a question about the legitimacy of the verdict of the tribunal of reason. If reason is the plaintiff, the defendant, and the judge, how can an impartial verdict be given? How can we ensure that the agreement of the reader and the author of the *Critique* is a mutual, uncoerced (i.e., republican) agreement? In short, how can we ensure that the republic of reason is not despotic?

On the first page of the preface to the first edition of the *Critique of Pure Reason*, Kant gives us a clue: "It [reason] begins with principles which it has no option save to employ in the course of experience, and which this experience at the same time abundantly justifies it in using."[54] Reason justifies itself by appealing to the unavoidable laws of its own experience. It is not clear what sort of justification this would be, however, because it is not clear why the laws of reason are themselves unavoidable—in fact this is the very question being asked in the *Critique*. In other words, how do we know that the necessity of the categories is a legitimate necessity and not a despotic decree of a tyrannical reason?[55] How can reason judge itself when its own criteria are themselves in question? What justifies the republican practices appealed to by the *Critique* and prevents these practices from being viewed as dogmatic impositions and despotic decrees?

The epistemological problem here is how we can guarantee that universal agreement really is the "touchstone" of truth if we still do not have immediate knowledge of the thing in itself—we could all agree wrongly after all. The moral parallel here is the problem of how we can guarantee that universalizable maxims are good and not evil. Finally, the political problem is how we can guarantee that universally agreed upon laws are not themselves unjust or tyrannical. As we shall see, these problems were confronted by Fichte, Hegel, and Marx as they attempted to clarify the political entanglement at the heart of Kant's system. Kant, for the most part, simply assumes that all knowers, as citizens of the political republic, would agree freely (without being coerced) to the method of his deduction. He makes this assumption explicit, as mentioned above, at the very beginning and very end of the *Critique* (A xxi, B 884), where he asks the reader to judge for him/herself whether the *Critique* has been successful. This basic principle of free and equal agreement is not justified by the *Critique*. Rather, the justification of such a method points beyond the *Critique* to Kant's political thought.

CHAPTER 4

Kant's Political Philosophy: Progress and Philosophical Intervention

> It is not to be expected that kings will philosophize or that philosophers will become kings; nor is it to be desired, however, since the possession of power inevitably corrupts the free judgement of reason. Kings or sovereign peoples (i.e., those governing themselves by egalitarian laws) should not, however, force the class of philosophers to disappear or to remain silent, but should allow them to speak publicly.
>
> —Kant, *Perpetual Peace*[1]

Kant lived and wrote during a turbulent political epoch. Much of his explicit political philosophizing occurs under the shadow of two important political events: the end of "enlightened despotism" in Prussia with the death of Frederick the Great in 1786 and the symbolic birth of a new liberal era with the French Revolution of 1789. With the ascension of Frederick Wilhelm II to the throne, Prussia entered a period of regression and reaction against the enlightenment, seen most clearly in Wöllner's edicts of 1788 instituting strict censorship and requiring pledges of faith on the part of theological faculty. At the same time the French Revolution held out hope that enlightenment would finally dawn across Europe. Kant's writings during this period reflect his hopeful view of political life and his concern to defend the autonomy of critical reason, which for Kant was the very mechanism of enlightenment, against state censorship. Although Kant did retreat somewhat in response to Frederick Wilhelm's rebukes, he continued to defend freedom of thought in his political writings and in his *Religion within the Limits of Reason Alone,* a political book published in the midst of the Wöllner censorship. Despite continuing to challenge the political authorities to become more enlightened, Kant did not allow himself to become a martyr for the enlightenment and remained profoundly ambivalent about the efficacy of the philosopher's voice as a catalyst of historical change.[2]

Kant continually advocated advancement toward enlightenment, even though he recognized that the revolutionary content of the philosopher's voice should be constrained by the philosopher's duty to obey the law. Given this constraint on political activity, Kant limits philosophy to an educational role inspired by hope for moral and political progress. Although the voice of philosophy is the voice of enlightened progress, this voice should not become overtly political. The above epigraph, taken from Kant's essay, *Perpetual Peace* (published in 1795 in the midst of this era), shows us how acutely Kant was aware of the conflict between philosophy and politics. Kant's solution to this conflict is to separate philosophy and politics in order to preserve the autonomy of philosophy.

Nonetheless, as we saw in chapter 3, Kant views philosophy and politics as intertwined. His critical methodology points philosophy back toward political life: the republican transformation of political life can be understood as the propaedeutic for the completion of the critical project.[3] Moreover, as Kant recognizes in *Perpetual Peace,* the republican transformation of political life will also serve to make the completion of the practical moral project possible. Although in the *Critique of Practical Reason,* Kant resolves the antinomy of happiness and morality by appealing to "the postulates of pure practical reason," (freedom, immortality, and God), in his political essays, Kant endeavors to resolve this antinomy in practice.[4] Nonetheless, since Kant's critical philosophy is oriented toward seeing the limits of knowledge, he recognizes that there are no final assurances about an enlightened outcome to the political struggle. Instead, Kant relies upon what might be called a "postulate of political philosophy," hope. Hope, based upon the fact of the French Revolution, allows Kant to continue to advocate enlightenment even as Prussia becomes reactionary.

Kant thus seems to have inverted the traditional Platonic notion of the relationship between theory and practice. The traditional interpretation of Plato holds that philosophical enlightenment is prior to political transformation and that, indeed, moral insight is required for a just critique of political life. For this reason, in the *Republic,* Plato maintains that the just state will be the state that is organized according to the wisdom of the philosopher-king. Kant's notion of the relation between theory and practice is more organic and republican, by which I mean that he recognizes a reciprocal interaction between philosophy and politics. While he does argue that the philosopher plays a significant role as the catalyst for political transformation, Kant recognizes that philosophical reflection is itself dependent upon these very political transformations. This is why he argues for a division of labor between philosophy and politics, and concludes that it is not to be expected that "kings will philosophize or that philosophers will become kings."[5] There is a two-sided development in the history of enlightenment. On the one hand, moral and scientific development are dependent upon republican political transformation. On the other hand, republican political transformation is itself dependent upon the moral and theoretical projects of enlightenment. While the moral and theoretical projects require a free, law-governed public sphere for their completion, republican politics requires theoretical insight into the moral truth that all human beings are free and have the equal right to consent to the laws that govern them.

The circle which thus appears to result is the very problem of perpetual peace that Kant returns to not only in his essay by that name but also in his other political essays, the *Rechtslehre* of the *Metaphysics of Morals,* and even in his *Religion within the Limits of Reason Alone*. This problem is an instantiation of the general problem of the relation between philosophy and politics: how do we convince pragmatic politicians that the proper end of political life is not the perpetual war of Machiavellian politics but rather the perpetual peace of the kingdom of ends? This is a problem because the Machiavellian logic of political life reinforces itself such that the truth of political life in which Machiavellian princes vie for power is in fact a state of perpetual war, not perpetual peace: enlightened political realists thus seem justified in continuing to prepare for war, not for peace. If this were the case, if there were no hope that the Machiavellian cycle could be broken, then there would be no hope for moral progress or for the attainment of the republican conditions for the possibility of the completion of the critical project. Enlightenment requires that republicanism burst forth and shatter the cycle of war.

While Kant's defense of enlightened despotism shares something with the Hobbesian resolution to the problem of Machiavellian politics, Kant's liberal republican sympathies ultimately conflict with this despotic approach. The catalyst that triggers the dissolution of the Machiavellian cycle for Kant is not the Leviathan, but rather the philosopher's voice, which freely criticizes the immoral practices of political life, thereby mediating the conflict between moral truth and political pragmatics. What is needed for this mediation is not a philosopher-king but philosophers who are free to speak about political matters and enlightened moral politicians who are willing to permit free philosophical criticism.[6] Kant makes it very clear in numerous places that the solution to the problem of perpetual war is solved by the free public exercise of the philosopher's voice.

The treatise, *Perpetual Peace,* can thus be read as an address to the Prussian authorities in defense of philosophy. He states explicitly in what he calls the "secret article of a perpetual peace" that "the maxims of the philosophers on the conditions under which peace is possible shall be consulted by states which are armed for war."[7] There is considerable irony in the fact that this strong claim about the political power of the philosopher's voice must be called a "secret" article. He realizes that this bold statement may "seem humiliating for the legislative authority of a state, to which we must naturally attribute the highest degree of wisdom, to seek instruction from subjects (the philosophers) regarding the principles on which it should act in its relations with other states."[8] Kant concludes, then, that the state may keep its reliance on philosophy a secret. This is done by merely allowing the philosophers to "speak freely on the universal maxims of warfare and peacemaking."[9] Although Kant admits that the state is under no compulsion to submit to the will of the philosopher, the philosopher's advice should nonetheless be listened to by the enlightened state interested in perpetual peace. "The philosopher should be given a *hearing*."[10] Thus the key to the transformation of political life is not the coming of the philosopher-king but, rather, the enlightenment of the king such that the king will "allow them [philosophers] to speak publicly."[11] Kant gives us no direct indication about what sort of historical transformations would follow from philosophical freedom, although he does indicate that the further transformation of political life will be effected by what he calls the "moral politician." It is not much of a leap to conclude that the moral politician is a politician who has heard the philosopher's voice.

In what follows I will examine the way in which, for Kant, the philosopher's voice functions as the catalyst that stimulates progress toward the completion of the enlightenment project. I will then examine the apparent contradiction between Kant's teleological view of history and his claims about the transformative power of the philosopher's voice. I will consider what Kant says about the prophetic function of the philosopher's voice. I will then contrast this prophetic function with Kant's natural teleological view of history and argue that there is an antinomy in Kant's notion of progress: progress is a natural occurrence, and progress is the result of philosophical intervention in history. To resolve this antinomy I maintain that we must consider the intimate organic relation between philosophical and political enlightenment. I will argue that Kant was aware of his own role within the autocatalytic process of enlightenment: it was this awareness and the hope that it inspired that encouraged Kant to undertake his task of enlightening political life even in light of the repressive tendencies in his native Prussia. With this understanding of Kant's self-consciousness of his own political voice, we will be poised to move beyond Kant to consider the deliberate political intervention of Fichte, the regressive philosophical politics of Hegel, and the prophetic politics of Marx

History and Hope

> But man is represented as having fallen into evil only through seduction, and hence as being not basically corrupt (even as regards his original predisposition to good) but rather as still capable of an improvement, in contrast to a seducing spirit, that is,

> a being for whom temptation of the flesh cannot be accounted as an alleviation of guilt. For man, therefore, who despite a corrupted heart yet possesses a good will, there remains hope of a return to the good from which he has strayed.
>
> —Kant, *Religion within the Limits of Reason Alone*[12]

Kant's ethical, religious, historical, and political writings are nothing, if not optimistic. Of course Kant is acutely aware of the difference between optimism and knowledge. The goal of his critical project is to define the limits of knowledge in order to "make room for faith."[13] Hope and faith serve as crucial motivating forces behind Kant's political activity. Kant has faith that history is a progressive development toward the eventual conjunction of duty and happiness. This ideal conjunction is characterized as a state in which human beings will be fully moral and will thus deserve happiness. It is also characterized as a state in which the political system will be just and will thus reward moral agents with what they deserve. In short, this is the state of complete justice in which those who are just are also those who are happy. In one of his more prophetic moments, Kant describes the completion of the historical progress toward justice as follows:

> Violence will gradually become less on the part of those in power, and obedience towards the laws will increase. There will no doubt be more charity, less quarrels in legal actions, more reliability in keeping one's word, and so on in the commonwealth, partly from a love of honor, and partly from a lively awareness of where one's own advantage lies; and this will ultimately extend to the external relations between the various peoples, until a cosmopolitan society is created.[14]

Here Kant envisions a utopian synthesis of the two opposing forces of morality and happiness in the cosmopolitan society of perpetual peace. This completion of history will occur when civil law is organized according to the formal principle of right, i.e., the political formulation of the Categorical Imperative intended to prohibit the state from using unjust force against persons who are ends in themselves. Indeed, in *Perpetual Peace,* Kant offers the Categorical Imperative as an antidote to Machiavellian politics in which the ends justify the means. As it is formulated by Kant there, the Categorical Imperative asks politicians not to subordinate goodness to expedience: "Act in such a way that you can wish to have your maxim to become the universal law (irrespective of what the end in view may be)."[15] Kant's ideal will be completed when the "moral politician" takes this formal principle up as the principle of civil right. The moral politician, moreover, should turn to civil legislation as a moral task whose end is the completion of the kingdom of ends that would result in and from the achievement of perpetual peace. In

Kant's utopia, human beings will finally see that their own "advantage," i.e., their happiness, lies in morality itself. This concurrence of morality and prudence will result in a just society within the nation-state as well as peace in international affairs. This ideal is the object of Kant's hope throughout his political writings.

Despite his optimism, Kant recognizes that the road toward the ideal is as long and arduous as is the process of redemption from original sin. Indeed, it is instructive to compare what Kant says about original sin in his *Religion* with what he says about progress in political history. We can hope for progress because reason is both the cause of our fallen state and the cure for this fall. Reason was culpable when human beings first asked the question of why we had to follow our innate moral sensibility; likewise, reason is able to tell us why we should return to the moral law. Hope for progress is the same as hope for autonomy. "Man himself must make or have made himself into whatever, in a moral sense, whether good or evil, he is or is to become. Either condition must be an effect of his free choice; for otherwise he could not be held responsible for it and could therefore be morally neither good nor evil."[16] The two opposing human drives "toward happiness and toward duty" have been and will continue to be at odds; it is reason's task to harmonize these, both within the individual and within society.

Kant recognizes that the seemingly unendless struggle between these two opposing forces is the creative tension of human culture, education, and history. Kant's optimism is thus tempered with his recognition that the length and difficulty of the path we have followed through recorded history to the present was necessary for the development of truly human culture. Human development is the result of the dialectical strife between the objective moral demand for justice and the subjective demand for happiness. In various places, Kant explicitly recognizes that this dialectic is a necessary stage in the education of the human race. Without this conflict, human beings would live a "pastoral existence of perfect concord, self-sufficiency, and mutual love."[17] However, contra Rousseau, Kant maintains that in this Arcadian setting "all human talents would remain hidden forever in a dormant state, and men, as good-natured as the sheep they tended would scarcely render their existence more valuable than that of their animals."[18] Here Kant seems to foreshadow Nietzsche's claim that with the advent of Christianity, "human beings become interesting," for it is the conflict between a moral world of justice and the human world of self-interest that propels humans forward and that gives us ideals according to which we can direct and shape our lives. Moreover, Kant argues, foreshadowing Humboldt, that nature herself has contributed to division and strife among nations by creating linguistic and religious differences.[19] These differences among nations contribute in the short run to "mutual hatred" and war. In the long run, however, these differences stimulate "an equilibrium of forces and a most vigorous rivalry."[20] Diversity and competition thus work against that type of moribund perpetual peace—the peace of the graveyard—to which Kant ironically alludes in the introduction to *Perpetual Peace.* Diversity and competition prevent history from ending in the graveyard of freedom that could result from a despotic form of universality that denies individual difference.

Historical development results from the strife that originates with the possibilities implicit in the idea of human freedom: the conflict between self-interested instinct and the moral law. While Kant admits that this strife will continue indefinitely into the future, he also claims that as history progresses, we continually approach the point at which morality and happiness will converge. Our task is to become more fully human by struggling to mediate between the conflicting demands of happiness and morality: we must suffer and labor to become fully human.[21] Such struggle is the very mechanism of progress that is further mediated by philosophical reflection upon the nature of this struggle, a reflection that gives us hope that the struggle is worth undertaking. "A philosophical attempt to work out a universal history of the world in accordance with a plan of nature aimed at a perfect civil union of mankind, must be regarded as possible and even as capable of furthering the purpose of nature itself."[22] Philosophy furthers this task by helping us understand the mechanisms of history and by giving us hope that these mechanisms will lead to progress.

Kant's optimism about human progress is not completely naïve. In his religion book, for example, he argues that the possibility of evil is a necessary precondition for human freedom. He does not claim that human development will be completed all at once in a millennial apocalypse. Nor is he sanguine about the efficacy of philosophy as an engine for development. He admits that "no philosopher has yet been able to bring (the principles of states) into agreement with morality."[23] He concludes:

> Nor (sad to say) has any philosopher been able to propose better principles which at the same time can be brought into harmony with human nature. The result is that the *philosophical millennium* which hopes for a state of perpetual peace based on a league of peoples, a world-republic, even as the theological millennium, which tarries for the competed moral improvement of the entire human race, is universally ridiculed as a wild fantasy.[24]

Thus Kant claims that progress, like the strife out of which it develops, is an ongoing process not simply to be completed by the invocation of the rhetoric of "perpetual peace" and "the kingdom of ends." Although the philosopher's voice can work to further progress toward these ends, Kant realizes that to put our entire faith in philosophy would be to live in a fantasy world of unrealistic hope regarding the practical power of philosophical speech.

Although philosophical speech may be the catalyst for future progress, practical political transformations are also required, at least to the extent that such practical transformations are what make it possible for philosophical speech to be freely and publicly expressed. Indeed such political transformations themselves make enlightened philosophical critique possible.

Despite his recognition of the limits of philosophy's power to change the world, Kant remains hopeful because he views progress as a natural process guided by a teleology implicit in nature. Progress occurs as we come to affirm the natural basis of the conflict between morality and happiness and the teleological unfolding of this conflict in history. Again, such affirmation of the teleological organization of history requires philosophical insight, including insight into the inherent limits of teleological judgment. For Kant, teleological judgments occur under regulative principles for judging parts as united in a purposive whole. Such judgments go beyond the limits of theoretical cognition in the same way as hope and faith do. Nonetheless, these judgments, like hope and faith, are essential for us as free moral beings. "Faith is trust in the attainment of a design, the promotion of which is a duty, but the possibility of the fulfillment of which (and consequently also that of the only conditions of it thinkable by us) is not to be comprehended by us."[25] Thus Kant's faith in the possibility of progress is part of his moral duty to the regulative ideal of enlightenment. This delineates for him the proper exercise of the philosopher's voice as both clarifying and carrying out the project of enlightenment.

Reason and experience show us that strife cannot be overcome by a miraculous epiphany that brings sudden enlightenment to the human race. Rather, human beings overcome strife by recognizing its natural basis and by having faith that it can be overcome. Once we are critically enlightened about the causes of strife and the moral necessity of hope, we will then be in a position to create a society in which strife is diminished and in which perpetual peace is attained. Despite the necessity of hope, we must also recognize that progress is painstaking and requires struggle, diligence, and patience.

Kant completes his description of his utopian ideal with the following disclaimer:

> Such developments do not mean, however, that the basic moral capacity of mankind will increase in the slightest, for this would require a kind of new creation or supernatural influence. For we must not expect too much of human beings in their progressive improvements, or else we shall merit the scorn of those politicians who would gladly treat man's hopes of progress as the fantasies of an overheated mind.[26]

Here Kant acknowledges again that his own hopes could seem fantastic to practically minded politicians. Politicians will raise all sorts of practical objections to the work of progress, that is, until they have been enlightened by philosophy about the moral necessity of hope.

Autocatalytic Publicity and the Antinomy of Progress

> The dominion of the good principle begins, and a sign that "the kingdom of God is at hand" appears, as soon as the basic principles of its constitution first become *public*; for (in the realm of the understanding) that is already here whose causes, which alone can bring it to pass, have generally taken root, even though the complete development of its appearance in the sensuous world is still immeasurably distant.
>
> —Kant, *Religion within the Limits of Reason Alone*[27]

Kant's task as a philosopher of progress is to show us how progress is possible without losing sight of the very real difficulties found at the level of practical politics. Although it is easy to see that for Kant the key to progress is the publicity of the principles of progress, it is more difficult to see how these principles are to be made public. In his discussion of the founding of the religious commonwealth or the church, which is analogous to the cosmopolitan state of perpetual peace, Kant recognizes that we encounter a problem as we attempt to create that moral community that is the condition for the possibility of further moral development:

> to found a church as a commonwealth under religious laws seems, however, to call for more wisdom (both of insight and of good disposition) than can well be expected of men, especially since it seems necessary to presuppose the presence in them, for this purpose, of the moral goodness which the establishment of such a church has in view.[28]

The religious problem may seem easier to solve than the problem of constituting the cosmopolitan society because the very content of religion tends in the right direction, i.e., toward morality. National political societies are, of course, constituted by respect for law in the form of the civil constitution. Even though this may be merely external conformity to law, there is hope for progress toward a subjective appropriation of the moral content of the civil law.

Once human beings are constrained to be good by justified civil laws under a republican government, they will no longer fear the self-interested motivations of their neighbors; their hope for progress will itself thus begin to become justified. They will have entered into a condition of peace and will be able to focus on the execution of moral duty without having to worry about practical political disadvantages that might have resulted from moral activity done in an immoral environment. In this way, Kant argues that even a "nation of devils" may be formed into a civil society such that the "public conduct of the citizens will be the same as if they did not have such evil attitudes."[29] Thus Kant concludes that political transformation is the propaedeutic for moral transformation. This is especially true when we include the sphere of international justice. This sphere is little better than the situation of the "nation of devils" because international relations are constituted by self-interested nations reaching an uneasy peace based upon mutual self-interest and the balance of power. Kant concludes with regard to relations between states that "we cannot expect their moral attitudes to produce a good political constitution; on the contrary, it is only through the latter that the people can be expected to attain a good level of moral culture."[30] In other words, the development of morality relies, in part, upon the establishment of political peace in terms of both a civil constitution and the league of nations.

Thus Kant argues in the *Contest of the Faculties* that the state should realize that it is in its own interest for its citizens to be enlightened about the moral content of the civil law. This enlightenment will best occur when it is not done by state officials but, rather, when it is undertaken by "free teachers of right, i.e., philosophers."[31] Philosophers are to be the educators of mankind. Kant defends this enlightenment idea against the encroachment of state authority. Free philosophical teachers of right help us develop toward enlightenment by showing us practical ways in which moral hope might be completed.

Kant thus thinks that philosophical ideals can stimulate progress. According to Kant, the key moment in progress is the moment at which philosophical ideals become public: "But truth and goodness do not fail to communicate themselves far and wide once they have become public, thanks to their natural affinity with the moral predisposition of rational beings generally."[32] In other words, Kant believes that once the truth of progress has been publicly communicated, this truth will begin a chain reaction that leads toward continual future progress. This is why Kant repeatedly emphasizes the importance of free public expression of philosophical critique. Such public expression of philosophical insight acts as the catalyst that begins the chain reaction of progress: public expression of philosophical critique transforms the public sphere, thus making the further public expression of philosophical critique possible, and so on in an ever increasing autocatalytic progress. Kant's practical agenda is to begin the process within the nation-state, such that the state at least listens to the philosopher's voice, even in if only in secret. As politicians become accustomed to attending to the philosopher's voice, they will become "moral politicians" and will then work for a similar transformation of international relations.

A philosopher such as Kant who looks to the future with the hope of human progress and interprets the past and the present in terms of this hoped-for future, is as much a prophet as a philosopher. Kant was self-conscious of this prophetic possibility implicit in public philosophy. In *The Contest of the Faculties,* Kant asks the following crucial question about his own historical interpretation: "But how is it possible to have history a priori?" In other words, Kant wonders how it is possible to make prognostications about the future progress of human history based upon a priori scientific truths. He responds to his own question with the following pregnant phrase: "The answer is that it is possible if the prophet himself occasions and produces the events he predicts."[33] An idea of future history is possible to the extent that the historian is himself part of history and, in fact, works to bring his own vision of the future into actuality. In other words, the prophetic work of the philosopher's voice is undertaken with the hoped-for progress serving as a regulative ideal for the philosopher's activity. This is similar to the way in which faith and those other postulates of practical reason are essential to moral progress. Kant's diagnosis of the present condition and his analysis of history is based upon his ideal vision of the future and certain facts about the present. Indeed, the very fact that Kant is able to publish his views and the great symbol of the French Revolution make it clear that history was actually progressing in the direction Kant hoped for. Kant attempts to avoid the fantastic, by using empirical details to support his claims about progress.[34] However, even his interpretation of these empirical facts is tied up with his larger regulative ideal of history as progressive and his desire to help accomplish this development.

This recognition of the prophetic nature of the philosopher's voice raises several difficulties with regard to questions about the *truth* of history and politics. The problem for Kant is that if his historical account has an influence upon the present or upon the future development of the human race, then it is not yet known to be a true account, i.e., the truth of Kant's prophetic history will itself only be known in the future, as the result of Kant's own intervention in history. This seems to preclude Kant's political and historical writings from claiming to be true in the literal sense. At most Kant claims that it is certain that the human race will at some indefinite time or another achieve enlightenment: he says that "it is tenable within the most strictly theoretical context."[35] However, he realizes that he cannot say exactly when enlightenment will be attained: "the precise time at which it will occur must remain indefinite and dependent upon chance."[36] Here we see a tension within Kant's historical view. On the one hand, it is certain that enlightenment will be attained; on the other, the attainment of enlightenment is not certain at any given moment in history. In other words, the historical ideal of enlightenment is an object of rational faith: it is a moral duty, based upon certain empirical facts, to believe in enlightenment. And this faith in enlightenment is itself part of the process that will help to actualize it.

It might seem as if Kant's view of progress seems to be stuck on the horns of his own Third Antinomy. On the one hand, enlightenment is equivalent to freedom and thus should be independent of the causal series of history. On the other hand, enlightenment is a result of the contingent causal progress of history. In the first *Critique* Kant resolves this antinomy by way of his transcendental idealism and by appealing to the moral law: we are transcendentally free despite the fact that we are empirically determined; we must consider ourselves to be free because we can treat human beings as responsible moral agents. Kant resolves the antinomy of history in the same way: enlightenment is *both* a causally dependent event and a spontaneous act of transcendental freedom. Moreover, even philosophical reflection on history is caught up in this transcendental dilemma. On the one hand, philosophical reflection is the product of history; on the other, it is the free intervention of reason into history.

This is what leads us to what I call the *antinomy of progress:* on the one hand, progress will occur naturally; on the other hand, progress requires philosophical intervention in history. The antinomy of progress is a problem because the first thesis allows that the intervention of the philosopher's voice is not necessary for progress to occur. If progress did not require philosophical education, then Kant should have given up his struggles against the Prussian authorities. However, Kant recognized that both natural progress and philosophical intervention are necessary for progress. Indeed, each implies the other. Philosophical intervention is only possible when the public sphere has naturally evolved to a point at which free public philosophical speech has been vouchsafed; the public sphere will only become republican and progress toward the cosmopolitan society when philosophical speech makes clear the articles of perpetual peace.

Although Kant does not elucidate this antinomy, he is explicitly aware of the fact that free philosophical discourse itself can impact the future development of the human race, despite the fact that history is supposed to be a necessary causal order. We saw this above in an example from *The Contest of Faculties.* We also see this in his "Idea for a Universal History," for example, in his Ninth Proposition on World History: "A philosophical attempt to work out a universal history of the world in accordance with a plan of nature aimed at a perfect civil union of mankind, must be regarded as possible and even as capable of furthering the purpose of nature itself."[37] Here Kant recognizes that his own philosophical history of the world is part of the movement which leads to the progress of world history. As the philosopher interprets history, he also forecasts the direction that future history will take and thus pushes history forward. Like the prophet who creates the future by speaking of it, Kant's historical and political reflections create the future by elucidating its direction. Kant, however, is at pains to distinguish his own work from that of the prophets. He says, for instance, that "philosophy too may have its chiliastic expectations; but they are of such a kind that their fulfillment can be hastened, if only indirectly, by a knowledge of the idea they are based on, so that they are anything but overly fanciful."[38]

Philosophical knowledge of history, when it is teleological knowledge under the regulative ideal of progress in history, can work to move history forward on its course of progress. But philosophical knowledge is not a kind of deus ex machina of the historical play. It is not the panacea that will solve all problems. Rather, philosophical knowledge of the orientation of history merely contributes to the unending work of historical progress. The philosopher's voice is the catalyst that interrupts the Machiavellian cycle of war, but this interruption is itself possible only because the possibility of perpetual peace has already been partially prepared by the natural teleology of history. This is an autocatalytic process in which the results of either part of the reaction—philosophical intervention or natural teleology—make the unfolding of the other part of the reaction possible and so on in a progressive chain reaction. As Kant describes this autocatalytic process, he begins to use the language of self-development and self-fertilization that foreshadows Hegel's *Phenomenology of Spirit*. He says, for example, with regard to the completion of the religious commonwealth, that it will begin to appear once the idea of the kingdom of God on earth "has become general and has also gained somewhere a public foothold." Once the public acknowledgment of this idea has occurred, progress is underway because "since this principle contains the basis for a continual approach towards such a consummation, there lies in it (invisibly), as in a seed which is self-developing and in due time self-fertilizing, the whole, which one day is to illumine and to rule the world."[39] The self-developing, self-fertilizing unfolding of the idea of the whole is catalyzed by the philosopher's public invocation of the regulative idea of the whole within a public sphere that has itself been prepared by the natural teleology of history.

Development and Revolution

> We should be content with providence and with the course of human affairs as a whole, which does not begin with good and then proceed to evil, but develops gradually from the worse to the better; and each individual is for his own part called upon by nature itself to contribute towards this progress to the best of his ability.
>
> —Kant, "Conjectures on the Beginning of Human History"[40]

Kant's recognition of the way in which the philosopher's comprehension of history has a reflexive impact upon history places the philosopher in an ambiguous relation to history and to the political world he inhabits. On the one hand, progress in history seems to rely upon the intervention of the philosopher. On the other hand, history is a natural teleological unfolding. This ambiguity will be resolved when we understand the historical necessity of philosophy. Kant barely begins to scratch the surface of this question, although this question will become central for Fichte, Hegel, and Marx. However, Kant does explicitly recognize the fact that reason had a historical origin. In "Conjectures on the Beginning of Human History" Kant considers the "fall" from Edenic natural unity as a result of the natural human instinct to conduct experiments, even when these experiments lead to the contradiction of other natural instincts.

> The initial incentive to abandon natural impulses may have been quite trivial. But the outcome of that first experiment whereby man became conscious of his reason as a faculty which can extend beyond the limits to which all animals are confined was of great importance, and it influenced his way of life decisively.[41]

Although reason had a natural origin, it remains the task of reason to become fully conscious of itself: this is the task of the philosophy of history.

The antinomy of progress forces us to reassess the role of the philosopher within history, leading to the radical, "system-exploding" conclusion that philosophical activity is the focal point of historical development.[42] This conclusion thus gives a fateful importance to the philosopher's voice. By locating the philosopher within history and understanding the philosopher's activity as itself part of the movement of social and political history, Kant brings a historical element into his supposedly transcendental system. Kant recognizes that historical progress is a necessary condition for the possibility of the completion of transcendental philosophy: as we saw in the last chapter, the critical method relies on the real political freedom of both the philosopher and his critical audience.

Kant's transcendental philosophy and his philosophy of history require a free public space in which thought can freely struggle to reach the truth.[43] A book like the *Critique of Pure Reason* could only be conceived and published in an "enlightened" era in which a free public sphere exists in which we can struggle for truth. Transcendental philosophy was made possible by the historical situation in Prussia under Frederick and Zedlitz and was threatened under Frederick Wilhelm II and Wöllner. It was under Frederick that freedom of critique was vouchsafed by the enlightened dictum: "Argue as much as you like and about whatever you like, but obey."[44]

And yet, enlightenment will only be complete when the people have been enlightened by Kant's reflections on history and, indeed, by the whole of the transcendental philosophy, which is, after all, a philosophy of freedom and the republican spirit. Philosophy, as the educator of mankind, must educate the state about itself and about the fact that human beings ought to be respected by the law. This was especially true under the reactionary state of Frederick Wilhelm II. Stated in its most extreme form, this is a paradox. Kant's philosophy seems to be impossible because it can only occur when political life has become enlightened, while it is Kant's philosophy itself that makes enlightenment possible. In the *Rechtslehre* of the *Metaphysics of Morals*, published during the reactionary period, Kant claims that progress will occur as the state strives to become just, where justice is defined in terms of the following idea of justice: "every action is just that in itself or in its maxim is such that the freedom of the will of each can coexist together with the freedom of everyone in accordance with a universal law."[45] If the state is reasonable, it ought to recognize its obligation to justice. But if the state is not yet rational, then it will not yet recognize its obligation to the principle of justice. Thus the state will have no reason to listen to the philosopher (even in secret). Nor will it have a reason to permit the philosopher of enlightenment to speak at all. Kant's goal is for political authority to allow philosophers to speak freely: "This subterfuge of a secretive system of politics could, however, easily be defeated if philosophy were to make its maxims public, would it but dare to allow the philosopher to publicize his own maxims."[46] The problem is that if the state is not yet enlightened, it will not allow the free expression of philosophical critique and so will not hear the voice that speaks for enlightenment.

The unenlightened state is not bothered by the contradictions that ensue when it violates the categorical imperative and violates the freedom of its citizens. The state must be enlightened if it is to become just. The problem is that if the state is not yet enlightened, it will not easily acquiesce to Kant's republican view of justice. Indeed, the unenlightened state has every reason to resist the promulgation of the Kantian philosophy because this philosophy amounts to a call for revolution against the unenlightened state.

Kant is very careful, however, not to state his revolutionary view of the philosopher's voice too strongly. Practically, Kant had to be careful not to offend the political authorities so that his message could be heard. This is why he cleverly begins *Perpetual Peace* by undermining his subsequent claims about the political power of the philosopher's voice. Since, as many politicians are wont to claim, philosophy is impractical, then Kant ironically claims, politicians should have nothing to fear in permitting the free exercise of the philosopher's voice.[47] Moreover, Kant's theory of republican politics recognizes that political revolutions are counterproductive to his goal of perpetual peace. At the end of his *Rechtslehre,* for example, Kant explicitly condemns revolution because it destroys law, and law is what is necessary for the attainment of perpetual peace.[48] The most important point to note about Kant's denial of the right to revolution is that revolutionary activity results in the destruction of the legally constituted public sphere in which the philosopher's voice could be heard and is thus counterproductive to progress. For Kant, the possibility of public expression is the criterion by which we can judge whether a maxim is right: "All actions affecting the rights of other human beings are wrong if their maxim is not compatible with their being made public."[49] It would be impossible to publicly call for the dissolution of public law because it is public law which itself makes possible such a public declaration. The ultimate practical problem of revolution is that revolutionary states of affairs dissolve the public sphere in which the philosopher's voice could be heard. For rational progress to occur, philosophy must defend the legally constituted public sphere while striving to reform this public sphere such that it includes the possibility of publicly sanctioned critique.

For Kant, enlightened philosophical critique is the focal point of historical progress. However, historical progress toward the free, enlightened public sphere is what makes philosophical critique possible. Kant avoids the revolutionary implications of this by returning to faith in progress found in the view that history has its own natural teleology. It is this natural teleology that has led to the occurrence of Kant's singular critical voice. However, Kant does not view his own voice as the only possible historical catalyst. Rather, according to Kant's hopeful view of history, progress would occur even if something called the "Kantian" philosophy had never occurred. However, on the other hand, since the "Kantian" philosophy would be by definition the philosophy of enlightenment, even if someone named Kant had not devised it, its *content* is a necessary part of the historical movement of enlightenment: there could be no progress, natural or otherwise, without the advent of enlightened philosophical critique of political life. While Kant's humility keeps him from making grandiose claims about his own philosophical efforts, his theory of history and his theory of enlightenment make it clear that the "Kantian" philosophy, whether it is called that or by some other name, is the philosophy of enlightenment, itself the result and cause of enlightenment. In other words, Kant's voice is the voice of the general spirit of enlightenment in history.

Reply to the Transcendentalist Objection: Natural Teleology and Education

> It is consequently very easy to lay the basis of enlightenment in individual subjects by means of education; one must merely begin at an early stage to accustom young minds to this reflection. To

> enlighten an era, however, is a very protracted process; for there are numerous external obstacles which either preclude that mode of education or make it more difficult to implement.
>
> —Kant, "What is Orientation in Thinking"[50]

I have argued that Kant's teleological view of history includes the idea that the critical transcendental philosophy is itself a result of historical progress. This conclusion may be difficult to digest for those of us used to conceiving Kant's transcendental philosophy as a-historical. The truths of transcendental philosophy are supposed to be universal and a priori—they are not supposed to be affected by contingent historical events. It is important to note, however, that I am not claiming that the *content* of the transcendental philosophy is itself historically contingent: the transcendental conditions for the possibility of experience remain safely ensconced within the transcendental deduction. Rather, as I claimed in chapter 3, I am arguing that there are necessary empirical and/or historical conditions for the possibility that empirical subjects could attain knowledge of the transcendental conditions of experience. This conclusion is easy to understand by way of analogy with developmental/educational processes. Truths that are to be imparted to students by education do not themselves change as students attain higher developmental stages. Rather, empirical and developmental changes in the student make it possible for the student to know these necessary, a priori truths.

The problem of education is analogous to the other problems we have discussed in the present chapter, including the antinomy of progress. What is the catalyst for progress in education? This problem is perhaps best stated as the problem of who will educate the educators. As Kant states it in the *Contest of the Faculties,* "But those responsible for the desired education are also human beings who will therefore have to have had a suitable education themselves."[51] As we shall see in the next two chapters, Fichte confronted this problem and offered a solution that involved using the philosopher's voice to actively intervene in and re-organize the educational system of Germany. Kant does not go this far, perhaps in part, because he is reluctant to claim that he or any philosopher could have all the answers to the problem of education. Although he admits that we might have a good idea about how to educate individual pupils, he claims that it is difficult to educate an era. Far from offering a radical educational agenda, Kant claims that what is needed first of all is the opening of the public sphere to the gradually reformative influence of the philosopher's voice.

The developmental process that occurs within individual pupils is similar to the teleological process of history. According to Kant, the unchanging end of history is perpetual peace and the attainment of the "kingdom of ends" on earth. Although this end was itself uncovered by the historical development of theology, morality, and historical sciences, the historical development of these sciences did not change the nature of the moral truth of history. Thus the republican ideal of political justification remained true throughout history, even when it was obscured by unjust political regimes. Kant is very clear about his teleological view of history: "The history of the human race as a whole can be regarded as the realization of a hidden plan of nature to bring an internally—and for this purpose also externally—perfect political constitution as the only possible state within which all natural capacities of mankind can be developed completely."[52] Although Kant realizes that such a teleological judgment about history itself requires delimitation (such as he provides in the *Critique of Judgment*), this teleological conception of history gives rise to the hopeful view of progress, which itself is the catalyst for further progress and thus actualizes the hoped-for teleological development. More than this, however, Kant appeals to real historical events and to the logic of natural self-interest. He contends, for example, that perpetual peace will develop out of the economic struggle of natural human self-interest. This idea is forcefully stated by Kant in his famous claim that the problem of constructing a civil constitution "could be solved even by a nation of devils (so long as they possess understanding)."[53] This is so because even completely self-interested beings, if they are rational, will agree to the Hobbesian necessity of creating a civil society. Moreover, Kant concludes that the cosmopolitan state will itself result out of the natural inclination toward self-interested competition, what he calls, "the spirit of commerce."[54] We might ask then why and in what sense, philosophy is needed within this natural teleological system?

Again, it is important to note that Kant makes no special claims about the power of his own singular voice, nor indeed about the power of his own generation of educators and philosophers. Rather, the task of development is the common task of human being, with particular educators merely working to contribute to the autocatalytic process of history.

> If we now ask what means there are of maintaining and indeed accelerating this constant progress towards a better state, we soon realize that the success of this immeasurably long undertaking will depend not so much upon what we do (e.g. the education we impart to younger generations) and upon what methods we use to further it; it will rather depend upon what human nature may do in and through us, to compel us to follow a course which we would not readily adopt by choice.[55]

The voice of philosophy is indeed the voice of human nature or reason. The importance of the philosopher's voice in historical progress is thus to make us conscious of the teleology implicit in this progress in order that we may then take up the cause of progress in earnest and transform political life so that the philosopher's voice can be heard. When the philosopher's voice is heard, we will further transform political culture and so on in continual progress. Understanding the end of history by way of philosophical reflection on morality and politics makes it possible for us to have hope that this end may be attained:

> But if we assume a plan of nature, we have grounds for greater hopes. For such a plan opens up the comforting prospect of a future in which we are shown from afar how the human race eventually works its way upward to a situation in which all the germs implanted by nature can be developed fully, and in which man's destiny can be fulfilled here on earth.[56]

Although one might reject this as the folly of a self-fulfilling prophecy, it is supposed to be understood as a natural autocatalytic process in which the catalyst is consumed and produces further material and energy, which contributes to the ongoing reaction. Moreover, in this autocatalysis, the content is not corrupted, i.e., the truths of transcendental philosophy are not undermined; rather, this content is uncovered, as the end of history is continually revealed by hopeful progress toward that end. The true catalyst in this case is the *content* of the philosopher's voice and its transformative, educative effect upon political life.

Reply to the Revolutionary Objection: The Work of Hope

> Yet he has reasonable grounds for hope as well. Since such improvements, if only their underlying principle is good, ever increase his strength for future advances, he can hope that he will never forsake this course during his life on earth but will press on with ever-increasing courage.
>
> —Kant, *Religion within the Limits of Reason Alone*[57]

Kant recognized that the conflict between selfish interest and moral duty is a natural conflict: human beings are naturally predisposed toward both happiness and morality. Thus we require inspiration and perspiration to continue to strive to complete the task of uniting morality, happiness, and law. However, Kant's teleological conception of history tells us that within the larger eternal order of the cosmos, happiness and morality will ultimately coincide. Thus hope functions like those other postulates of reason that Kant describes in the second critique: it is a necessary presupposition of morality (and of political progress). Kant's hope is not naive then, because it is based upon an argument about human motivation and the natural order within the cosmos. We require hope (and indeed fear as well) in order to stimulate us toward further progress.[58] Since progress is natural, Kant claims, we can thus legitimately hope that it will naturally occur and indeed this hope itself stimulates progress.

One might object, however, that Kant's "retreat" to hope leaves him without a truly revolutionary political agenda: the turn to hope leads to political acquiescence, such as occurred in Kant's confrontation with Frederick Wilhelm II. On the contrary, I argue that Kant's "retreat" to the hope of his natural teleological view shows how acutely he was aware of the problem of the philosopher's voice. Kant's recognition of the problematic status of the philosopher's voice actually stimulates a further transformation of both theory and practice. Indeed, Kant's critical approach is always to delineate the limits of a given mode of thinking in order to help clarify the proper relationship between different fields of human activity. Although Kant does ultimately invoke hope to solve the problem of the philosopher's voice in history, his virtue is that he was willing to admit the difficulties that lead him to this invocation. Most importantly Kant uses his voice to mobilize hope as a political strategy by making it apparent that the project of perpetual peace is already on the way to completion.

Kant's optimistic political hopes are based upon four factors: (1) his faith in the benevolent ordering of nature by the divine creator and in the creative power of grace;[59] (2) his own experience of historical and political progress in this revolutionary era;[60] (3) his intuition of the "sole fact of reason," i.e., the intuition that there is a moral law;[61] and finally (4) upon his recognition that hope itself can play a decisive role in history. Since Kant knows intuitively that there is a moral law, since he has faith that nature is also guided by divine grace, and since he has seen progress in history in his own era, his hope is justified. More importantly, Kant has seen progress that was inspired by hope itself, in the events of the French Revolution: "for a phenomenon of this kind which has taken place in human history can never be forgotten, since it has revealed in human nature an aptitude and power for improvement of a kind which no politician could have thought up by examining the course of events in the past."[62] Of course Kant had no way of knowing that the progress of Europe toward a cosmopolitan society would take at least two more centuries, would be hindered by numerous bloody wars, and would cost millions of lives. Although Kant's hope was perhaps premature, one may argue that it was not entirely irrational, for we are continually inspired by hope to bring philosophical insight about structures of political life to bear upon those very structures.

One might argue, however, that Kant had no right to be hopeful about political progress given that his hope is based in part upon two rationally unjustified premises: his faith in the divine benevolence of grace and his intuition of the moral law. Kant himself admits that there is no rational proof of either of these premises. One might also wonder whether the actual historical progress that Kant witnessed at the end of the eighteenth century justified his hope: after all, the French Revolution devolved into terror, the "enlightened" Prussian state had regressed, and most of the world still suffered under ignorance and despotism. It seems as if Kant's hope was spun out of the thinnest of threads.

Indeed, the robust movement beyond hope toward action that characterizes the political thinking of Fichte and Marx can be seen as a rejoinder to Kant and the limitations on political intervention implied by his invocation of hope. Kant's historical and political hope can seem to give rise to conservative political theory and practice. If progress is natural, it seems that it is also inevitable and that we may simply wait for it to happen. Thus Kant's chiliastic view of history seems to result in political conservativism. This optimistic view of the natural inevitability of progress may explain why Kant refuses, for example, to advocate revolution. If progress is natural and inevitable, revolution is, at least, an unnecessary expedient. At worst, revolution is: "the greatest and most punishable crime in a commonwealth, for it destroys its very foundation. This prohibition [against revolution] is *absolute*."[63] While Kant's view of revolution has remained controversial, the practical political problem that arises with Kant's view of the natural inevitability of progress has an even broader scope. The problem is that, if progress is natural and inevitable, there seems to be no need for political concern or action, indeed there seems to be no need for political philosophy itself. If human beings will eventually realize, on their own, that happiness and morality can be synthesized within the cosmopolitan state, then there is no need for the philosopher to tell them so. This problem is even worse than the problem that Kant responds to in "Theory and Practice." There he is attempting to answer a skeptic who claims that theory is unable to have a practical impact. The problem as I've stated it is worse: theory is itself unnecessary because practical problems will resolve themselves naturally, if given enough time.

Kant resolves this problem in his *Religion* book. There he claims that our faith in Providence does not lessen our obligation to actually work for our own salvation. Kant maintains that the Christian message is one that provides hope while simultaneously requiring work: "Accordingly he [Christ] destroys the hope of all who intend to wait upon this moral goodness quite passively, with their hands in their laps, as though it were a heavenly gift which descends from on high."[64] The point here is that Kant's invocation of hope does not remove from us the responsibility of work. Just as Kant's resolution of the Third Antinomy leaves us with a restless dualism, so Kant's resolution of the antinomy of progress leaves us with a hope that demands action. This hope is both justified and enacted by Kant's use of his voice: his very ability to speak publicly shows us that progress has been made; the content of his voice stimulates further progress.

Conclusion

> For enlightenment of this kind, all that is needed is freedom. And the freedom in question is the most innocuous form of all—freedom to make public use of one's reason in all matters.
>
> —Kant, "What is Enlightenment?"[65]

Kant hoped that the results of increased freedom in the public employment of reason would lead to a convergence of morality and happiness, truth and opinion. In an enlightened state, the moral politician would contribute toward a gradual reform of political institutions that would encourage the public use of reason in a progressive autocatalytic process. This ideal of public philosophical activity inspired subsequent generations of German philosophers, as we shall see. Moreover, Kant's discussion about the philosopher's public role resulted in a distinction between the public and the private use of reason, a distinction that would be called into question subsequently. Kant's view was that in our *actions* as citizens of the polis, we must submit to authority and fulfill our duties. However, within the enlightened republic, the public employment of reason, public *speech*, ought to be free from the constraints of authority. Philosophy thus becomes political to the extent that it is speech addressed to a public audience. We saw this political context in Chapter 3, even in the depths of Kant's theoretical philosophy. In his political writings Kant claims that philosophy should thus be protected by the civil laws. Similarly, enlightened politics is philosophical to the extent that it ought to aim at the eventual conjunction of morality and law. Philosophy becomes political to the extent that it must work to transform politics in order to bring forth the conditions for its own completion. Philosophy addresses the universal concerns of all human beings including the question of the role of the philosopher's voice.

I have argued in the last two chapters that Kant was critically aware of the political impact of his own voice and that he was aware of the impact of political life on his philosophical system. This self-consciousness of the intersection of politics and philosophy is revolutionary, even if Kant's own political activity was less than revolutionary. For Kant, progress toward enlightenment will not occur by way of weapons and war but, rather, by way of philosophical discourse. In addressing himself to political life as to a reasonable entity, Kant expresses his greatest hope that the voice of philosophy could actually have an impact on the course of history. This hope was taken up by Fichte and Hegel and eventually rejected by Marx.

CHAPTER 5

Fichte: Philosophy, Politics, and the German Nation

It is the vocation of the scholar to be the teacher of the human race.

—Fichte, "Some Lectures Concerning the Scholar's Vocation"[1]

After Kant, philosophy took up the task of unifying theoretical and practical reason into a system. Such a system, to be complete, must account for its own ground in the seemingly extraneous regions of history, language, and politics. Kant's reflections on these areas remain scattered among his "occasional" essays and can seem to be secondary to the project of the three *Critiques*. However, as I argued in Chapters 3 and 4, Kant was aware of the need to account for the empirical ground of his own philosophical activity, he understood the political ramifications of his critical philosophical activity, and he struggled to defend his project against the political authorities of his native Prussia. Although Kant was reluctant to use his voice directly to transform political life and resolve the antinomy of progress, hope for progress, as symbolically realized in the French Revolution, was a postulate of his political thinking. At most Kant claimed that political life should allow philosophers to voice their opinions in public. He did not demand that philosophers become kings nor that kings become philosophers.[2]

Kant's deliberately restrained response to the question of the philosopher's voice was eventually rejected by Fichte who actively attempted to inspire political actuality by using the poetic creative activity of his voice to cultivate the philosophical imagination of the German nation. Fichte's deliberate political activity reflects a Platonic interpretation of the relationship between philosophy and politics: the philosopher should be the leader of the nation. Unlike Kant, Fichte believed that philosophical thought and political activity should converge to produce a nation based upon the educational authority of the philosopher. For Fichte, the philosopher who knows the truth has both the obligation and the mandate to use his voice to transform political life in order to bring the ideal into actuality. This conclusion follows from both Fichte's theoretical and ethical systems, as well as from his conception of the linguistic basis of philosophical and political activity.

In the present chapter I will set Fichte's work in its political context. I will discuss Fichte's commitment to the project of systematic completion including the practical component that lies in the heart of his *Science of Knowledge (Wissenschaftslehre).* I will further discuss Fichte's explicit consideration of language and its relation to philosophical imagination, individuality, and political life. In the next chapter I will consider the development of Fichte's approach to language and to politics, as it is manifest in his *Addresses to the German Nation,* a text that represents a reversal of the restrained approach to politics found in Kant. In this text, we find a complete picture of Fichte's notion of the relation between philosophy, politics, and language, which led Fichte to the radical idea that the philosopher's task was to change the world, in a philosophical direction, by using his voice to inspire the nation.

Situating Fichte's Work

> The scholar is especially destined for society . . . Accordingly, it is his particular duty to cultivate to the highest degree within himself the social talents of *receptivity* and the *art of communication.*
>
> —Fichte, "Some Lectures Concerning the Scholar's Vocation"[3]

In his *Addresses*, we witness Fichte using his voice in a poetic manner to recreate political life according to the philosophical ideal. This philosophical ideal held that human beings could be liberated by a process of philosophical and moral education. While Kant turned to political activity as a moral task restrained by respect for moral autonomy, Fichte turned to politics as a philosophical task inspired by a new conception of the relation between philosophy, politics, and language. His radical mission was to prepare the ground for that form of philosophical insight that was necessary for the completion of the moral development of historical actuality. Fichte's proselytizing activity pushed him beyond the limits of Kantian liberalism and filled his voice with the evangelical fervor of what G. A. Kelly calls "Fichtianity."[4] Fichte turns to political activity because he believes, as Tom Rockmore points out, that "since philosophy is concerned with the rational analysis of reality, it follows that this discipline enjoys a political role as a means to bringing about human liberty."[5]

Unfortunately, Fichte's enthusiasm for educational enlightenment leads to an un-philosophical attempt to reduce the difference between philosophy and politics by employing poetic rhetoric to inspire the nation in an outburst of nationalistic fervor. Much has been made of Fichte's nationalism as it appears in the *Addresses*. While we cannot simply ignore the nationalistic elements in Fichte's *Addresses,* these elements must be understood as part of his larger philosophical project.[6] Fichte's project shares the Kantian hope for the dawning of perpetual peace and for the eventual conjunction of universal morality and political life. The nationalistic development of this project occurs within a changed political situation and within a newly developed understanding of the way in which transcendental philosophy can respond to the metacritical problem of language.

In the 1790s, Fichte was already aware of the problem of language. In 1795, at the same time that he was working on his *Science of Knowledge (Wissenschaftslehre),* he wrote an article on language, "On the Linguistic Capacity and the Origin of Language." Moreover, at this same time Fichte was involved in an educational project in Jena, which linked the transcendental philosophy to popular education in a context colored by enthusiasm for the French Revolution. Upon his arrival at the University of Jena in 1794, Fichte organized a series of popular lectures, "The Vocation of the Scholar."[7] These lectures had a political content insofar as they argued that scholars were the engines of progress toward enlightenment. It is important to note that Kant was articulating similar ideas at around the same time in his political essays. Fichte took it a step farther than Kant however by being actively involved in the political-educational activity which he advocated. In the 1790s Jena was a focal point for radical intellectuals, and Fichte, who had already published pamphlets in defense of the French Revolution, was a mentor and inspiration for students who were sympathetic to the ideals of the revolution. Fichte was also aware of the difficulties of putting the transcendental philosophy into popular form and began to encounter resistance to his political views. This culminated in the atheism controversy of 1799 in which his views were misrepresented for political reasons. Fichte's supposed atheism—really a variety of Kant's idea of a religion of morality—was linked to his republican political disposition. As Fichte lost his chair at Jena as a result of this controversy and moved on to Berlin, he became increasingly aware of the complicated problem of educating a nation for enlightenment. He realized that the public would misunderstand the system because of political and psychological impediments, as seen in his Introductions to the *Wissenschaftslehre* and his "Crystal Clear Report to the General Public Concerning the Actual Essence of the Newest Philosophy: An Attempt to Force the Reader to Understand." Additionally, his reflections on language developed in a more nationalistic direction perhaps as a result of his encounters, in Jena, with Romantics such as Friedrich Schlegel and the comparative linguist Wilhelm von Humboldt—both of whom were also in Berlin with Fichte. Finally, enthusiasm for the French Revolution became transformed during the early years of the nineteenth century, as Napoleon became a conquering emperor. All of this culminates in the *Addresses* in which we find linguistic nationalism tied to the cosmopolitan ideal of educational enlightenment.

Fichte realized that for the system of reason to complete itself, the empirical conditions (historical, linguistic, and political) must be accounted for and, if necessary, transformed by the creative will of the philosopher. Fichte was acutely aware of the sound of his own voice as well as the mode of reception of his audience. Fichte came to embrace the Romantic idea that the philosopher's voice, imbued with the transformative power of poetry, could be used to stimulate imagination and change the world. Just as the Romantic poet viewed himself as a genius of freedom and imagination, Fichte viewed himself as a political poet, a genius who might synthesize morality and politics by way of philosophical education. Fichte's *Addresses* are groundbreaking in the double sense of poetically cultivating the ground for the construction of the critical edifice and simultaneously shattering the rational ground of transcendental philosophy. The *Addresses* move transcendental philosophy from out of the transcendental realm into the empirical realm in order to bring about the empirical conditions necessary for the completion of the transcendental project. The mechanism for this movement is the philosopher's voice.

Significantly, Fichte attempts to account in a philosophical manner for the inspirational power of his own voice. Fichte's political activity raises questions about the linguistic limitations of the transcendental philosophy, language as the medium of exchange between the philosopher and his audience, language as the constitution of national cultural and spiritual identity, and finally, questions about the very language of the philosopher who speaks. Indeed, the question of authorial voice is itself one that is found at the heart of transcendental philosophy. Given Kant's distinction between the transcendental ego and the empirical ego, we wonder which ego belongs to the author. In the preface to the *Vocation of Man* (1800), Fichte writes, for example, "the 'I' who speaks in the book is by no means the author."[8] This is so because the 'I' of the author is supposed to be the same as the 'I' of the reader. By 1807, in the *Addresses,* Fichte locates the speaker's voice within the organic whole of the linguistic nation. In the *Addresses,* however, he is less sanguine about the reader's ability to comprehend because he sees the degradation of the German and European spirit under the failure of the Revolution that led to the Napoleonic conquests. He says pregnantly in response to the question of why he, Fichte, has the right to reorganize and reeducate Germany, "I answer that, of course, everyone would have the same right as I have, that I am doing it solely because not one of them has done it before me, and that I would be silent if another had already done it."[9] The enlightened philosopher has the authority to speak of transforming the nation. The project of establishing a systematic unity of theory and practice required that the philosopher use his voice to revolutionize the empirical conditions under which an education in the transcendental system of freedom could be completed.[10]

Fichte's *Addresses* can be read as both concrete political action aimed at liberating Germany from the French invaders and as a philosophical prolegomenon necessary to prepare the ground for the eventual acceptance of the truths expressed philosophically in the *Wissenschaftslehre*. The first interpretation has been developed, for example, by Friedrich Meinecke, who sees Fichte as a pivotal character in the historical liberation of Germany.[11] However, we must be skeptical of claims about Fichte's impact on the political life of Germany during the Wars of Liberation. Engelbrecht has argued convincingly that Fichte's *Addresses* did not have any immediate impact upon the German people.[12] This is true for a variety of reasons including meager attendance at his lectures and a lack of publicity. Most notably, the French authorities simply ignored Fichte, despite the fact that they had cracked down on German resistance, for instance executing Palm, the liberal Nürnberg bookseller. The myth that Fichte bravely and defiantly delivered his *Addresses* in the face of the French authorities and that the *Addresses* inspired the Germans to rise up against the French was invented by his biographer and son, I. H. Fichte, and by later German nationalists eager to find a philosophical hero whom they could pervert for their own purposes.

It is thus the second interpretation that will primarily interest us in the rest of this chapter, for it shows the philosophical necessity of cultivating the political ground of philosophical speculation. In Fichte's political activity we hear the philosopher's voice reach its limit as philosophy succumbs to the temptation to take up rhetorical means to achieve philosophical, political, and moral ends.

The Practical Components of the Science of Knowledge and the Theoretical Demand for the *Addresses*

> What sort of philosophy one chooses depends, therefore, on what sort of man one is; for a philosophical system is not a dead piece of furniture that we can reject or accept as we wish; it is rather a thing animated by the soul of the person who holds it.
>
> —Fichte, *Science of Knowledge*[13]

The above quote, taken from the First Introduction to the *Wissenschaftslehre* is an ad hominem against dogmatists. Fichte was willing to mount such an ad hominem attack in the introduction to his system because he admits that the system is practical and that a person's moral character is an issue for theoretical philosophy. A "dogmatist" who rejects the transcendental account of freedom is not capable of comprehending the philosophical system. Fichte explicitly admits in the Introduction that the idealist philosophy requires proper education.

> If idealism should prove to be the only true philosophy, it is necessary to be born, raised, and self-educated as a philosopher; but one cannot be made so by human contrivance. Our science expects few converts, therefore, among those already formed; if it may have any hopes at all, they are set, rather, upon the young whose innate power has not yet foundered in the indolence of our age.[14]

Fichte thus pointed the way toward his more vigorous interventions in political life. Fichte's goal is to educate those young philosophers who would be able to move with him beyond dogmatism. Fichte was thus willing to sacrifice the circumspection of philosophy on the altar of rhetoric and politics in order to create the conditions under which philosophical activity could be completed.

A philosophical demand thus leads Fichte to intervene in politics and take up the persuasive techniques of rhetoric and the creative imaginative work of political poetry. The *Addresses* aim at solving this problem by proposing practical political changes that would help to educate his audience so that they could comprehend the truth of transcendental idealism. Since, as Fichte claims, philosophical depth is the birthright of the German spirit, his goal in the *Addresses* is to elicit the German spirit such that Germans will be able comprehend the greatness of German philosophy. Unfortunately, the German spirit was not yet ready to comprehend the truth of German philosophy. "This philosophy is not at home in our age . . . It must give up on all claim on the present generation."[15] His system has not been understood because of the defective imaginations of the reading public. In his "Crystal Clear Report" of 1801, Fichte recognizes that some will comprehend the *Wissenschaftslehre,* and others will not: "So the Science of Knowledge presents itself to those who, in and for themselves, are able to possess it. Those who are not capable of this are steeped in the Science of Knowledge by those who are led by it, by the regents and school teachers."[16]

There are two conditions for comprehending transcendental philosophy: a free and creative imagination which allows us to "philosophize with spirit" and political freedom to utilize this imagination.[17] Without freedom in these two senses, we will fail to comprehend the system. "If this failure to understand has a reason, whatever it may be, the *Wissenschaftslehre* itself contains a reason why to certain readers it must forever pass their understanding: namely, that it assumes them to possess the faculty of freedom (*das Vermögen der Freiheit*) of inner intuition."[18]

In the *Addresses,* Fichte blames these lapses in his audience upon a lack of education and upon the present, corrupt political system. We can see, then, that Fichte's philosophical enterprise depends upon the education of free spirit. This in turn relies upon a certain social and political structure, which supports this educational enterprise. It is this social and political element within the system that leads Fichte to explicitly address ethics, politics, and indeed the German nation itself. His *Addresses to the German Nation,* like all of his popular works, can be understood as an attempt to address the real basis of philosophy, those living, breathing human beings who must come to know the truth of philosophy and enact its principles in real political life.[19]

The creative imagination is the key faculty for philosophy because it is the faculty that allows us to think two opposed theses at once: "the state, in which totally opposed directions are united, is simply the activity of imagination."[20] Imagination is the faculty which allows us to hover (*schweben*) between opposites, and this power "determines whether or not we philosophize with spirit."[21] A lack of imagination and the inability to philosophize with spirit is the result of that type of education that stifles imagination in order to promote mere understanding. Thus the inability of the subject to acknowledge the truth of Fichte's idealism is accounted for in the *Wissenschaftslehre* as a result of poor education. The *Addresses* are Fichte's attempt to rectify the empirical problem that underlies the philosophical difficulty: man must be remade socially, politically, and culturally so that the type of freedom and imagination necessary for philosophy can flourish.

In the *Wissenschaftslehre* we see an explicit connection between philosophy, politics, and morality. Reason is the dialectic between the theoretical and the practical: "reason cannot even be theoretical if it is not practical."[22] It is a practical demand of reason that grounds Fichte's idealist system because it is a matter of duty for the ego to demand that the unity of the system be grounded on freedom. Being *should* be interpreted in terms of the activity of the self. The model of reality is the activity of the moral self: "All reality is active; and everything active is reality."[23] The basic model of being is thus moral activity, which is freedom within self-imposed laws and limitations. Fichte concludes by saying that "all theoretical laws are based on practical laws . . . it follows that, even in the context of theory, there is an absolute freedom of reflection and abstraction, and the possibility of directing one's attention to something and withdrawing it from something else is a matter of duty, without which there can be no morality whatever."[24] Just as Kant maintained that freedom is conformity to the law of reason, Fichte says that the laws of reason are "brought forth by means of free but law-governed thinking."[25] In other words, the law to which freedom must conform is itself the product of freedom. Thus freedom must conform itself to itself, must give itself its own laws. It is the nature of freedom to limit itself. This is what he means, for example, when he states that "every striving must therefore be limited by a force opposed to that of the striving itself."[26] Even if there were no opposition to freedom, freedom would posit its own opposition in the form of the moral law by which it determines itself.

This is circular. Indeed, just as Fichtean ontology admits the circular self-determination of self by way of the self-posited not-self, so the Fichtean theory of freedom admits the circularity of the self-determination of freedom by way of freely posited laws. We determine ourselves by the circular relation between self and other (where the other is either an object or the moral law). "A system that pays no attention at all to this circle, is dogmatic idealism; for it is indeed the aforesaid circle which alone confines us and makes us finite beings; a system which fancies itself to have escaped therefrom, is a transcendent realist dogmatism."[27] As discussed in the chapter on Kant, this circularity describes the basic structure of republican self-government: the people give themselves laws to which they then must conform. In the *Wissenschaftslehre*, Fichte openly acknowledges this circularity, beginning from the free ego and deducing all of the categories from this ego, including the moral imperative that governs the freedom of the ego from which he began. Kant tried to avoid this circle by locating freedom beyond the scope of knowledge, as a necessary moral postulate.[28] Fichte's task is to make the interconnection between theoretical and practical reason explicit: to make reason conscious of its own structural presuppositions. In order to complete this task, Fichte turns to political action: the systematic task requires that real empirical egos become politically free to take up the moral challenge of transcendental philosophy.

Fichte explicates the systematic interrelation of epistemology and politics in a more detailed manner than does Kant. As a keen observer of the contemporary political landscape at the end of the eighteenth century, Fichte was acutely aware of the potential for devolution from democracy to despotism. This can be linked to his concern, articulated in the *Wissenschaftslehre*, with avoiding what he calls "dogmatism." Dogmatism is a type of philosophical despotism in which the systematic unity of opposites is established by force.[29] Dogmatism is a denial of the circular nature of the mutual determination of subject and object. Fichtean idealism seeks to avoid dogmatism by starting from the assumption that all thinkers are free and that freedom involves self-limitation. Fichte then tries to generate from this assumption a self-determining system.

This type of idealism is republican in spirit: enlightened free participation will lead to agreement. Dogmatism, on the contrary, is despotic: it assumes some principle to which not all thinkers will agree and seeks to establish agreement by way of persuasion, manipulation, and, if necessary, coercion. The distinction between coercion, manipulation, and other forms of persuasion is not clearly articulated by Fichte, as far as I can tell. He is, however, aware of a distinction among types of persuasion. In the "Lectures Concerning the Scholar's Vocation" Fichte says, for example, that the "scholar may employ none but moral means to influence society. He will not be tempted to use *compulsory* means or physical force to get men to accept his convictions . . . But neither should the scholar employ *deception*."[30] At issue in the moral vs. immoral means of persuasion is respect for the autonomy of the one to be persuaded.

Fichte attempts to refute dogmatism by appealing to a republican conception of human being: "We start from freedom, and in fairness presuppose it also in them [the dogmatists]."[31] Despite Fichte's occasionally acerbic criticisms of common sense, he believes that his system is open to public scrutiny and approval. In his "Crystal Clear Report" he emphasizes the fact that education is open to all who are capable. Moreover, in this text at least, he uses the rhetorical form of a dialogue between himself and his reader, as if to emphasize the fact that all educated readers should be able to see the truth of his system. He concludes that "each and every person must find it [the truth of the system] by himself and it can be expected of him at once. Everyone who only awakens to self-possession and steps forth from the intermediate position between plant and man finds it to be this way."[32] In an enlightened era, reasonable people will agree to the truths of the transcendental philosophy. However, this is not yet an enlightened era: "many will misunderstand it, and more will not understand it at all."[33]

The difficulty for Fichte is to uphold his republican principles in the face of ignorance and political despotism. By the time of the *Addresses*, Fichte approaches the task of enlightenment from a more authoritarian perspective: coercive education is needed to prepare the ground for enlightenment. This conclusion is foreshadowed by Fichte's discussion of defective philosophical imagination in the *Wissenschaftslehre*. In one of the most remarkable statements in his *Wissenschaftslehre,* Fichte uses an ad hominem argument against his critics.

> The science of knowledge is of a kind that cannot be communicated by the letter merely, but only through the spirit; for its basic ideas must be elicited, in anyone who studies it, by the creative imagination itself . . . in that the whole enterprise of the human spirit issues from the imagination and the latter cannot be grasped save through the imagination itself. Anyone, therefore, in whom this whole aptitude is already weakened or deadened beyond hope of recall will admittedly find it forever impossible to make headway in this Science; but the ground of this inability he should look for, not in the Science itself, which is easily grasped, if it is ever grasped at all, but rather in the want of capacity in himself.[34]

Fichte here pushes the Science of Knowledge beyond ontology back into psychology, sociology, and educational theory. Fichte completes the above thought with the following footnote: "The Science of Knowledge cannot become a generally accepted philosophy, so long as education has the effect, in so many men, of killing off one capacity for the sake of another . . ."[35] The cultivation of the human imagination via proper education thus becomes a focal point for Fichte's philosophical endeavors and leads him to intervene in political life: the goal is the reorganization of political life such that philosophical imagination can properly develop. Fichte, much like Schiller in his *Letters on the Aesthetic Education of Man,* calls for a new form of education. Unfortunately, however, Fichte disagrees with Schiller as to the means by which human beings are to be educated: it is not by play but by authority.

The tension between authority and freedom becomes a recurrent theme for Fichte. In his explicitly ethical essays, Fichte sought to bring the republic of reason into existence by advocating a coercive political regime, the *Notstaat* of his *Science of Ethics* (1798). The coercive state is needed as the means toward the humanization of man. It administers society in order to let human beings move from out of barbarism toward freedom. Once freedom has been achieved, however, the *Notstaat* would be replaced by the republic of reason or the system of freedom. Significantly, Fichte views the chief goal of the coercive state as education: philosophy requires that individuals be educated by the state. This view becomes the essence of the educational state advocated in the *Addresses:* universal education for all under a coercive authority dedicated to the creation of the spirit of morality and philosophy.[36] Despite his pronouncements against dogmatism and despotism, coercive authority becomes the precondition for the completion of the republic of reason. The malignance of these seemingly despotic means is supposed to be ameliorated by the fact that this despotism is to be guided by philosophical insight and respect for the autonomy of those who are to be educated. The educator's task is to make us free so that we may then fully participate in further moral, political, and philosophical activity.

This tendency toward dogmatism can be seen in the very structure of Fichte's theoretical work. Fichte recognized the problem of the justification of the critical method and attempted to resolve it by beginning from the assumption of "the Act… that lies at the basis of all consciousness and alone makes it possible."[37] I have interpreted this above as the basic idea that the self is self-positing and self-limiting, i.e. the autonomous activity of the self is its own self-limitation under self-imposed laws. From this first principle we are supposed to be able to deduce the further principles of ontology. Fichte admits that this first principle is merely a postulate, that it "can be neither proved nor defined, if it is to be an absolutely primary principle."[38] Fichte further denies that it is necessary to discuss this first principle at any length because everyone with sufficient education and imagination would agree to it. This essential principle will eventually be proven in the course of the exposition of the system itself. It turns out that the proof for this first principle is that it is a necessary principle of morality: morality demands that we assume that the self is activity. Fichte's argument for this methodological assumption thus stems from the claim that agreement about the nature of the self is a matter of morality and character. "What sort of philosophy one chooses depends, therefore, on what sort of man one is; for a philosophical system is not a dead piece of furniture that we can reject or accept as we wish; it is rather a thing animated by the soul of the person who holds it."[39] If the methodological assumption is a matter of character, this explains why Fichte must resort to ad hominem arguments about defective imaginations in establishing agreement for his science and eventually why he must take up the task of moral education.[40]

Just as we saw with Kant, Fichte also relies upon a shared set of basic concepts such as justice and justification. In the Preface to the *Wissenschaftslehre* of 1795, written the same year that Kant published *Perpetual Peace,* Fichte writes:

> It will be necessary first to obtain a view of the whole before any single proposition therein can be accurately defined, for it is their interconnection that throws light on the parts; a method which certainly assumes willingness to do the system justice (*freilich den guten Willen voraussetzt, dem Systeme Gerechtigkeit widerfahren zu lassen*), and not the intention of merely finding fault with it.[41]

He makes this statement to interdict a reading of his science that would not view the system as a whole. Such a reading would be, in these terms, unjust. However, as discussed with regard to a similar problem in Kant's first *Critique*, it will be impossible to do the system justice, i.e., to view it as a whole, until human beings have been properly educated so that they share the idea of justice with which they should approach the system. According to Fichte, justice demands consistency within the circle of the whole system, i.e., justice demands that the first principle be considered within the whole. It is but a small leap from this assumption of an idea of "doing the system justice" to the claim that the apparently unjustified first principle will be justified when political life is such that human beings are able to freely assent to it. The conception of justice evoked here in the Preface is one that implies the law-governed freedom of the creative imagination. In short, it is the conception of justice implicit in the republic that is to be the result of Fichte's educational *Notstaat*. In order to arrive at this republican conception of justice, however, we must go through the coercive educational mechanisms of the educational state.

Fichte's entire system is thus caught up in the tension between the ideals of the republic of reason and the material reality of lived political life. Like

Kant, Fichte asserts that the system must be open to free criticism by all knowers considered as equal. His goal is freedom, even if the means to this end is coercive education. He says, for instance, "The *Wissenschaftslehre* should in no way *force* itself upon the reader but should *become a necessity* for him, as it has for the author."[42] This is so because comprehension of the *Wissenschaftslehre* requires the "capacity for freedom": "If this capacity for freedom (*Vermögen der Freiheit*) is not already present and employed, the *Wissenschaftslehre* can make no headway with a person."[43] A despotic system would not be self-grounding because it would reject the capacity for freedom and equality of the egos of its "citizens." And yet, Fichte realized that most of his readers were not free and did not yet possess the requisite degree of philosophical imagination to comprehend the conception of freedom implicit in the science itself; they had to be made free and needed to be forced to cultivate their imaginations by the coercive educational state.

The *Ursprache*, Poetry, Politics, and Destiny

> Of the means of introducing into the lives of all the thought that has begun in the life of the individual, the highest and best is poetry; hence this is the second main branch of the spiritual culture (*geistigen Bildung*) of a people. The thinker designates (*bezeichnet*) his thought in language, and this . . . cannot be done except by images of sense and, moreover, by an art of creation extending beyond the previous range of sensuous imagery. In doing this the thinker is himself a poet . . .
>
> —Fichte, *Addresses to the German Nation*[44]

Given that Fichte remained committed to Kant's cosmopolitan morality, one wonders why Fichte felt it was necessary to specifically address the *German* nation. After all, Fichte was aware that the history of culture is a European, if not a global affair: his first Address locates the *Addresses* within the context of his speculations about European or world history as found in his 1806 text, *The Characteristics of the Present Age*. However, for Fichte the decisive moment that confronted world history in 1807 was uniquely German: it is the Germans who were to usher in a new epoch in history by creating a new, more spiritual world and by uniting against the French in defense of the ideal of the revolution, which was betrayed by Napoleon. In the *Addresses* Fichte both attempts to prove that the proper manifestation of the new spiritual world is the German nation and attempts to show the, as yet, nonexistent German nation how it might come to create this new world. The means of creating the new world are political, philosophical, and poetic. The new era will be a German era, Fichte argues, because only in the German language and culture are politics, philosophy, language, and imagination organically connected.[45]

While there are certainly chauvinistic and contingent historical reasons why Fichte's *Addresses* are addressed specifically to the Germans, Fichte attempts to provide a philosophical justification for the fact that "it is first of all the Germans who should be recognized as those who begin the new era—as forerunners (*vorandehend*) and exemplars (*vorbildend*) for the rest."[46] In this formulation of the German task it is clear that Germany is not to be a conquering nation but a model or image of the new epoch of history.

Fichte's philosophical justification of his claims about the unique historical mission of Germany is based upon what he claims is the uniquely philosophical nature of the German language and way of thinking. We will develop this more fully in the next chapter. For the moment let us note that the essence of German is that it is a living primal language, an *Ursprache*, in which alone truth can be authentically uttered. The *Ursprache* connects living German speakers with their original destiny and provides the means for completing this destiny, the means for making life into that which it ought to be. Most significantly, this *Ursprache* is a living connection between theory and practice, between life and thought:

> In this way, I say, spiritual culture (*geistige Bildung*)—and here is meant especially thinking in a primal language (*Ursprache*)—does not exert an influence on life; it is itself the life of him who thinks in this fashion. Nevertheless it necessarily strives, from the life that thinks in this way, to influence other life outside it, and so to influence the life of all about it and to form this life in accordance with itself. For, just because that kind of thinking is life, it is felt by its possessor with inward pleasure in its vitalizing (*belebenden*), transfiguring (*verklärenden*), and liberating (*befreienden*) power.[47]

Fichte claims that theory and practice are united in the spirit of the *Ursprache*. Thinking in the *Ursprache* leads to the real invigoration, transfiguration, and liberation of political life.

In the *Addresses,* Fichte defends the political, philosophical, and poetic power of language. The goal of the *Addresses* is to use the poetic power of language to inspire the German spirit and bring forth the German nation. Only in an *Ursprache* is living philosophical thought possible because in such a living language, "the symbol is directly living and sensuous; it represents (*wieder darstellend*) all real life and so takes hold of and exerts an influence on life."[48] Creative advancements in thought must be tied to real life and this is only possible when such thought is articulated in an *Ursprache*. This leads Fichte to conclude that the spirit of the German nation is found in the unifying power of the German language. This spirit is the depth of the philosophical imagination that is accessed by the organic semantics of the German *Ursprache*. Fichte claims that there is a "national power of imagination (*Nationaleinbildungskraft*)" and that words in the *Ursprache* (as opposed to foreign words introduced into this language) stimulate this imagination directly.[49] Since the power of the imagination is the root of philosophical and moral activity, Fichte's argument leads to the conclusion that German makes possible progress in philosophy, politics, and morality.

By 1807 Fichte has become more Romantic in defense of the German against the corrupting influences of the French. Although he is still an advocate of progress and enlightenment, he understands progress in terms of a living connection to the origin of human culture. This only happens in a living language in which philosophical, artistic, and even political investigations are linked to the transcendental ground of language in "spiritual nature itself (*geistigen Natur selbst*)."[50] This connection is, Fichte claims, only found in the German spirit, and Germany thus ought to be the forerunner of progress in history.[51] French civilization seems to have failed to live up to its promise by exchanging the ideals of revolution for the lust of empire. Fichte links the failure of French culture to the remnants of imperial Roman culture in the French language. German language remained unpolluted by Roman culture. Instead, it remains linked, as an *Ursprache*, to the basis of language in the intersubjectivity of human freedom and the synthetic power of imagination.

Fichte's comments about the importance of the *Ursprache* are significant for both his political and philosophical agendas. He claims that philosophy and all of spiritual culture grow out of real, historical, political life and that only a certain type of political life will lead to the full fruition of philosophy. In particular, for Fichte, making the German people into a real political nation in which thinking in the *Ursprache* can proceed without external constraint will open the possibility of the completion of a living mediation between politics and philosophy. For the living truth expressed in the *Ursprache* to become self-conscious and complete, this truth must be made real by way of real political transformations in the lives of those who speak the *Ursprache*. The philosophical truths, which can only be thought in the *Ursprache,* will be completed and comprehended when the Germans are politically and spiritually free. This will, in turn, be an example for the rest of mankind, who will then follow Germany into the new epoch in which mankind will freely "fashion itself by means of itself."[52] One can see here the linkage to Fichte's more theoretical work in which freedom is understood as the ego positing itself. Fichte understands the new German epoch as a philosophical epoch because such freedom can only be enacted "through knowledge."[53] Such philosophical self-determination can only occur within an *Ursprache* because only within such an *Ursprache* is thinking organically connected to its origin in freedom and the creative imagination.

When the living truth that is implicit in the *Ursprache* is finally allowed to express itself, when thought determines itself in accord with its origin, it will do so, Fichte claims, by means of the transformative power of poetry. Fichte agrees with his contemporaries Schiller, Schelling, and Hölderlin when he claims that "the thinker (*der Denker*) . . . is a poet (*Dichter*)."[54] A truly original thinker represents in images, as the poet does, the truth of sensual life and in this representation is able to overcome remaining oppositions between subject and object in order to create a newer, more spiritual, more comprehensive whole. Within an *Ursprache* in which thought and life are organically connected, poetic thought thus has direct political consequences: "to such a language, therefore, poetry is the most excellent means of flooding the life of all with the spiritual culture that has been attained."[55] Fichte justifies his own flurries of poetic rhetoric by stating that poetry is at least as useful as philosophy for cultivating the creative imagination. Fichte thus moves beyond Kantian rationalism in claiming that progress will be achieved by the power of persuasive speech and the poetic art of imagination. This is Fichte's crucial contribution to the problem of the philosopher's voice. Fichte's philosophy of language and his recognition of the philosophical need for political transformation lead him to the idea that the philosopher can and should use his voice as political poetry that stimulates the imagination with language in order to create political transformation, philosophical comprehension, and the development of moral freedom.

Fichte concludes his remarks on language in the *Addresses* with a brief account of "the golden age." This golden age would be reached when life, language, and thought interpenetrate each other mutually.[56] Fichte notes, however, that with such a completion comes a subsequent decline. Fichte acknowledges that it is possible for poetry, politics, philosophy, and life to be completed at a given stage of historical development. However, such completion inevitably results in death; after a people celebrates its golden age, "the source of poetry runs dry."[57] This source is the force of nature that leads us to strive to produce new poetry, philosophy, and politics, i.e., it is human freedom. In the *Addresses* Fichte concludes that at the present stage of historical development, the German spirit alone remains close to this source and thus has a unique task in the future of the development of the human race. Indeed, Fichte states that the criterion for being called "German" is whether or not "you believe in something absolutely primary and original in man himself, in freedom, in endless improvement, in the eternal progress of our race (*unsers Geschlechts*) . . ."[58] German politics, philosophy, and poetry thus point beyond the golden age promised by spiritually dead languages toward the eternal progress that is the work of freedom.

Conclusion

As we shall see in the next chapter, Fichte collapsed the distinction between philosophy and politics because of the implication developed out of his philosophy of language. Moreover, as we shall see, Fichte's elision of the difference between philosophy and politics leads to his flirtation with an excess of rhetoric that belies the philosophical pretensions of his work and goes against the grain of modern republicanism. This excess is seen in his move from an early transcendentalist account of language in general as the condition for the possibility of thinking to the chauvinistic account of the *Addresses* in which only the German language facilitates spiritual development. As we saw in the present chapter, Fichte turns to politics because of serious theoretical and practical concerns. Since the philosopher is the one who best understands both the theoretical and practical demands of political intervention, this intervention and its justification are the philosopher's task. Moreover, since both theory and practice are intimately connected with language, the philosopher's task is to speak to his audience in their living language. In the next chapter we shall see that Fichte makes the voice of the philosopher—his own voice—an object for systematic philosophical reflection.

CHAPTER 6

Fichte's Voice: Language and Political Excess

> Among the people with a living language (*lebendige Sprache*), spiritual culture (*Geistigesbildung*) influences life; whereas among a people of the opposite kind, mental culture and life go their separate ways.
>
> —Fichte, *Addresses to the German Nation*[1]

In the *Addresses,* Fichte synthesizes the projects of moral development, national self-assertion, and the cultivation of the philosophical imagination. This synthesis occurs within a theory of language that grounds Fichte's attempt to use his own voice to complete this synthetic project. Given the political context in which Fichte delivered his *Addresses*, it is easy to understand why Fichte might occasionally overstate his case about the virtue of the German spirit. After the French defeated Prussia at Jena and Auerstadt in 1806 and marched unhindered into Berlin, it seemed as if the German spirit had suffered a complete moral collapse. The army had offered little resistance, and the population easily complied with French authority. Remaining enthusiasm for the ideals of the French Revolution could no longer be supported under the obvious imperial aspirations of Napoleon. Amid this crisis, Fichte called for the rebirth of the German nation under the guidance of German philosophy. "Only a complete regeneration, only the beginning of an entirely new spirit (*eines ganz neuen Geistes*) can help us."[2] In this context, his rhetorical flourishes make sense, even when they verge on the absurd. He claims, for example, that enthusiasm for the French ought to sound ludicrous when uttered in the German language. "Good, earnest, steady German men and countrymen, far from our spirit be such a lack of understanding, and far be such defilement from our language, which is formed to express the truth (*zum Ausdrucke des Wahren Gebildeten Sprache*)!"[3] This nationalistic rhetoric finds its basis in the immediate political context but also in Fichte's understanding of language and its connection to both philosophy and politics.

As we saw in the last chapter, serious practical and theoretical concerns led Fichte to take up political activity in earnest. These same concerns led him to make a "linguistic turn" and take up the issue of language as a matter for serious philosophical consideration.[4] In the present chapter I will examine the shift in Fichte's philosophy of language from his early attempt to discover the transcendental ground of language to his later attempt to locate this ground in the force of nature that gave rise to the German *Ursprache*. I will also discuss the limits of Fichte's later nationalism. Finally, I will examine Fichte's claims about the prophetic power of his voice and his attempted philosophical justification of the political tone of his voice in the *Addresses*. Unfortunately, Fichte's awareness of the importance of voice leads him to those excesses of nationalism, which violate the very spirit of his philosophy by negating the difference between philosophy and politics in an attempt to bring them together.

The Development of Fichte's Philosophy of Language

> What an immeasurable influence on the whole human development of a people the character of its language may have.
>
> —Fichte, *Addresses to the German Nation*[5]

In 1795, in the midst of developing his *Wissenschaftslehre*, Fichte took up the issue of language. Unlike Kant, Fichte seriously considered the metacritical question about language as the medium of thought. The goal of developing a philosophical system thus requires that philosophy account for this linguistic medium. Fichte's basic claim in both his early and late philosophies of language is that the transcendental condition for language, the "force of nature" that gave rise to language, was human freedom. Fichte develops this view in a Romantic direction, so that in 1807 he emphasizes that this force is a creative power and is not merely a representational activity.

There are three main differences between Fichte's early philosophy of language and its subsequent development.[6]

1. In the *Addresses,* Fichte extends his consideration of language in an explicitly social, cultural, and political direction, explicitly linking language to the concept of spirit and of the nation.[7]

2. In the *Addresses,* Fichte ties his whole argument about the political nature of language around his view that language is, in a sense, the transcendental ground for the possibility of both nationality and individuality.[8]

3. This leads to the following conclusion significant for our current project. Fichte maintains that the voice of philosophy, uttered in the *Ursprache* of the nation, can change the world by inspiring political activity and by cultivating the philosophical imagination.[9]

In 1795, as Fichte wrote his first essay on language, he was caught up in an attempt to discover the transcendental ground of language in order to establish the possibility of doing transcendental philosophy in a finite historical language. In 1807, as Fichte addressed his German audience under the French occupation, he was concerned with finding a way to renew the German spirit and inspire the creation of the German nation in order to establish the necessary empirical ground for the completion of his philosophical project. While these two projects are quite different in intent, they are related. If thinking is linguistic, then it is only a small step to the conclusion that good thinking requires proper language. It is a further step to the conclusion that the proper use of language requires a political transformation of those who speak the language proper to philosophy. The final step is the claim that political transformation should be inspired by the philosopher speaking in the philosophical *Ursprache*.

Fichte's conclusion in the *Addresses* that the philosopher's voice can inspire the German people is thus centered around a claim about the spiritual nature of language and the creative spiritual and political power of the philosopher's voice. Fichte conceives the German spirit in terms of language; it is not primarily a racial or geographical concept.[10] The spirit of a people is the connection between its language and the original source of language, which, Fichte maintains, is the human need to communicate. This need to communicate is ultimately linked back to the problem of imagination mentioned by Fichte in the heart of the *Wissenschaftslehre:* the "creative imagination" or "spirit" is the ground for the possibility of communication by the "letter."[11] Fichte goes so far as to explicitly define "spiritual culture (*geistige Bildung*)" as "thinking in an *Ursprache*" because such a primal language remains linked to the living root of human life.[12] This living root is human intersubjectivity, freedom, and the power of the imagination. In an *Ursprache,* Fichte says in the *Addresses,* spiritual culture "is itself the life of one who thinks in this way."[13] The life of spirit is simply the power of imagination to hover between opposites. This power is contained in the *Ursprache,* which connects sense and idea.

Although Fichte's comments on language in the *Addresses* represent the changed focus of his thought toward very practical political matters, he does not reject the conclusions of his earlier transcendental account of language. In 1795 Fichte understood the transcendental basis of language in terms of the intersubjective nature of human reason. This pointed him toward a social interpretation of language that he left undeveloped in the 1795 essay. In 1807 Fichte extended this reflection on language and reached the radical conclusion that language is the basis of both nationality and individuality. It would not have been possible to reach this conclusion if he had not already rejected an asocial theory of language in 1795. In the early essay, Fichte rejected both the view that language was given to man by God and the view that language evolved from primitive animal instinct. Instead he understands language as a necessary consequence of the social nature of the human spirit: it results from the struggle of free human beings to be recognized by other free human beings. Thus Fichte's social interpretation of language and the political practice of the *Addresses* stem from the view that he developed in 1795, i.e., that the transcendental ground of language is the intersubjectivity of human freedom.[14]

However, in the *Addresses* Fichte goes beyond his basic transcendental claims about language and thus further politicizes his project. For example, Fichte seems to hint that the history of language can influence the history of philosophy and vice versa. Thus Fichte flirts with a metacritical view that runs counter to the spirit of transcendental idealism. Fichte also claims that different languages can be more, or less, philosophical. From this he reaches the conclusion that the philosophical imagination is best cultivated in certain original languages that are semantically organic, such that they facilitate the synthesis of opposites. More generally, Fichte redefines the relation between thought, language, individuality, and culture. He rejects the view that individuals are atomic selves who come up with ideas prior to language and who then search for words with which to express their thoughts. Rather, Fichte has a social interpretation of thought, language, individuality, and culture. Fichte claims that spirit speaks through individuals and that individuality must thus be understood in relation to a given historical culture, language, and philosophical tradition. This last conclusion leads to the radical notion that philosophers must cultivate the spirit that exists within the linguistic nation. The philosopher's voice, speaking in an *Ursprache,* has the power to use this language to cultivate both national unity and individual imagination. Indeed, the philosopher's voice is indispensable in this regard because the philosopher has the original insight into the unity of language, nation, individuality, and spirit.

In 1795 Fichte claimed that the transcendental basis of language is the communicative nature of free human beings: language originates in the human desire or drive to communicate with and be recognized by other human beings.

> As soon as he has actually encountered a being of his own kind in a reciprocal relation, it is precisely this drive that would have to produce in him the wish to indicate his thoughts to the other with whom he has become connected, and, on the other hand, to be able to obtain from the other a clear communication of the other's thoughts.[15]

This intersubjective origin has different levels of empirical expression: the family and the tribe. Signs develop and are used within a family; these signs are then exported to the larger community of the tribe. The social and political development of empirical languages can be traced back to an original *Ursprache,* which is the first way in which human beings express thoughts to one another. The aim of language is "signification (*Bezeichnung*) . . . for the sake of mutual reciprocity of our thought."[16] Fichte further clarifies this by stating that "through association with human beings, there awakens in us the idea of indicating our thoughts to one another through arbitrary signs—in a word, the idea of language."[17] This basic desire to communicate is the ground of the *Ursprache,* the immediate expression of inner thought that is developed further in both familial and tribal interaction.

In the early text Fichte described the *Ursprache* as a primitive language that was a direct imitation of nature: "Just as nature signified something to men through sight and hearing, exactly thus did they have to signify it to one another in freedom.—One might call a language constructed on this basic principle the *Ursprache* or Hieroglyphic language."[18] In this early essay, Fichte did not claim any special ontological or spiritual status for the *Ursprache.* While all languages remain connected to their origin in some way, Fichte claimed that this connection to the origin of language was gradually effaced by the progress of culture. As culture progresses, the *Ursprache* "will gradually perish and be replaced by another which carries in itself not even the slightest trace of the former."[19] This progress occurred as the original words of the *Ursprache* "were replaced by signs which better corresponded to the civilized spirit of the people."[20] In this early text, then, Fichte sees the overcoming of the *Ursprache* as a sign of spiritual progress. This is not so in the *Addresses,* where progress is understood as keeping alive the original spiritual power of the *Ursprache.* In the *Addresses* Fichte claims that German culture is progressive because the actually existing German *Ursprache* affords Germans the most comprehensive appropriation of the original "force of nature" that is at work in language. This claim is in direct contradiction to his earlier claim that the *Ursprache* is overcome by civilization.

In this early essay, Fichte leaves unanalyzed the explicitly political development of language, i.e., the development of diverse national languages. He does not extend his account of the development of language beyond a primitive tribal level and does not consider the connection between language and the modern nation-state. While he does point beyond the *Ursprache* toward a more advanced, more "spiritual," cultured, or civilized language, he leaves this undeveloped.[21] Almost at the end of the 1795 essay, Fichte claims that a more culturally advanced language would eventually "supplant (*verdrängten*)" the *Ursprache:* "For as the nation (*die Nation*) advanced further in its culture, it would necessarily have to find new forms adequate to its concepts and soon forget about the older ones while using the new ones."[22]

In the *Addresses* Fichte extends the political context of language to an explicit consideration of the link between the nation, its language, and the spiritual development of its culture. Fichte says in the *Addresses* that it is crucial for a nation to remain in touch with its proper linguistic heritage, its living language.[23] Fichte here attempts a taxonomy of peoples based upon the *Lebendigkeit* of their various languages. This criterion is linked to the spiritual depth of the creative imagination. The more vital languages and nations also have the deepest philosophical insight, the most vigorous sense of moral freedom, and the most advanced spiritual culture.

Although the nationalist tone of Fichte's taxonomy in the *Addresses* represents a crucial shift away from his analysis in the 1795 essay, this nationalistic approach is still limited to a universalist idea of the transcendental condition for the possibility of language in the intersubjective nature of human freedom.[24] In the *Addresses,* however, Fichte extends the notion of intersubjectivity in a radically political direction by recognizing that the creative power of human freedom is always tied to some national spirit. "This making of itself deliberately, and according to rule, must have a beginning somewhere and at some moment in space and time . . . In regard to the space, we believe that it is first of all the Germans who are called upon to begin the new era . . ."[25] In the *Addresses* Fichte links the transcendental project of freedom to the German nation and especially to the German language. He concludes that the German language is the language that is closest to the completion of the project of human freedom because it remains most clearly linked to the transcendental ground of language. German is the proper language in which to comprehend the essence of human freedom because German remains tied to the "force of nature (*Naturkraft*)" from which language first issued forth.[26] The task of articulating this connection and actualizing it in politics and imagination was taken up in the *Addresses*.

Fichte's Final Philosophy of Language

> Men are formed by language far more than language is formed by men (*mehr die Menschen von der Sprache gebildet werden, denn die Sprache von den Menschen*).
>
> —Fichte, *Addresses to the German Nation*[27]

What then is Fichte's philosophy of language as articulated in the *Addresses*? As we have seen, this question is not tangential to his project in the *Addresses* nor indeed to the more theoretical project of the *Wissenschaftslehre*. Fichte explicitly states that "a consideration of the nature of language in general (*das Wesen der Sprache über haupt*)" is necessary as part of his larger project of inspiring the German people.[28] Fichte's philosophy of language can be summed up in the above epigram about the way in which language forms us as individuals. There are two ways in which Fichte develops this view, a strong version and a weak one. In both of these he is arguing for a reversal of the common-sense view of the relation between language and individuality, language and the community, and indeed language and thought. The common-sense view holds that individuals, communities, and thoughts exist prior to language and that we learn particular languages in order to express our inner thoughts to other members of our community. Such for example is Augustine's view (famously used as a foil by Wittgenstein in *Philosophical Investigations*) that both will and thought are prior to language and that we learn language in order to be able to express our thoughts and our wills.[29]

In the *Addresses,* Fichte rejects this theory of language. In the strong version of his theory, he claims that language is the basis of individuality, community, and thought. He states that with regard to individuals: "They do not form language, it is the language that forms them (*so bilden nicht sie die Sprache, sondern die Sprache bildet sie*)."[30] Individuals and their most deeply held thoughts are all formed by language. Fichte further elaborates this claim in a more political direction: "the people does not express its knowledge, but its knowledge expresses itself out of the mouth of the people (*nicht eigentlich dieses Volk spricht siene Erkenntniss aus, sondern seine Erkenntniss selbst spricht sich aus aus demselben*)."[31] This claim is, in turn explained by the following: "It is not really man that speaks, but human nature that speaks in him and announces itself to others of his kind (*Nicht eigentlich redet der Mensch, sondern in ihm redet die menschliche Natur, und verkündiget sich anderen sienes Gleichen*)."[32] According to this strong claim, individuals are merely conduits for the life of spirit that is found in the totality of language and community. It is these sorts of claims that allow Fichte to maintain his strong version of forced education: since the individual is merely a vessel, spiritual content may be put into the individual by force. The nation thus creates moral individuality by way of authoritarian coercive education because the nation as a linguistic-spiritual entity is prior to the individual.

The weaker form of Fichte's claim can be found in the following:

> What an immeasurable influence on the whole human development of a people (*eines Volkes*) the character of its language may have—its language, which accompanies the individual into the most secret depths of his mind in thought and will and either hinders him or gives him wings, which unites within its domain the whole mass of men who speak it into one single point and common understanding (*gemeinsamen Verstanden*), which is the true point of meeting and mingling for the world of the senses and the world of spirit (*der Sinnenwelt und der der Geister*), and fuses the ends of both in each other in such a fashion that it is impossible to tell to which of the two it belongs itself . . .[33]

Here Fichte moderates his view slightly and recognizes that there is a mutual interplay between the individual and the spirit of his/her community. Notice that this interplay is quite similar to the hovering faculty of imagination, which occurs in the heart of the theoretical philosophy. Language is crucial, for it acts as the medium in which individual and community are interrelated. Indeed, Fichte concludes that there is no way to dissolve the mediating function of language and that we cannot tell whether the individual or the community is prior to their juncture in language. Thus, even this weaker claim, which allows some room for the individual beyond or in opposition to language, still maintains that individual consciousness is at least partially determined by social language. In both versions of this theory, then, it is clear that Fichte rejects the view that individuals and their thoughts are somehow prior to or distinct from language and the community.

In the *Addresses* Fichte provides us with two arguments for the priority of language: a transcendental argument and a practical/moral argument. The transcendental argument is similar to the argument he made in the 1795 essay on language. In that essay, Fichte claimed that language originated in the human drive to be recognized by another human being: the transcendental condition for the possibility of language is the intersubjective nature of human freedom. In the *Addresses,* Fichte claims that language originates in a force of nature that is unitary and necessary: "it ever remains nature's one, same, living power of speech, which in the beginning necessarily arose in the way it did (*bleibt es immer dieselbe Eine, ursprünglich also ausbrechenmüssende lebendige Sprachkraft der Natur*)."[34] He even goes so far as to claim that there is a "fundamental law" according to which "every idea becomes in the human organs of speech one particular sound and no other."[35] Fichte does not explain this fundamental law in any detail, but it might, perhaps, be explained as a law of onomatopoeia wherein human speech originates out of an imitation of sounds in nature.[36] Behind this must be however, the transcendental condition of human intersubjectivity which makes imitation of nature in speech necessary to begin with. In the *Addresses* this transcendental condition seems to be what he calls the "force of nature," which he refers to as "language in its original emergence from life (*der ursprüngliche Ausgang der Sprache*)."[37] Language emerges from the intersubjective basis of human freedom. It is thus prior to individuality because individuality can only form on the basis of communication between selves, which is itself only made possible by language and imagination.

The practical/moral argument is linked to Fichte's call for a new form of education. Fichte's *Addresses* are dedicated to inspiring the German nation. This will occur, Fichte claims, when Germany creates a new form of education for its youth. According to Fichte, there could be no such thing as moral education if the individual were a selfish atom that comes into existence somehow prior to his/her community. If it were true that children were naturally selfish and viewed themselves as atomic selves, it would be impossible to educate them:

> Nothing can be created from nothing, and the development of a fundamental instinct, no matter to what extent, can never make it the opposite of itself. How then could education ever implant morality in the child, if morality did not exist in him originally (*ursprünglich*) and before all education? It does, therefore, actually exist in all human children that are born into the world; the task is simply to find out the purest and most primitive form in which it appears.[38]

Fichte claims that he knows that children have this fundamental moral disposition both as the result of empirical observation and as the result of his own speculative philosophical thought. Speculative philosophy in the *Wissenschaftslehre* reaches the conclusion that the self and the not-self mutually determine one another and that the self strives to recognize and to be recognized by the not-self. In the *Addresses* Fichte explains this as "the most primitive form of morality," what he calls "the instinct for respect."[39] He further elaborates this: "The bond, therefore, which makes men of one mind, and the development of which is a chief part of education for manhood, is not sensuous love, but the instinct for mutual respect."[40] This instinct for mutual respect is linked to the intersubjective nature of human freedom and thus to Fichte's discussion of language. Language is the medium that allows individuals to respect one another by allowing us to express ourselves to others for recognition. According to Fichte, then, we do not acquire language because we are preformed homunculi looking for the means of expressing our selfish desires. Rather, language occurs because we are moral and social beings whose basic instincts require that we create a medium in which we can respect one another.

The details of Fichte's view on language thus changed significantly between 1795 and 1807, while its underlying kernel did not. Fichte revises his estimation of the *Ursprache* and argues that the best language is the language that stays closest to its roots in the intersubjective nature of human being. Nonetheless, Fichte retains his view that language originates in intersubjectivity. In the later text he argues more vigorously for the view that language is prior to the development of finite individuality and that society is thus, in some sense, prior to the individual. It is this view that allows him to call for a radical authoritarian social project of reeducating individuals.

Rhetoric, Transformation, and Excess

> Only a complete regeneration (*Umschaffung*), only the beginning of an entirely new spirit (*eines ganz neuen Geistes*) can help us.
>
> —Fichte, *Addresses to the German Nation*[41]

Fichte deserves a unique place within both the history of German politics and the history of German Idealism because he undertakes the quite extraordinary task of unifying philosophy, poetry, and politics in both theory and practice in order to create a new spirit in European history. Unlike Kant, who was skeptical of persuasive political rhetoric, Fichte deliberately employed the bombastic poetry of political speech in his *Addresses to the German Nation*. While Kant stated that political reasoning which "admits an incentive other than the idea of duty itself," is "pathological," Fichte recognized that political action is as much a matter of inspiration as it is a matter of deliberation.[42] While Fichte does not deny Kant's claims about the transcendental nature of morality, he felt the need, resisted by Kant, to use his voice in a poetic and political manner to begin the process of instituting morality by way of the educational state. Even though Kant thought of the philosopher's voice as the catalyst for historical change, Kant resisted the temptation to use his voice as an active agent for change. Fichte, on the other hand, viewed his voice as more than a catalyst: Fichte wanted to use his voice in a creative act of political poetry. For the Kantian theory of morality to become practically effective, Fichte claims, political life must be imbued with the new spirit that is the power of the German language and its intimate connection with the philosophical imagination. The task that Fichte undertakes in his flights of rhetoric in the *Addresses to the German Nation* is to facilitate the creation of a public spirit by way of education: this spirit, once posited by the philosopher's voice, will be able and willing to recreate itself upon spiritual ground. This creative task requires the inspirational intervention of the philosopher in political life.[43]

Like his contemporaries, Schiller, Schelling, and the young Hegel, Fichte held that poetry as well as philosophy was needed to complete the modern political project. Given his considerations on language and his emphasis on the philosophical imagination, it is easy to see that, for Fichte, poetry is what links philosophy and politics. As the young Hegel states in the "System-Fragment" (1796): "Until we make ideas aesthetic, i.e., mythological, they hold no interest for the people, and conversely, before mythology is reasonable, the philosophy must be ashamed of it."[44] While philosophy comprehends the truth of spirit, poetry and the active mythology of nationalism makes this truth interesting to the people and thus actively inspires the people. Thus, unlike the older, more conservative Hegel, who claimed that philosophical reason finally transcends poetry and can thus have only a retrospective interest in political life, Fichte deliberately took on the mantle of philosopher-poet and actively intervened in political life. Throughout his career Fichte had seen the philosopher's task as political. As early as 1794 Fichte stated that "the true vocation of the scholarly class is the supreme supervision of the actual progress of the human race in general and the unceasing promotion of this progress."[45] By 1807 Fichte came to the realization that the philosopher can only promote progress by using the inspirational power of poetic speech. The conjunction of poetry, politics, and philosophy that occurs in the *Addresses* is intended to give birth to a new spirit. It is not clear whether the offspring of this conjunction is the higher spirit of Kantian enlightenment or the monstrous spirit of German nationalism.

What is at issue in considering this conjunction of philosophy, poetry, and politics is the traditional distinction between political rhetoric and philosophical argumentation. The rhetorical art of political persuasion is unphilosophical, while the reasoned conclusions of philosophy are not politically expedient. When the opposition between rhetoric and philosophy is stated in this extreme manner, it is clear that rhetorical persuasion must be included as one of the un-philosophical, "pathological grounds" for action that Kant rejects in the *Metaphysics of Morals*. Rhetoric appeals to pathos—interest and inclination—without regard for proper reason and argumentation. Indeed Kant routinely claimed that his critical project is dedicated to the endeavor of helping people to overcome the irrationality of superstition and zealotry by helping them to reason for themselves. Moreover, Kant claimed that critical philosophical thinking alone—not poetry or political rhetoric—would lead to the political goal of increased freedom.[46] For Kant, philosophy ought not to persuade by using rhetoric, it ought rather to instruct by using reasoned argument.

In the *Addresses* Fichte attempts to overcome the distinction between philosophy and rhetoric. Given his spiritual nationalistic interpretation of language, Fichte claims that authentic philosophy is political and that authentic political life ought to be philosophical. To achieve this authenticity, philosophy must make use of the poetic power of the *Ursprache*, its rhetorical force. The philosopher must persuade and inspire political action, even though this political action is supposed to result in a form of political life that will be governed by reason. The philosopher must thus use rhetoric to lead beyond rhetoric to philosophy, just as the educational project must use authority and coercion to lead to freedom. Fichte thus borrows from Plato a recognition of the need for the "noble lie": the philosopher-king, in order to inspire and unite his people, must use the unphilosophical expedient of rhetorical persuasion.

While Fichte claims that political life needs to be inspired by philosophy, he also claims that philosophical enlightenment can only be established within an enlightened political culture. This gives rise to an interesting problem with regard to the dialectic between the universal content of philosophy and its particular manifestation in time and space: while the content of philosophy is supposed to be the universal truth about human being, this truth can be known only by those specific individuals who inhabit a particular, historically and geographically located, political life and who speak a certain original language. Fichte finds himself caught in a dilemma between Kant's humanistic cosmopolitanism and his own recognition that thinking is always historically located. Fichte attempts to resolve this difficulty by hypostatizing the German nation as *the* philosophical nation. And yet, Fichte continues to claim that this true philosophy is itself the cosmopolitan philosophy of Kant and the universal morality of rational Christianity. Fichte's struggle to reconcile the cosmopolitan perspective of critical philosophy with his own recognition of the local, national place of philosophical reflection forms the basis of the tensions that appear in Fichte's *Addresses*.[47] Moreover, these tensions are ultimately a matter of the difference between philosophical enlightenment and inspiration. Fichte's virtue (as well as his vice) is that he tries to unite these differences within his own voice.

With his recognition of the transformative power of poetry, Fichte also recognizes the transformative power of speech and voice. In a few places, Fichte even goes so far as to claim that it is the creative power of his own voice that will inspire and invoke the German nation, for example, "Throughout the entire domain of the whole German language (*Zunge*), wherever our voice (*Stimme*) rings out free and unrestrained, it thus invokes (*ruft zu*) Germans by the very fact of its existence."[48] The very sound of his voice and the impassioned rhetoric of his address is supposed to give birth to the newly spiritualized German nation. Fichte thus positions himself as the incarnate conjunction of poetry, philosophy, and politics—quite an extraordinary and excessive claim.

Fichte's postulation of the organic relation between poetry, thought, and politics in the German language is intended to inspire the German people to rise up and reclaim their right to self-determination, a right that the French had revoked. It is easy to understand the historical need for Fichte's *Addresses,* given the fact that French troops were stationed outside of the lecture hall in which Fichte spoke. However, one must admit that Fichte's attempted conjunction of philosophy, poetry, and politics leads to excesses of nationalism. The poetic license that Fichte claims in light of the political crisis leads to a conflict with the philosopher's task of pursuing the truth. In his attempts to philosophically justify his claims about Germany, its *Ursprache,* and its historical destiny, Fichte's poetic rhetoric leads him away from truth toward exaggeration and falsehood.

Nonetheless, what makes the *Addresses* an interesting text and more than just an exercise in incendiary rhetoric is the fact that they attempt to offer a *philosophical justification* for the excesses of rhetoric found in inspirational political speech. As a political actor, Fichte utilizes inflammatory rhetoric and inspirational poetry; as a philosopher, he attempts to give a philosophical justification for this revolutionary political rhetoric. Indeed, according to Fichte's claims about the *Ursprache,* German politics and philosophy consist in just this implausible conjunction of politics, poetry, and philosophy. The excesses of poetic rhetoric that occur in political speech lead to a violation of philosophical argumentation and the search for truth. Fichte's attempt to persuade the German nation leads him to make statements that are plainly false. In the Fourth through Eighth Addresses, Fichte provides three arguments for the unique German position in the history of European culture. These arguments are intended to establish that German culture is the origin of modern European political life. Each of these arguments is flawed.

First, Fichte praises the line of culture begun with Luther and the Protestant Reformation, implicitly situating himself in that lineage. It was Luther, claims Fichte, who was able to comprehend the truth of Christianity because he contemplated it using the insights of one who speaks an *Ursprache*. German thinking is able to surpass the level of thinking that occurs in Romance languages—the lifeless methodical thinking of the Catholic Church—because by thinking the truth of Christianity in the *Ursprache,* truth comes to life. This argument is at least plausible because it is true that the Lutheran Reformation was premised on the attempt to bring the truth of Christianity back to its roots in the people and that one method by which Luther sought to accomplish this goal was to translate the Bible into the vernacular German. However, this argument seems to flagrantly disregard the possibility that a non-German speaker could have a proper understanding of Christianity. Here Fichte's political desire to bolster the German culture leads to a seriously overstated argument.

Fichte further disingenuously ignores philosophical and historical truth in his two other arguments about the cultural importance of the German people. In his second argument, Fichte deliberately discounts the historical importance of the Italian city-states of the Middle Ages and claims that the Germans were the first to develop bourgeois culture in the Middle Ages with the development of middle-class towns. Fichte thus concludes that German culture is the original model for modern European culture. In this argument Fichte grossly overstates his case: it is simply not true that bourgeois culture is a uniquely German invention. His political poetics thus result in a seriously jaundiced view of history. In his third argument, while Fichte acknowledges that it was the French who first undertook the task of forming a rational republican state, he claims that the French Revolution was itself inspired by German philosophy. He then glibly notes that the French experiment in republican government failed. He concludes that the task of completing the modern world is a uniquely German task because only the Germans can comprehend the philosophical basis of political revolution. This argument is also historically inaccurate and seriously prejudiced. Not only does he falsely claim that the ideas on which the French Revolution were based were entirely German ideas, he also ignores philosophical and constitutional developments in England and America.

While Fichte attempts to defend his claims about the uniqueness of German culture by appealing to historical arguments about the German origins of modernity, this defense leads to some blatantly absurd arguments. His desire to inspire his German audience and the poetic license he uses in his inspirational speeches cloud his philosophical judgment and lead him to make inaccurate historical claims and to overstate the importance of Germany and its *Ursprache* in both history and philosophy.

The difficulties encountered in attempting to unite political rhetoric with philosophical argument lead one to wonder whether philosophy and politics can ever be conjoined without violating philosophy's devotion to the truth. Fichte's philosophical justification of his poetic license relies upon his claims about the *Ursprache*. However, if we realize that his claims about the value of the German *Ursprache* are themselves part of an attempt to inspire the German nation, this justification remains doubtfully circular. While the poet and the politician may claim to be the voice of the *Ursprache,* and while they may make bombastic claims about the power of the *Ursprache*, it seems that the philosopher's duty is to remain skeptical of such claims in the pursuit of truth. Fichte's political goal thus leads him to violate his philosophical duty. The Fichtean conjunction of philosophy, poetry, and politics seems to lead to the creation of a monster of ideology: one who is willing to sacrifice philosophy's search for truth, while persuading us that this sacrifice is necessary for the eventual completion of philosophy.

Fichte's Voice

> I was the first one to see it vividly; therefore it fell to me to take the first step . . . There must always be one who is first; then let him be first who can!
>
> —Fichte, *Addresses to the German Nation*[49]

Fichte's *Addresses* are paradoxically addressed to the German nation, an entity that in 1807 was not yet actual in the sense that the German people had not yet freed themselves from the cultural and political hegemony of France. Moreover, the philosophical imagination—the spirit—of his audience is itself undeveloped and in need of education. Since a developed imagination is required to comprehend the depths of Fichte's system in all of its manifestations as either theoretical, political, or moral, the ostensive audience of Fichte's *Addresses* cannot comprehend the depth of Fichte's words. This paradox is resolved when we consider the rhetorical form of the text as a poetic act of inspiration. To stimulate the German spirit, Fichte must utilize the rhetorical form of patriotic speechifying: he must motivate and inspire his audience so that they can willingly engage in the educational project through which the proper audience for the *Wissenschaftslehre* and Fichte's moral and political systems will be created. "Formerly there lived in the majority naught but flesh, matter and nature; through the new education alone spirit shall live in the majority, yea, very soon in all and spur (*treiben*) them on; the stable and certain spirit, which was mentioned before as the only possible foundation of a well organized state shall be produced everywhere."[50]

For Fichte, philosophical truth requires that real human beings be educated so as to nurture the dialectical function of imagination. This is what Fichte means when he says in the *Addresses* that education must move beyond rote memorization to become real knowledge. Education can easily produce mere "knowledge (*Erkenntniss*)" by "stimulating regular and progressive mental activity."[51] But mere knowledge is not enough to produce the new type of human being envisioned by Fichte's educational revolution, "knowledge is only incidental to it (*die Erkenntniss fällt derselben nur zu*)."[52] Rather, what is important for the new education is cultivation of the spontaneous mental activity of the pupil. This spontaneous mental activity to be created by education is, in effect, the activity of the imagination and spirit.

Fichte openly acknowledges in the *Addresses* that "as yet this generation cannot believe our words; it is inevitable that they seem to it like fairy tales."[53] Moreover Fichte claims that the failure of the Germans to comprehend his *Wissenschaftslehre* and their failure to unite politically is a failure of the Germans properly to understand themselves. Thus the political crisis and the philosophical crisis of Germany will be resolved by way of a proper comprehension of Fichte's words and a proper enactment of his creative proposals. Toward the end of his Fourth Address, Fichte takes up the issue of the connection between political and philosophical transformation.[54] Since Fichte's philosophy is not yet at home in the present age, it must thus give up its claims on the present generation and must, instead, "undertake the task of fashioning for itself the generation to which it does belong." Then, making the connection between politics and philosophy explicit Fichte states: "The education which we have hitherto described is likewise the education for this philosophy." While the Germans must educate themselves and must assert themselves as free moral beings, Fichte recognizes that this is an impossible task for the current German generation. Rather Fichte concludes that philosophy itself speaks in a prophetic voice and through a creative act ushers in the new age: "Yet in a certain sense it (philosophy) alone can be the educator in this education; and so it had to be a forerunner neither understood nor acceptable." Fichte concludes the Fourth Address by offering an analogy with the prophet Ezekiel who prophesied that God would reanimate the dead bones of the Israelites. Fichte puts himself in the same position as Ezekiel. Fichte's

Addresses are the prophetic words that will awaken the German people and will produce the completion of the political and philosophical rebirth of spirit. As the result of this new education, "therefore, a totally new order of things and a new creation would begin."[55]

Fichte occasionally tries to downplay the importance of his own words by turning to the question of history. Much of his text is dedicated to proving that the task of creating the new epoch in history is a task that can only be undertaken by the Germans. Fichte also recognizes, alluding to his theoretical philosophy, that this new creation will be a process of self-positing.

> Formerly mankind became just what it did become and was able to become; the time for such chance development has gone by; for where mankind has developed most it has become nothing. If it is not to remain in this nothingness, it must henceforward make itself (*sich selbst mache*) all that it is yet to become. The real destiny of the human race on earth . . . is in freedom to make itself what it really is originally (*es mit Freiheit sich zu dem mache, was es eigentlich urprünglich ist*).[56]

Political transformation is a matter of the Germans adequately understanding themselves and their historical destiny. Fichte's words alone are insufficient to transform German culture. The Germans must make themselves what they originally are by overcoming their ignorance and learning to assert themselves freely. This task will be completed when the Germans properly understand Fichte's words. The problem remains, however, as Fichte points out in his considerations of the failure of his *Wissenschaftslehre*, that since the Germans are not yet free and since they lack creative imagination, they cannot adequately comprehend Fichte's words.

Fichte's goal is freedom, both political and spiritual. On the one hand, Fichte's political addresses assume that his audience possesses freedom of philosophical insight so that they are able to comprehend the need for political action. On the other hand, philosophical insight is only possible when the audience is politically free. This circle seems to pose a problem for Fichte because he acknowledges that, in Germany at the time, both philosophical insight and political freedom were lacking. Fichte attempts to resolve this problem by insisting upon the creative power of his own voice.

He recognizes that both his philosophical reflections and his political interventions may fall upon deaf ears. Both the actual formation of the German nation and the spiritual elevation of the German people depend upon proper education within a free political society. The question remains, however: who is to educate the educators? Fichte wrestles with this problem in both his theoretical and political texts and clearly believes that he himself is the one who has seen the light and whose task it is to enlighten and free the human race both spiritually and politically. In the Introduction to the *Wissenschaftslehre*, Fichte explains the unique capacity of one who knows the truth as a "special grace of nature" and as "philosophical genius."[57] In the *Addresses,* Fichte clearly implies that he is the philosophical genius, the new Ezekiel who will enlighten humanity. Fichte states in the last Address: "This was the first step to the goal of a thorough reformation (*Verbesserung*); someone or other had to take it. I was the first one to see it vividly; therefore it fell to me to take the first step . . . There must always be one who is first; then let him be first who can!"[58] Fichte's words in the *Addresses* act as the moment of genius or grace that will allow the Germans to exit the closed circle of traditional education and lead the human race into the new age.

Throughout the *Addresses* Fichte explicitly refers to the fact that he is addressing a real audience and that the call of his voice is a creative act which creates its proper audience by inspiring the real human beings who hear his words. In the first Address he states that he is addressing the whole nation through its representatives in the immediate audience. He goes on to say that he presupposes that both he and his audience "consider ourselves simply Germans, that we be not held captive even by pain itself, that we wish to see the truth and have the courage to look it in the face."[59] This claim is ironic because Fichte diagnoses the problem of Germany as an unwillingness to face up to the painful truth. It is thus clear that Fichte's immediately present audience is called upon by Fichte to transform itself into the spiritually free, self-consciously German audience that alone can rise up and create the German nation. In the last Address Fichte enumerates the various really existing people *to whom he speaks*: young men, old men, men of business, scholars, and princes. Fichte seeks to inspire these men to rise up and create the new age. He also claims that his voice *speaks for* his audience's ancestors, their comrades fallen in battle, their descendants not yet born, and indeed all of humanity. All of these voices urge the individuals who hear Fichte's voice to become conscious of themselves and to reclaim their political and philosophical birthright. Fichte's *Addresses* can thus be understood as a creative act, an invocation that brings its audience into existence in the act of addressing it. If philosophical thinking and poetic speech have creative power, then Fichte's speech is creative poetry addressed to those who are not yet spiritually actual in an effort literally to inspire: to breathe spirit into them by way of the force of nature found in the German language.

What Fichte says about the *Ursprache* in the *Addresses* and what he says about the spiritual power of imagination in the *Wissenschaftslehre* can help clarify this inspirational activity. He claims that in the *Ursprache,* "the symbol is itself directly living and sensuous; it is re-presentative (*wieder darstellend*) of all real life and so the symbol takes hold of and exerts an influence on life [or life takes hold of and exerts an influence on the symbol—both translations are possible and Fichte probably meant this to be ambiguous—the German reads: *und so dasselbe ergreifend und eingreifend in dasselbe*]. To the possessor of such a language spirit (*Geist*) speaks directly and reveals itself as man does to man."[60] Spirit has a direct influence on those who speak and think in an *Ursprache*. Fichte goes so far as to claim that the *Ursprache* has a special creative power over life: "the words of such a language in all its parts are life and create life (*schaffen Leben*)."[61] With regard to the people who speak such a language, Fichte states that "they do not form the language; it is the language that forms (*bildet*) them."[62] The *Ursprache* can create a higher, more spiritual life for the people who speak it. This seems to be especially true for *philosophy* that is spoken in the *Ursprache*, which has creative poetic power. In the *Wissenschaftslehre*, as we saw above, Fichte makes it clear that philosophy, the *Wissenschaftslehre* itself, cannot be communicated by language alone, but that one "philosophizes with spirit" only when one appeals to the "creative power of imagination."[63] Fichte concludes: "The *Wissenschaftslehre* is of a kind that cannot be communicated by the letter merely, but only through the spirit (*durch den Geist*); for its basic ideas must be elicited (*hervorgeberacht*), in anyone who studies it, by the creative imagination itself."[64] Here Fichte clearly indicates that spirit is only brought forth by the creative power of imagination. When conjoined with what Fichte has to say about the creative power of the *Ursprache* and the poetic power of thought in the *Ursprache*, it is clear that Fichte believes that his own poetic/philosophical speech in the *Addresses* is that which will bring forth the spirit of the German nation.

Fichte claims that past German philosophy was an ineffective form of preaching. This left the German spirit without a proper home: "it is now sufficiently clear that these sermons (*Predigten*) have vanished without result into thin air, and the reason for this is evident too. A living thing affects only something living."[65] For philosophy to flourish it must be addressed to a living, freely creative audience. According to Fichte, the German nation, as it exists under the influence of foreigners invaders, was as good as dead; uninspired, uncreative, dead philosophy will do nothing to resurrect the German spirit and influence political life. This is the reason that the Germans neither adequately comprehend the truth of German philosophy nor recognize their unique historical mission. In response to this, Fichte proclaims that he and his listeners must undertake the task of "fashioning (*bilden*) the generation to which it does belong."[66] This work of creating spiritual humanity is begun with the creative poetic, rhetorical activity of Fichte's addresses. These addresses, if they are to have their intended effect, must be more than just empty sermons; they must be a poetic act of creation, a lively call for political action, and an inspiring activity of philosophical self-consciousness.

Conclusion

Fichte's *Addresses* have both a theoretical and a political import: they poetically attempt to create in speech the political ground on which theoretical philosophy can flourish, thus opening the way toward further political and philosophical enlightenment. As we have seen, Fichte's attempt to unify theory and practice in the sound of his voice leads to some disquieting conclusions. His view of the German language and culture is nationalistic. His proposed method of reeducation is authoritarian. And his claim that theory and practice can only be united by the will of the philosopher who posits this unity in the *Ursprache* reeks with hubris. Fichte saw himself as the Promethean genius of German culture who alone would be able to posit the unity of theory and practice by at once comprehending the future of humanity and creating it. As Sluga interprets Fichte's estimation of his role within world history:

> Fichte thought the ego could construct and reconstruct both itself and the world. Fully convinced that he was the first philosopher to recognize these facts and to see through the errors of dogmatic philosophizing, and certain that the history of humankind was in effect the history of reason, Fichte concluded that he himself was necessarily occupying a pivotal place in world history.[67]

This view of his own self-importance as the one who brings forth spirit in both theory and practice is the height of hubris, a hubris that prefigures a similar hubris on the part of both Hegel and Marx. Fichte saw himself as a philosophical politician, placing himself at the center of the process of political and philosophical creation. He clearly thought that he was the one who should properly addresses the German nation in the first person. While we should justly indict Fichte for his hubris, let us note in closing, that Fichte's goal was not to recreate the German spirit in his own image but rather to bring forth the *true* German spirit that would be the vanguard of European cosmopolitan morality. Like Plato's philosopher-king, Fichte believed that he was the one who knew the truth and whose task it was to inspire the people with this truth.

Let us further note three valuable insights about the philosophical enterprise and its relation to politics that can be distilled from our consideration of Fichte's voice. 1.) Fichte understood that political life is the ground for philosophy and that philosophy is the ground for politics. He thus, quite correctly I think, saw the philosopher's task as a political one. 2.) Fichte claimed that the philosopher and the politician are like poets engaged in a process of creation. Human beings are not born free in either the spiritual or political sense; rather, we must be educated into freedom. Just as it is the politician's task to develop the human capacity for political freedom, it is the philosopher's task is to inspire the human capacity for spiritual freedom. 3.) Fichte acknowledged that the creative power of philosophy and politics rests upon the creative power of speech. Philosophy and politics both occur "only" in speech, and yet this speech can have profound transformative power over the real lives of human beings. These insights, perhaps, led Fichte to overestimate his own importance as a philosopher-politician. However, by examining the excess of Fichte's *Addresses,* we can see the awesome responsibility that philosophy has to its audience. While we ought to continue to strive to unite philosophy, poetry, and politics, we must recognize that this struggle cannot be overcome by the voice of a single speaker. To claim otherwise, as Fichte did, is to violate the republican spirit of enlightenment that leads us to strive for this unity. As we turn to Hegel, we shall see that Hegel's firm distinction between philosophy, politics, and poetry was an attempt to avoid the excesses of Fichte's inspirational philosophical politics.

CHAPTER 7

Hegel: Philosophy and the Spirit of Politics

> The cultivation (*Bildung*) and the flowering of the sciences is here one of the essential moments itself in the life of the state; at this university, the university of the focal point, philosophy, the focal point of all cultivation of the spirit, of all science and truth, must find its place and its principal furtherance.
>
> —Hegel, "Inaugural Lecture at the University of Berlin"[1]

With Fichte, the voice of philosophy went beyond its proper limit by appropriating political rhetoric, albeit for the philosophical purpose of jump-starting progress toward enlightenment. Fichte could not rest easily with the antinomy of progress that resulted from the Kantian approach to the dichotomy between philosophy and politics. Nor could he abide the distinction between philosophical speech, political rhetoric, and poetic inspiration. While Kant postulated infinite progress toward a reconciliation of the difference between morality and politics, Fichte attempted to collapse this infinity with the poetic creative power of his own voice. Hegel saw this and was skeptical of Fichte's attempts at what Hegel called, "popularity." He recognized that Fichte continued the philosophical revolution in Germany with his brand of subjective idealism. However, for most people, this philosophy became too arid and uninspiring. Thus Hegel claims that although previously "men of culture," including businessmen and statesmen, would be interested in philosophy, now philosophy had become insipid and superfluous.[2] As a response to this, Fichte turned to popular forms that were also inadequate because, according to Hegel, they culminated in "poetic and prophetic tendencies, in vehement aspirations, in excrescences which grew out of the Fichtian philosophy."[3]

Hegel and Fichte were both involved in the same project of enlightenment found in Kant. They both thought that philosophical education was the key to progress toward republican politics. However, they disagreed about the proper method by which philosophy could lead the way toward political progress. The largest distinction between the two can be found in their efforts to "popularize" philosophy. While Fichte was not above reaching out to his audience by employing poetic political rhetoric, Hegel demanded that his audience do the hard work necessary to climb up the ladder to the philosophical perspective. Part of this difference can be understood in terms of the historical circumstances under which Fichte and Hegel lived and worked. The eight years that separated Fichte and Hegel in age made an enormous difference in terms of the political situation in Germany and in Europe. Fichte lectured and agitated in Jena during the heady days immediately following the French Revolution. Hegel celebrated the French Revolution secretly as a youth in Tübingen with his friends in the seminary, Schelling and Hölderlin. Hegel arrived in Jena after Fichte and his Romantic followers had begun to leave, and after Napoleon had begun to transform the revolutionary French republic into an empire. While Hegel completed his *Phenomenology of Spirit* as Napoleon defeated the Prussians at Jena, Fichte was in Berlin and would soon deliver his *Addresses*. Eventually Fichte was involved in the founding of the University of Berlin as part of the national education project of a reformed Prussia, while Hegel came to Berlin and took over Fichte's chair at the University after the Congress of Vienna had mobilized forces of reaction throughout Europe. By the time Hegel published his treatise on politics, *The Philosophy of Right,* a reactionary censorship, the Karlsbad decrees, was already in place. While we can understand Fichte's enthusiasm about the role of philosophy in political life in light of the spirit of 1789, Hegel's more circumspect point of view can be understood in terms of the reactionary period in which he reached his philosophical maturity.

Hegel's career as a political philosopher can be read as a response to Fichte and to the failed hope of the French Revolution. Just as Hegel sought to articulate the complexity of contemporary social life and the modern idea of freedom, he also attempted to find a non-dogmatic way to maintain the differences between philosophy, politics, and poetry that Fichte had ignored. Moreover, for Hegel, the philosophical activity that articulated this distinction was itself always already both political and poetic to the extent that it shared the same spirit found in politics and poetry. Hegel thus resolved the antinomy of progress by locating the philosopher's voice within the history of spirit as the culmination of the totality of cultural life. For Hegel, philosophy develops out of politics, is located within political life, and helps complete the political project of freedom by making political life conscious of itself.

In the present chapter I will examine Hegel's general systematic methodology and his ideas about expression, systematicity, and philosophy. I will consider the way in which Hegel locates philosophy within political life. I will then attempt to locate his *Philosophy of Right* within political life in terms of the audience he addresses in this text. In the next chapter, I will discuss Hegel's methodology and role as a teacher, and his philosophy of language and voice.

The Need for Expression

> Man as spirit reduplicates himself (*der Mensch als Geist verdoppelt sich*)
>
> —Hegel, *Lectures on Aesthetics*[4]

For Hegel, philosophical activity comprehends the representational activity of spirit as it occurs in politics, art, and religion.[5] Human (or in Hegel's terms, spiritual) activity is expressive: it aims to express itself by way of various representational strategies. These representational activities lead beyond themselves toward philosophical comprehension because the need that drives human beings to produce works of art and to create explicit political constitutions also leads us to philosophize about both art and politics. "The universal and absolute need (*das allgemeine und absolute Bedürfnis*) out of which art arises, has its source in the fact that man is a *thinking* consciousness, i.e. that he draws out of himself and makes explicit for himself, that which he is, and generally, whatever is."[6] The need to create, to speak, and to think, is the need to make the implicit explicit so that it might become an object for further contemplation. It is, as Hegel states in the above epigram, a process of "reduplication" by which the outer world is brought into the inner spirit and in which the inner spirit expresses itself into the outer world.[7]

Despite the ubiquity and uniqueness of this need for expression and of the process of reduplication, Hegel recognizes the importance of the differences found in the different media in which this need is expressed. Unlike Schiller, for example, who, even more than Fichte, sought to unify the totality of human experience under the guise of "aesthetic education," Hegel recognized that the process of unifying the totality requires a continual recognition of the necessity of differences within that totality. Thus Hegel is not willing to collapse the difference between philosophy, poetry, religion, and politics, although he does attempt to articulate the way in which these share an essential spiritual content.[8] The tension created by this difference between modes of expression creates the drive that leads to the systematic nature of philosophical activity. Awareness of difference creates the need for that type of philosophical activity that can at once unite and differentiate within a system of the whole. Within the system, then, there are various ways in which the whole can be approached: Hegel repeatedly states the whole of philosophy is a circle of circles each of which provides an entry into the system.[9] One way of approaching Hegel's philosophical system, then, is to comprehend the way in which it originates from and returns to political life. The goal of philosophy, from this perspective, is to use the ordinary language of political life to express its difference from political activity and its sameness with the spirit of political life. The philosopher speaks from a vantage point within the polis and addresses a political audience. However, the philosopher must resist the temptation to collapse the distinction between philosophy and politics in the way that Fichte did. The recognition of the sameness and difference of philosophy and politics will help to complete the project of freedom: freedom consists in the comprehension of the various ways in which freedom expresses itself.

The activity of expressing the sameness and difference among things is the heart of Hegel's system. His dialectical method is dedicated to reconciling differences without destroying them: this is the idea behind the methodological concept upon which Hegel grounds his system, i.e., the process named by the German word *Aufhebung*. "To sublate (*Aufheben*) has a twofold meaning (*gedoppelten Sinn*) in the language: on the one hand it means to preserve, to maintain, and equally it also means to cause to cease, to put an end to."[10] Hegel's system is this attempt to preserve differences while canceling them by uniting them under more universal ideas. Thus Hegel's work is concerned in general with mediating the difference between philosophy and the world, between philosophy and political life, without negating either of the opposed moments. Indeed, his earliest work announces itself as a response to the remaining unresolved differences left by Fichte's attempts to complete the Kantian system.[11] Kant had merely formulated the difference between philosophy and politics. Fichte ultimately subordinated one to the other. Hegel attempts to see them together in their difference. His mature system does this by locating philosophy (as part of Absolute Spirit) as the culmination or self-overcoming of political life (as part of Objective Spirit). Although it is philosophy that expresses the difference between philosophy and politics, the need for such expression and the language in which it is to occur comes from political life. The comprehension of political life, which results from the philosophical exposition of the idea of political life, thus both leads beyond political life and actualizes its inner content.

For Hegel, the human spirit becomes free and rational by taking the outer world into the inner world and expressing the inner world to the outer world, which includes other human beings. The activity of appropriation and expression is the realization of individuality and freedom: one becomes a real individual by making the world one's own but also by expressing this unique appropriation to the world so that it can be known. This occurs in the work of art and in politics. In politics, it is the spirit of the people that is appropriated and expressed in law. Although Hegel is skeptical about democracy and the anarchy that would ensue with universal suffrage, he is in favor of representational government and a written constitution, for these are the expression of the spirit of a people.[12] During Hegel's lifetime the question of a constitution for the German people as a whole or at least for individual German principalities was an urgent one. For Hegel, this question had to do with an objective expression of the idea of freedom found in contemporary political life. This idea is most fully actualized by philosophy, which comprehends the significance of the need for expression.

Spirit and its Modes of Expression

> That the true is actual only as system, or that substance is essentially subject, is expressed in the representation of the absolute as spirit—the most sublime concept and the one which belongs to the modern age and its religion.
>
> —Hegel, *Phenomenology of Spirit*[13]

Spirit is the double movement of self-appropriation and self-expression characteristic of art, politics, religion, and philosophy. As Hegel says in his early lectures on the philosophy of right, spirit is, "what knows and what is known, and this knowledge is itself self-conscious."[14] The philosopher's voice is the expression of the self-consciousness of spirit. In political philosophy, the philosopher's voice expresses the basic ideas of political life. The movement of appropriation and expression that occurs in Hegel's philosophical system is spirit. The systematic enterprise thus occurs as linguistic expression or voice. In the broadest sense, Hegel conceives of philosophical activity as spirit speaking to itself in its otherness. As John McCumber claims, "If the absolute is not other than the System which expresses it; and if the System is not other than that expression itself; then we can see just how self-referential Hegelian philosophy is. For the Absolute is not other than the teacher (Hegel) lecturing to (his) students."[15] I agree with McCumber's analysis, although, as we shall see in the next chapter, Hegel's pedagogical style is problematic. Nonetheless, Hegel's systematic enterprise must be understood as a project of *Bildung*, education, in which the teacher and the student are engaged in the task of communicating the self-consciousness of spirit via a linguistic medium of expression and appropriation.[16] As noted in the epigram with which we began the present chapter, this activity is the focal point of the state, embodied in the philosophical faculty in the state-sponsored university.

How can we make sense of this conception of philosophy? As preliminary, it is important to understand the way in which Hegel connects his systematic project to the idea of spirit. A system of knowledge should contain the necessary and universal ideas of all phenomena. For Hegel, the necessary universal idea is free spirit itself, for spirit is both the substance of historical actuality and the subject, which reconstitutes this in the system of philosophy. Moreover, it is by way of spirit that the system is linked to ethics and politics, for spirit is not only a religious term but is also an ethical and political term.[17] Spirit is the activity of human beings freely expressing themselves. Such free expression should not be, however, wild, arbitrary, Romantic "free spiritedness." Rather, it should be a systematic struggle for self-consciousness of ourselves in all of our activities.

In his *Phenomenology*, Hegel defines spirit as individuated self-conscious, free thought. This definition has four parts. First, spirit is thinking: "it is thinking which has its being in spirit alone."[18] Spirit is that which is capable of the activity of thought. The universal essence of all phenomena, after Kant, is whatever is able to think this essence as system. Second, thinking only occurs in concrete individual human beings. It is the individual human thinker who is the subject of this thinking activity. However, these individual human thinkers carry on the activity of thinking in community with others through the medium of human language. Third, spirit is self-conscious. Modern philosophy, following Descartes and Kant, requires that individual thinkers think about themselves: "science on its part requires that self-consciousness should have raised itself into this Aether [of thinking] in order to be able to live."[19] In other words, thinkers must be aware of the nature of their own activity, its social context, and the limitations of the media (language, art, politics, religion) in which thinking occurs. The sociohistorical context constitutes the thinkers who reflect upon this context. The thinker is thus the self-consciousness of his age. Finally, this self-conscious thinking must be free. Self-consciousness must result from the free development of the subject matter; it must not be imposed dogmatically by manipulative rhetoric or coercion. Thus the modern idea of spirit demands that we freely understand the ways in which we are determined by our sociohistorical context. This self-consciousness makes us free and thus completes the modern project. "The individual has the right to demand that science should at least provide him with the ladder to this standpoint, should show him this standpoint within himself. His right is based on his absolute independence [*absolute Selbständigkeit*], which he is conscious of possessing in every phase of his knowledge."[20] The individual thinker has the right to demand to know how and why her finite standpoint differs from the standpoint of the universal. In concrete terms, the individual thinker has the right to be shown the way in which her own limited perspective and imperfect medium of exchange limits her in her pursuit of the absolute. In short, the finite determinate nature of individuality and the finite determinate nature of the media of expression must themselves be made self-conscious and seen in their relation to the universal comprehensive view of the philosophical system.

We can see now the basic link between Hegel's system and the Kantian project that I called previously, "the republic of reason." Hegel's idea of system is based upon a republican conception of justice in which individuals have certain rights within the system. The most basic right possessed by individuals is the right to know how and why their individual vantage point differs from the systematic one. This, for example, is why an explicit constitution is a necessity for modern political life. All rational individuals have a right to demand access to the truth. Two problems confront Hegel. First, the system must be expressed in a finite historical medium that is not itself yet fully rational or self-conscious. Second, most individuals are not yet rational. These two problems converge in the project of education. Education is the process by which individuals come to understand the limitations of the finite mode of expression that inhibits their own development toward self-consciousness. This is "the ladder" Hegel mentions in the *Phenomenology:* the ladder leads us beyond the limits of finite historical language, politics, art, and religion by accounting for the limitations of these media.[21] Moreover, Hegel links his educational project to the modern republican political project that played itself out in his lifetime. The difficulty for Hegel was to educate his contemporaries about contemporary movements of spirit so that they might better understand themselves and their political task.

In this way Hegel responded to the metacritique in a more systematic way than did Fichte, who simply hypostatized German as the philosophical *Ursprache*. Hegel attempted to systematically account for the necessity of the apparently contingent expressions of spirit in politics, art, religion, history, and language. Hegel was not unaware of the systematic problems that led Fichte to turn explicitly to political agitation. Like Fichte, Hegel was aware that many individuals would not be able to comprehend his system. However, unlike Fichte, Hegel does not give up on philosophical expression. Rather, he strives to express in philosophically pregnant language the necessary difference between spirit and its modes of expression. He thus explains why spirit is self-estranged and self-estranging: spirit is expressed in the difference between its content and its mode of expression; by expressing itself it distances itself. It is the task of philosophy, not to annihilate this difference, but to express its necessity. Hegel's mature political philosophy, his *Philosophy of Right,* is an attempt to explain the way in which philosophy arises necessarily from modern political life in response to political life's demand for reconciliation of its own unresolved antinomies. By exposing the political necessities that ground philosophical reflection, Hegel defends the apparent strangeness of the philosopher's voice as it encounters its political audience: philosophy sounds odd because it develops the language of political life into a self-conscious, systematic whole that is both of politics but alien to politics.

One of the tasks of philosophy is for the philosopher to comprehend the unique content of philosophical language and its difference from and basis in the representational modes of ordinary life. With regard to politics, the philosopher's task is to articulate the implicit ideal of freedom in modern political life. Despite the fact that this task derives from the very idea of freedom it describes, it seems alien to political activity. Like Kant and unlike

Fichte, Hegel realizes that philosophical activity must keep itself distinct from politics. However, Hegel goes beyond Kant in arguing that this uniquely critical form of philosophical activity is the result of the demands of the modern political spirit. Hegel thus expected that enlightened modern political life would support the efforts of political philosophy. Although he was perhaps a bit naïve in this expectation, his own personal life served as proof of this idea. His position at the University of Berlin in the 1820s brought his political philosophy to the mainstream of Prussian (and hence German) politics.

Dichotomy and the Need for Philosophy

> Dichotomy is the source of *the need of philosophy* (*Entzweiung ist der Quell des Bedürfnisses der Philosophie*); and as the culture of the era, it is the unfree and given aspect of the whole configuration of the era.
>
> —Hegel, *The Difference between Fichte's and Schelling's System of Philosophy (Differenzschrift)*[22]

The Kantian project of creating the republic of reason runs into problems when its theoretical demands for freedom and equality conflict with the lack of freedom and equality found in real political life. The outcome in our less-than-perfect world seems to require that philosophy become political if it is to be anything other than merely hopeful exhortation. Thus Fichte was willing to abandon the philosophical method in order to use rhetoric to move political life toward the actualization of Kant's hoped-for political ideal. If it is true, as I argued previously, that the critique of pure reason assumes the freedom and equality found in republican political life, and if it is true, as Fichte discovered, that human beings are not yet enlightened, then it seems that the systematic project reaches an impasse. The philosopher must either become despotic (as in Fichte) or must retreat from the intractable irrationality of political life. Both alternatives have been ascribed to Hegel. He has been vilified as a protototalitarian, and he has been seen as a conciliatory and quietistic defender of the status quo.[23] Both of these accusations are off base. Hegel's project represents a third alternative located somewhere between the passive hopefulness of Kant and the vigorous activism of Fichte. To arrive at this third alternative, we would have to consider whether there could be a nondogmatic justification of the basic intuition that the freedom and equality of knowers ought to ground the system. We would further have to consider what would be the best political resolution of this impasse for a philosopher who is aware of the lack of rationality and freedom in political life. This double consideration formed the basis of Hegel's project.

Hegel's system originates from the recognition of dichotomy and the spiritual need to overcome it. Hegel's dialectical approach aims to reconcile opposites by viewing them together as mutually determined and determining from within the perspective of a more comprehensive totality.[24] Dialectic aims toward a final reconciliation, which would be absolute knowing. It is important to note that absolute knowing is not merely the reconciliation of opposition within the world of appearance in which the reconciling activity views the world, as it were, from an external perspective. Rather, the final stage in the dialectic requires that we comprehend the opposition between the original appearance of the dichotomy and the reconciling activity itself. In other words, absolute knowing requires that we comprehend the way in which philosophical activity is itself different from and yet reconciled with the dichotomous world of appearance, the way in which dichotomy and its reconciliation are themselves reconciled.[25] According to Hegel, then, the fundamental need for philosophy is the basic need to resolve the dichotomy between the appearance of the absolute and the absolute itself. As he concludes the above quote from the *Differenzschrift*: "In culture, the appearance (*Erscheinung*) of the Absolute has become isolated from the Absolute and fixated into independence."[26] In the *Science of Logic*, he explains this more clearly as the apparent distinction between the philosophical method and the content to which it is applied. However, he claims that the method itself is "not something distinct from its object and content; for it is the inwardness of the content, *the dialectic which it possesses within itself*, which is the mainspring of its advance (*denn es ist der Inhalt in sich, die Dialektik, die er an ihm selbst hat, welche ihn fortbewegt.*)."[27] In other words, for Hegel, philosophy and its method is the inner truth of whatever content it considers. The philosopher's voice expresses the inner truth of this content and is, indeed, driven toward expression by the content. However, the mode of exposition of the system is itself external to the content precisely because it is expository.

> The divisions and headings of the books, sections, and chapters given in this work as well as the explanations associated with them, are made to facilitate a preliminary survey and strictly are of only historical value. They do not belong to the content and body of the science but are compilations of an external reflection which has already run through the whole of the exposition and consequently knows and indicates in advance the sequence of its moments before these are brought forward by the subject matter itself.[28]

Hegel's point is that there is a crucial difference between truth and the verbal exposition of truth in a book or a lecture.

In the same way there is a crucial difference between the ideals of political life and the philosopher's expression of these ideals. Hegel aims to keep this distinction in mind in the exposition of the system. His philosophical activity demands that he be self-conscious of the sound of his own voice in its difference from the content which it expresses. With regard to political life, Hegel maintains (1) that the philosopher's voice expresses the inner truth of political life, (2) that the method of philosophical comprehension is itself the method demanded by the subject-matter, and (3) that philosophy and politics are nonetheless distinct. The absolute goal of political philosophy is to comprehend the unity in the difference between philosophy and politics.

With regard to political life, the easiest form of dichotomy to grasp is the apparent difference between the ideals of modern political culture and the reality of modern political life. This dichotomy demands to be understood in terms of the very ideals of political life. This is the point of the (in-)famous *Doppelsatz* from the *Philosophy of Right:* "What is rational is actual; and what is actual is rational."[29] In other words, there is a reason for the dichotomies of political life: it is these dichotomies that are actual and yet rational. The *Philosophy of Right* attempts to comprehend such dichotomies by elucidating the connections between modern political actuality and the ideals of modern political life. This elucidation is itself required by the ideals of modern political life, which give the individual the right to comprehend himself and his perceived alienation from political life.

In the *Science of Logic* Hegel explicates the political consequences of this method of expressing the idea of self-conscious individuality very clearly in his discussion of The Idea.

> But if an object, for example the state, did not correspond at all to its Idea, that is, if it was not the Idea of the state at all, if its reality, which is the self-conscious individuals, did not correspond at all to the Notion, its soul and its body would have parted . . . But because the Notion of the state so essentially constitutes the nature of these individualities, it is present in them as an urge (*Trieb*) so powerful that they are impelled (*gedrungen*) to translate it into reality, be it only in the form of external purposiveness, or to put up with it as it is, or else they must needs perish.[30]

What Hegel means here is that it is the idea of the state, an idea which maintains that individuals should be self-conscious of the idea of the state, that impels these individuals to become conscious of the idea of the state. Moreover, this idea impels the state to actualize its idea in the same way that it urges individuals to do whatever it takes to translate the idea into reality. It is the modern idea of right that thus demands the philosophical activity that would bring individuals to self-consciousness, and it is this same modern idea that would lead the state to become more rational. Political progress is thus facilitated by philosophical education about the remaining dichotomies in political life.

Such a project of reconciling appearances and reality need not require, as Fichte had thought, that the philosopher abandon philosophy for politics. Rather, for Hegel, only philosophy adequately comprehends the apparent contradiction between the appearance of reality and the ideal form of reality. Moreover, Hegel maintains that there is a *political need* for more and better philosophical comprehension. Hegel's project attempts to reconcile the difference between modern political life and its implicit ideals but it also attempts to explain how and why political life needs philosophical comprehension. Hegel's claim is that the philosopher's voice arises from a political need. This need includes the need to explain why political life needs the political philosopher. In other words, Hegel's philosophical voice expresses self-consciousness of its own basis in the needs of political life.

While Kant and Fichte were both aware that political life needed philosophy, neither of them recognized this need as the very ground of philosophical activity. Kant and Fichte remained stuck in the dichotomy, which Hegel criticizes as the problem of transcendental philosophy. Hegel, on the contrary, attempts to comprehend the political ground of philosophical activity. Going beyond Fichte's "linguistic turn" and its recognition of the empirico-historical *form* of philosophical activity, Hegel begins a political turn. He claims that philosophical activity *develops out of* political life and that philosophical comprehension is the *self-conscious overcoming* of political life. The philosopher's voice is thus the self-conscious expression of the implicit consciousness of political life. It is the republican ideal of modernity that makes the expression of the philosopher's voice necessary as the completion or actualization of the ideal, for this ideal demands that all members of the political community be able to comprehend themselves as free. Thus modern political life demands that political philosophy be publicly articulated, so that human beings can come to know the way in which they are free within modern political institutions. "In right, the human being must encounter his own reason (*Vernunft*); he must therefore consider the rationality of right (*die Vernünftigkeit des Rechts*), and this is the subject (*Sache*) of our science."[31]

This last sentence contains an ambiguity that is useful for understanding Hegel's project. On the one hand, it demands that right be reasonable. On the other hand, it demands that individuals be educated so that they might comprehend the right. Hegel's task is thus two sided: to make law more rational and to educate us so that we might comprehend this rationality. In this way, Hegel's project amounts to education for self-consciousness. It is the philosopher's voice—as it *speaks for* the laws that determine the community and as it *speaks to* the community that is determined by these laws—that makes this self-consciousness possible. Modern political life and its republican ideal of self-conscious freedom make the philosopher's task necessary.

Hegel thus rejects Fichte's dogmatic approach because it presupposes an unresolved dichotomy between the philosopher and his audience, between philosophy and political life. Hegel explicitly criticizes those works in which Fichte tries to be "popular." He claims that these popular works are characterized by their use of a "language most impressive to a cultured, religious temperament (*Gefühl*)."[32] However, they are not truly worthy of philosophical consideration because of this affective language. He rejects the "affecting" and "edifying" approach associated with Fichte's popular lectures for what he sees as the more strenuous work of the concept: serious philosophical comprehension, which includes expressing its sameness and difference from ordinary political language. Hegel's goal is to recuperate the public role of philosophy itself in all its serious complexity. He thinks that philosophy abandoned its public role under the hegemony of certain Kantians who alienated philosophy from its essential task under the delusion that philosophy must become popular. Indeed, it is the popular form of philosophy, Hegel claims, that made philosophy itself seem superfluous to the general public. "The public was through the philosophy of Kant and Jacobi strengthened in its opinion that the knowledge of God is immediate and that we know it from the beginning and without requiring to study."[33] Kant's transcendental idealism leads, in its "popular" form, to the justification of faith and hope without knowledge. Hegel rejects Kant's unresolved dualism, his theological and political hope, as a *gedankenlose Synthesis*—a "synthesis devoid of thought."[34] While Hegel praises Kant's work as a "good introduction to philosophy" for having ignited the "yearning desire (*Sehnsucht*) for content, for truth,"—the desire to comprehend the object as subject, the desire to see the rationality in things—he claims that Kant had failed to satisfy this desire.[35] In the same way, this conception of philosophy was itself so one-sided that it led Fichte to abandon philosophy completely for the rhetorical excesses of his popular works. For Hegel, what was needed was not a hopeful and popular approach to politics nor an abandonment of philosophy for politics but, rather, a reconstruction of both sides: an attempt to make philosophy live again and an attempt to educate the people, so that they might comprehend this living philosophy and thus come to know themselves.

The problem with Kant and Fichte was that they failed to see that philosophical activity was both the subject and object of history. In other words, they failed to see that philosophy occurs as the result of human history's demand for self-consciousness. Without this recognition that the philosopher's voice is the voice of history expressing itself to itself, Hegel believed, we end up with philosophers who either become too subjective and withdraw from politics for a life of contemplation (what he calls mere philosophers of the understanding) or we end up with philosophers who become too objective and give up on philosophy for the life of political activity. Hegel maintains that the demand of philosophy is to comprehend the limitations of each approach. When the philosopher speaks, then, he is the voice of political life that addresses political life in order to complete the demand for self-consciousness implicit in political life. It is thus the philosopher's task to become self-conscious of the sound and location of his own voice in history and politics.

Philosophy and the Modern Idea of Right

> The principle of the modern world at large is freedom of subjectivity . . .
>
> —Hegel, *Philosophy of Right*[36]

Historical knowledge formed a major part of Hegel's systematic enterprise in both his study of politics and his study of philosophy. In the *Philosophy of Right,* Hegel states that "the history of spirit is its own deed; for spirit is only what it does and its deed is to make itself—in this case as spirit—the object of its own consciousness, and to comprehend itself in its interpretation of itself to itself."[37] Hegel recognizes that philosophy arises from out of history as does the ideal of freedom—the freedom of subjectivity—that grounds modern political life. The goal of his political philosophy is to comprehend the modern spirit in its historical manifestation.

To overcome the passive hope of the Kantian project without slipping into that type of active enthusiasm that led Fichte toward despotism, Hegel needed to discover the determinate location of the philosopher's voice in the political activity of his time. Hegel remained committed to the basic principles of republican politics and thus needed to locate the philosopher's voice within these principles without reducing philosophy to politics. This claim about Hegel's commitment to republicanism might seem surprising given his arguments in favor of constitutional monarchy. Hegel's discussion of constitutional monarchy, however, is aimed at establishing basic republican principles. What is important for Hegel is the "constitutional" aspect of "constitutional monarchy": the constitution makes explicit the self-consciously limited protection of liberal rights demanded by the modern idea of right. A solid constitution that respects the mediating institutions of modern life (family and civil society) should serve as the antidote for that form of enthusiasm for liberty that led, for example, to the excesses of the French Revolution.

In the *Philosophy of Right* Hegel maintains that such excessive enthusiasm occurs because of the tendency to view one of the determinations of Objective Spirit as absolute in isolation from the others. This occurs when abstract, indeterminate, freedom is emphasized, as with the French revolutionaries or when, with Fichte, a form of "positive" or self-assertive freedom is emphasized.[38] For Hegel, it is the whole of Objective Spirit in the identity and difference of its negative and positive aspects that must be recognized. This occurs most obviously in the constitution that protects liberal values while preventing them from slipping into revolutionary zealotry. Hegel's republicanism thus centers on the proper definition of freedom that includes both negative freedom and positive commitment. In the *Phenomenology* Hegel indicates that so-called "absolute freedom"—what he calls in the *Philosophy of Right*, "abstract" or "arbitrary" freedom—can result in terror, as the general will destroys all opposition in what he calls "the fury of destruction."[39] This terror results when the principles of republicanism are implemented by force, rather than achieved as the result of the organic development of society. In Hegel's interpretation, The Terror of the French Revolution occurred because there was "no reciprocal action between a consciousness that is immersed in the complexities of existence, or that sets itself specific aims and thoughts, and a valid external world, whether of reality or thought."[40] This is the same idea behind what Hegel calls in the *Differenzschrift*, the dichotomy in culture between the appearance of the absolute and the absolute, i.e., the republican ideals of modern culture and the lived reality of modern political life. The problem of the French Revolution is that freedom was seen as absolute without reference to other goods such as community or justice. Hegel recognized that republican principles can become dogmatic or despotic when they are divorced from reality, i.e., when the general will fails to take account of the lived experience of autonomous individuals. This lived historical experience includes disagreements between individuals and the so-called general will; it also includes the mediating institutions of ethical life. Dogmatists and despots in general fail to take account of the community as a historically given "free object standing over against it."[41] They also fail to respect the rights of individuals against the community.

In the *Philosophy of Right* Hegel argues that only a differentiated constitutional system is able to hold individual rights together with communal good. Within such a system, the philosopher's voice completes the modern project by elucidating the way in which individuals are both free and determined within the constitutional system. Moreover, the modern political project should guarantee that individuals have the right to be educated to freedom by the philosophy of right. Hegel is acutely aware of the problems that can arise when philosophy attempts to impose its ideals upon a form of political actuality, if that form is not yet prepared to receive and implement these ideals. Hegel's solution is to call for more and better philosophical activity, which does not however impose its utopian ideals upon an unwilling public. The philosopher's task is education as development from within, not education as imposition from without. The goal is for philosophy to make it possible for the people to comprehend their own implicit ideals.

While Fichte's educational project became despotic, Hegel remained committed to a method of self-discovery and self-development. He rejects Fichte's claim that education requires that we sequester the next generation to protect them from corruption by the decadent present generation. Rather, Hegel maintains that education demands engagement with the reality of the present. Hegel quite clearly states in the *Philosophy of Right* that children, although they need discipline and guidance, have a natural predisposition to overcome their natural, subjective, childish disposition and enter freely into the world of ethical life. "The need for an upbringing is present in children as their own feeling of dissatisfaction within themselves at the way they are—as the drive (*Trieb*) to belong to the adult world whose superiority they sense, or as the desire to grow up."[42] Thus when Hegel claims that "education is the art of making human beings ethical," he means that education fulfills the human need to belong to the ethical community.[43] Education should thus allow individuals to comprehend the idea of right under which they are determined in the ethical community. While education, in its preliminary stages, is the inculcation of the habits of the community, ultimately, in the modern world, these habits are habits of freedom and self-consciousness. Habits are shortcuts on the way toward the full complexity of philosophical education, which is necessitated by the modern idea of right.[44]

Hegel claims that the demand for philosophy is already incipient in the most immature members of the modern political community. Children want to become moral and to be members of the ethical community. Moreover, the modern ethical community is based upon the idea of right, which includes universal respect for the freedom and self-consciousness of individuals such that children ought to become educated. The task of education is to enable children to comprehend their own universal desire to become members of the ethical community as itself part of the republican spirit of modern ethical life. Philosophical education is the process of becoming self-conscious of the way in which we belong to the ethical spirit of our age even in the depths of our feelings and drives. The philosopher's voice is not addressed from the outside of the ethical community back toward the public. Rather the philosopher's voice is the voice which each and every member of the ethical community would share, if they had attained the completion of philosophical self-consciousness. In short, the philosopher's voice is the voice of the spirit of the age.

The spirit of modernity is the spirit of individual freedom. The community must respect the individual differences that constitute it. We see this explicitly in the community's support for that type of education that leads to philosophical comprehension of the spirit of the age. Within the republic of reason, the right of individuals to their own opinions must be respected because the modern republic is based upon moral respect for individuals that preserves individual autonomy even while locating it into the ethical community.[45]

Nonetheless, individuals must be educated to see that their individual autonomy is itself supported and justified by the social norms that they have inherited from the ethical community. The goal of philosophy is to make us conscious of the rationality of these inherited ideals, so that we may become active participants in the ongoing life of the community and the future development of these ideals.[46] Although Hegel recognizes that we are historically situated, he rejects historicism insofar as he maintains that our historical situation can be rationally comprehended according to universally acceptable norms of justification.[47] Right becomes valid by being comprehended by those who are subjected to it and who share its norms of justification.[48] Modern European ethical life thus demands that individuals be educated, so that they can comprehend the idea of right as it is embodied in the actual community in which they live. This idea cannot be imposed on the community, as Fichte might have suggested. Rather, it is the result of an organic historical development, the completion of which is philosophical comprehension of this development by way of the norms implicit in it. Philosophy is reflection after the fact (*Nachdenken*) on the rationality of the real. Our history, our tradition, and our culture provide us with the concepts and language with which we begin. The task of philosophy is to rightly understand these concepts, their interconnections, and the spiritual history in which they are located. Despotism is avoided by recognizing the fact that the demand for a republic of reason, the demand for an explicit constitution, and the demand for systematic philosophical comprehension of ethical life are all demands that modern individuals already make.

For Hegel, the truth is not immediate but mediated by way of education into culture—the idea of *Bildung*.[49] This process of mediation must be understood in historical and political terms. Education and culture are historical, political processes. Progress occurs by way of political contestation—the so-called cunning of reason. It is comprehended by the dialectical reconstruction of history. The philosopher's task is to clarify historical development, its relation to the real lives of empirical individuals, and its relation to the spirit that unifies history. However, this dialectical process cannot be completed, as Fichte proposed, with the implementation of the coercive state because this would violate the idea of freedom implicit in the dialectic. There will always be estrangement and dissent within political life: this is the consequence of a nondogmatic republican view, which respects the rights of moral individuals. Moreover, the educational process will itself be an activity in progress. Each individual must be spoken to as a distinct individual with a unique vantage point that must be accounted for by the system. The task of spirit is thus to *strive for* agreement. As Hegel says in the Preface to the *Phenomenology*: "For it is the nature of humanity to press onward to agreement (*Übereinkunft*) with others; human nature only really exists in an achieved community of minds (*zu Stande gebrachten Gemeinsamkeit der Bewußtseyn*)."[50] Such a community of minds can only be achieved within the continuing practices of a free political community. However, it is important to note that for Hegel, such striving cannot be the source of the endless progress that he criticized in Fichte as the result of a one-sided dogmatism that would not allow itself to be reconciled with its opposite without recourse to despotic means. Rather, for Hegel, each moment of the political contest includes its own piece of the truth that can be comprehended by philosophical reflection that attempts to locate each piece within the totality. It is also important to note that this view of the totality need not be totalitarian, quietistic, or conciliatory, as Hegel's critics have claimed. Rather, Hegel admits that the totality moves and develops through history, while also claiming that at the present moment the task of philosophy is to comprehend the presently configured totality. The result of this should be an ongoing educational dialogue between the philosopher and his political audience.

Hegel's Political Voice

> For us philosophy is not, as it was for the Greeks, practiced as a private art, rather it has a public existence of concern to the public (*eine öffentliche, das Publikum berührende Existenz*), especially or solely in the service of the state (*im Staatsdienste*).
>
> —Hegel, *Philosophy of Right*[51]

Philosophical reflection upon political life is always already part of political life. The philosopher speaks from within political life to a politically located audience. Hegel explains this more concretely by claiming that modern political life demands the services of philosophical reflection. In the preface to the *Philosophy of Right,* he explicitly states that political philosophy is both a discipline that transcends political life and an essential political activity. On the one hand, philosophy cannot "issue instructions on the how the world ought to be" because it "comes too late."[52] On the other hand, philosophy "has a public existence of concern to the public."[53] Hegel does not think, however, that philosophy should be merely passive reflection upon the status quo; nor does he think that the state can be properly served by a superficial and conciliatory science of law. Rather he states that the modern state needs rigorous philosophical insight into itself: "the state also contained the need (*Bedürfnis*) for a deeper education and insight, and demanded (*forderte*) that this need be satisfied by science."[54] What Hegel criticizes as "the superficial (*die Seichtigkeit*)" form of political philosophy leads to confusion about the nature of politics that ultimately has grave consequences for political life, as, for example, Hegel contends happened in France at the time of the revolution.[55] The *Philosophy of Right* argues that political life needs rigorous philosophical reflection and that such reflection is political activity.

The *Philosophy of Right* is *both philosophical*—it tries to know the truth of political life—*and political*—it actively participates in political deliberation and contestation. This explains what Hegel means when he states that philosophy is a public concern in service to the state. The process of knowing the truth of political life is both a political and a philosophical activity because the state itself is a spiritual being that bases its activity upon knowledge.[56] Moreover, when Hegel states, for example, that philosophy is "the self-thinking idea, the truth aware of itself," he is not denying that philosophy is involved in political life.[57] Rather, Hegel acknowledges that philosophical reflection always occurs from within a political context: the self that becomes self-conscious is a politically located self.

The truth of political life is that it requires philosophical reflection; the truth of philosophical reflection is that it participates in political activity. The problem is that we ordinarily assume that the subject matter of political life is essentially irrational and conflictual. On the one hand, politics seems to proceed by way of contingent historical circumstance and self-interested action. On the other hand, philosophical reflection proceeds by way of reasoned argument and dispassionate self-consciousness. It seems that these two methods have very little in common. Hegel, however, offers us a historical argument that claims that these methods have converged in modernity in what he calls in the *Philosophy of Right*, "the Germanic Realm" and what he calls in his lectures on history "the Modern Time." In his lectures on World History, Hegel concludes that after the Enlightenment, "the consciousness of the spiritual is now the essential basis of the political fabric, and philosophy has thereby become dominant."[58] The modern era is one in which political practice has become philosophical to the extent that political life now demands its own philosophical self-consciousness. At the same time, philosophical reflection has come to admit its own political and historical location.

The methodological ambiguity of Hegel's political philosophy has been neglected by commentators. It seems that most commentators understand the *Philosophy of Right* in terms of the exclusive disjunction between political practice and philosophical reflection.[59] On the one hand, there are commentators who interpret the *Philosophy of Right* as engaging in "social theodicy" or "social ontology" and who ultimately view Hegel as politically conservative.[60] This interpretation fails to see Hegel's text as political activity and also fails to recognize that Hegel also wrote explicitly political works such as "The German Constitution" (1799–1802) and "The English Reform Bill" (1831).[61] Habermas, who is aware of the seeming antinomy between the journalistic works and the *Philosophy of Right,* concludes by characterizing this as an unresolved contradiction in Hegel's thought between the supposed "superiority" of theory as philosophical reflection and its "impotence" as political practice.[62] On the other hand, some interpreters emphasize the political aspect of the *Philosophy of Right,* understanding the text as an example of "legal interpretivism" that aims at clarifying political practice or as an articulation of the beliefs and aspirations of the bourgeoisie.[63] Such interpretations fail to tie Hegel's political writings to his larger philosophical project. However, to do justice to Hegel, we must view him as a philosopher of freedom, while emphasizing freedom as *both* a political and philosophical idea.[64] We cannot reduce the ambiguity identified in these interpretations. Hegel is engaged in both philosophical and political activity, and attempts throughout to make it clear how these are both the same and different.

One way to approach this problem is to emphasize the pedagogical goal of Hegel's text. Hegel's overall goal in both the political writings and the *Philosophy of Right* is education. Education, however, must be tailored to its audience.[65] Thus a proper understanding of Hegel's pedagogical goal in both the *Philosophy of Right* and the political writings requires that we consider *who* is being instructed. As the audience shifts, so does the relation between theory and practice. The intended audience of Hegel's journalistic writings, for example, is different from the intended audience of Hegel's *Philosophy of Right.* Thus Habermas is wrong when he claims that Hegel's journalistic writings lead him "into contradiction with his system."[66] Hegel's educational endeavor admits of different practical expressions depending upon the different needs of his audience. The audience of the *Philosophy of Right* demands one type of voice; the audience of the political writings demands another. Like Fichte and Kant, Hegel is aware of his audience and speaks in a voice suitable to it. Unlike Fichte, however, Hegel argues that his voice, in its difference from political life, is nonetheless the self-consciousness or self-development of political life. He not only speaks *to* his audience, he also speaks *for* it.

Addressing *The Philosophy of Right*

> A plastic discourse demands, too, a plastic receptivity and understanding on the part of the listener; but youths and men of such a temper who would calmly suppress their own reflections and opinions in which original thought is so impatient to manifest itself, listeners such as Plato feigned, who would attend only to the matter in hand, could have no place in a modern dialogue; still less could one count on readers of such a disposition.
>
> —Hegel, *Science of Logic*[67]

Hegel is clearly aware of the presence and limitations of his audience. He is also clearly aware of the unavoidable complexity of philosophical thought that attempts to be self-conscious of its identity with and difference from its audience. For us to grasp this complexity it will be useful to break down the various addresses of Hegel's text into four general categories (although this becomes complicated when we recognize the connection between these four as well as other, less perspicuous, addresses of the text).

The Students

The text known as the *Philosophy of Right* was a handbook for Hegel's lecture course of the same name. Hegel says in the first line of the Preface to the published text of 1821: "the immediate occasion for me to publish this outline is the need to provide my audience (*meinen Zuhörern*) with an introduction to the lectures on the philosophy of right which I deliver in the course of my official duties."[68] Here Hegel explicitly indicates that his text is addressed to those who listen to his lectures, i.e., his students.

Hegel lectured on the philosophy of right seven times from 1817 up to his death in 1831. The text that has been handed down to us as the *Philosophy of Right* was completed in 1820 and published in 1821. Different versions of Hegel's lectures reflect variations in the historical circumstances in which they were delivered. Hegel's political philosophy was affected by changes in political life in a way that his logic or philosophy of nature was not.[69] The most obvious of these political influences on Hegel's philosophical thinking was the censorship laws known as the Karlsbad decrees (of 1819). Hegel was a professor in a public university in the capital of the Prussian empire. His political philosophy was addressed explicitly to students at this university, and the university was a political institution. Hegel was thus actively engaged in political life. The education of students at a public institution is political activity. And Hegel was very close to running afoul of the authorities in several instances.[70]

Discrepancies between the officially published version of the lectures and Hegel's other lectures can also be understood in terms of the changed audience that was addressed by these various lecture courses. Indeed, the audience of Hegel's lectures changed in two significant ways from 1817 to 1831. First, the political climate changed over the course of these years as the defeat of Napolean and the Congress of Vienna opened the door for Prussian reaction. These were turbulent political times in Germany including: the symbolic rebellion of the *Burschenschaften* during the Wartburg festival of 1817; the assassination of the reactionary Kotzebue and the repressive reaction to this in the Karlsbad decrees of 1819; Prussian censorship surveillance through the 1820s; German enthusiasm for the July Revolution of 1830 in

France; and subsequent repressive decrees of the German federal diet in the summer of 1832, six months after Hegel's death. The needs and interests of his students as participants in political life must have changed over the course of these years. For example, in response to the July Revolution, his students wanted a more radical political philosophy than Hegel was willing to provide.[71] Second, Hegel's own significance changed over the course of these years. After being appointed professor in Berlin, Hegel's lecture courses became increasingly more popular. Hegel became something of a celebrity, and his audience came as much to hear Hegel, the man, as to learn political philosophy.[72] Additionally, his lectures on the philosophy of history, aesthetics, and the philosophy of religion were formulated in a popular fashion and addressed to a wider audience than his original version of the *Philosophy of Right* or his *Encyclopedia.* Although he did not appropriate the bombastic oratory of Fichte, he nonetheless altered his style to suit his expanded audience.

So who was this immediate audience, those students who actually attended Hegel's lectures? In his lectures, Hegel was in fact addressing the ruling class, as Marx would later contend. In a letter to Creuzer (October 30, 1819) Hegel states that "one even finds majors, colonels, and privy councilors attending one's lectures here."[73] Hegel's goal, when understood in terms of the real students he was addressing, was to educate future and current members of the ruling class about the political world they were to rule. Indeed, in the text, Hegel makes it clear that there is a substantial difference between the ruling class that was his audience and the "rabble" who had no capacity for education.

When the text is understood within this context, its goal is obviously not critical truth about political life that would lead to radical political action. Rather, it aims to help his students understand political life so that they may develop into productive members of the ruling elite. Education, from this perspective, is directed toward refining the self-consciousness of those who are already part of the state and members of civil society: "human beings should have respect for the state as that whole of which they are the branches, the best way of achieving this is, of course, through philosophical insight into its essence."[74] To be a branch of the state, is already to be a part of the state, i.e., to be a colonel or privy counselor or at least to be the son of one of these. As a text addressed to the young bourgeoisie, the *Philosophy of Right* merely systematizes the knowledge of ethical life that these young men implicitly possessed, although of course for Hegel modern ethical life is based upon the idea of freedom.

Hegel was not unaware of the antithesis of his immediate audience. He recognizes that "the rabble," those who are not members of the ruling elite, will feel alienated from society because their poverty drives them toward "inward rebellion against the rich, against society, the government, etc."[75] Indeed during this time of social tumult, when war had dislocated much of the population, it would have been obvious that there was a growing class in society who could not be easily educated and integrated into the status quo. The dislocated and disgruntled "rabble" could not be educated according to Hegel's definition of education because they lacked an organic relation to the state and civil society which would create in them the drive to be educated, which we previously discussed. As an example of this, throughout the *Philosophy of Right,* Hegel links individuality to citizenship and the ownership of private property—something which the "rabble" lacked.[76] Although Hegel advocates the Kantian moral view of the intrinsic worth of human being qua human being, *education* seems to be reserved for those who are members of civil society and who are full citizens of the state. Education is only possible for those who properly inhabit the spheres of family life, civil society, and state. Hegel even goes so far as to indicate that women ought not to hold political power and that women should be educated in a different manner than men: "women may well be educated, but they are not made for the higher sciences, for philosophy and certain artistic productions which require a universal element."[77] Thus, women and the rabble are excluded from the address of the *Philosophy of Right* in the same way that non-Western peoples are excluded from the course of World History: only those who are constituted by the modern Western idea of right are properly the audience of Hegel's voice. Hegel's voice cannot properly *speak for* these "others" and so cannot either *speak to* them. In this sense, Hegel's voice is thus the voice of the laws and customs of the dominant force in history.

This way of addressing the text succeeds in understanding the text as primarily a political document. It is influenced by and responds to the needs of the dominant party or class in political life. Understood in this way, Hegel's text is susceptible to ideological critiques such as Marx's as well as feminist critiques such as Elshtain's: Hegel's text educates young bourgeois men about their patriarchal bourgeois society without questioning the basic assumptions of this society.[78] The philosopher's voice thus expresses a partisan, political idea and fails to live up to its philosophical pretensions.

The State

The above interpretation of Hegel's text makes the most sense when we consider what Hegel says about the role of the bourgeoisie within the state as property owners, moral agents, family members, civil servants, and members of the estates and corporations of civil society. It is significant that Hegel demands a proper upbringing prior to philosophical education. Failure of education and subsequent lack of freedom is blamed on poor preparation.

Indeed, Hegel was suspicious of the educational preparation of his students.[79] He seems to acknowledge that his own students may not be able to grasp his philosophical thought. His students are thus not the only audience of his text. Hegel's text is also aimed at educating the educators. Following the structure of Hegel's text, there are three determinations in which educators must be educated: family, civil society, and state. Hegel clearly addresses all three of these in his text. With regard to family and civil society, fathers and business leaders must learn to understand their role in bringing up the youth. However, since the state is said to be the ground of the whole of *Sittlichkeit*, and since the state is, for Hegel, ultimately the end and source of "the individual's knowledge and activity," let us focus on the state as a further address of the text.[80]

Hegel devotes a substantial portion of his text to the monarch. It is clear from Hegel's defense of hereditary monarchy that the bourgeoisie can have no aspiration to attain to the office of king. At best, if we confine our attention to the bourgeoisie as the address of the text, it seems that the section on the monarch is designed to help members of the bourgeoisie understand their place within the monarchic system of government. However, the *Philosophy of Right* could also be interpreted as a text addressed to the monarch or the state itself in an attempt to educate the monarch about the proper need for education within the state. There are two ways in which we may approach the issue of philosophy's service to the state: (A) institutionally and (B) substantively.

A.) Hegel's professorship at Berlin was part of the institutional bureaucracy of Prussia. Indeed in the first sentence of the Preface Hegel acknowledges the fact that he is a servant of the state: the lectures that he gives on the philosophy of right are delivered in the course of his "official duties" (*sienem Amte gemäss*).[81] These lectures were prepared according to the demands of his office—as professor at the Royal University at Berlin. In letters written to the royal ministers who oversee the university, Hegel explicitly addresses the text to the state. In a letter that accompanied a copy of the text sent to von Altenstein, Hegel said that "the printing of this text at once gives account of the scope of the principles I teach in my lectures on the subject" and that "I consider myself duty-bound as a publicly appointed professor at the Royal University to render such an account to you. . . ."[82] Hegel here acknowledged that his professorship is a political office. His appointment at the University of Berlin was a public matter that brought with it certain duties and which was ostensibly approved by the king himself by way of the Royal Ministry of Ecclesiastical, Educational, and Medical Affairs.

Hegel freely acknowledged his duty to the state. However, it is clear in his letters to the royal ministers that Hegel believes that the Prussian state was still a liberal regime and not a repressive autocracy. In a letter to von

Hardenberg, Hegel states that the *Philosophy of Right* is designed to glorify the Prussian state's liberal policies with regard to philosophy and the sciences. Moreover, he claims that in the text he has demonstrated "the harmony of philosophy with those principles generally required by the nature of the state," and that "philosophy in its own sphere of action, may give immediate support to the government's beneficent intentions."[83] Such statements may be interpreted as providing evidence either of Hegel's political naivety or of his fawning conciliation with the Prussian bureaucracy. However, as Ilting has pointed out, letters such as these, and indeed, the Preface to the officially published version of the text may have only been a natural reaction on Hegel's part to the changed political atmosphere caused by the Karlsbad decrees.[84] He may have had no choice but to bend his knee before the state. Institutional structures required that he acknowledge his service to the state and address the state directly. Nonetheless, letters such as these make it clear that Hegel offered his voice in service to the state.

B.) Aside from these external, institutional connections, there is more evidence, internal to the text, that indicates that Hegel was addressing the Prussian state. Philosophy's service to the state is understood by Hegel as an attempt to provide the monarch with some idea of the nature of his power within the modern constitutional state. Instead of a manual for helping Hegel's bourgeois students understand themselves, the text may be read as a treatise designed to help the monarch understand the nature of his power within a constitutional monarchy. Thus the *Philosophy of Right* can be understood, as Ernst Cassirer understands it, as a text in the lineage of Machiavelli's *The Prince*: it is a manual addressed to the monarch with the purpose of helping the monarch to consolidate his power.[85] As discussed in chapter 2, early in his career Hegel was fascinated with Machiavelli and for a moment wanted to see himself as a German Machiavelli.

However, much of what Hegel says about the monarch argues against this reductive interpretation. Hegel states explicitly that the monarch need not be educated in the way that the bourgeois need to be. It is clear, for instance, that Hegel does not require the sovereign to have extraordinary intellectual gifts. Rather, all the monarch must do is bring the rationality of the constitution together in his will as the one who merely dots the "i's."[86] It is the constitutional whole that is rational, not the will of the sovereign. All that matters for Hegel's conception of the monarch is the functional or formal element of the unified will. The monarch need not be educated, intelligent, or benevolent. This is true because the monarchy is understood as an office defined by the constitution in much the same way as Hegel's official duties were defined by the constitution. Hegel claims that the monarch is not even "responsible" for his decisions because the subject matter which the monarch must say yes or no to is brought before him by his advisors.[87] Hegel does not require that the monarch be self-conscious about himself or about what he does. Modern life requires a more complex division of labor. The king need not be a philosopher. Nonetheless, for the state to be justified, the institutional role played by the will of the sovereign must be philosophically comprehensible. In other words, the official duties of both monarch and philosopher must be rationally defined. Moreover, the division of labor requires that there be a philosopher who comprehends the notion of sovereignty and explains this to the state, its functionaries, and its citizens so that each of these may understand the rationale that determines them. Justice does not require that the philosopher become king but only that the institutional role of the monarch be comprehensibly defined.

This limits the claim that the monarch or the state is the only address of the text. While it might be nice to have a sovereign who is self-conscious, it is not necessary. The monarch's power is defined by the constitution, and he can continue to blithely dot the "i's" without ever having read the *Philosophy of Right*. The service that philosophy performs for the state is not then to help the monarch consolidate his power, as in Machiavelli's *The Prince*. Rather, this service is a necessary function of the division of labor within the modern concept of the state: to make it possible for the monarch, his ministers, and subjects to comprehend the constitutionally defined institutions in which they participate.[88] Hegel thus resists the Platonic ideal of the philosopher-king, claiming even that Plato's *Republic* is "the proverbial example of an empty ideal."[89] Philosopher and monarch are both necessary parts of the life of the whole, their respective spheres need not coincide, even though the modern concept of freedom requires that individuals whose lives are affected by the monarch be able to comprehend the modern idea of a constitutional monarchy.

The Philosophers

Hegel clearly believes that philosophers have an essential role to play within the division of labor in society. There is a philosophical class within society whom Hegel addresses in the text. As educators who must bring individuals to self-consciousness and freedom, philosophers themselves must be educated about their role within the division of labor. Hegel concludes in his introduction to the *History of Philosophy:* "Philosophy only appears in history where and insofar as free institutions are formed."[90] However, such institutions are free only if philosophy can comprehend the concept of freedom implicit within them. Thus it is crucial that Hegel address other philosophers so that they may comprehend the historical and political function of philosophy. In this sense, Hegel's *Philosophy of Right* can be read as a methodological treatise on the proper function of philosophy within modern political society.

Throughout the *Philosophy of Right,* Hegel addresses his philosophical predecessors and his contemporaries. He speaks to past philosophers such a Plato and Montesquieu and also to contemporary thinkers engaged in then-current debates about constitutional, political, and moral questions in Germany. This dialogue with other philosophers helps to situate his text within the history of Western political thinking; it also locates Hegel's theory within the contemporary debate. He addresses his living contemporaries—Fries, Hugo, von Haller, the Schlegel's—by name in the text (although he does not mention his rival on the law faculty in Berlin, Savigny, by name anywhere in the officially published version).[91] While there are political implications of these various addresses—Fries, for example was a political liberal who was persecuted by the state—the importance of Hegel's references to these other political theorists is the fact that Hegel did not simply address his text either to his students or to his institutional superiors. Rather, he also addressed it to other philosophers engaged in the project of reflection on the truth of political life. The most important implication of this address is that Hegel was at pains to distinguish his own philosophical treatise from other accounts of the same phenomena. Hegel's rejection of Fries, for example, is based in part upon what Hegel calls Fries "superficial" theory of moral and political education. Where Fries emphasized the creation of a feeling of solidarity by way of "immediate perception and contingent imagination," Hegel emphasizes the strenuous work of the philosophical concept.[92] Hegel's text is addressed to fellow philosophers in order to demonstrate to them the proper form of philosophical education. The philosopher must not only understand the rationality of contemporary political life, he must also comprehend the way in which his philosophical contemplation is determined in relation to past and present philosophical thought.

Spirit

While Hegel's philosophical voice can be located in time and space in the ways that we have just seen, it is also a reflection on political life that can be understood as moving beyond merely *political* philosophy. This is obvious if we consider the text as part of Hegel's larger project of bringing spirit to self-consciousness. The *Philosophy of Right* as *philosophy* is part of absolute spirit and seeks to comprehend the total system of ethical life as well as the systematic relation between ethical life and the rest of reality. Hegel is engaged in the arduous task of educating spirit about itself. Thus despite the various ways in which philosophy is tied to the political realm (as addressed to students, in service to the state, even in politically fueled debates with other political philosophers), philosophy also attempts to comprehend the political realm in a universal and objective manner in its connections with other determinations of spirit, including its connection with those forms of self-consciousness that occur in Absolute Spirit.

In this sense, Hegel understands political philosophy as aiming beyond political life. The *Philosophy of Right* is supposed to be part of the *total* education of spirit. It is supposed to overcome the partisan debates of political life by comprehending them. Hegel states that the proper end of education (*Bildung*) and of reason is

> to work to eliminate natural simplicity, whether as passive selflessness or as barbarism of knowledge and volition—i.e., to eliminate the immediacy and individuality in which spirit is immersed, so that this externality may take on the rationality of which it is capable, namely the form of universality or of the understanding. Only in this way is spirit at home (*einheimisch*) and with itself (*bei sich*) . . .[93]

Spirit comes to be at home with itself by way of the education afforded to it by the *Philosophy of Right*. Thus the text is addressed to spirit in a way that seeks to overcome partisan politics in order to achieve universality and objectivity by comprehending the way in which spirit itself consists of the diversity that leads to these partisan struggles. Here is where the famous Owl of Minerva passage from the Preface becomes relevant. Philosophy is reflection on political life from a perspective that hovers above political life at the end of the day and that comprehends itself in its difference from and identity with political life.

So when we ask who or what "spirit" is for Hegel, it is clear that it includes all of the various audiences we have just considered, as well as the recognition of the differences and similarities among them. Spirit, as self-consciousness, is located in the selves of those individuals whom Hegel addresses. However, it is not constrained to the particularity of these selves, nor is it simply the universal idea common to all. Rather it is all of these: individual, particular, and universal. Thus Hegel maintains that spirit is political and that political life is spiritual. Spirit is political insofar as it is determined by the diversity and particularity of concrete historical life. Political life is spiritual insofar as it demands its own self-consciousness and is constituted by a need for philosophical comprehension. Spirit occurs in Hegel's students' understanding of their political situation. It also occurs in the state's substantive need for philosophy as well as its institutional practice of philosophical education. Finally, spirit is the attempt of philosophers to reflect upon the universal truths of political life and to comprehend the political basis of this reflective activity. When Hegel thus addresses his diverse audience, his voice is the voice of spirit speaking to itself in its difference from and identity with itself.

CHAPTER 8

Hegel's Voice: Language, Education, and Philosophy

> We also express (*sprechen...aus*) the sensible as universal... We do not freely imagine (*stellen...vor*) the universal "this" or being in general, but we *express* (*sprechen...aus*) the universal; in other words, we simply don't say (*sprechen*) what in this sense-certainty we really *mean*. Language (*die Sprache*), however, as we see, is the more truthful; in it we ourselves refute directly and at once our own "meaning"; and since universality is the real truth of sense-certainty, and language merely expresses this truth (*die Sprache nur dieses Wahre ausdrückt*), it is not possible that we could even say (*sagen*) the sensuous existence which we "mean."
>
> —Hegel, *Phenomenology of Spirit*[1]

We have seen that Hegel addresses a definite audience and that he is self-conscious of the fact that his political philosophy is a politically located form of address. His goal is to use his voice to stimulate his audience to become self-conscious by thinking the universal truth expressed in the particular language of the philosopher's voice. For complete self-consciousness to occur, his audience must comprehend the difference between the historical contingencies of the philosopher's voice and the necessary content that it expresses. Thus the audience needs to understand the totality of Hegel's system, including its conception of philosophical activity and its philosophy of language, in order to become completely self-conscious and free. The challenge for Hegel's audience is to hear the universal truth that is "expressed" in the historical and contingent medium of Hegel's voice. As Hegel indicates in the passage from the *Phenomenology* quoted above, universal truths are already expressed in ordinary language, even when ordinary language attempts merely to say something particular and contingent.[2] Hegel's philosophical activity is, in part, an attempt to clarify the difference between what is said and what is expressed, the difference between the ordinary meaning of words and their philosophical exposition.

I will examine Hegel's mature linguistic theory in some detail at the end of the present chapter. Before this I will discuss Hegel's early thoughts about language and philosophical style and his understanding of the uniqueness of philosophical activity. I will examine the methodological structure of Hegel's approaches to philosophy and politics, and the relation between monologue and dialogue, authority and freedom in Hegel's thoughts about education. I will discuss Hegel's claims about *philosophy* as the unique culmination of the modern spirit's quest for self-consciousness, as well as his argument that political life *needs* philosophy. The thesis that will be defended in the present chapter is that Hegel's voice in his political philosophy is the expression of the implicit truths of political life, which is addressed to political life in order to bring political life to self-consciousness and that this mode of expression is itself necessitated by the very idea of self-conscious freedom that is found in modern political life.

Philosophy, Communication, and Language

> Consciousness first exists as recollection (*Gedächtniß*) and its product, language (*die Sprache*).
>
> —Hegel, *Jena System*[3]

Philosophy is the activity of giving voice to truth—an activity of expression and externalization, which makes implicit ideas explicit. It helps us make sense of the words that we already use to identify and remember representations and concepts. But philosophy must also clarify the fact that its voice is historically situated and speaks a contingent historical language. Philosophy is discursive and requires the externalization that occurs as the human voice speaks in time, in a historical language, to a real audience. Hegel uses ordinary language that his audience already understands to lead it to further self-consciousness of the relation between the content and its form of representation. Throughout his career the presence of the audience and the question of language were a concern for Hegel. As a youth, Hegel envisioned himself as an enlightened "educator of the people" along the lines established by Lessing.[4] Although he eventually adopted a deliberately rigorous and notoriously difficult writing style, Hegel still maintained his vision of enlightenment education—even as his mature philosophical system deliberately avoided superficial popularity in order to stick to the complex truth of systematic dialectic. In the *Encyclopedia* and even in the *Science of Logic*, Hegel repeatedly notes ways in which the ordinary language coheres with and differs from its philosophical employment. When Kant and Fichte addressed their audiences directly, this was a move away from transcendental philosophy; when Hegel addressed his audience, this was philosophy itself, for, as we saw in the last chapter, spirit simply is this conversation between philosopher and audience. Thus, for example at the conclusion of the lectures known as the *History of Philosophy*, Hegel says to his audience: "I have tried to develop and bring before your thoughts (*vor Ihren Gedanken vorüberzuführen*) this series of successive spiritual forms pertaining to philosophy in its progress, and to indicate the connections between them."[5] He then claims that this series is the life of that spirit "which lives in us all" and which strives for self-consciousness. Finally he concludes with the following.

> We have to give ear to its urgency (*Auf sein Drängen haben wir zu hören*)—when the mole that is within forces its way on—and we have to make it a reality. It is my desire that this history of Philosophy should contain for you a summons (*Aufforderung*) to grasp the spirit of the time, which is present in us by nature, and—each in his own place—consciously to bring it from its natural condition, i.e., from its lifeless seclusion (*Verschlossenheit, Leblosigkeit*), into the light of day.[6]

It is clear from these passages and others like it that Hegel was aware of the fact that philosophy is the activity of the lecturer or writer who uses language to call forth the implicit truth that inhabits each of us. This educational calling forth takes place in an intersubjective dialogue mediated by language. Hegel is thus clearly aware of what Habermas calls "communicative action" or of what Pinkard calls the "sociality of reason."[7] Moreover, Hegel is explicitly aware of the problem of language, communication, and the need for poetic inspiration. As early as 1796/97, in the "System-Fragment," Hegel, writing under the influence of Hölderlin, demanded that philosophy must become poetic and "mythological," so that it could inspire the people and transform political life. He writes: "The philosopher must possess just as much aesthetic prowess as the poet." And: "Until we make our ideas aesthetic, i.e., mythological, they hold no interest for the people, and conversely, before mythology is reasonable, the philosopher must be ashamed of it . . . mythology must become philosophical and the people reasonable, and philosophy must become mythological in order to make philosophy sensual."[8] It is important to note that Hegel's recognition of the importance of language and its poetic inspirational power thus antedates Fichte's discussion of language and the poetic power of the philosopher in the *Addresses* and probably reflects the influence of Herder or possibly even Fichte's 1795 essay on language. Let us recall that in Fichte's early essay on language, he maintained that language arose from the social nature of the human spirit: the transcendental ground of language is the intersubjectivity of human freedom. For Fichte, language was the necessary consequence of the social nature of the human spirit: it results from the struggle of free human beings to be recognized by other free human beings.

However, five to ten years after Hegel celebrated the poetic power of sensual language, he came to explicitly reject it. In his journals in Jena, Hegel states for example that one should "not want to combine philosophizing with poeticizing" because one should "resolve on a necessary separation and observe it strictly."[9] Indeed Hegel goes on to say that philosophy which is focused on comprehensive concepts rather than on mere immediate thoughts must occur in a unique form of writing that demands a "painful effort."[10] In his so-called Jena System (of 1803–1804), Hegel systematically located the mediating function of language in the philosophy of spirit as an aid to memory and thus thinking (as seen in the epigram with which we began the present section). Hegel's consideration of language here is much like that of Fichte's early essay: reason occurs as a dialogue between diverse selves mediated by language. However, Hegel's interpretation of language makes the community even more primary as the ground for the development of spirit. Thus, for Hegel, spirit occurs as the *result* of the mediated experience of the community, language, and ultimately philosophical education. Indeed, even within the self-conscious individual, linguistic mediation takes place. The self-consciousness of each individual is made possible by language as the instrument of memory and thus of thinking: names allow us to represent objects to ourselves in order to think about them. Thus individual self-consciousness is always mediated by some historically contingent real language, appropriated from the community. Furthermore, Hegel links self-consciousness to historical actuality as it occurs in the language of the people in which individuals find their identity and difference.

> *Language only exists as the language of a people* (*die Sprache ist nur als Sprache eines Volks*), likewise for Understanding and Reason. Only as the work of a people is *language* the ideal existence of *spirit*, in which spirit itself expresses (*sich ausspricht*) what its essence and being is. Language is something universal, something granted recognition in itself, something that resounds in the same manner in the consciousness of all; within it every speaking consciousness immediately comes to another consciousness.[11]

Hegel thus clearly locates language as that which mediates between the universal and the individual, between philosophical reflection and historical actuality.

In this way, it is the activity of speaking—the living voice in relation to its audience—which enacts the social process that is reason. The importance of the mediational role of language remains with Hegel throughout his career, from the *Phenomenology's* dialectic of sense-certainty up through his discussion of language, memory, culture, and history in his mature *Encyclopedia*. Going beyond Fichte, Hegel systematically locates language as the basic medium in which all other mediational and social activities find their ground, from labor and property (as in the Jena System) on up to religion and philosophy.[12] Moreover, he makes it clear that his task is to use language to make the mediational activity self-conscious. The philosophy of language and the question of voice are thus not superficial matters for Hegel. It is in language that philosophical truth becomes objective, and it is in Hegel's voice and its interaction with its concrete historical audience that spirit comes alive and leaves its "lifeless seclusion." Philosophy is the externalization of truth, its expression in words. These words are the objectivity of thought that expresses the self-consciousness of those individuals who comprehend those words that embody the spirit of the community. This self-consciousness is made possible by the philosophical language, which explicates the mediation between word and object, inner and outer, subject and object, individual and community.

Authority and Philosophy

> What, therefore, is important in the study of science, is that one should take on oneself the strenuous effort of the concept.
>
> —Hegel, *Phenomenology of Spirit*[13]

The mediational activity that results in self-consciousness is education. We become conscious of the spirit that inhabits us by educating ourselves about it. Although Hegel has a discursive, dialogical conception of the sociality of reason, he also conceives of the educational activity of philosophy along authoritarian lines. Although Hegel's philosophy of mind denies that the student's appropriation could be entirely passive, philosophical expression occurs, for Hegel, primarily as lecture or treatise, as monologue in which the teacher expresses content, which the student then appropriates. For Hegel, the teacher should not speak the popular language of his audience in order to manipulate and inspire (as in Fichte's *Addresses*). Rather, it is the audience's task to raise itself to the level of philosophy by way of diligent effort. If some are unable to do this (perhaps because they are among the rabble, women, or foreigners—as we saw in the last chapter), it is not the philosopher's fault. The complexity of the truth cannot be reduced to the level of ordinary consciousness without damaging it. Despite this authoritarian model, Hegel clearly moves beyond Fichte and Kant in his recognition of the teacher's need to consider the determinate nature of his audience. Hegel wanted the philosophical enterprise to recognize that empirical differences are significant, including the different ways in which individuals are determined within the sphere of Objective Spirit. Thus Hegel's approach to education cannot be, like Fichte's, simply the imposition from above of the universal moral law. Rather, Hegel's lectures include a dialogical element, at least to the extent that he recognizes different needs among the members of his audience.[14] In fact, Hegel's notoriously difficult style of writing and lecturing is such that it forced his audience into an active dialogical response in a way that a more polished and transparent style would not have.[15]

Hegel would respond to the charge of authoritarian education by claiming that his philosophical project is, in fact, the antidote for those types of inherited, external, authority under which most of us live our lives. Self-consciousness is a circular relation, where the self is both the subject and object of knowledge. In the *Philosophy of Right* we see this in the distinction between spirit as it exists in objectivity and the philosophical comprehension of this objectivity. The inherited "truths" of ordinary life are not in fact truths in the fullest philosophical sense. These truths must be justified for free thinking—they must become self-conscious. Moreover, this goal of self-consciousness will only be possible if in fact the laws do embody freedom. This goal can lead us to further critique actuality. Nonetheless, this critique can only be justified if it comes from within ethical life and uses the terms of ethical life. Hegel's project rejects unjustified, contingent historical authority and attempts to replace it with the justified authority found in the necessity of the idea. The result of this philosophically justified authority is self-consciousness and freedom.

Hegel provides us with a list of the ways in which the structures of political life that we inherit *appear* to be justified or true: by the positive authority of the state, by mutual agreement among human beings, by the authority of inner feeling, or by the testimony of spirit.[16] These modes of justification are only apparent. The task of philosophy is to question such old truths, sacred authorities, and seemingly transparent agreements in order to comprehend these merely apparent modes of justification. The *Philosophy of Right*, when viewed from the most general perspective, is Hegel's attempt to carry out a task initiated with Socrates' interrogation of the laws of Athens. The specifically modern twist on this task is the attempt to found the law on grounds to which all rational beings would assent. "Proper to philosophy is what has been produced under the form of free thought and not through authority."[17] Philosophy transforms that which is immediately given by authority and experience by elevating it into the self-consciousness of philosophical thought. The move from dogma to free thought occurs as we become conscious of the merely apparent modes of justification found in political life and replace them with a comprehension of their internal necessity.

It is modern political life itself that demands this movement from authority to philosophical self-consciousness. This is what Hegel calls the "right of subjective consciousness" to know the laws that determine it and to know how these laws are actualized in specific cases.[18] Hegel's treatment of the constitution is a paradigm example of this right. Individuals have a right to know the laws that determine them. Thus the constitution ought to be publicly posited. Hegel praises, to cite another example, the public nature of jury trials by saying that members of civil society have a right not only to be physically present in court but also "to be present in spirit and with their own knowledge (*Wissen*)" otherwise, "the right which they receive will remain an external fate for them."[19] In short, for the law to be justified, it must be known as rationally necessary for the individuals who live under it—it must be recognized as valid by those individuals. Throughout Hegel's analysis of political life he emphasizes the publicity of law and the ability of citizens to become conscious of the laws that determine them. This emphasis on public know-ability is the basic modern idea of right, which allows external authority to be transformed into self-conscious freedom.

It is important to note here that Hegel admits that there can be a difference between *positive* law and *justified* law and that Hegel is not, then, merely an apologist for the status quo. Hegel indicates a place of difference in which we are able to critique our positive laws: "what is law (*Gesetz*) may differ in content from what is right (*Recht*) in itself."[20] This difference occurs because positive laws are subject to a variety of contingencies, not the least of which is the "contingency of self-will" of the legislators. While Hegel emphasizes that the *form* of positive law (positive laws must be made explicit to the public) is right in itself, he nowhere says that any particular positive law is right in itself. Rather, Hegel, who is aware of the practical limitations of legislators, admits that we may question the *justification* of specific positive laws. Perhaps this difference can be explained by way of the different concepts of *legitimacy* and *justification*. Publicly propagated laws are legitimate and have authority, although they may not be just or right. Hegel considers knowledge of the legitimacy and authority of positive laws to be a matter of history, limited to the finite considerations of the understanding. Justice or *Recht* involves the further consideration of the unity of content and form wherein it is determined whether the laws are rational.[21] One of the criteria for determining whether a law is justified is that the law must be posited: it must be made publicly explicit. Legitimacy in the external, historical sense is a prerequisite for philosophical justification. This is so because the law must, first of all, be publicly knowable. However, justification involves a further examination of the content of the law in relation to the idea.

Hegel maintains that the content of the modern political idea is this idea of publicity, which leads to self-consciousness. In the *Philosophy of Right* he states:

> The *truth* concerning *right, ethics, and the state* is at any rate *as old* as its *exposition and promulgation* in *public laws (Öffentlichen Gesetzen) and in public morality and religion.* What more does this truth require, inasmuch as the thinking spirit is not content to possess it in this proximate manner?

> What it needs is to be *comprehended* as well, so that the content which is already rational in itself may also gain a rational form and thereby appear justified (*gerechtfertigt*) to free thinking.[22]

Hegel continues to say that free thinking does not stop at what is legislated or given but "demands to know itself as united in its innermost being with the truth." Hegel's methodology in the *Philosophy of Right* is thus circular. The demand for justification of the given laws of society with which Hegel's philosophical text begins is a demand for knowledge of the truth of the law; this demand for knowledge is part of the very notion of justification implicit in our concept of law. However, this concept can only be known after the philosophical explication of it. The *Philosophy of Right* is the explication of the implicit idea that necessitates the philosophical explication of it. In other words, the same spirit, which demands that the laws be public, also demands that they be philosophically comprehensible. Our concept of law involves the idea that law should occur as a publicly accessible code of laws and that each individual has the right to know these laws. The demand for knowledge of the justification of the laws with which the *Philosophy of Right* begins is a demand that comes from the very nature of the laws that it sets out to study. We have a right to demand knowledge of the laws because the laws themselves postulate that right.

Despite Hegel's recognition of diversity within the state, his conception of spiritual organism holds that a living spiritual organism must be united by an idea.[23] The modern idea requires that individuals *know* this basic idea that unites them. This self-consciousness is the modern idea of freedom. As Hegel states in §270 of the *Philosophy of Right*, the final goal of the state is to become conscious of the idea of freedom:

> This very substantiality is however spirit which knows and wills itself (*sich wissende und wollende Geist*) as having passed through the form of education (*Bildung*). The state therefore knows (*weiß*) what it wills, and knows (*weiß*) it in its universality as something thought (*als Gedachtes*). Consequently, it acts and functions in accordance with known (*gewußten*) ends and recognized (*gekannten*) principles, and with laws which are laws not only in themselves but also for consciousness (*fürs Bewußtsein*); and it likewise acts in determinate knowledge (*Kenntnis*) of existing circumstances and relations in so far as its actions have relevance to these.[24]

Here we find Hegel straying into what seems like obscure metaphysical territory. He says that the state knows and wills itself. He says that the state has been educated. He claims that the state acts and functions according to known ends and recognized principles. He says that the laws are laws for consciousness. He claims that the state acts in light of knowledge. All of these seem to ascribe a subjectivity to the state that it does not seem to have. Hegel seems to be saying that the state is a giant self-conscious subject.

And yet, if we reflect on these claims a bit, it is not so clear that the state is not a subject. The state can be said to know and will itself insofar as it self-consciously (i.e. with certain ends which are explicit) protects itself by laws, police, and the military. The state can be said to be educated about itself insofar as it is self-conscious of its own history by way of archives, state historians, historical monuments, perhaps even by state philosophers (where, as in Hegel's Berlin, universities and professors are functions of the state). The state acts according to recognized principles and ends insofar as it has a set of explicit goals and procedures for action (e.g. the goal of protecting its citizens by way of due process of law). The state can even be said to be conscious of its laws insofar as the legislature, the judiciary, the executive, the monarch, and even the citizens reflect upon, criticize, and consciously alter the laws.

One may object that this does not make the state into a self-conscious entity because the supposed self-consciousness of the state really relies upon the self-consciousness of the individuals who are the state's historians, judges, legislators, monarchs, and citizens. Hegel, however, would not dispute this. He says, "In these spheres (of the state) in which its moments, individuality (*Einzelheit*), and particularity have their immediate and reflected reality, spirit is present as their objective universality which manifests itself in them as the power of the rational in necessity."[25] In other words, particular persons belong to the state rationally and necessarily: the state needs to be embodied in particular persons. The rational necessity that is manifest in the relation between state and individual is, as Hegel says above, spirit. This rational necessity becomes fully spiritual when it is comprehended by self-conscious individuals. Moral subjects or individuals are thus a necessary part of the spiritual state because their reflective subjectivity is one of the modes of self-consciousness of the state insofar as they know and will the universal idea expressed in the laws and institutions of the state:

> Individuals (*Individuen*) as a mass are themselves spiritual natures, and they therefore embody a dual moment, namely the extreme of individuality which knows and wills for itself (*für sich wissenden und wollenden Einzelheit*), and the extreme of universality which knows and wills the substantial (*das Substantielle wissenden und wollenden Allgemeinheit*).[26]

The particular individual is a part of the state whose subjectivity is the subjectivity of the state. Indeed, the self-consciousness of the state must occur in the self-consciousness of those individuals who are citizens, judges, legislators, and most importantly, philosophers. The philosopher uses his voice to educate his audience about the philosophical idea, which constitutes both himself and his audience. This education may *seem* authoritarian at first. However, since its source and its goal is *self*-consciousness, it is not authoritarian, according to Hegel. Rather, philosophy leads to autonomy by helping individuals understand themselves, even helping them to understand why this strenuous philosophical self-consciousness *appears* authoritarian, i.e., because the self of the individual is more complex than the individual initially knows.

Self-Consciousness as a Uniquely Philosophical Task

> The coming into being of philosophy out of the need that has been mentioned has experience, the immediate and argumentative consciousness, as its starting point. With these needs as stimulus, thinking conducts itself essentially so as to raise itself above the natural, sensible, and argumentative consciousness into its own unadulterated element . . .
>
> —Hegel, *Encyclopedia*[27]

The demand for comprehension of the truths of political life grows out of the content of political life itself. This is why the education that occurs in the *Philosophy of Right* is not authoritarian, i.e., because it is the result of the need for self-consciousness implicit in political life. In the present section we will discuss why Hegel thinks that *philosophy* is required to fulfill this demand and not some other form of mediation. The third section of the *Philosophy of Right*, called *Sittlichkeit,* contains a progression from narrow to broad forms of self-consciousness. The family produces independent persons who negate the family by leaving home, entering civil society, and willingly and consciously producing new families of their own. Civil society is a self-reflective entity concerned with education and the publicity of the laws. The state is a conscious being with its consciousness occurring in the citizens, the laws, and the will of the monarch. These forms of consciousness are incomplete, however: the monarch's consciousness occurs merely as natural will; the citizens are finite individuals; and the laws are mute. The modern idea of right, as implicitly self-conscious, demands that there be a philosophy of right in which this self-consciousness becomes complete. This demand is articulated in his concern with the justification of the given laws of ethical life: only when these laws are explicitly comprehended will they finally be known as justified. For this to occur, philosophy is needed, because it is philosophy alone that is able to comprehend the implicit interconnections among these diverse determinations of self-consciousness.

Hegel begins with the modern demand that the *Philosophy of Right* be written. This demand grows out of the modern form of *Sittlichkeit* that the *Philosophy of Right* discusses. The circular relation between ethical life and philosophy of right indicates a few points of resistance to the task of comprehension. First, since the idea of right comes from ethical life, philosophy must continually return to the concrete phenomena of ethical life in a dialectical process. Second, since ethical life contains various parts such as abstract persons, moral individuals, and family members, philosophical comprehension can only occur as a system. Third, since ethical life propagates itself by way of natural reproduction, the task of comprehension is temporally infinite: each new generation must be educated. Philosophy of right, therefore, is a continual, systematic, dialectical task—not a static or complete artifact.

In *Philosophy of Right* § 270, quoted above, Hegel claims that the essence or "substantiality" of the state is "the spirit which knows and wills itself as having passed through the form of education (*Bildung*)." Education leads the spirit to know itself, its own will, its laws, and actions. It is only insofar as the state knows itself in this way that it is justified. Hegel's philosophy of right is the form of education necessary for the justification of the whole of modern ethical life. Why is this the case? In the long Remark to § 270, Hegel gives us an extended discussion focusing on this process of education. Here Hegel contrasts the state, religion, and science (philosophy). He concludes that philosophy alone is the real process of education. Hegel first considers the claim that religion is the foundation of the state. Hegel is ambivalent about this claim. On the one hand, religion is supposed to be absolute truth. Hegel claims then that "everything else should be seen in relation to this [i.e. to religion's claims to absolute truth] and should receive confirmation, justification (*Rechtfertigung*), and assurance of certainty from this source."[28] The state could then be justified by religion. However, on the other hand, religion is often antagonistic to the state. The objective institutions of the state are of no lasting value when considered from the perspective of religion. In fact, religion often undermines the state by denigrating the world of ethical life in favor of some other world beyond this one. The form that absolute truth takes in religion cannot adequately embrace the form of truth that occurs in the state. The state is described as "an organism within which lasting differences (*Unterschieden*), laws, and institutions have developed." Religion, in opposition to the state, is "the relation to the absolute in the form of feeling, representational thought and faith, and within its all-embracing center, everything is merely accidental and transient." Religion does not adequately comprehend the systematic truth found embodied in the state because it denies the significance of the concrete determinations of political life and because it does not make its own mode of expression explicit. In order to adequately comprehend the truth of the state, we would need to see the state as the "transition of the inner to the outer" or the "incorporation (*Einbildung*—a term related to *Bildung*, education) of reason into reality". This truth can only be comprehended by a *philosophy* of right that is able to express the identity and difference between the idea of right, its concrete embodiment, and the linguistic mode of expression in which this is expressed.

In the *Philosophy of History,* Hegel does speak of God in history: "God governs the world; the actual working of his government—the carrying out of his plan—is the history of the world."[29] However, Hegel concludes there that it is *philosophy* that comprehends this: "This [divine] plan philosophy strives to comprehend . . . Philosophy wishes to discover the substantial purport, the real side of the divine idea, and to justify the so much despised reality of things; for reason is the comprehension of the divine work."[30] The project of comprehension cannot be undertaken by religion, which is self-satisfied, immediate, focused on inner feeling, and which occurs by way of the mere "picture-thinking" language of ordinary experience. Rather, what is needed to see this truth is "mastering one's opinions by the labor of study and subjecting one's volition to discipline so as to elevate it to free obedience."[31] In short, what is needed is philosophy because philosophy is able to explain the difference between the absolute and the appearance of the absolute, the difference between the form and content of its expression.

Hegel goes on in the Remark to § 270 to say explicitly that it is philosophy alone that comprehends the difference between the true as it appears objectively in the state and the more subjective form of truth that occurs in religion: "It is philosophical insight which recognizes that Church and state are not opposed to each other as far as their content is concerned, which is truth and rationality, but merely differ in form." In the Addition to this section Hegel claims that the state is supposed to be self-conscious, not for the purpose of more actively oppressing people but for the purpose of making people free. He concludes: "One means then that men ought to have respect for the state, for the whole of which they are the branches. The best way of freely achieving this is through philosophical insight into the essence of the state." While religion differentiates its idea of freedom from the political idea of freedom, philosophy is able to express the identity in this difference.

In the long Remark to § 279, Hegel indicates that the idea of the monarch needs to be comprehended by philosophy because religious interpretation of this has led to a misunderstanding of the idea of right found in the idea of the divine right of kings. "The misunderstandings associated with this idea are familiar enough, and the task of philosophical enquiry consists precisely in comprehending (*zu begreifen*) this divine quality." In other words, although religious terminology can provide a superficial understanding of the majesty of the monarch, only philosophical comprehension fully grasps what the metaphor of "divine authority" truly means. This does not mean that the arbitrary will of the monarch is divine, but that the divine idea of right must be embodied in some finite, particular, official will.

In the Remark to § 280 Hegel makes this point even clearer: "For these reasons, philosophy alone is in a position to consider this majesty [of the monarch] by means of thought, for every method of enquiry other than the speculative method of the infinite and self-grounded idea annuls the nature of majesty in and for itself." Only philosophy can do justice to the concept of monarchy in its relation to the idea of right. This is exactly why the *Philosophy of Right* is required by ethical life itself: it alone undertakes the task of bringing the state (and ethical life in general) to self-consciousness, thereby engaging in the task of actualizing freedom in the world.

Finally, in the very last section of the text, § 360, Hegel states that it is philosophy (more precisely *Wissenschaft*) that will bring about the reconciliation of free spirit to itself in the state. This reconciliation is made possible by two different factors. First, the modern state has actually become implicitly rational: free, self-conscious spirit can now feel at home within the state because the state is based upon the principles of respect for freedom in abstract right, respect for self-consciousness in morality, and respect for publicity in constitutional law. Second, spirit has matured to the level where it can begin to comprehend the essence of the state. Now, finally, "the spiritual realm brings the existence of its heaven down to earth in this world."[32] This seems to mean that the truth of religion, i.e., universal freedom, has finally come into the world and entered political life. However, Hegel notes in § 359 that the "otherworldly and intellectual realm"—even though it is "indeed the truth of spirit"—"has not yet been thought." What is lacking in the interaction between religion and the state is thought itself. This mode of thinking only occurs when *Wissenschaft* or philosophy breaks upon the scene, for it is the philosopher's voice that makes explicit the identity and difference between politics, morality, religion, and the idea upon which they are grounded. At the very end of § 360 Hegel finally states the relation between state, religion, and science:

> In the *state*, self-consciousness finds the actuality of its substantial knowledge and volition in organic development; in *religion*, it finds the feeling and representation of this truth as ideal essentiality; but in *science* (*Wissenschaft*) it finds the free and comprehended cognition (*freie begriffene Erkenntnis*) of this truth as one and the same in all its complementary manifestations, i.e. in the *state*, in *nature*, and in the *ideal world*.[33]

In other words, it is only philosophical science that gives us free, comprehensive knowledge of the whole. Spirit is only free when it is self-conscious. It is most freely comprehended and self-conscious in the science of itself, in philosophy, because only the philosopher's voice is able to express its own identity with and difference from politics, religion, and nature.

The *Philosophy of Right* as Issuing Forth from the State

> The very substantiality [of the state] is the spirit which knows and wills itself as having passed through the form of education. The state therefore knows what it wills, and knows it in its universality as something thought.
>
> —Hegel, *Philosophy of Right*[34]

In the last section we examined some places where Hegel says explicitly that it is philosophy alone that brings spirit to self-consciousness in the state. In the present section I will show that philosophy is not external to the state but is itself a product of the state. This is important because it leads to the conclusion that philosophy must distinguish itself from political life and yet comprehend the ways in which it remains united to political life.

In the Remark to § 270 Hegel assumes that the state is a spiritual entity. As spiritual, the state is interested in knowledge. Thus, Hegel claims that the state supports science in a way that even religion does not. Hegel is aware that there is an intimate connection between the modern state and scientific inquiry, while religion has often been opposed to science. This is interesting given the fact that, in the *Encyclopedia*'s account of Absolute Spirit, religion is supposed to be higher than the state and is supposed to give way to philosophy.[35] In one of the notes to the Remark to § 270 in the *Philosophy of Right,* Hegel indicates that the progressive structure of the *Encyclopedia* breaks down. "*Religion*, like *cognition and science*, has as its principle a distinct form which is different from that of the state . . ." Nonetheless, Hegel continues: "In both respects [science and religion], the principles of the state are applicable (*anwendend*) to them. A comprehensive treatise on the state would also have to consider these spheres, as well as art, purely natural circumstances, etc., in their relation to and position within the state."[36] Here Hegel says that the concept of the state is applicable to religion and philosophy and that these have a relation to and a position within the state. Religion, science, art, and even nature can be understood from the point of view of the state, just as the state can be understood from the perspective of each of these.

Philosophy can be understood as a product of the state's interest in knowledge and self-consciousness. This interest makes the state the place in which science and philosophy blossom. Such a blooming is possible, on the one hand, because the doctrines of the modern state and the doctrines of modern science do not conflict: the doctrines of science for the most part do not make claims that interfere with objective social life. Hegel notes, however, that the doctrines of the church and the state do conflict because the church is not content to limit itself to the inner spiritual life of the moral conscience, which is its proper sphere. Rather, the church attempts to set itself up in opposition to the state, placing the city of God over against the city of man. On the other hand, science is encouraged by the state because the ends of science help to foster the ends of the state. By bringing individuals to self-consciousness of themselves and by educating them about the nature of the state, philosophy helps to create better citizens, better legislators, and better monarchs. Indeed, this is the very idea of the University of Berlin. While the universal respect for human freedom characteristic of Christianity also corresponds to the doctrines of the modern liberal state, problems occur when the church (Hegel undoubtedly has in mind the Roman Catholic Church) steps beyond its proper limits and tries to usurp the power of the state by asserting a theocracy or when religion undermines the state by claiming that personal freedom only matters in some world beyond the state.

Hegel goes so far as to claim that modern science owes its progress to the modern state. While religion has been opposed to science (as for example in Galileo's forced recantation), the state has supported it. As Hegel says in the Remark to § 270: "it is from the state that freedom of thought and science first emerged."[37] This is so because the state is based upon the universal freedom of consciousness that also forms the basis of scientific research and philosophical cognition. Hegel says that the state, for the most part, is indifferent to the opinions of subjective self-consciousness and allows freedom of opinion.[38] This is quite different from the antagonistic relationship between religion and science, in which religious dogma is opposed to freedom of opinion.

The state, then, actually encourages the growth of science. This stems from the fact that the state demands self-consciousness. The state wants to know itself and wants its citizens to know the idea of right that determines their freedom. Citizens' knowledge of the state occurs by way of education. Thus, Hegel maintains that the state has an interest in education including, ultimately, an interest in philosophy. In ancient times, perhaps, the family served as the locus of education.[39] However, the size and complexity of the modern state demand a "direct education in ethics and in thought" such as occurs in university education.[40] Through this process of philosophical education, the particular individual overcomes his finite subjectivity and learns to see the unity of his own freedom with the freedom of the state. This education is primarily devoted to the middle class, which makes up most of the executive branch of the government and the civil service—this is the student audience of Hegel's lectures. Education is important, Hegel says, as "the point at which the laws and decisions of the executive come into contact with individuals and are translated into actuality."[41] The state itself should be interested in supporting the process of education, including philosophical attempts to articulate the truth of the state because the very idea of the modern constitutional state demands this form of justification. Moreover, as we shall see in the next section, only philosophy is explicitly self-conscious of the very medium—its words and voice—in which it expresses itself. Thus when the philosopher uses the language of political life or religion, he is aware of the limitations of this contingent medium in a way that the politician, clergyman, or theologian is not.

Hegel's Philosophy of Language

> We only know our thoughts, only have definite, actual thoughts, when we give them the form of objectivity, of a being distinct from our inwardness, and therefore the shape of externality, and of an externality, too, that at the same time bears the stamp of the highest inwardness. The articulated sound, the word, is alone such an inward externality.
>
> —Hegel, *Encyclopedia*[42]

What makes possible the ambiguity of Hegel's address? How is he able to speak to so many different audiences—his students, other philosophers, the state, spirit itself—at once? Moreover, how is Hegel able to overcome the limitations of political, religious, and poetic speech in order to express the limitations of the mode of expression? All of this requires recognition of the systematic nature of philosophy and especially the location within his system of a philosophy of language that makes his audience conscious of the sound of his voice and the philosophical significance of its mode of expression. Hegel's philosophy of language makes it clear that language is the medium that allows expression of complex thought to a diverse audience.

The task of Hegel's political philosophy is to express the truth of political life to the various individuals within political life. To do this, he must speak the language of those individuals while using this language to lead these individuals beyond their own finite viewpoints. The philosopher's use of language must thus be more self-conscious than the use of language in political or religious speech. The philosopher does not use language to persuade or inspire. Rather, he uses language to guide spirit in its quest to become self-conscious. Hegel's philosophy is, in general, a self-consciously ambiguous enterprise insofar as it is an attempt to articulate, in a historical language, the unity in difference of the totality of phenomena, which includes the necessity of using spirit's contingent historical language to express the universal idea of spirit. Hegel must be able to express both sides of a given phenomenon in its opposition to and unity with other phenomena. This dialectic must also be applied to the medium of expression: Hegel must express the identity and difference of philosophical speech and ordinary language. To this end, Hegel locates language explicitly within his system in the section called Subjective Spirit because language is the necessary accompaniment of subjectivity and thought.[43] Language and voice are not, then, superficial issues for Hegel. Indeed Hegel writes that "we think in names" and "to want to think without words . . . is a manifestly irrational procedure."[44]

Philosophy must be expressed, articulated, made objective. Moreover, and this brings us to the issue of voice, thinking must be communicated to others. Hegel's criticism of Kant and Fichte came from his rejection of their transcendentalist emphasis upon the sameness of transcendental egos, which seems to reject the need for philosophy to be communicated. Although Fichte moved beyond Kant in his social interpretation of language and his recognition of the intersubjectivity of freedom, his reductive approach to education in the *Addresses* indicated a remaining transcendentalism that Hegel finally rejected. For Fichte the problem of communicating his system was to be resolved by radically transforming society and reeducating the people, so that they might overcome the limitations of their contingent empirical decadence. For Hegel, the system itself must be able to account for the differences in social life, which give rise to the problem of communication. Hegel's social theory recognizes diversity within social life, just as his ontology recognizes diversity even in the mode in which Absolute Spirit expresses itself. The crucial task for Hegel was not to reduce this difference to an abstract sameness; rather, he had to develop a theory of communication in which these differences can be interrelated without losing their uniqueness. The medium for this interrelation between individuals and social and ontological spheres is language and the voice of the philosopher in which these differences are cancelled and preserved. The form of thinking that remains stuck within the inward experience of the monological subject is inferior because it lacks substantiality (it is not yet actual) and because it lacks substantiation (it is not yet verified). Philosophical thinking needs to express itself in its difference from other forms of thinking. Fichte attempted to resolve this problem by sanctifying German as the *Ursprache* in which language remains close to its spiritual source. He claimed that if Germans properly understood their language, they would understand the spiritual destiny that would allow them to know the truth of the *Wissenschaftslehre*. Hegel, on the contrary, maintains that no contingent historical language can necessarily fulfill the spiritual task. Rather, philosophy must overcome the limits of contingent historical languages by articulating the identity and difference between philosophy and ordinary speech. Hegel maintains that thought must overcome its inwardness and become objective, not by hypostatizing its contingent medium as absolute but rather by expressing its difference from and identity with this medium.

Hegel makes us explicitly aware of the fact that the medium in which thinking occurs is language and especially its verbal manifestation as voice. With regard to voice, Hegel says, for example, that the voice (*die Stimme*) "is the principal way in which a person makes public his inner nature; what he is, that he puts into his voice (*was er ist, das legt er in seine Stimme*)."[45] Hegel's emphasis here is the sound (*Ton*) of the voice which has an affective capacity. "Sounds," Hegel says, "evoke in us a corresponding mood."[46] The voice of the philosopher would be, according to this account, the point at which the "inner" spirit of philosophy enters the real "external" world of political life and has an affect upon it. In this transition of inner to outer, or spirit to matter, the conflict between philosophy and rhetoric, philosophy and politics arises. For the most part, a political audience is persuaded by the *sound* of a voice: its quality as a sensation. This rhetorical element is, however, notoriously unstable. This is so because sound, according to Hegel, vanishes as quickly as it appears. "Therefore, in the voice, sensation obtains an embodiment in which it dies away just as fast as it is expressed (*als sich äußert.*)."[47] Hegel equates the voice with the expression of the merely animal side of human nature: the cries, laughs, and other spontaneous expressions of emotion and sensation. In fact, Hegel says that the expression of inner content associated with "voice" completes itself as it becomes an "externalization (*Entäußerung*) in which the inner is completely evacuated into the outer and thus dissipates immediately."[48] The limitation of voice is that it alienates itself from its inner content as soon as it enters into the externality of sound. Thus laughter and crying—the original externalization of voice—carry no further content: they are the inner immediately externalized.

The voice becomes stable only as it overcomes itself in what Hegel calls "language" or "articulate speech" or "words." The immediate vocal externalization of the inner self becomes a process of communicating determinate content. In language, the speaker and the hearer can come to share a determinate objective experience. An object can be expressed by a word in the sense that the object itself is represented. In this sense, even subjective experiences can become objects for representation, as soon as we use words to express them rather than mere vocal cries or laughs.

> Man, however, does not stop short at this animal mode of expressing himself (*Sichäußerns*); he creates *articulate* speech (*die artikulierte Sprache*) by which his internal sensations are turned into *words*, are expressed in their entire determinateness, are objective to him as subject, and at the same time become external and extraneous to him. Articulate speech is thus the highest mode in which man externalizes (*entäußert*) his internal sensations.[49]

The crucial aspect identified by Hegel in this account of words and articulate speech is the fact that mere sound—voice—becomes significant for us and for others when it is used to express determinate objects of experience. This is the objective element referred to above. In speech, we externalize our experience and thought in a medium that has lasting significance for ourselves and for others. In this way we can recognize our experience as an object and so can others who speak our language. Words are intuitions (sounds) that have a significance other than their immediate sensible manifestation (their sound). This significance is reproducible in different subjects who share the same linguistic habits as we do. This activity of representation of objects of experience is the essence of communication. The movement from voice to language involves mediation by way of the contingent inherited language of a culture by which the self becomes an object for itself. Unfortunately, Hegel does not consider the importance of this link between language and political life in any detail.

Hegel's theory of language emphasizes the contingent nature of the connection between sound and significance. This is a rejection of Fichte's theory of the organic connection between language, spirit, and nature in the *Ursprache*. Hegel leaves open the problem of explaining the difficulty of the contingent sound of the philosopher's voice in a way in which Fichte does not. Hegel indicates quite clearly that there is no intrinsic connection between the sound and its significance: "the arbitrary nature of the connection between the sensuous material and a general idea occurring here, has the necessary consequence that the significance of the sign must first be learned. This is especially true of language signs."[50] What has to be learned is the historically contingent yet determinate way in which a culture connects meaning to sound. The importance that Hegel places upon this learning process and the difference and identity between the contingent historical language and its absolute content have been subject to dispute among commentators.[51] Suffice it to say that Hegel recognizes the complexity of this problem in a way that Fichte did not. Hegel attempts to account for the unity and difference of both the natural and the cultural, the unity and difference of the subjective and the objective. There are two different elements always at play in language: sound and its system, language.

> The sound [*Ton*] which articulates itself further for determinate representations—speech [*die Rede*] and its system, language [*die Sprache*]—gives to sensations, intuitions, conceptions, a second and higher existence than their immediate existence— it gives them an existence which is valid in the realm of representation [*im Reiche des Vorstellens*].[52]

The higher existence is the existence that these sounds have in the culture of significance in which they are meaningful. Nonetheless, this higher existence never fully escapes from its natural affective antecedent and the concrete historical location of the voice that speaks.

The same movement from "lower" to "higher" occurs as the historically contingent ordinary language is appropriated by philosophy and given an even higher spiritual significance. The content of philosophy must be expressed in some language, even though the representational language of real speech will itself be limited by the associations and meanings that occur in ordinary usage. Philosophy is thus always connected with its historical, political, and natural source of expression, even as it strives to express universal and necessary truths in this particular and contingent language. One of the tasks of philosophy is to express this distinction between the contingent ordinary language and its necessary philosophical employment by using the ordinary language in whatever way is appropriate to express the content of philosophy. "Philosophy has the right to select from the language of common life which is made for the world of pictorial thinking, such expressions as seem to approximate to the determinations of the concept."[53] However, the philosopher must be self-conscious of the differences between his own philosophical appropriation of the language and the common usage. This is seen most clearly at the very end of the *Encyclopedia*, in the section entitled Philosophy (§§ 572–573). Hegel makes it clear here that philosophy is the movement beyond the mere representational thinking of art or religion. Philosophy's advantage is that it comprehends both the necessity of the content and the necessity of using the contingent forms of representational thinking to express this content. "Philosophy thus characterizes itself as a cognition of the necessity in the content of the absolute representation (*Vorstellung*), as also of the necessity of the two forms (art and religion) . . ."[54] What is significant here is that Hegel states this in representational language—he must, for he must use real, historical language. Thus he tells us *in language*, that the task of philosophy is to comprehend the necessity of using language to tell us what philosophy is. In other words, philosophy must be self-conscious of its own mode of expression.

Hegel clearly believes that vocal language is original, insofar as voice is the immediate expression of the inner.[55] This is quite similar to Fichte's later account of the *Ursprache* as a vocal language in which spiritual nature speaks. For Hegel, written alphabetic language is derivative from the original expressive activity, as the alphabet consists of written signs for spoken sounds that do not have any intrinsic connection with the sounds they represent. Hegel thus claims that alphabetic language retains the dynamism of spoken language and avoids the static tendency of what he calls "hieroglyphic" languages. It is not clear however, whether Hegel maintains that written language is better or higher than spoken. In one sense, written language is higher: it involves a further mediation by which the visible signs must be translated into spoken sounds and then into their signification. But this mediational activity is supposed to become automatic as we acquire the habit by which we no longer have to "utter aloud" the words that we are reading in order to "catch their meaning in the sound."[56] Thus Hegel seems to imply, in another sense, that reading an alphabetic language and speaking are essentially the same thing, although consisting of different habits by which we transform subjective experience into objective symbols. Although Hegel does not resolve the problem of the status of writing and spoken language, it is clear that both of these are habits or shortcuts, acquired by education and training, by which we make inner experience objective. Finally, in a third sense, Hegel states that "the visible language is related to the vocal only as a sign, and intelligence expresses itself immediately and unconditionally by speaking."[57] In this context it remains unclear whether the immediacy of voice is itself a limitation that is overcome by written language or whether the immediacy of expression remains at the ground of written language. In passing, I suggest that the difference between voice and written word has to do with the two forms of intuition. Voice is primarily communication across space: Hegel bridging the distance between himself and his students. Written language is primarily communication across time: Hegel sending his words to the future by writing them down. Although the subsequent history of philosophy has emphasized written language over spoken as the locus for hermeneutical self-understanding, Hegel remains ambivalent about the philosophical significance of the written word.[58] This is perhaps best understood by Hegel's fear that the merely written language can remain static and dead. Rather what is required is interpretation, and this occurs by way of the voice of the philosopher in interaction with his audience.

Despite the fact that the philosopher always has a voice in the sense that he or she must use sounds (or words) to externalize his/her thoughts and despite the material basis of philosophy in the embodied human voice, philosophers use their voices to point beyond the material power of sound toward the "higher" more spiritual content of what Hegel calls "language [*Sprache*]."[59] The spiritual content transmitted (sent across space by voice and across time by writing) by the material medium of voice or writing is *logos* or reason, that which Hegel equates with the identity and difference of speech (*die Rede*) and its system, language (*die Sprache*). There can be no communication without speech; speech remains insignificant without language. Philosophy is the ability to comprehend both the necessity and the contingency of the medium in which thought is communicated. Hegel's analysis leads us to the general problem of communication. How can material sound communicate the "higher" inner stuff of spirit without corrupting this spiritual content? The difference between language and sound indicates a problem in distinguishing that which is to be sent (language, *logos*, reason) from the medium in which it is sent (voice, sound). The effort to distinguish the form and the content is the very task of the philosopher, and Hegel repeatedly attempts to make his audience aware of the complexity of this task.

Conclusion

This brings us back to Hegel's political philosophy. In political *philosophy,* the philosopher must continually call attention to the difference between philosophical speech (or writing) and political speech. The philosophical task is to make this distinction clear in language that is itself the language of political life. Philosophy develops out of political life as an attempt to resolve conflicts within political life by making them self-conscious. This comprehensive task should not be confused with the political task of changing social reality, even though it may have this result. This was the confusion to which Fichte succumbed. Hegel attempts to avoid this problem by clearly distinguishing the philosophical mode of expression from its contingent political and historical medium.

Hegel maintains that his philosophical task is mandated by modern political life. Structures of modern political life demand their own self-comprehension by way of political philosophy. This is a recurrent theme in Hegel's text. With regard to the monarch, for example, Hegel says: "philosophy alone is in a position to consider the majesty of the monarch by means of thought."[60] With regard to conflict between church and state, Hegel says: "It is philosophical insight which recognizes that Church and state are not opposed to each other."[61] It is *philosophy* that brings structures of political life to self-consciousness. It is *philosophy* that reconciles us to the actuality of dichotomies within political life. For Hegel, the voice of the philosopher externalizes the truth of political life in the language of political actuality in order to make that actuality conscious of the dichotomies that remain within political life—even including the dichotomy between political practice and philosophical comprehension. In this sense, Hegel's voice both transcends the conflicts of political life and remains engaged in real political practice as a catalyst for political change. Hegel's advance over Kant and Fichte, however, is his attempt to express to the public the very difference between his own philosophical activity and its political implications. Hegel mounts this effort to distinguish between philosophy and politics in order to help political agents become aware of the way in which modern political life is based upon the universal freedom of the human spirit. Unlike Fichte, Hegel refuses to impose this upon his audience, for such an imposition would violate the spirit of freedom. Unlike Kant, he wants to make the political role of philosophy apparent to his audience so that they might become aware of the philosophical idea that constitutes their lives and thus complete the republican project of modernity.

Hegel makes it clear that spirit cannot fully transcend political life. Rather spirit is both political action and philosophical reflection: "The history of spirit is its own deed; for spirit is only what it does and its deed is to make itself . . . the object of it own consciousness, and to comprehend itself in its interpretation of itself to itself."[62] This sentence is necessarily convoluted: the truth it tries to articulate is the truth of spirit, which is both the historical actuality of political life and the interpretation of this actuality that is political philosophy. This shows us that the various addresses of the *Philosophy of Right* must be considered in concert as necessary parts of political philosophy. Political philosophy is politically active in that it serves the state, addresses the public, and engages in theoretical debates about the state. However, it also attempts to bring the totality of this political action to self-consciousness by, in Hegel's words above, "interpreting itself to itself." Self-consciousness is an organic part of the diversity of political life: Hegel's students, the ministers of state, and indeed the general reading public are political agents to whom political philosophy is addressed in order to clarify what it is they already do. Part of what they do is engage in the continual contestations of political life. In Hegel's terminology, in this sense, political philosophy is part of Objective Spirit: it too participates in this contestation by directly addressing political agents and helping them to understand themselves. However, political philosophy is also a scientific endeavor that seeks to rise above the diversity of political life in order to comprehend this diversity within a systematic totality. In this sense, it is part of what Hegel calls Absolute Spirit. Even while acknowledging that philosophy (like art and religion) is politically located, Hegel claims that it is more than mere political activity. For Hegel, the philosopher's voice hovers ambiguously between philosophy and politics: it is reflection on political life that is also part of ongoing political activity. The ambiguity of this hovering will be the focal point of Marx's rejection of Hegel's political philosophy.

CHAPTER 9

Marx: Politics, Ideology, and Critique

> One of the most difficult tasks confronting philosophers is to descend from the world of thought to the actual world. The immediate actuality of thought is language (*die Sprache*) . . . The problem of descending from the world of thoughts to the actual world is turned into the problem of descending from language to life.
>
> —Marx, *The German Ideology*[1]

We have seen various responses to the tension between philosophy and politics. Despite their differences, however, each of the philosophers we have considered has remained committed to an ideal of progress toward universal cosmopolitan enlightenment guided by the philosopher's voice. Each was also located within the political establishment, to one degree or another, as philosophical voices speaking for and to the German nation. Each of them thus struggled with the problem of how best to conceive of national identity, language, and political struggle within a cosmopolitan context. However, after Hegel's death in 1831, the enlightenment idea that there could be a universal *philosophical* solution to the problems of political life appeared to young thinkers interested in pushing forward with the political ideals of modernity as a conciliatory and conservative approach.[2] In the 1830s the question of linguistic diversity, national identity, and the universality of the categories of consciousness—issues that stretched back to Herder and Fichte—again became an explicit matter for concern with the posthumous publication of Wilhelm von Humboldt's essay *On the Diversity of Human Language Construction* in 1836. This essay tied together ideas about language as the medium of thought and ideas about language as the locus of national identity. It concluded ambiguously that although some languages are "better" than others, all languages represent valuable aspects of human mental capacity.[3] The ambiguities of Humboldt's conclusion are similar to the ambiguities of Hegel's system of Objective Spirit, which attempted to locate the various particular aspects of political life under one general systematic scheme. Marx's claim that we must descend from language to life can be read in this context:

philosophical conundrums about unity amid difference fail to respect the genuine human problems of misery, oppression, and strife.

In the 1840s the conciliatory nature of this ambiguity became the object of criticism by the so-called Young Hegelians including Feuerbach and Marx. The Young Hegelian critique of Hegel's system emphasized the historical, anthropological, critical, and revolutionary side of Hegel's systematic endeavor. As Feuerbach said in 1843 in his *Principles of the Philosophy of the Future*, "The task of the modern era was the realization and humanization of God—the transformation and dissolution of theology into anthropology."[4] This anthropological turn was accompanied by a revolutionary mood throughout Europe in midcentury that culminated in the revolutions of 1848. For Marx the historical and materialistic response to Hegel pointed toward socialism and a Hobbesian conception of politics. Marx's understanding of political life thus represents a decisive turn away from the enlightenment models of Kant, Fichte, and Hegel. For Marx, the conflicts of political life could no longer be ameliorated by philosophical education. Indeed, Marx's radical revolutionary point of view was justified by the fact that the political establishment explicitly rejected the philosophical theories of the Young Hegelians.[5] Marx himself was forced into exile by the Prussian authorities and eventually renounced his Prussian citizenship in 1845. He returned to Germany briefly to take part in the revolutionary activity of 1848 and then retreated to London to continue organizing the theoretical, rhetorical, and practical activity of what he saw as a universal revolution. Since radical philosophy was at odds with the political ideology of the time, since historical anthropology indicated the prevalence of diversity and division in political life, and since the authority of Hegelian philosophy had been appropriated by the political authorities, Marx's approach to the task of philosophical education became linked to the practical political expedient of fostering a political revolution from a position outside of the political establishment.

Marx's demand that we "descend from language to life" is a demand that philosophy become political. For Marx, a philosopher should not—indeed cannot—hover above political life, unifying its diversity in his voice, as Hegel had suggested. Rather, since language and thought are social products and since society is constituted by division, oppression, and strife, the philosopher's voice is located amid these struggles. Marx reaffirms the project of progress toward universal justice begun by Kant but follows Fichte's lead in taking this project in an active political direction. Moreover, Marx recognizes that in the midst of political struggle, a philosophical discourse of universal justice is inexpedient. Rather, what is required is an active critique of the dominant ideology that is tied to a practical attempt to use rhetoric to stimulate concrete political activity.

In what follows I develop Marx's view by looking at his explicit critique of Hegel and his early neo-Hegelian humanism. I stop to consider several problems of interpretation that arise from Marx's critique of humanism, most notably the problem that Marx speaks in multiple voices. I then turn to Marx's underdeveloped "philosophy of language." At the end of the present chapter I consider a couple of criticisms that we might make of Marx. In the next chapter I turn to the clearest expression of Marx's understanding of the political nature of the philosopher's voice, the *Communist Manifesto*. I interpret this text in terms of the multiplicity of its voices and audience. I then consider how Marx's more "theoretical" work, *Capital*, also represents a political approach to philosophical theory. Finally, I conclude by explicating the political nature of Marx's voice.

Hegel and Humanism

> Hegel's standpoint is that of modern political economy . . . The only labor which Hegel knows and recognizes is abstractly mental labor. Therefore, that which constitutes the essence of philosophy—the alienation of man who knows himself, or alienated science thinking itself—Hegel grasps as its essence.
>
> —Marx, *Economic and Philosophical Manuscripts of 1844*[6]

As seen in the previous two chapters, Hegel represents the zenith of the philosophical attempt to arrive at systematic self-consciousness of the interrelation of voice, politics, and philosophy. He uses language self-consciously to comprehend the identity and difference between philosophy and politics. We saw fissures in the totality that spirit was meant to comprehend, most notably in the political nature of Hegel's address in the *Philosophy of Right*: he speaks to an audience with a determinate position within society, and he deliberately excludes, for example, women and the "rabble" from his address. Despite his attempts to systematically include the totality of political life within the philosophical concept, the determinate nature of his voice made this impossible. His philosophical voice remained politically located despite his efforts to climb the ladder of ordinary language beyond politics toward the idea of political life.

Marx was aware of the political location of Hegel's philosophical activity and criticized Hegelian philosophy as part of the struggle for power in Germany. For Marx the relation between philosophy and politics was resolved entirely in the direction of politics: he views "philosophy" (which for Marx means *Hegel's philosophy*) as the voice of one party—the bourgeoisie—in its struggles against both the *ancien régime* and the burgeoning proletariat.[7] Marx's extended criticism of Hegel's *Philosophy of Right* (of 1843) provides a jumping-off point for the subsequent discussion of Marx's approach to the problem of the philosopher's voice.

Marx criticizes Hegel's political philosophy as "logical, pantheistic mysticism."[8] What he means by this is that Hegel's approach to politics is idealistic to the extent that Hegel considers political life abstractly from the perspective of the categories of his logic: political life is viewed by Hegel, according to Marx, as a mere "parenthesis within logic."[9] For Marx this means that Hegel does not allow concrete political life to establish its own rational system: "it is not rational on account of its own reason."[10] Hegel is unable to descend "from language to life" because he does not hear the voices of those who speak languages other than his own spiritual dialect and does not recognize the rationality of those who reject his dialectical logic. Rather, Hegel imposes the ideal order of his logical system upon political life while maintaining ideologically that this is simply the explicit development of the immanent logic of political life. For Marx, this can be seen most clearly in the way in which "the state" is supposed to be the reconciliation of the opposition between "family" and "civil society." This dialectical *Aufhebung* is structurally similar to the movement from the opposition between being and essence to the reconciliation of the concept in Hegel's logic. For Marx, Hegel's imposition of this structural logic represents a form of idealism that leads Hegel to badly misunderstand political life. To real participants in political life, the state is not the idea in which their alienation is reconciled, rather it is the representative of the interests of the dominant class who continue to alienate and oppress them. Thus when Marx concludes that Hegel's "philosophical work does not consist in embodying thinking in political definitions, but in evaporating the existing political definitions into abstract thoughts," he demands that we reject this notion of philosophy.[11] Rather, for Marx, philosophy must become political by recognizing the lived experience of those who are alienated from the state.

Marx understands the state as a part of civil society that tries to resolve the struggles within society by idealizing the interests of the dominant class. The state is not the ideal reconciliation of difference; it is the result of power politics. Hegel defends the interests of the dominant class by couching these interests in an account of the state as the idea of the whole. This idealism prohibits the Hegelian "philosophy" from acknowledging the remaining oppositions that continually disrupt political life. In other words, Hegel's idealism ignores the difficult political questions of power and domination that formed the basis of Marx's approach. From this follows Marx's condemnation of Hegel's philosophy of law. Marx rejects Hegel's "deification of authority," his "idealization of bureaucracy," and the "religious" nature of Hegel's defense of private property and primogeniture.[12] Hegel's retreat from politics to his formal consideration of the structural logic of the determinations of Objective Spirit leads him to ignore conflicts and struggles that negate this logic. It is this unpolitical implication of Hegel's political philosophy that is condemned by Marx throughout.

Marx thus claims that Hegel's philosophy of politics ignores politics by simply stipulating the abstract agreement of all individuals. For Marx, such unanimity is not forthcoming. Rather Marx poses "democracy" as the antidote for Hegel's idealized constitutional monarchy. "Hegel starts from the state and makes man the subjectified state; democracy starts from man and makes the state objectified man."[13] This means that Marx must thus turn to "man" in order to see what democracy and democratic politics might look like. In his early unpublished essays Marx comes back to "the human" as the antidote to the metaphysical and the social as the antidote to the philosophical. Marx concludes in his 1843 critique of Hegel: "Man does not exist for the law but the law for man—it is a *human manifestation*; whereas in the other forms of state man is a *legal manifestation*."[14] What this means for Marx is that political life must be understood by looking at concrete human social life, not by abstractly considering the idea of law.

What Marx discovers in his examination of "man" in his early manuscripts is not the same thing that his "philosophical" predecessors Kant, Fichte, and Hegel had discovered. This leads Marx to a supposed break with humanism.[15] As Marx turns to "man," he discovers that there is no transcendental essence of human being. Rather, human beings are material, social, and historical. Thus to discover the essence of human being (and thus the essence of law), we must consider the nature of human beings in their relation to the material world, in society, and at a given time in history. What Marx discovers in his social/historical/material analysis of "the essence" of human being is that human beings in the contemporary world are "essentially" alienated. This recognition leads Marx to overcome philosophical (i.e., Hegelian/universal) humanism. Marx's turn to a situated analysis of "man" leads to the recognition that one cannot say anything universal about man's essence because man today has become alienated from his essence. Althusser describes this conclusion as "theoretical anti-humanism."[16] Marx's "humanistic" account of alienation in 1844 includes the following claims: man is alienated from himself, from other men, from his productive activity, from the product of his labor, from nature, and indeed from his essence (or "species-being").[17] This alienation is a matter of the power struggle between two social/economic classes: the property owners and the propertyless workers, capitalists and proletarians. Marx indicates that the owners and those who defend the capitalist system—the bourgeois political economists—fail to comprehend this fact of capitalism because they are not alienated in the same way that the proletarians are. This leads to the conclusion that one cannot make a universal claim about man without identifying the ideological address of such a claim. In this way, theory remains connected to its political location and the practical struggle for power in which it participates. As Marx states in 1845 in his second Thesis on Feuerbach, "man must prove the truth, i.e., the reality and power, the this-worldliness (*Diesseitigkeit*) of his thinking in practice."[18] In other words, following upon his realization of alienation as the "essence" of man, Marx realizes that theory is political: theories about the so-called "essence of man" are part of the struggle for power that constitutes capitalist society.

It is important to note that in the *1844 Manuscripts* Marx reaches his conclusions by way of an immanent critique of capitalism and its ideology. He claims that he has arrived at the fact of alienation by considering the very concepts of bourgeois political economy. "We have accepted its language and its laws . . ." Or: "On the basis of political economy itself, in its own words, we have shown . . ."[19] The concepts and language of capitalism create alienation, even as they theorize the essence of man. For Marx, however, capitalism is not the result of man's "essential" greed or competitiveness. Rather, greed and competitiveness are the result of the language and concepts of capitalism. Moreover, Marx recognizes that language differs according to social class: the words of the political economist mean one thing to the bourgeoisie who profits from them; they mean quite another thing to the proletariat who is exploited by them.

Ideology, Language, and Philosophy

> The ideas of the ruling class are in every epoch the ruling ideas: i.e., the class which is the ruling material force of society is at the same time its ruling intellectual force.
>
> —Marx, *The German Ideology*[20]

By 1845 Marx had developed his notion of ideology: political interests are expressed as universal truths. "The ruling ideas are nothing more than the ideal expression (*der ideelle Ausdruck*) of the dominant material relationships, the dominant material relationships grasped as idea; hence of the relations which make the one class the ruling one, therefore, the ideas of its dominance."[21] Marx's approach to the problem of the philosopher's voice is tied to his view of alienation, his view of the social and political location of consciousness, and his theory of ideology. When Marx states in the *1844 Manuscripts* that "the element of thought itself—the element of thought's living expression (*das Element der Lebensäusserung des Gedankens*)—language (*die Sprache*)—is of a sensuous nature" and when he connects this to the "social reality of nature," we must be aware that for Marx this living social reality is characterized by alienation and structured by domination.[22] Language, the living expression of thought, reflects the political conditions under which thought is formed for both bourgeoisie and proletariat by way of domination, oppression, exploitation, and exclusion. Consciousness under contemporary capitalism is characterized by alienation and political struggle. Thus contemporary language, like contemporary society, is divided and conflictual: different classes speak differently. This is connected to that democratic interpretation of politics, which Marx opposed to Hegel. "The state is an abstraction. The people alone is what is concrete."[23] The concrete life of the people in contemporary society is characterized by alienation and class antagonism. If human beings are divided, if political life is a struggle for power, then consciousness and language are equally divided and part of the political struggle. In other words, for Marx there can be no such thing as the philosopher's voice per se, which reconciles these struggles by comprehending the difference between philosophical idea and political actuality. Rather, for Marx "the philosopher's voice" is always already divided, partial, and political. To say this is at once to put Marx in opposition to the "philosophical" party, which claimed that the philosopher could overcome the partisan struggles of political life either by knowing (as in Kant) the transcendental ideas of justice, the state, and man, by speaking these ideas in a living *Ursprache* (as in Fichte) or by comprehending (as in Hegel) the spirit that guides the development of these ideas in history.

A logical conundrum arises at this point for Marx: how can Marx claim that all theory is ideological without undermining the supposed truth-value of his own theory. Justin Schwartz both states and resolves this problem quite nicely in "The Paradox of Ideology."[24] Schwartz indicates that Marx is not making a global claim about all truth-claims. Rather, Marx's point is that some truth-claims are the product, not of concern for the truth, but of self-interest (whether conscious of this or not) and can thus be criticized from another perspective—one which is not self-interestedly concerned with defending these "truths" for "non-cognitive" reasons. Schwartz indicates that the proletariat thus has a better (i.e., nonself-interested) perspective on capitalism. While I agree with Schwartz to the extent that Marx remains committed to "truth" and "science"—that is, Marx remains committed to what Allen Wood calls "common sense realism"[25]—I want to emphasize that Marx's understanding of the social role of this commitment leads him to understand his own project in political terms. Marx claims that it is a commonsense fact that different social classes have different interests in the truth: the bourgeoisie, for example, is not interested in discovering the truth about capitalism, which Marx discloses. Stimulating interest in the truth is a matter of political struggle and not only a matter of theoretical activity. Just as Fichte recognized that his audience had no interest in transcendental philosophy and turned to politics in order to create this audience, so Marx recognizes that the bourgeoisie has no interest in criticizing its ideals and practices. The difference is that Marx gives up on the attempt to create a universal audience for his critique. Rather, he addresses an audience—the proletariat and its leaders—that already has an interest in the truth about capitalism. In the long run—as a result of revolutionary politics—the bourgeoisie will be forced to hear the truth about its ideology. The bourgeoisie will not gladly embrace this truth, which goes against its self-interest, without first struggling to resist it.

Ideology is not about *what* we believe as the truth or falsehood of logical or empirical claims (it is not ideological to claim that "2+2=5" or that "snow is black"; these are simply false). Rather, ideology is about *why* we believe: the political self-interest that leads us toward (or away from) truth.[26] Ideology occurs when we claim that social preferences are "natural" and "universal" in order to subvert criticism and ignore questions of truth (it is ideological to claim that "competition is natural," when this is meant to forestall inquiry into the "nature" of competition in order to protect competitiveness from criticism). "Philosophy"—the supposedly disinterested pursuit of truth—becomes ideological when its claims about "truth" are used to justify political power. It is a clever political ploy to use the language of disinterestedness to justify one's own interests. In Elster's words: "to win power a class must speak the language of universality and rationality, not the language of petty interests."[27] This is most insidious when such claims are not conscious at all, as for example in Hegel's political philosophy. When Marx claims that the ruling class "imagines" its ideas to be the eternal truth detached from class interests as "an independent existence," this is not to claim that this class is lying to itself; rather, like Hegel, they actually believe that their interests represent the interests of the whole.[28]

Marx politicizes philosophy by claiming that the ideology of capitalism prevents further critique to the extent that the ideals of the ruling class are postulated as eternally true. Philosophy must thus become practical in order to make possible the empirical conditions under which critical discussion could proceed. This is not itself an ideological claim (contra Althusser who seems to maintain that there is no nonideological perspective from which one might speak). Rather, Marx claims that it is simply a fact of historical actuality that class divisions and ideological defenses exist. Likewise it is a fact of politics that social transformation must be accompanied by ideological critique if it is to be successful.

Interpretive Problems

Marx rejects the "philosophical" approach to politics so strenuously that understanding the political location of a philosopher's voice becomes crucial for evaluating its content. Marx's awareness of the way in which supposedly disinterested philosophical "truth" can be ideological leads him to locate his own voice in the concrete struggles of political life: Marx's own "philosophical" critique of ideology thus explicitly announces itself as political action. Marx does not hide the fact that he speaks for and to a particular party in the struggles of political life. The claim that voice is a focal point of Marx's theoretical work is, however, a questionable one. There are three problems for interpreting Marx that stem from this explicit turn to politics. First, Marx's own voice is unclear: Marx's texts demand that we ask seriously—in a way that we did not have to with Kant, Fichte, or Hegel—who is Marx. Second, Marx's audience is questionable. The problem of ideological mystification makes it unclear who Marx's audience is. We must be careful in considering the variety of audiences that Marx addresses. Third, Marx does not make language or voice the explicit subject of any of his published works. Almost all of Marx's comments on language occur in unpublished manuscripts. We must ask why this is and whether it is significant for a discussion of Marx's voice. Before we further examine Marx's critical project, I will discuss each of these points in turn.

Who is Marx? Does he have "a voice"?

The problem we encounter when interpreting Marx is that Marx does not have a unified authorial voice. Unlike Kant or Hegel, Marx did not leave a systematic corpus. Nor did he explicate in a systematic way—as Fichte and Hegel did—his own views on the nature of language and its relation to politics and philosophy. This problem becomes acute when we stop to consider the texts from which Marx's "philosophy of language" can be most easily unpacked: the *1844 Manuscripts*, *The German Ideology*, and the *Grundrisse*. These texts were not published by Marx in his lifetime (a significant point to which I will return shortly). Moreover, Engels and Marx jointly authored *The German Ideology* and *The Communist Manifesto*. Since much of my subsequent argument about Marx's "philosophy of language" and about the political nature of his "voice" will hinge on *The German Ideology* and the *Manifesto*, it is important to note that these texts do not simply record Marx's voice. Indeed recent scholarship on *The German Ideology* has made this text even more enigmatic than it already was. According to Terrell Carver, *The German Ideology* consists of "dialogue and debate" between Marx and Engels and is not a "smooth text" in which the authors merge as one voice.[29] This and the fact that the *Manifesto* is "an unambiguously joint effort" in the sense that Marx and Engels supposedly agreed to its final version leads Carver to claim that there is not one thing that can be called "Marx's voice" *simpliciter*. Rather there is a multiplicity of voices that could be called Marx's. It is important to keep in mind that Marx's voice might also be Engels speaking for or through Marx, it might be the two of them speaking together, it might be them debating each other, and it might also be satirical, parodic, or ironical.[30] The idea of the philosopher's voice thus breaks down at the level of authorship when we turn to Marx. This is not just a superficial matter. The breakdown of authority is in fact part of the content of Marx's thought. Human beings are alienated and involved in struggles for power within a class society. Marx's "authority" is itself alienated and engaged in political struggles that require collaboration and a variety of rhetorical strategies. Unlike Fichte, for example, who spoke to his political audience with the authority of a transcendental philosopher who understood the creative poetic power of his own voice, Marx speaks with the voice of one who is in the process of criticizing the ideological nature of transcendental authority. Although for convenience in what follows I will speak of Marx's voice as "one," we must keep in mind that Marx's "voice" is deliberately multivocal.

Who is Marx's Audience?

Given the fact of alienation and ideological mystification, Marx cannot speak directly to an audience that will understand him. Indeed, as we shall see when we discuss the *Communist Manifesto*, Marx's intended audience, the proletariat, did not yet exist as an audience. Moreover, Marx wrote on a series of levels for a variety of audiences: he wrote newspaper articles intended for general audiences, party platforms intended for both party leaders and for rank and file members, and theoretical economics intended for the community of philosophers and political economists. Unlike Kant, who directed his thought toward the general reading public, Marx recognized divisions within this public: class divisions, intellectual divisions, and ideological divisions. Marx's voice thus becomes plural to the extent that he engages in rhetoric appropriate to each of his different audiences. Like Fichte, who was willing to use inflammatory rhetoric when necessary, Marx consciously speaks in a political voice when the context demands it. Since his critical theoretical approach is political, Marx's voice takes on the political sound appropriate to his audience. Unlike Fichte who at least could appeal to the linguistic unity of his German audience, Marx speaks to an international audience divided not only by language but also by levels of economic and political progress.

The working class of England or of New York must be addressed differently than the German proletariat, not only because of a difference in language but also because of a difference in progress toward liberal political reform and socialist economic reform. Again, Marx's recognition of this difference in his audience indicates a further politicization of philosophy. The audience of philosophy is, for Marx, a plural political one. Unlike Hegel who speaks to and for the universal spirit of political life, Marx speaks for and to the people in their plurality. Marx's audience is not unified by an interest in enlightenment (as in Kant), a philosophical *Ursprache* (as in Fichte), or by participation in the life of spirit (as in Hegel); its divisions reflect the divisions found in contemporary European life.

Why does Marx seemingly ignore "the philosophy of language"?

Marx does not ignore language as an issue. However, he never states an explicit philosophy of language and does not publish most of his reflections on language. Indeed, Ulrich Erckenbrecht states at the beginning of his comprehensive book on Marx's philosophy of language that Marx's "tendencies toward linguistic theory yield no gapless, contradiction-free, complete system."[31] Not only are Marx's sporadic notes on language unpublished and unsystematic, but the "materialistic theory of language," which Erckenbrecht derives for Marx, owes much to Engels' works such as *Dialectics of Nature*. Reiterating the problem mentioned in # 1 above, Erckenbrecht treats Marx and Engels as one voice when it comes to the philosophy of language.[32] I maintain that we must seriously consider why Marx refrained from publishing an explicit philosophy of language. Clearly Allen Wood is correct when he states that "Marx's writings have very little to say directly about epistemology."[33] Moreover, despite wanting to follow Erckenbrecht in ascribing to Marx a "materialist" theory of language or wanting to ascribe to Marx a form of what Wood calls "linguistic behaviorism," I think Wood is correct when he concludes that "the only sensible thing to say here is that the texts do not justify ascribing any definite theory of mind to Marx and Engels."[34]

So why does Marx refrain from developing a theory of language? I maintain that Marx's rejection of the universal strain of "philosophy" associated with the German Idealist tradition led him to ignore the systematic necessity of developing a complete philosophy of language. Indeed, the content of what he does say about language leads him beyond language to society and economics. In his unpublished notes known as the *Grundrisse*, Marx states:

> With regard to the individual, for instance, it is evident that he himself relates to his language (*Sprache*) as his own only as the natural member of

> a human community. Language as the product of an individual is an absurdity. But this is equally true of property. Language itself is just as much the product of a community as in another respect it is the being of the community, its articulate being, as it were.[35]

Marx ignores language in his published texts because he is not so much interested in the "product" of society as in the mode of production, i.e., the way in which society organizes itself so as to produce language. We might also note that Marx neglects to offer an explicit account of individuality and consciousness as well, perhaps for the same reason. The best explanation of this—one that I must admit is not very satisfactory—is that since Marx's work aims at clarifying society and economics to his political audience, he leaves these fundamental questions out of his published work because they are too "abstract" to be of practical political value. In fact, we must admit that what is lacking in Marx's project is an explicit theory of language, despite numerous implicit hints.

Marx's notes on language always locate language in the concrete historical community as well as in the mode of production characteristic of a society. "Membership of a *naturally evolved society*, a tribe, etc., is a natural condition of production for the living individual. Such membership is e.g. already a condition of his language (*Bedingung für seine Sprache*), etc. His own productive being can only have existence under this condition."[36] Such hints beg to be clarified by an account of the way in which Marx's own theoretical activity is itself conditioned by the society in which he lives and writes. The problem for Marx, however, is that in modern European society individuals are alienated from themselves and from each other. It is impossible truly to formulate a complete systematic account of language in the same way that it is impossible to formulate a complete system of society. Rather, the philosophy of language, like Marx's own economic theory, is caught up in political struggle. Since language is derivative of productive activity and from social interaction, Marx leaves the idealistic project of a theory of language, subjectivity, and consciousness undeveloped and turns to his critique of economy and society. In his early "humanist" stage and in his collaboration with Engels—who was more concerned with the question of "consciousness" and "subjectivity" than Marx—in *The German Ideology*, there is a discussion of language and its relation to consciousness. However, he does not follow up on this discussion satisfactorily. The best explanation of this lapse is that Marx maintains that language, subjectivity, and consciousness are themselves "philosophical" sidetracks that lead away from the concrete historical problem: the social dominance of the bourgeoisie and the cultural hegemony of the language of capitalism. While the Idealists' concern with language stemmed from their concern—following Kant's encounter with the metacritique—for the medium in which ideas or spirit can be communicated and realized, Marx's concern with language is as the medium in which political practice unfolds. Once this has been established, Marx drops language and turns to the real problem: political action.

Language and Voice

> "Spirit" is from the outset afflicted with the curse of being "burdened" (*behaftet*) with matter, which here makes its appearance in the form of agitated layers of sounds, in short, of language. Language is as old as consciousness, language *is* practical, real consciousness that exists for other men as well, and only therefore does it also exist for me; language, like consciousness, only arises from the need (*Bedürfnis*), the necessity (*Notdurf*) of intercourse with other men.
>
> —Marx, *The German Ideology*[37]

So how does Marx justify his transformation of philosophy into politics? We can answer this question by examining Marx's undeveloped "philosophy of language." Marx's materialism makes him acutely aware of the way in which theoretical activity is tied to language. The above description of the "curse" that burdens consciousness—a curse not for Marx but for his idealist opponents—shows that for Marx "spirit" necessarily must appear in and as language. Marx's materialism extends so far as to claim that language and consciousness are merely "agitated layers of sound" that occur in a social context. Marx's debt to Hegel is apparent here in the way he understands language in terms of sound and in terms of the need that gives rise to language. Indeed, Marx uses Hegelian language to express the relation, mediated by language, between thought and nature. In the *1844 Manuscripts* he states that "the element of thought itself—the element of thought's living expression (*das Element der Lebensäusserung des Gedankens*)—*language*—is of a sensuous nature."[38] Marx, like Hegel, recognizes the necessity that thought express itself in language. He also recognizes that language is itself the connection between thought and nature. Language is sensuous. It is material. It is "agitated layers of sound" that is "thought's living expression." However, Marx's view is an inversion of the Hegelian view. Hegel understood voice as the externalization of spirit that was necessary for spirit to become objective. Marx understands sound as the material basis of "spirit," by which he means that spirit is itself the result of material forces. Thus Marx understands spirit as the subjectivity of objective forces, a view quite the opposite of Hegel's. The irony of Marx's statement that spirit is "burdened" by its material appearance is further clarified by Marx's recognition that spirit simply is its material appearance. Indeed, Marx goes so far as to identify consciousness (at least developmentally) with language. As he says above, "language is as old as consciousness." Both the Hegelian idea that spirit is something other than its material objectivity, its origin, or its result, and Hegel's attempt to use ordinary language to speak for that self-consciousness which is other than the grammar and syntax of ordinary language are rejected by Marx as part of the bourgeois ideology in which wage-slavery is freedom, in which oppression is equality, and in which exploitation is profit.

Although Marx's discussion of language is not as systematic as Hegel's (or, for that matter, Fichte's), it is clear that Marx has some idea of the Hegelian account of language. Marx agrees with Hegel in his recognition of the fact that language and spirit are social products. Indeed, Marx's account of the evolution of language shares much in common with both Hegel's and Fichte's accounts of the social nature of language. Fichte had grounded transcendental philosophy in the fact that language was the condition for the possibility of human freedom as intersubjectivity. This led him eventually to recognize the social and historical location of thinking. He thus recognized that thinking must use finite historical language to complete the system of itself. However, Fichte took the easy way out and simply hypostatized the German language as the philosophical *Ursprache*. Hegel too had grounded consciousness in language. However, Hegel argued that the completion of the philosophical system would occur as thinking became self-conscious of the necessity of its determination by finite historical language. For Hegel, freedom resulted, as spirit became aware of the necessity of its own historical and social manifestation.

The crucial difference with Marx is that Marx recognizes that if language and consciousness are understood as the result of concrete practical social interactions, then philosophy itself is a political activity. Marx claims that "consciousness is, therefore, from the beginning a social product, and remains so as long as men exist at all."[39] Hegel and Fichte might agree to this, although they would use the concrete social determinacy of language and consciousness as a springboard to leap to the universal. Here Marx would balk and demand that we stop to recognize that there is no uniformity in social experience. Just as Fichte recognized differential national experiences within national languages, Marx recognizes differential social experiences within social class. Hence, for Marx, there is no a priori transcendental ego that overcomes the "burden" of expressing itself in ordinary language by speaking in an *Ursprache*; there is no universal spirit that attains self-consciousness of the relation between ordinary language and philosophical comprehension. The universal is yet to come and can only arrive by a political transformation. The Fichtean appeal to the transformative philosophical power of the *Ursprache* and the creative power of the philosopher's poetic voice would have appeared to Marx—despite his own rhetorical flourishes—as an ideological mystification of the material basis of language and consciousness.

Although language is material, language alone cannot change consciousness because mere language cannot change the material basis of consciousness. Rather what is needed is practical transformation. Although practical transformation, too, will be accompanied by language, mere words remain impotent if they are not tied to political activity. What is necessary for the completion of progress toward freedom is not mere theory—as in Hegel—but, rather, more and better practice. While Hegel believed that the completion of history occurred when spirit became aware of itself as historically determined, Marx believed that this self-awareness was just the beginning of history. Moving forward from Fichte and Hegel's recognition of the material, social, and historical basis of language and consciousness, Marx took up the task of transforming this basis in line with the needs and interests of one part of contemporary society.

Hegel's attempt to maintain the rigor of philosophy against the enthusiasm of Fichte's rhetorical dogmatics led Hegel into what Marx saw as philosophical isolation—the proverbial retreat to the ivory tower. In the *Rheinische Zeitung* in 1842, Marx makes this clear in his discussion of press censorship, philosophy, religion, and the popular press. "Philosophy," Marx says, "has an urge for isolation, for systematic seclusion, for dispassionate self-examination which from the start places it in estranged contrast to the quick-witted and alive-to-events newspapers, whose only delight is in information."[40] He goes on to say that philosophy is "unpopular," "unpractical" and that "philosophy has never taken the first step towards exchanging the ascetic frock of the priest for the light, conventional garb of the newspapers."[41] In his own political interventions Marx self-consciously defrocked himself by returning language to life.

The practical quest of Marxian philosophy will be achieved, in part, by teaching philosophy to properly understand the nature of its connection to language and to life. In *The German Ideology* Marx opens a discussion of the way in which philosophy under Hegel has misunderstood itself and its relation to language. The problem of philosophy is that it ignores its dependence upon language. As Marx says, "language is the immediate actuality of thought."[42] Marx claims that the philosophers do not recognize this linguistic basis. As we have seen, this polemic is perhaps unjust. Both Fichte and Hegel were aware of the linguistic basis of thinking. Hegel, moreover, tried to locate language and its connection to thinking within his systematic project. Hegel, at least, knew that he had to account for the linguistic medium in which philosophy occurred. Marx goes deeper than this in his criticism. Marx's conclusion is that philosophy ignores the fact that its very language is a reflection of the social system and the social class occupied by the philosopher. "German philosophy is a consequence of German petty-bourgeois conditions."[43] The problem for philosophy was that it did not yet properly recognize its social and political location: Hegel did not realize that he spoke only for and to the bourgeoisie when he called the ideals of this class the universal ideals of humanity. We might object at this point that Hegel was aware of the fact that he spoke to and for the bourgeoisie as seen in our discussion of the address of Hegel's *Philosophy of Right*. However, this only proves Marx's point. Hegel's deliberate neglect of the rabble (and women) as an address of his political philosophy only proves Marx's point that Hegelian philosophy is bourgeois (and patriarchal).

Marx concludes this discussion of language in *The German Ideology* by claiming that the remaining task for philosophy is to understand its own ideological mystifications by understanding the nature of language.

> The philosophers have only to dissolve their language into the ordinary language (*gewöhnliche Sprache*), from which it is abstracted, in order to recognize it as the distorted language of the actual world, and to realize that neither thoughts nor language in themselves form a realm of their own, that they are only *expressions* (*Außerungen*) of actual life.[44]

The theme of connecting philosophical language with ordinary life was one that we saw in both Fichte and Hegel. While Fichte connected thinking to the *Ursprache*, and while Hegel wanted to make spirit self-conscious of its sameness and difference with its linguistic mode of expression, Marx, like Feuerbach, demands that philosophy understand itself and its language within the actual life of real human beings. Marx's description of this actual life recognizes that it is constituted by suffering, oppression, and exploitation of the working class. Distorted philosophical language is used by a dominant class to carry out the oppression and exploitation of the suffering class. Where Hegel had said that language was the expression of the implicit spirit, Marx says that language is the expression of the actual conditions of life. The distortions of philosophical language are thus of more than mere philosophical interest because they serve, as ideology, to justify the inequities of class society. In order to return to the problems of material life, one must interpret the material basis that expresses itself in the ideologist's language.

Despite this criticism of philosophy, Marx maintains respect for the universal aspirations of philosophy. Just as capitalism has its virtues in terms of increased productivity, so bourgeois philosophy has its virtues in terms of its idea of universal freedom. The problem is that philosophy has not yet properly understood itself and the consequences of this idea. Marx remains committed to philosophy (which he prefers to call theory or science) to the extent that it is more and better philosophy—including a better understanding of the ideological nature of language and theory—that undermines ideology and accompanies concrete political practice. In another article from the *Rheinische Zeitung*, Marx writes that philosophy should not become a species of relativism. Rather philosophy's virtue is its universal aspiration.[45] This universal aspiration is progressive. The problem with Fichte was that he remained committed to a nationalism that belied this universalism; the problem with Hegel was that he was blind to the class biases inherent within his universalism. This universal aspiration cannot be realized while there are classes that are excluded from the address of the philosopher's voice. Marx turns to political activity in order to prepare the ground for further progress. Such a preparation requires, however, the recognition that the philosopher's voice can only, as yet, speak for and to a given class within our divided society. To claim otherwise is to succumb to the temptations of the bourgeois ideology.

The Ambiguity of the Philosopher's Voice

> The head of this emancipation is philosophy, its heart is the proletariat.
>
> —Marx, "Contribution to the Critique of Hegel's Philosophy of Right"[46]

Marx wants philosophers to recognize the social and linguistic location of their philosophical activity. The heart of his theory is the experience of the proletariat. In articles from the *Rheinische Zeitung* Marx discusses both of these in a defense of philosophy against its superficial journalistic detractors. This is remarkable because Marx also claims that, in general, philosophy is not yet aware of its social and linguistic determinations. On the one hand, philosophy tends toward isolation and seclusion. Nonetheless, on the other hand, Marx claims that "philosophers do not spring up like mushrooms out of the ground; they are products of their time, of their nation, whose most subtle, valuable and invisible juices flow in the ideas of philosophy."[47] By 1844 in his "Economic and Philosophical Manuscripts" Marx has arrived at the conclusion that theory itself is a social activity. This conclusion is linked to the claim that thinking is a social activity because it is mediated by language, which is itself a social product. "Not only is the material of my activity given to me as a social product—as is even the language in which the thinker is active (*die Sprache, in der Denker thätig ist*)—my own existence is social activity . . ."[48] Like Fichte and Hegel, Marx recognizes the social nature of language and the self. He goes beyond both Fichte and Hegel by recognizing that theory itself, i.e., philosophy or science, is a social activity. This is true because language is social. The meaning of those "agitated layers of sound" that make up language is socially constituted; the activity of using sound to transmit meaning is social activity.

Marx is thus sympathetic to philosophical activity that recognizes its own social nature. Although Marx ignores both Fichte and Hegel's linguistic philosophies, these would have been viewed as steps in the right direction. The remaining task was to express the social nature of language and of theory in general in its connection to the lived experience of social reality. Philosophy must thus recognize oppression, exploitation, and suffering in real life. It must also use the language of ordinary life to express this. The article from 1842 makes it clear that the young Marx was hopeful about the possibility that philosophy might yet realize its universal aspirations by becoming aware of its own social and linguistic components. "Since every true philosophy is the intellectual quintessence of its time, the time must come when philosophy not only internally by its content, but also externally through its form, comes into contact and interaction with the real world of its day."[49] Philosophy must learn to express itself in popular form and to understand its connection to the experience of living individuals. Marx concludes that philosophy must take up the popular form of newspaper articles and popular manifestos if it is to participate in the actualization of its ideals. The remaining problem, however, is that philosophers speak differently than journalists and politicians. Addressing journalists and politicians explicitly, Marx says:

> But philosophy speaks about religious and philosophical matters in a different way than you have spoken about them. You speak without having studied them, philosophy speaks after studying them; you appeal to the emotions, it appeals to reason; you anathematize, it teaches; you promise heaven and earth, it promises nothing but the truth; you demand belief in your beliefs, it demands not belief in its results but the testing of doubts; you frighten, it calms.[50]

The virtue of philosophical language is its patient aspiration toward the truth. Marx's discussion of the philosophical way of speaking sounds surprisingly Hegelian and seems to be opposed to Fichte's sort of dogmatic political intervention. It is important to note that Marx's defense of philosophical language is itself expressed in polemical terms with great rhetorical effect and appears in a newspaper. Marx himself has thus begun the process of breaking down the distinction that he just drew between philosophy and journalism. In the subsequent six years from this discussion to the publication of the *Communist Manifesto*, Marx's theory of language and the relation between theory and practice become more radically focused around the idea that the isolation and seclusion of philosophical practice and the remoteness and aridity of philosophical language are functions of ideology. Philosophy's pursuit of universal truth is impotent because philosophical language remains aloof from political actuality.

The difficulty for Marx is to bring language into accord with the world of concrete experience, to express the lived truth of this concrete experience without slipping yet again into the isolation and seclusion of philosophy. In1847 in *The Poverty of Philosophy*, for example, Marx argues that Proudhon's problem is that he has not grounded his theory in the concrete reality of economic life. Indeed, one of Marx's most memorable criticisms of Proudhon is the claim that Proudhon had misunderstood the question of the "value of labor." Proudhon, according to Marx, avoided the question of the value of labor by considering it a matter of linguistic carelessness to ascribe value to labor. Of course, Marx claims that the value of labor as commodity is a social fact that cannot be erased simply by using different language. "In labor as a commodity, which is a grim reality, he sees nothing but a grammatical ellipsis."[51] Proudhon's retreat to linguistic considerations can do nothing to alter the "grim reality" of capitalism and its tendency to treat human labor as an abstract commodity. In *The Poverty of Philosophy,* Marx criticizes the tendency of philosophy to abstract from lived reality by retreating to philosophical language and logic. Proudhon's problem is that, as an isolated and secluded philosopher immersed in the German tradition, he deals only with abstract logical categories. These abstractions are impotent to the extent that they speak a language that is divorced from the concrete reality of human individuals. Philosophical language is, according to Marx, "the language of this pure reason, separate from the individual. Instead of the ordinary individual with his ordinary manner of speaking and thinking, we have nothing but this ordinary manner in itself—without the individual."[52] Here we see the opposite view of the apology for philosophy expressed in the *Rheinische Zeitung*. Now Marx claims that philosophy's problem is its inability to speak for and to the suffering masses of the material world. The problem, according to Marx, is that although philosophy claims that it remains tied to the concrete, its play of abstractions leads it beyond the concrete. It retreats to a consideration of language and logic while neglecting to connect these back to the misery of ordinary people. Whereas Hegel wanted to lift the individual up to the level of spirit by way of the "ladder" of the *Phenomenology*, Marx fears that philosophy leaves the suffering individual behind.

Worse than this, the process of abstraction reifies the status quo by making present conditions appear as necessary, the very idea of the rationality of actuality that was expressed in Hegel's infamous *Doppelsatz*. This is at once a problem of language and a problem of politics. Marx goes so far as to claim that different classes have different languages, or at least, different understandings of the practical implications of theory and its language. In

The German Ideology Marx considers some of the arguments of "bourgeois ideologists" as mere etymological mystifications. These defenders of capitalism use etymology supposedly to refute communism without, however, noticing that language itself serves the ruling class. They argue for the impossibility of abolishing private property on the ground that property (*Eigentum*) in the sense of possession and property in the sense of individual characteristic (*Eigenschaft*) are etymologically linked—as if one could not be an individual without also being an owner. These "ideologists" make the same argument with regard to other important economic and psychological terms in several languages including German, French, and English. Marx concludes that "for the bourgeois it is all the easier to prove on the basis of his language the identity of commercial and individual or even universal, human relations, as this language itself is a product of the bourgeoisie, and therefore both in actuality and in language the relations of buying and selling."[53] This reification of the status quo thus leads to the conclusion that these bourgeois ideologists only speak for and to the bourgeoisie, even as they claim to aspire to truth.

Philosophy, Politics, and Critique

> Man is a *zoon politikon* in the most literal sense: he is not only a social animal, but an animal that can individuate (*vereinzeln*) itself only within society. Production by an isolated individual (*vereinzelten einzelnen*) outside society—something rare, which might occur when a civilized person already dynamically in possession of the social forces is accidentally cast into the wilderness—is just as preposterous as the development of language without individuals who live *together* and speak to one another.
>
> —Marx, *Grundrisse*[54]

The philosophers we previously examined each had a unique response to the problem of the relation between philosophy and politics. Kant tried to avoid confronting this problem directly by deferring to the hoped-for resolution of the impasse between morality and politics in the kingdom of ends. Fichte celebrated the fact that philosophy could be made political and that political life could be made philosophical in the medium of the philosophical *Ursprache*. Hegel attempted to comprehend the nature of the entanglement and to unite political action and theoretical *Nachdenken*. These three responses remained committed to the idea that progress in both philosophy and politics would occur by way of properly mediating this complex interaction of voice and audience, form and content, idea and actuality by using reason, as if reason were itself still other than this conflict, the universal toward which philosophy and politics strove. Kant's problem of mediating between the morality of pure practical reason and the politics of empirical life, Fichte's problem of preparing the empirico-historical ground for the completion of transcendental philosophy, Hegel's problem of locating philosophy in history—each of these problematics assumed that there was one universal principle by which philosophy and politics could be united: transcendental ego, *Ursprache*, spirit. Each also assumed that the problem of the philosopher's voice was not intractable. Kant, avoiding the metacritical question of language, assumed that philosophy and politics both spoke the republican language of reason, which infiltrated the metaphorics of his critical project. Fichte responded to the metacritique by claiming that the German *Ursprache* was the voice of reason through which transcendental idealism could transform political life. Hegel asserted that the ladder from ordinary to philosophical language could be discovered and mounted because the spirit that expressed itself in ordinary language was also the spirit that knew itself in logic. With Marx, however, the problem of philosophy was not to resolve the conflict between philosophy and politics by way of some universal medium but, rather, to understand the fissures that remain within this medium. The political nature of philosophy can be understood in terms of the divisions in the medium through which universal reason was supposedly transmitted. For Marx, since language is social, and since society is fractured, language is fractured too. Marx thus rejects the dogmatics of a universal reason that ignored the conflicts that disrupted the totality of ego, *Ursprache*, or spirit. Marx's goal in this context is to make explicit the political nature of the philosopher's voice.

This interpretation runs counter to a facile interpretation of Marx, which claims that he offers us a theory of politics that strives to complete the Hegelian system.[55] I maintain, on the contrary, that Marx rejects the Hegelian philosophical approach to politics in favor of a political approach to philosophy. Marx's goal is critical and his critique shares something in common with the Kantian critique. However, Marx politicizes the Kantian critical method. Marx rejects the totalizing trend that he critiques in the philosophical tradition, i.e., the Kantian method, which uses critique to discover the a priori universality of pure reason. Critique for Marx is understood as a political activity involved in struggles for power in the real world of concrete living individuals. For Kant, critical philosophical activity had been the proper method in which republican politics could progress because critique, like republican politics, was concerned with developing human autonomy. However, Kant's critique aimed at an abstract universal autonomy that had no immediate political implications. While Kantian critique had attempted to remain aloof from political activity understood in terms of concrete political struggles for the same reason that it remained aloof from the arational struggles of history, Marx's critique announces itself as political just as it conceives of history as the locus of struggles for power. For Marx, theory is political in the sense that it is always involved in the ongoing power struggles that determine the meaning of the language used in articulating the critical theory.[56]

Marx politicizes critical activity by criticizing its transcendental aspirations and by locating his own voice within the struggles of political life. He speaks for the proletariat against the bourgeoisie, and he admits that his voice will sound terrible to a bourgeois audience. Marx is not interested in critique as the reconciliation of society with its spirit (as in Hegel) or in critique as part of a process of republican reform of society under the aegis of universal reason (as in Kant). Rather, for Marx, critique is an act of (possibly violent) protest, practiced against the oppressors on behalf of the oppressed.[57] Marx does not define "politics" in terms of friendly dialogue and debate (as in Kant's republican vision). Despite his praise for democracy in his *Critique of Hegel's Philosophy of Right* and other places, democracy requires revolution. The problem of the Kantian republican ideal is that it remained merely an ideal contradicted by reality, an ideology that must be criticized. Revolution was Marx's political solution because Marx rejected the Kantian legacy of rational hope and came to understand politics as a concrete struggle for the power to define concepts like "morality," "justice," and "reason." For Marx, the philosopher's voice must become part of this struggle for power and should see through the ideological illusion which claims that reason is somehow above the fray.

Marx criticizes the Kantian critical project and its attendant hope that the universality of reason will produce a moral politics. Indeed, he views such universal rationalism as the hollow core of German bourgeois ideology. Marx's reductive materialist understanding of Kant gives us an insight into the political nature of Marx's own method. In *The German Ideology* Marx claims that since the German bourgeoisie was "impotent" politically, it retreated to the Kantian idea of "the good will" in order to console itself for its own impotence.

> Kant was satisfied with 'good will' alone, even if it remained entirely without result, and he transferred the realization of this good will, the harmony between it and the needs and impulses of individuals, to the world beyond. Kant's good will fully corresponds to the impotence, depression and wretchedness of the German burghers . . .[58]

According to Marx, Kant divorced liberal theory from political practice because liberalism was not yet viable in Germany. This would explain, for example, the trouble that Kant had vis-à-vis revolutionary activity, as I discussed in Chapter 4. Marx diagnoses this problem as resulting from the Germans' inability to properly understand the practical significance of their own theoretical aspirations. Because of their political impotence, they divorced thought from will, interest, and activity, such that they could not understand the force with which the liberal ideas of freedom and equality ripped through France during the revolution. "Kant, therefore, separated this theoretical expression (*Ausdruck*) from the interests which it expressed (*ausdrückt*)... Hence the German petty bourgeois recoiled in horror from the practice of this energetic bourgeois liberalism as soon as this practice showed itself, both in the Reign of Terror and in shameless bourgeois profit-making."[59] For Marx, in opposition to Kant, critique is political activity.

Indeed, for Marx, it is not too much to say that the revolutionary political will of the oppressed gives rise to the critical theory of capitalism. As Marx states in the *Manifesto,*

> the theoretical conclusions of the Communists are in no way based on ideas or principles that have been invented, or discovered, by this or that would-be universal reformer. They are merely general expressions (*allgemeine Ausdrücke*) of actual relations springing from an existing class struggle, from a historical movement going on under our very eyes.[60]

According to Marx, the proletariat already experiences its own degradation. The critical theorist simply makes this experience explicit. Just as Hegel held that philosophy was the explicit comprehension of the implicit unity of subject and object, Marx holds that Communism is the explicit comprehension of the implicit revolutionary will of the proletariat. Unlike Hegel, however, this process of expression and explication is, for Marx, unavoidably political. By making the subjective will and experience of the proletariat explicit, Marx's critical theory of capitalism enters into conflict with the theory and experience of the bourgeoisie. In this sense, Marx's critique of political economy and his revolutionary activity are linked: both are engaged in the political struggle that results as the experience of the proletariat becomes objective.

Critical Responses to Marx's Critique

> I am speaking of a ruthless criticism of all that exists, ruthless both in the sense of not being afraid of the results it arrives at and in the sense of being just as little afraid of conflict with the powers that be.
>
> —Marx, "Letter to Ruge, September 1843"[61]

Marx explicitly opens himself to criticism, noting that his theory must not be afraid of those it antagonizes. Indeed, the spirit of his critical project invites us to continue in this spirit to raise criticisms against him. Two questions arise with regard to the interpretation of Marx I am propounding in the present chapter. First, what description of the relation between thought and reality allows Marx to reject, in the name of critique, the Kantian critical project? Second, how can Marx reject the universal rationalist project of Kantian critique without contradicting himself? I will discuss these each in turn.

How does Marx reject the Kantian critical project?

> The *task of history*, therefore, once the *world beyond the truth* has disappeared, is to establish the *truth of this world*. The immediate *task of philosophy* (*Aufgabe der Philosophie*), which is at the service of history, once the *holy form* of human self-estrangement has been unmasked, is to unmask self-estrangement in its *unholy forms*. Thus the criticism of heaven turns into the criticism of earth, the *criticism of religion* into the *criticism of law*, and the *criticism of theology* into the *criticism of politics*.
>
> —Marx, "Contribution to the Critique of Hegel's *Philosophy of Right*"[62]

Marx conceives of history as inherently conflictual and of critique as immersed in this conflict. There is no universal endpoint of historical development, nor of criticism. Rather, history and criticism are political struggles. He recognizes, as early as 1843, that his project will lead to a collision with his own philosophical predecessors and that this collision will be political. "Now philosophy has become mundane, and the most striking proof of this is that philosophical consciousness itself has been drawn into the torment of the struggle, not only externally but also internally."[63] Political struggle infects the supposed purity of philosophy. Contra Kant who had postulated, from the standpoint of transcendental reason, an infinitely deferred convergence between justice and morality, Marx sees this claim as itself a political one. It was this point of convergence, the kingdom of ends, which provided Kant with a transcendental position from which to criticize political actuality. Marx rejects this idea of the transcendental point of convergence, claiming instead that the transcendent standpoint is used to defend the bourgeois ideology. In other words, Marx's rejects what has been called "the moral point of view" as distinct from the merely legal point of view. Marx goes so far as to equate the Kantian ideal with the values of the social class to which it appeals: it is a bourgeois ideology. The problem with the moral point of view, according to Marx, is that it deceitfully postulates a universal morality when, in reality, this morality is simply the view of a minority social class.

Questions of justice, goodness, etc. are, for Marx, political questions to be resolved by way of political contestation.[64] Moreover, Marx recognizes that some of the antagonisms between rival moral viewpoints will be intractable and will ultimately lead to violence. Despite his "common sense realism," Marx rejects Kant's critical moral project and returns us to a Hobbesian universe in which Kant's transcendental critical reason has no role to play. This throws the traditional distinction between philosophy and politics into doubt. As Miller concludes, reflecting a now familiar critique of liberalism, "there are conflicting conceptions of the good that cannot be resolved through rational persuasion."[65] For Marx, philosophy is no longer abstract theory patiently persuading political agents by appealing to the abstract truth about morality. Rather, philosophy is politicized to the extent that the very language of morality and reason has been appropriated by ideology in defense of the power of the dominant class. This leads Marx, finally to the famous conclusion that "the arm of criticism cannot replace the criticism of arms."[66] In other words, political activity—struggle for power—and philosophical activity—criticism of ideology—work in tandem, each addressing a different aspect within the strategies of political revolution. Despite this reduction of philosophy to power politics, philosophical activity remains essential. "Material force can only be overthrown by material force; but theory itself becomes a material force when it has seized the masses."[67] Theory is a vital adjunct to practice, although as Marx makes clear, the goal is no longer merely the truth as such. Rather, theory must address its political audience in its own language in order to stimulate the development of self-consciousness in this audience. Philosophy for Marx is interested activity addressed to the needs of a political audience, not disinterested passivity addressed to spirit. Marx states clearly that "Theory is only realized in a people so far as it fulfills the needs of the people."[68] Theory that is to realize its ideals must make itself practical by addressing itself explicitly to the needs of the class it represents. This leads us to the second question of whether Marx, in rejecting the Kantian project, contradicts himself by stating a universal claim about the necessary particularity of philosophical activity.

Is Marx inconsistent in his rejection of universality?

> Right can never be higher than the economic structure of society and its cultural development.
>
> —Marx, "Critique of the Gotha Program"[69]

Given the content of his claims about the practical interested particularity of theoretical activity, Marx has to give up on the universalist aspirations of the Kantian project. He states quite plainly in his "Critique of the Gotha Program" that ideals such as fairness, equality, and right are bourgeois ideals:

their supposed universality belies the limited scope of their application. Although such ideals have rhetorical force in stimulating revolutionary activity, Marx is wary of confusing these bourgeois ideals with the as yet-to-be-determined ideals of the proletariat. "What a crime it is to attempt to force on our Party again, as dogmas, ideas which in a certain period had some meaning but have now become obsolete verbal rubbish, while perverting the realistic outlook, which it cost so much effort to instill into the Party . . ."[70] Marx recognizes the changeable nature of consciousness in its relation to the mode of production, class, historical development, etc. His critique is thus supposed to be an immanent critique in which the supposed universality of the bourgeois ideals is exposed as a fraud. The problem is whether Marx can consistently claim that universal truths are ideological. I examined this problem earlier under the discussion of ideology and concluded that Marx's critique of ideology is not universal but local and political: it is the capitalists who self-interestedly make false claims about the universality of morality.

At his most extreme—and therefore at his politically most effective—Marx reduces moral concepts to the economic structure in which they arise and are meaningful. "Right can never be higher than the economic structure of society and its cultural development."[71] This theme broadens what he says in the *Manifesto* and in *The German Ideology* about the "ruling ideas being the ideas of the ruling class." Marx rejects the notion that there is a standard higher than or exterior to social life from which moral ideas derive their validity. When political struggle exists, it is obvious that rival moral ideas are in conflict. Marx claims that the struggle between proletariat and bourgeoisie is a historical fact and that both sides will disagree about the meaning of moral concepts. Within this struggle, Marx's "moral theory" is addressed to a particular audience—the proletariat—and derives its validity from the experience of that audience. Marx does not claim that his audience is the universal human audience. Indeed the content of Marx's own theory—its social determinism—will only be accepted as valid for a particular audience: the bourgeoisie will misinterpret Marx if they claim that his theory is "philosophical" or "moral" in the Kantian sense and ignore its political nature. For the most part, only the proletariat will understand Marx's claims about the socially determinate nature of theoretical activity, and thus the theory is primarily addressed to them. This psychosocial claim about cognitive differences among social classes is supported by the fact that only the proletariat concretely experiences those forms of oppression and alienation, which are the content of Marx's theory. Proletarians live the experience of alienation, which is the basis of conflict and struggle in both theory and practice. Marx rejects the Kantian/bourgeois notion of a "pure" individual who is not divided against himself: proletarians do not experience themselves in this way. Rather, current social institutions create, for the proletarians at least, "a cleavage in the life of each individual, insofar as it is personal and insofar as it is determined by some branch of labor and the conditions pertaining to it."[72] Thus only the proletarian will agree with Marx's account of the way in which theoretical determinations are always involved in a struggle between opposed forces. While the bourgeois might claim that there is a universal truth about human being and the moral good, the proletarian experiences the world and himself as self-divided and thus rejects this claim.

Marx places theory firmly in the midst of political struggle. Indeed, he concludes that the proletarian experience of the political nature of division (its origin in struggles for power) leads the proletariat to become revolutionary. "Thus they find themselves directly opposed to the form in which, hitherto, the individuals, of which society consists, have given themselves collective expression (*Gesamtausdruck*), that is, the state; in order, therefore, to assert themselves as individuals, they must overthrow the state."[73] The proletariat experiences itself as self-divided and sees that this self-division is created by the dominant mode of production and its institutions. The proletariat is revolutionary in the sense that it implicitly understands itself as opposed to the dominant interests of the ruling class and is not constrained by the liberal humanism of the bourgeois ideology. Kant's reluctance to espouse revolution on moral grounds would thus be seen by Marx as an example of morality serving the interest of the dominant ideology. The proletariat would acknowledge Marx's claims about the necessity of revolution because their experience of the world is structured by disunity and conflict and not by the experience of the unity of reason, which the Kantian critical theory presupposes.

Allen Wood makes the revolutionary character of Marx's politicized philosophy clear in his interpretation of Marx's "concept of justice" as caught up in political struggle.[74] The claim that someone knows the truth about justice is a political claim: it is a comment on current social and political institutions and one's status within them. We must consider for whom the philosopher or politician speaks when they make their claims about justice: which class? under what mode of production? Wood ignores this politicized conclusion in his attempt to interpret Marx as an "immoralist," i.e., one who is concerned with alleviating nonmoral evil.[75] Wood nonetheless explains quite nicely the nature of Marx's nonmoral critique of moral concepts: "A higher mode of production is not 'more just' than a lower one; it is only just in its own way."[76] I agree with this: Wood is right that Marx's theory does not impose an a priori notion of justice upon society.

It is important to emphasize, however, that the "adjustment" of moral concepts to mode of production of which Wood speaks is a revolutionary political process.[77] Marx's idea of the political situatedness of moral concepts is essential for understanding the political nature of his own theory: he speaks for and to a politicized audience and makes no pretense of appealing to a universal audience. Despite his more mature "reformist" or "gradualist" revisions of his revolutionary goal, we must take Marx's radical politics seriously, as when he writes to the bourgeoisie in the famous Red Edition of the *Neue Rheinische Zeitung*: "We are ruthless, we ask no mercy from you. When our turn comes we will practice terrorism without trying to prettify what we do."[78] Marx's theoretical activity is thus predicated upon the necessity of radical political activity.[79]

Conclusion

This brings us to the question of whom Marx is addressing in his texts. I will take this question up in earnest in the next chapter. It should be clear already, however, that Marx has a complex audience in mind, even though his primary addressee is the proletariat. This audience is necessarily complex because the proletariat, as Marx envisioned it, was not yet existent. We can see that this leads to a troubling problem for Marx: Marx addresses an audience that does not yet exist and yet claims that he speaks for that audience. The problem is whether Marx claims to have constructed a universal philosophy of history that comprehends the totality of history, as Habermas says, from "a point of view outside this process from which the system as a whole can be comprehended critically and convicted of its obsolescence."[80] Habermas views Marx as the last great practitioner of the enlightenment project of critique. He claims, moreover, that for us the totalizing view presupposed by this critical project has become problematic. I maintain, however, that Marx is the end of the critical project in the sense that he politicizes the totalizing aspirations of this project.

Marx's implicit theory of language contains an epistemology that locates consciousness within social determinations. However, this theory remains implicit for strategic reasons. Marx resists the temptation of becoming mired in abstract epistemological debates. Thus his rhetoric about the experience of the proletariat as "the universal class" must be interpreted as politically motivated, despite Lukács's attempt to locate Marxian "science" in the universal experience of this class.[81] Marx does not want to engage in a battle of abstract universals with the Idealists; rather, he uses their language to inspire the proletariat to engage in concrete political struggles for power. Nonetheless, the implicit epistemology found in Marx's sporadic notes on language and consciousness transform totalizing philosophy into concrete political activity. Marx's claims about the scientific nature of his theory must be reassessed in light of the fact that Marx's social theory of language forces him to admit that concepts are socially determined and thus leads him to reject the epistemological problematic of Kant, Fichte, and Hegel. Marx's socialist critique of ideology and the "realist theory of knowledge" ascribed to him by Habermas and Wood go hand in hand.[82] It is Marx's materialist empiricism that leads him to the conclusion that language is politically powerful and socially located. This further leads him to reject the Idealists' epistemological problematic as another ideological obfuscation of the political location of philosophical activity. The subject-object problem obscures the important empirical fact that words are abbreviations for social relations. Marx's goal is not to accompany Kant, Fichte, and Hegel into the a priori universality of idealism—an approach that leads to ideological blindness to the lack of universality in concrete political life. Rather, his goal is to help the proletariat attain consciousness of its political identity within the hegemonic struggles of modern social life. Starting with the immediate experience of the proletariat, Marx claims that this class experiences the world as essentially alienated and alienating. Marx realizes that attempts to defend his socialist interpretation of mind, language, and morality would be rejected by the ideologists who use idealism to defend the bourgeois status quo. Moreover, such epistemological ramblings would distract from the concrete task of constructing political identity for a class whose experience is based upon a lack of such an identity.[83]

Marx, like Fichte, acts as a prophet: his goal is to unite his audience, albeit not under the universal idea of transcendental idealism but rather under the concrete fact of class oppression and socially constituted alienation. He uses language to inspire and inflame his audience with consciousness of their oppression. Unlike Fichte, Marx gives up on the claim that his audience is universal. He does not claim that the universal truth can be expressed in an *Ursprache,* which functions as the medium for the truths of cosmopolitan enlightenment. Nor does he maintain that his political audience will ultimately be reconciled to the universal moral truth. Rather, Marx carries Fichte's nationalistic conclusion forward into the struggles of international class politics. For Marx, the philosopher's voice is the voice of a part of humanity, not the voice of the whole.

CHAPTER 10

Marx's Voice: Political Action and Political Language

> Far from it being true that "out of nothing" I make myself, for example, as a "speaker" (*als sprechenden*), the nothing which forms the basis here is a very manifold something, the real individual, his speech organs, a definite state of physical development, an existing language and dialects (*vorhandene Sprache und Dialekte*), ears capable of hearing and human environment from which it is possible to hear something, etc., etc..
>
> —Marx, *The German Ideology*[1]

Marx's legacy is mixed. If we discount Marx's economics, if we view his revolutionary political practice as either sadistic or naïve, if we look at his theory of class-politics as hopelessly reductive, we must still confront the fact that Marx opens the question of the historical and social basis of philosophical activity. For Marx, the philosopher's voice is, like all voices, understood as a material product. Rather than conceiving his own voice as the expression of some transcendent subjectivity or the universal spirit of history, Marx locates his own voice within concrete struggles for power. This interpretation, the one I will defend in the present chapter, runs counter to the one offered by Seyla Benhabib who claims that Marx inherited from Hegel a monological theory in which "purposeful or intentional activity is described with the help of a prelinguistic model."[2] Benhabib's concern is that Marx's emphasis on alienation within productive processes assumes that human productive activity is teleologically governed by subjective intentionality in which the products of labor are objects of human will. The result is, according to Benhabib, that Marx denies the plurality of human experience by uniting human beings, not under "spirit" or "ego" but under the "politics of class."[3] In what follows, I will not deny that Marx emphasizes "class" as opposed to concrete individuality: in fact I will argue that Marx views himself as the spokesman for the working class. However, I will argue that Marx's rejection of the universalist approach of the German Idealist tradition, when combined with his self-consciousness of the social location of his own voice, leads Marx to recognize that "the" philosopher's voice is unavoidably plural.

Ironically Marx's view of the unity of theory and practice has its roots in German Idealism. Whereas Kant and Hegel remained hopeful of the possibility of unifying theory and practice in the voice of the reflective philosopher, Marx maintains that this hoped-for unity requires philosophers to reinterpret their voices in terms of political activity. This is the meaning of his famous Eleventh Thesis on Feuerbach. This gives Marx much in common with Fichte.[4] While Kant and Hegel saw philosophy as distinct from action, Fichte had emphasized activity as the basis of the transcendental ego. Like Fichte, Marx does not give up on theory; rather, he recognizes that theory is itself a part of action. However, unlike Fichte, Marx acknowledges that human activity and voice are plural. Marx's goal is not to avoid theory but to locate it within the plurality of concrete political action.

Following Feuerbach's materialist response to Hegel, Marx recognized the necessity with which philosophy must enter into political struggle. One of the recurrent themes in Feuerbach's criticism of Idealism is the monological model in which reason is derived from the isolated ego. Feuerbach socializes reason in an inversion of the Hegelian dialectic, which progressed from the plurality of communal life to the unity of spirit. Feuerbach also recognizes the plurality of communal life. However, he demands that we recognize this plurality, not reduce it to the unity of spirit, because plurality is the material truth of human being.

> Only through communication and conversation between man and man do ideas arise. Not alone, but only with others, does one reach notions and reason in general. Two human beings are needed for the generation of man—of the spiritual as well as of the physical man; the community of man with man is the first principle and criterion of truth and generality.[5]

This social theory of truth has roots in Kant's discussion of the "touchstone" of truth, as I discussed in Chapters 3 and 4. Feuerbach develops the Kantian approach in the direction of a thoroughgoing empiricism which also recognizes that thinking is dialogical: "The true dialectic is not a monologue of a solitary thinker with himself; it is a dialogue between I and thou."[6]

Marx's debt to Feuerbach thus extends to a political interpretation of Feuerbach's rejection of the monological model of transcendental reason: the I and thou that carry on the dialogue are interpreted by Marx in terms of the divergent interests of opposed classes. This raises the political problem of whether different classes can speak one another's languages. Moreover, given Marx's awareness of the power of ideology to convert a limited perspective into the appearance of universal truth, the problem becomes one of preparing the ground for genuine dialogue by undermining the dominant ideology's appearance of universal truth. As early as his doctoral dissertation Marx claims that philosophy must confront the world of appearance with an act of will, "inspired by the urge to realize itself, it enters into tension against the other."[7] The point here is that philosophical critique appears to the world at large as untrue. It must combat this appearance by also combating that which appears as truth in the world. Like Fichte, Marx realized that philosophy cannot succeed unless it actively engages its other, i.e., the "appearances" of political life. This theme leads us all the way back to Socrates' trial. However, Marx's twist on this eternal conflict between appearance and reality is his recognition that the conflict results, not in the triumph of philosophy in the "real" world outside Plato's cave but, rather, in the politicization of philosophy "The result is that as the world becomes philosophical, philosophy also becomes worldly."[8] Since struggle is the commonsense fact from which Marx begins, he can thus claim that philosophy is always already political in the sense that it already engages—even if unwittingly—in struggles for influence and power. Marx thus further radicalizes both Fichte's move toward politics and Feuerbach's move toward dialogue: language cannot unify philosophical politics because language is plural and political.

Struggle, Politics, and Identity

> The mode of production of material life conditions the social, political, and intellectual life process in general.
>
> —Marx, *Contribution to the Critique of Political Economy*[9]

Marx's conception of the ideological nature of philosophy is tied both to his materialist conception of language and consciousness and to his materialist interpretation of the Hobbesian/Machiavellian understanding of politics. For Marx, consciousness is social interaction mediated by the material element of language. Consciousness, like politics, takes place within social and political institutions that are determined by the economic structures of power. This social structure is itself characterized by the antagonism of forces seeking control over the economic bases of society. Whereas Kant, Fichte, and Hegel, as followers of the enlightenment tradition of political thinking, shared a somewhat sanguine view of political life as ultimately reasonable, Marx shatters this view by understanding human life as fundamentally conflictual. Marx's understanding of politics is Hobbesian in its recognition of the intractable nature of the conflicts that result from human self-interested activity. It is Machiavellian in its recognition of the fact that political power is asserted not by logic and morality but by rhetoric and force.[10]

Marx's twist on these themes is to tie them to the question of the mode of production. For Marx, state power is not a matter of arbitrary will or personal interest. Rather, Marx concludes, "if power is taken as the basis of right, as Hobbes, etc., do, then right, law, etc., are merely the symptom, the expression (*Ausdruck*) of other relations upon which state power rests."[11] This can be linked to Marx's claim, quoted at the outset of the present section, that material relations determine "social, political, and intellectual life processes." Politics, language, and even philosophy can be understood in terms of their material basis.

Uniting these two claims—that consciousness is material and that politics is power-conflict—brings us to the conclusion that, for Marx, philosophical conceptions of right are themselves part of the process of transforming might into right. Marx negates Hegel's approach to the problem of the philosopher's voice and returns, via Feuerbach, to the Fichtean approach. He speaks to a political audience without, however, affirming Fichte's goal of creating a transcendental unity of morality and politics. Hegel rejected the dogmatism that resulted from Fichte's transcendental poetic-political-linguistic nationalism by systematically distinguishing and relating the different ways in which language can be used: the philosopher's voice was to be different from the poet's and the politician's, even though it used the same language. Marx negates this negation and returns to "dogmatism," however, of a more explicitly political order. It is Marx's virtue that he makes the philosopher's voice an explicit issue of both his practical and theoretical work. Although Marx's solution is like Fichte's to the extent that it asserts the need of the philosopher to take up the language of politics, it is more explicit about this need in the sense that Marx understands philosophy itself, including his own, in terms of its foundation in the concrete struggles of political life.

Marx rejects attempts to conceive of the philosopher's voice in nonpolitical terms. Against Kant's hopeful enlightenment project, Marx would claim that the Kantian project deliberately rejects its revolutionary content because it refuses to admit that theory is practical. Against Fichte's uneasy conjunction of linguistic nationalism and transcendental idealism, Marx would claim that these idealistic goals are limited bourgeois goals that can only be understood as such when we see that language, consciousness, and political nationalism are the result of struggle for control of the means of production. Against Hegel, Marx would claim that the attempt to assert a difference in theory between philosophy and politics has the practical result of producing an ideological mystification that undermines the radical force of practical political philosophy.

For Marx, philosophy gives voice to the material conditions of the class for which and to which it speaks. Marx's goal is to speak for and to this class in order to stimulate it self-consciously to engage in the political struggle in which it is already unconsciously engaged. This is a task of, in Feuerbach's words, a "philosophy of the future," which has returned from the "self-sufficient bliss of the realm of ideas" and has looked into the realm of "human misery."[12] The first task is to prepare the ground under which genuine human dialogue could flourish. Thus Feuerbach concludes, "to think, speak, and act in a pure and true human fashion will, however, be granted only to future generations."[13] Marx's task is to create the material conditions under which human speaking, thinking, and acting could be pure and true.

Contra Benhabib's accusation against Marx's supposedly monological approach, it is clear that the process of solidifying the implicit self-consciousness of the proletariat so as to create an explicit political identity for the proletariat cannot be completed as an imposition of truth. Rather, Marx rejects such impositions in order to prepare the way for a future in which genuine dialogue can unfold. The self-consciousness of the proletariat will develop dynamically as communist theory and practice interact within history. The "idea" of political life can only develop within political struggle; it cannot be imposed from without. Although Marx speaks for and to the working class, he does so with the recognition that there are other voices that claim to speak for and to this class and that his own voice is thus part of the struggle by which the proletariat develops its own identity from out of that "human misery" to which Feuerbach asked us to return.

Ambiguity of Philosophy and Politics in the *Communist Manifesto*

> Political power, properly so called, is merely the organized power of one class for oppressing another.
>
> —Marx, *Communist Manifesto*[14]

Let us turn then to Marx's attempt to speak for and to the proletariat in the *Communist Manifesto*. The *Manifesto* is a political text that criticizes the apolitical approach of philosophy by understanding theory as part of the material process of forming political identity. In what follows I will attempt to locate Marx's voice in the *Manifesto* in terms of the different audiences it addresses. It is important to note however, that the *Manifesto* is itself a historical artifact whose time is past: both its practical agenda and its theoretical claims about capitalism have been historically and theoretically superseded.[15] We turn to the *Manifesto* not to discover the truth about communism or to analyze its practical agenda. Rather, we turn to it to discern what happens when the philosopher's voice locates itself within concrete political struggles.

The philosophical significance of the *Communist Manifesto,* a clearly political work, lies in the conception of political philosophy upon which it is grounded: the materialist view, which sees both philosophy and politics as "superstructures" grounded in economic struggle. Its practical problem is a recognition that the working class needs to reject the dominant paradigm in both theory and practice. Since ideas have material consequences, Marx pushes the political struggle of the working class into the heart of its opponents' ideology by attacking the ideological claim that there is one universal answer to the question of the essence of human being. "Does it require deep intuition," Marx asks in the *Manifesto,* "to comprehend that man's ideas, views and conceptions, in one word, man's consciousness, changes with every change in the conditions of his material existence, in his social relations and in his social life?"[16]

This question lies at the heart of Marx's practical/theoretical problem. On the one hand, it is obvious that human beings have changed and that we continue to change as the mode of production changes. Thus, as a fact of history we must recognize that revolution is always a real possibility. On the other hand, this is not obvious at all to a culture wedded to the philosophical belief in those "eternal truths" that Marx criticizes in the *Manifesto.*[17] Marx's *theoretical* task is to demystify the "deep" philosophical belief in such eternal truths in order to return to the "superficial" truth that revolution is an enduring possibility. However, Marx's *practical* task is to stimulate the proletariat by giving them the sense that the revolution is inevitable.[18] This tension between theory and practice leads Marx into difficulties, most notably the problem of free will vs. determinism. If his goal is to inspire free activity by the proletariat, then why does he speak of the inevitability of the revolution? This problem is best resolved by noting the tension between theory and practice: he speaks to his audience(s) with multiple voices.[19]

The *Manifesto* links the theoretical and practical problematics in trying to inspire the Communist Party and the working class. What is unique about the *Manifesto* is its methodological ambiguity. The *Manifesto* rests on the border between politics and philosophy, thus calling the distinction between these two disciplines into question. As Stuart Wilks-Heeg concludes, the *Manifesto* "was as much a work of political propaganda as one of political philosophy."[20] It understands politics as determined by philosophy and philosophy as dominated by politics. It addresses the ambiguity between philosophy and politics and recognizes itself as caught up in this ambiguity. To properly understand the *Manifesto,* we must consider its multiple voices. I will show that there are at least three different audiences to which the *Manifesto* is addressed: the proletariat, the Communist Party, and other political theorists. The voice that Marx employs is different depending upon the interests and concerns of the audience. On the one hand, the *Manifesto* addresses political agents in a philosophical manner. It attempts to give the proletariat and the Communist Party a theoretical understanding of their political agitation. Here the *Manifesto* uses philosophy for the political task of inspiring these political agents toward further political action. On the other hand, the *Manifesto* addresses philosophical issues in a political manner. It attempts to show the way in which philosophical views are linked to political ideology and are best judged by the political practice to which they give rise. Here the *Manifesto* uses political action and commitment to evaluate philosophical theory.

In writing the *Manifesto* with Engels, Marx explicitly associates himself with a political party, the Communists, and even sets himself up as a spokesman for the party, writing its founding document, the *Communist Manifesto*. Marx is clearly a political partisan. And yet, in the *Communist Manifesto*, Marx offers what seem to be philosophical analyses of political life. It is natural to wonder, then, whether Marx is a political philosopher and whether the *Communist Manifesto* is a work of political philosophy. This question may seem ironic given that Marx rejects both philosophy and politics as outmoded practices of the bourgeoisie. Marx makes this clear in the *Manifesto* itself by claiming that the "ruling ideas of each age have ever been the ideas of its ruling class."[21] The ruling ideas of the capitalist epoch include politics, religion, morality, and philosophy. Marx attempts to transcend these bourgeois concepts with his materialist science of political economy and his revolutionary social agenda. Political economy is intended to go beyond philosophy; the Communist Revolution is intended to go beyond politics.

In this sense, the *Manifesto* is *neither* philosophical nor political—an extraordinary conclusion to reach for a work of political philosophy. In the *Manifesto* Marx claims that Communists reject both philosophy and politics. With the revolution, "the public power will lose its political character. Political power, properly so called, is merely the organized power of one class for oppressing another."[22] Politics, as Marx understands it, is a form of social organization that is oriented around a central authority called the state, which authorizes and defends the values of the ruling class.[23] Once class antagonisms have been abolished with the Communist Revolution, the political form of social organization will also be abolished. Moreover, Marx's materialism goes beyond philosophy and returns to real life. Philosophy, in its pursuit of transcendent truth, had forgotten the most important part of human life, "the real individuals, their activity and the material conditions under which they live."[24] In the *Manifesto* Marx takes seriously his claims about the limits of philosophy as stated in the *German Ideology* and in his "Theses on Feuerbach." The *Manifesto* is Marx's move from a mere philosophical interpretation of the world toward a serious attempt to change it. For Marx, serious thinkers ought to abandon philosophy in order to address themselves to the practical concerns of real people; they ought to engage in practical action; this practical action ought to be oriented toward the abolition of both politics and philosophy.

Nonetheless, Marx remains a political philosopher. His claims against politics and philosophy are strategic, located attacks on the theory and practice of the bourgeoisie. Marx does not leave theory behind: the *Manifesto* is a theoretical account of capitalism and its impending demise. Indeed this text addresses itself explicitly, in Part III, to other political theorists and falls inevitably into the trap of engaging in an abstract, seemingly *philosophical*, debate about "true" socialism. Moreover, the *Manifesto* presents a plan for *political* action, albeit as a preliminary step toward establishing communism and thereby overcoming politics. Thus, despite Marx's attempt to revolutionize theory and practice, he inevitably returns both to traditional theoretical concerns (that his theory is the *true* theory about political life) and to traditional political concerns (with practical recommendations about how the proletariat can obtain and consolidate *political* power). Thus we should interpret Marx's claims about overcoming philosophy and politics as rhetorical strategies designed to facilitate the formation of the political identity of the proletariat. Like Fichte, Marx adjusts his rhetorical voice according to his audience.

Commentators have continually wondered whether Marx was a political philosopher or a political actor, whether he was a metaphysician, a statist, or something more radical.[25] Recently Paul Wetherly has concluded that Marx's "theory of the state" is ambiguous because Marx views the state as both a servant of deterministically understood class interest and as a structural-institutional independent agency.[26] More critically, Karl Popper interprets Marx as propounding a paradoxical theory that claims both that politics is "impotent" and that political action is needed to overthrow politics. Popper finds Marx's position to be incoherent at worst and, at best, "fatally mistaken" because it reduces all social relations including the political to economic relations.[27] Robert Tucker concludes, after considering this problem in some detail: "in these terms, Marx both was and was not a political philosopher."[28] Such conclusions about Marx are provocative. One continues to wonder how Marx could both be and not be a political philosopher.

Joseph M. Schwartz's account of "Marx's hostility to politics" offers us a glimpse of a way of approaching Marx that can lead us further into this problem: "Consequently Marx's insistence on his analysis of capital as a "science" led to his downplaying the role of politics in social change in his formal and analytical writings such as *Capital*, although many of his journalistic and historical writings implicitly recognize a relatively autonomous, causal historical role for politics."[29] As Schwartz indicates, there is a crucial difference in tone, style, and method in Marx's different works. In some works Marx is more of a political philosopher in the traditional sense, in others he is more a political agitator and partisan. While most commentators agree with Schwartz that *Capital* is an example of what Marx, at least, called "science," it is also clear that a work like the *Communist Manifesto* is an example of partisan politics. What is at issue in making these determinations is the address of the text. *Capital* addresses, for the most part, those interested, for political reasons, in the truth about capitalism; the *Communist Manifesto* addresses, for the most part, those interested in taking concrete action to change the status quo. This qualification "for the most part" is necessary because in these texts, Marx calls the distinction between theory and practice into question.

Indeed, if there could be something called a Marxist "political philosophy," it could never be a disinterested search for transcendent truth about the polis. Rather, it is part of political practice within the polis. Theory functions to solidify the political identity of different parties in the political struggle for power. Political philosophy occurs as part of political contestation. But this claim about the epistemological status of political philosophy is itself ambivalent. Marx seems to admit that his own theory about political theory is only valid for that class that understands itself in terms of the struggle for power. Marx recognizes that the bourgeoisie will reject this claim about political philosophy. For Marx, the truth of a political theory is relative to the class that is interested in it, although for this class there is a definite "truth." This theory is correct for the proletariat not for the bourgeoisie. Thus the proletariat understands itself and its bourgeois opponents differently than the bourgeoisie understands itself and its proletarian antagonists. This ambivalent epistemology is what allows Marx to offer arguments against various non-Marxist forms of socialism in the *Communist Manifesto*. Given the political agenda in question, i.e., radical social transformation in the interests of the working class, these other socialist theories remain, to one degree or another, reactionary. Within a given political purview—within a set of class interests—Marx claims that there is a "correct" form of self-consciousness, i.e., the one that best explains the experience of this class. There can be, however, no objectively true synthetic view that transcends this experience because the synthetic approach is a bourgeois approach, which undermines the class interest of the proletariat by assuming a nonpolitical universal human experience.

Addressing the Proletariat

> Working Men of All Countries Unite!
>
> —Marx, *Communist Manifesto*[30]

Whom does the *Manifesto* address? Most obviously, the working class. Unfortunately, this obvious answer is not as transparent as it at first appears. The primary address of the *Communist Manifesto*, the proletariat, did not yet exist in 1848 as a self-conscious revolutionary class. This explains the conclusion of the

Manifesto, the famous cry, "Workers of the World Unite!" This cry is addressed to the workers as a command: in order to win the world, in order to lose their chains, the working class must unite and form itself into a revolutionary party. Although Marx uses the word "proletariat" throughout the essay, a careful reading makes it clear that the class-conscious revolutionary proletariat whom he addresses does not yet exist. Marx states that the liberal, bourgeois, revolutions begun in the eighteenth century and continuing into the nineteenth century are in the process of bringing the proletariat into existence. As the bourgeoisie grows and capitalism flourishes, the proletariat develops.

> Not only has the bourgeoisie forged the weapons that bring death to itself; it has also called into existence the men who are to wield those weapons—the modern working class—the proletarians. In the same proportion as the bourgeoisie, i.e., capital, is developed, in the same proportion is the proletariat, the modern working class, developed . . .[31]

Despite Marx's optimistic pronouncements about the power of the proletariat, in 1848 the proletariat was still in a process of development.[32] This makes it appear as if Marx was following in the tradition of messianic prophecy—prophesying the apocalyptical appearance of the revolutionary proletariat—a tradition of political philosophy with links to Fichte.[33] In the *Manifesto* Marx seems to recognize that the revolution could not be successful in 1848: the downtrodden workers have not yet united to form a revolutionary majority opposed to capitalism. This is why it was necessary to write the *Manifesto* in the first place, i.e. to bring the revolutionary proletariat into existence. Indeed Engels, writing in 1895, nearly fifty years after the first publication of the *Manifesto*, admits that "history has proved us, and all who thought like us, wrong. It has made it clear that the state of economic development on the Continent at that time (1848) was not, by a long way, ripe for the elimination of capitalist production."[34] Engels states that the problem was that capitalism still had a great capacity for expansion before the misery of the workers became acute enough to push the revolution from possibility toward inevitability. This explains why the working class, as developed under capitalism in 1848, was not a consciously revolutionary class: without an increase in exploitation and misery, the proletariat could not find it necessary to become conscious of itself as an international revolutionary class.

We would assume that Marx was aware of this in his call for the workers of the world to unite, a demand aimed at the future, directed toward the formation of the revolutionary proletariat. And yet, in the *Manifesto* Marx seems to contradict himself by saying, for example, that "the proletarian movement is the *self-conscious*, independent movement of the immense majority, in the interests of the immense majority."[35] This claim must either be false because, in 1848, the proletariat was not conscious of itself as a class independent of the bourgeoisie; or it must be addressed to another audience, i.e., the Communist Party, which is to unite and inspire the movement of the proletariat. Clearly, the proletariat, in general, was not aware that its interests were in opposition to the bourgeoisie, and the movement begun by the Communist Party was not yet a movement of the majority.

Marx exaggerates his claims throughout the *Manifesto*, unafraid of contradiction, because his goal is political inspiration, not philosophical reflection. Communists were not yet, in 1848, feared or even widely known. Thus the famous claim about communism as a "spectre haunting Europe" is, as David Felix notes, "a boastful lie."[36] The *Manifesto* was part of the process of creating a party that would provide self-consciousness to the proletariat. His boastful lies about the proletariat are thus political tricks, not truth claims. This rhetorical flourish is understandable if we recognize that throughout the *Manifesto*, Marx, in a kind of conjuring trick, addresses the so-called self-conscious majority in order to bring it into existence.[37] This is why, in the *Manifesto*, Marx places the revolution in a metaphorical future: "what the bourgeoisie, therefore, produces, above all, is its own grave-diggers. Its fall and the victory of the proletariat are equally inevitable."[38] The revolution is inevitable because of systematic tendencies within capitalism. But it will not happen until the proletariat is educated about itself as a class and until the workers of the world actually unite to form the revolutionary class. The *Manifesto* addresses itself to the task of executing this goal of educating and uniting the workers in order to hasten the demise of the bourgeoisie.

We see here a methodological problem with regard to political philosophy. If Marx speaks for and to the proletariat, but this class does not yet exist, we wonder what justifies Marx's claims about the proletariat. If the truth-claims he makes are supposed to be truths about and for the proletariat, but this proletariat does not yet exist, then what is the logical status of these claims? At best, they can be considered to be hypothetical claims—if the proletarians were to become self-conscious, this is what they would think about themselves. This is not a very satisfactory response, however, because Marx is not interested in a hypothetical proletariat. He repeatedly states that philosophy must return to real concrete life. In 1845 Marx states with regard to the proletariat that, "It is not a matter of what this or that proletarian or even the proletariat as a whole pictures at present as its goal. It is a matter of what the proletariat is in actuality and what, in accordance with this being, it will historically be compelled to do."[39] A vicious circle results here in that the proletariat to which Marx speaks only becomes real and concrete in response to Marx's text, while Marx's text is supposed to be addressed to the real concrete proletariat. The *Manifesto* is thus addressing the being or essence of the proletariat, even if this contradicts the present condition and self-consciousness of individual members of the working class. Here we return to the problem of which Benhabib accused Marx: he seems to address political life from the outside, with an unpolitical claim about the truth of the proletariat that runs counter to the actual condition in which the proletariat finds itself. The authority of Marx's prophetic voice seems to come from a claim about the being of the proletariat that transcends the concrete existence of that class.

Addressing the Communist Party

> The Communists disdain to conceal their views and aims. They openly declare (*sie erklären es offen*) that their ends can be attained only by the forcible overthrow of all existing social conditions.
>
> —Marx, *Communist Manifesto*[40]

Marx wants to locate his voice between fantastic prophetic rhetoric and dead historical fact. This middle path can be seen if we readjust Marx's address away from the proletariat to the Communist Party. Marx claims to be offering the truth. This truth is, however, only available to those who acknowledge the existence of the proletariat as a class whose experience is worthy of consideration, namely, the Communists. Marx addresses the *Manifesto*, not only to the nonexistent proletariat, but also to those Communists who already share Marx's understanding of the proletariat. The antidote to the spectral nature of the working class to whom the *Manifesto* is addressed is found in the reality of the Communist Party. Thus the truth claims made in the *Manifesto* are not merely truths about some nonexistent class. They state facts about the Party. Those who read and subscribe to the *Manifesto* have already agreed to the basic premise that capitalism is an alienating, dehumanizing system. The *Manifesto* addresses these party members in order to clarify the dissatisfaction they already feel with regard to the status quo in order to make them conscious of the movement in which they are already active and to clarify their task.

The task of the Communist Party and the intellectuals who are to lead the revolution is to form the proletariat into a self-conscious revolutionary class: "the immediate aim of the Communists is the same as that of all other proletarian parties: formation of the proletariat into a class, overthrow of the bourgeois supremacy, conquest of political power by the proletariat."[41] In other words, the proletariat, as a self-conscious revolutionary class, must be brought into existence by the Communist Party. Indeed, the *Communist Manifesto* is part of the formation of the party. The *Manifesto* was written specifically for the Communist Party and intended to articulate a "detailed theoretical and practical programme of the Party."[42] Thus, the *Manifesto* is not only addressed to the proletariat. It is also addressed to the Party. The concluding demand, "Workers of the World Unite!" is addressed to the members of the Party in order to clarify their task for them: they must help the workers of the world to unite by leading, organizing, and educating them.

The *Manifesto* is addressed to the intellectual leaders of the Party in order to "openly declare" (*erklären offen*) the political ambitions of the party. The *Manifesto* simply is the declaration of the existence of the party. Thus the *Manifesto* bridges the gap between political fantasy and philosophical truth: its language is a performative act of calling the Party into existence. Of course, along with this inauguration, Marx fills the *Manifesto* with laudatory descriptions of the virtues of the party (useful rhetoric for the political task of forming a party). Marx describes the intellectual vanguard of the party as members of the bourgeois ruling class who see the contradictions within capitalism and who "cut themselves adrift" and "go over to the proletariat."[43] Marx praises them as "bourgeois ideologists who have raised themselves to the level of comprehending theoretically the historical movement as a whole."[44] The members of the Party are understood as "the most advanced and resolute section of the working class parties of every country."[45] Moreover, "they have over the great mass of the proletariat the advantage of clearly understanding the line of march, the conditions, and the ultimate general results of the proletarian movement."[46]

Marx was thus speaking to the party leaders in order to inspire them and inflame their revolutionary zeal. In the *Manifesto* Marx sings the praises of the intellectual vanguard of the Party without considering the possibility that these intellectuals may be opportunistic manipulators merely seeking personal political power.[47] Indeed, such a consideration of the possible shortcomings of the Party would be inappropriate to the specific goals of the *Manifesto*: one does not inspire a party by mentioning ways in which the party members may be corrupt. Rather, the goal of inspiring the members is best served by praising them and by clearly spelling out their immediate task: "they never cease, for a single instant, to instill into the working class the clearest possible recognition of the hostile antagonism between bourgeoisie and proletariat . . . In short, the communists everywhere support every revolutionary movement against the existing social and political order of things."[48]

This last statement is both a description of what the Communist Party does and a normative claim about what it ought to do. Here again we see methodological tensions within Marx's address. He describes the Party as an already existing organization, even though the *Manifesto* is part of the process of bring it into existence. Although the Party already existed in cells in London and Brussels, Marx claims that "it is high time that the Communists should openly, in the face of the whole world, publish their views, their aims, their tendencies and meet this nursery tale of the specter of communism with a manifesto of the party itself." Thus, despite the fact that Communism already existed as a force, however paltry, in action, it had not yet organized itself into a self-conscious party. The task of the *Manifesto* then, is both to help the party members understand what they already do by making the actions of Communists explicit and to explain to them what they should do by setting forth a particular political agenda.

The methodological problem we encounter at this point is how the dissatisfaction felt by Communists can lead to a normative political agenda. A variety of agendas could result from the experience of dissatisfaction with nineteenth century social life.[49] What justifies the provisional ten-point political agenda on social change and Marx's claims about the inevitability of the coming revolution? Marx may claim that this issues forth from the contradictions he finds within capitalism. Unfortunately this pushes the issue back from the political to the philosophical: to support his claim that his practical political program is the best one or that it is inevitable, Marx must claim that his philosophical analysis offers the truth about history. As we saw in the preceding section, for Marx, this means the truth for and about the proletariat. Marx's political agenda must be supported by a philosophical account of the proletarian's experience and identity. To inspire the Communists he must convince them that they are right.

Addressing Philosophy

> Where speculation ends, where real life starts, there consequently begins real, positive science, the expounding of the practical activity, of the practical process of development of men. Empty phrases about consciousness end, and real knowledge has to take their place. When the reality is described, philosophy [*die selbständige Philosophie*] loses its medium of existence.
>
> —Marx, *The German Ideology*[50]

The *Manifesto* is not only addressed to political agents in the proletariat or in the Communist Party. It also addresses itself to other communists who are not members of the party, to other communist philosophers, and indeed to all political thinkers who care to listen. Part III of the text specifically takes up the issue of "Socialist and Communist Literature." In this section—an odd section to find in a supposedly untheoretical work designed to inspire action—Marx addresses political theorists in general in order to help clarify the position of the Communist Party in opposition to other parties. Thus Marx addresses the proletariat and the members of the Communist Party only indirectly in this section. The obvious goal of this section is to help the Communist Party understand itself by contrasting its ideology with other socialist ideologies. However, a more significant methodological implication of this section can be discerned in its recognition of the relation between political action and reflective philosophy. As Marx states in *The German Ideology*, there is no such thing as independent philosophy; rather, philosophical activity occurs in the service of political party. Clarifying ideology theoretically is a form of political action.

Marx is aware that the specific political agenda of the Communist Party needs a philosophical defense. As we shall see in the present section, this defense focuses on the way in which other socialist theories lead to nonrevolutionary practice. The implicit claim here is that we can judge a theory by looking at the political action to which it gives rise. This begs the question because it assumes that Marx's theory and its practical agenda is the best option without ever giving an argument to that effect. It assumes that revolutionary action is the only solution to social alienation. It seems, however, that Marx is not afraid to beg this particular question because he is already engaged in revolutionary political activity even in the theoretical portion of the text. Marx's understanding of philosophy as class-based ideology is itself a class-based ideology—the ideology of the Communist Party and the working class. Marx reduces the philosophical defense of the Communist political agenda to a political dispute between parties: the parties that disagree with the Communist agenda are labeled as bourgeois, and their philosophical positions are rejected as bourgeois ideology. The *Manifesto*'s theoretical critique of other socialist theorists is a political matter.

Throughout this section Marx resorts to crude ad hominem arguments. While Fichte had used ad hominem in the introduction to the *Wissenschaftslehre,* because his form of idealism was inherently linked to morality, Marx adopts the ad hominem as a self-consciously political strategy. "Theory is capable of seizing the masses when it demonstrates ad hominem, and it demonstrates ad hominem as soon as it becomes radical."[51] His claims about the reactionary bourgeois character of his opponents are useful because they go to the heart of the question of political identity: the type of man one is, i.e., the class to which one belongs. Marx criticizes "feudal socialism," for example, by saying that "in political practice, therefore, they join in all coercive measures against the working class; and in ordinary life, despite their high falluting phrases (*aufgeblähten Redensarten*), they stoop to pick up the golden apples dropped from the tree of industry…"[52] "Petty-Bourgeois Socialism" is criticized as reactionary for its support of guilds and patriarchal relations in agriculture. "German socialism" is seen as flowery rhetoric without political efficacy; German socialists only "increase the sale of their goods amongst such a public."[53] "Bourgeois Socialism" is socialism in name only, what Marx calls "a mere figure of speech (*bloßen rednerischen Figur*)."[54] It advocates free trade and other capitalist values, while claiming that all of these reforms are "for the benefit of the working class."[55] "Critical-Utopian socialists" seem to come close to being real communists. However, they are "doomed to failure" because they want to avoid revolution and retreat to painting "fantastic pictures (*phantastische Schilderung*) of future society."[56] In Marx's words, "they reject all political, and especially all revolutionary, action . . ."[57]

This shows us that for Marx, political philosophy is evaluated by examining the action that results from it. The ad hominem approach amounts to saying that one should only trust the Party whose theory creates that type of political identity that leads to radical political action: no other party or theory can adequately grasp the truth of the proletarian experience. Authentic political philosophy is political philosophy that results in revolutionary political practice. Any other practical result indicates a reactionary, bourgeois ideology. We can see here that Marx has moved philosophy squarely into political practice. However, this brings with it the negative consequence that arguments are neglected in favor of stereotyping and name-calling. Rather than arguing why these other forms of socialism are false, Marx resorts to calling them "reactionary" and "bourgeois." Marx gives us no nonideological (i.e. nonpolitical) reason why his political agenda and theoretical views are the best. We can see then that the *Communist Manifesto* is enmeshed in the problem with which we began. Marx's theory and practice are merely the theory and practice of one party within the polis. His political philosophy addresses the formation of political identity within concrete political struggle. It is not philosophy but politics. Marx understands himself as thus merely the spokesman for one Party within the political struggle. Marx is the philosopher of the working class in the sense that he speaks both for and to the working class.

Theory and Practice in *Capital*

> The centralization of the means of production and the socialization of labor reach a point at which they become incompatible with their capitalist integument. This integument is burst asunder. The knell of capitalist private property sounds. The expropriators are expropriated.
>
> —Marx, *Capital*[58]

The political interpretation of Marx I have proposed makes the most sense when applied to Marx's explicitly political works, such as the *Communist Manifesto*. To establish my thesis more clearly, I will examine the way in which Marx's less overtly political work is nonetheless engaged in political activity. To this end let us jump into the complexities of Marx's most theoretical work, *Capital. Capital*, written by Marx in his exile in London during the 1860s, is Marx's attempt to make the reality that grounds the revolutionary will of the proletariat manifest to itself in order to facilitate the political activity of the proletariat. The revolutions of 1848 had failed to bring about lasting universal change and had instead resulted in the nationalism and reaction characteristic of the Second Empire in France and the rise of Bismarck in Germany. Although Marx remained politically active during this period, founding, for example, the International Working Men's Association, his youthful political activity became tempered by a recognition of the need for a more thorough theoretical grounding for revolutionary politics. *Capital* is thus still political despite its theoretical concerns. As David Felix writes: "More than a classic study of the new industrial society, *Capital* was an instrument of power. Its creation had been revolutionary politics of the highest order."[59]

In *Capital*, Marx argues that what appears as a natural necessity to the bourgeoisie and its political economists is in reality the contingent result of exploitative social relations. The difficulty here is that such a distinction between appearance and reality is itself political. Beneath all of his complicated economic analyses and detailed accounts of contemporary division of labor, class relations, and the factory system, Marx utilizes a critical hermeneutical approach that treats the "objects" of capitalism as symbols to be deciphered from a point of view other than that of the bourgeoisie. Marx is quite fond of using occult language to describe capitalism. He approaches the objects of capitalism as talismans to be demystified. His goal is to expose the reality concealed beneath "the whole mystery of commodities, all the magic and necromancy that surrounds the products of labor on the basis of commodity production."[60] Like magical and religious objects, the objects of capitalism have real power to the extent that the social structure supports and responds to them. Money truly does make the world go round. Marx does not deny that these fetish objects have real power and significance. Indeed, he states that the categories of bourgeois economics are "forms of thought which are socially valid, and therefore objective."[61] The problem is that the contingent social origin of their objectivity is concealed by the symbolic structure, which treats them as natural necessities. The concepts of capitalism must be deciphered to show the social relations that constitute them. In a passage that calls to mind Hegel's philosophy of language, Marx states with regard to the concept of "value":

> Value, therefore, does not have its description branded on its forehead; it rather transforms every product of labor into a social hieroglyphic. Later on, men try to decipher the hieroglyphic, to get behind the secret of their own

> social product: for the characteristic which objects of utility have of being values is as much men's social product as is their language (*Sprache*).[62]

It is important to recall that Hegel had condemned hieroglyphic language because it was too static to express the living spirit of spoken language. For Hegel, hieroglyphic alphabets do not allow language to grow and develop in the way that alphabetic languages do. Moreover, the etymology of "hiero-glyph" is significant here: these are holy writings, symbols with supposedly sacred, mystical content. What Marx calls the "fetishism of the commodity" is an example of the process by which society creates a symbol of its values. As Marx indicates above, this is the same process by which society creates symbols in language: a historical process by which natural objects are infused with social significance. Marx's goal is to demystify this process in order to expose its social origin. Throughout this section Marx uses the language of mysticism, religion, and magic to describe the process of fetishism that results in "the magic of money."[63] His religious and mystical rhetoric even leads him to quote *Revelation*'s account of the regulation of commerce under the Antichrist according to the "number of the beast."[64] There is a rhetorical connection between this passage and the above quote about the description of value being branded on its forehead. Marx implicitly argues that fetishism of the commodity results in a secret evil that is at least as insidious as the explicit forehead branding that occurs in the Apocalypse of St. John. At issue is the proper understanding of the infernal mysteries that are hidden in the objects of our social life. Every product of labor is imprinted with a significance far deeper than the supposed "value" ascribed to the commodity in terms of money. Marx states that money is the most mysterious hieroglyph of all because it takes on the cloak of necessity as the universal medium of exchange: "it is however, precisely this finished form of the world of commodities—the money form—which conceals the social character of private labor and the social relations between the individual workers, by making those relations appear as relations between material objects, instead of revealing them plainly."[65] For Marx, the most cryptic symbols—the ones most in need of critical deciphering—are the ones that present themselves as natural necessities: those concepts like value, money, commodity, and property that conceal their own social origin.[66]

The critical social/materialist dialectic of *Capital*—exposing the social and material origins of the "natural" appearances of capitalism—forms the basis of the methodology that Marx inherited from Hegel by way of Feuerbach. The Hegelian dialectic was supposed to make concepts fluid by making the interrelations between concepts explicit. It thus demystified those concepts by making them comprehensible. Those concepts that our culture treats as metaphysical givens—value for Marx, God for Feuerbach, or spirit for Hegel—are explained in their identity and difference from other determinations. This process, quite similar to Kant's critical attempt to use the language of reason to clarify reason to itself, can be understood in terms of a criticism of language, for the concepts under scrutiny are linguistically determined.[67] Like Hegel, Marx rejects the sacred/mystical view of language—the hieroglyphic approach—and conceives of language and concepts in terms of their concrete sensuous and social origin. Hegel's goal was to use ordinary language to provide the ladder by which spirit could lift itself to the level of logic. Moving beyond Hegel, Marx claims that the concepts of not only capitalism and bourgeois political economy, but also the concepts of philosophy—Hegel's logic included—have a social origin. Marx's goal is to see through the supposed "objectivity" of these concepts in order to expose their social origin.

Again it is important to note that Marx does not completely reject the traditional interest in discovering the general truth about language, society, and economy. Despite his politicized approach to philosophy and his recognition of the importance of historical and social specificity, Marx does not deny that general concepts exist and are important. As he says in the *Grundrisse*:

> *Production in general* is an abstraction, but a reasonable abstraction in so far as it actually emphasizes and defines the common aspects and thus spares us the need of repetition. Still, this *general aspect* or the common element which is brought to light by comparison, is itself multiply divided and diverges into different determinations. Some features are found in all epochs, others are common to a few epochs. The most modern epoch and the most ancient will have [certain] determinations in common. Without them production is inconceivable. But although the most highly developed languages (*entwickeltsten Sprachen*) have laws and categories in common with the most primitive ones, it is precisely what constitutes their development that distinguishes them from this general and common element.[68]

The point here is that what is important is the differences that remain once the "common elements" have been sifted out. Unlike Fichte who wanted to maintain that there was continuity in the *Ursprache*, Marx recognizes differences in linguistic development. If we recall Hegel's account of language, Hegel also emphasized these differences. However, for Hegel, the differences could be united in an account of the way in which differences are necessary to the life of spirit. Marx resists this last move of the Hegelian dialectic. He claims that essential differences must not be forgotten and that the attempt to postulate the common element is itself an abstraction. What this means is that for Marx, the view that erases difference by moving to the universal—although a convenient way of speaking—forgets the fact that concrete social life is constituted by differences, even (contra Fichte) within the culture shared by speakers of a national language. This leads again back to a politicization of both theory and practice. According to the content of Marx's theory, the theory must not forget that it has a particular social origin that explains its difference—despite its similarities—from the theories of the bourgeois economists and Idealist philosophers. These differences are the focal point of the political struggle in which Marx's voice is engaged.

So how is *Capital* a political text? The critical method that recognizes the possibility of different interpretations of supposedly objective concepts gives rise to the possibility that appearances could be otherwise: it establishes the possibility of a revolutionary transformation of what political economists once saw as necessary natural laws. As Marx states in the Preface to the First Edition of *Capital*: "in all the civilized states of the European Continent, a radical change in the existing relations between capital and labor is as evident and inevitable as in England… Within the ruling classes themselves, the foreboding is emerging that the present society is no solid crystal, but an organism capable of change, and constantly engaged in a process of change."[69] In *Capital*, Marx gives us concrete historical examples of the way in which even the bourgeoisie is becoming aware of the fact that appearances are not as stable as they were once thought to be. The idea of free markets, for example, was changing even as Marx wrote. In his discussion of state regulation of child labor, for example, Marx makes it clear that child labor has lost "the appearance of a contract between free persons" even to the bourgeoisie.[70] The English Parliament's attempts to regulate child labor in one industry caused parents to sell their children into other industries where so-called "freedom of labor" still prevailed.[71] Parliament's attempt at regulation of child labor represents an acknowledgment by the ruling class of the fact that labor-exchange is not as free and equal as it seems to be. In this way, political concepts such as "freedom" continually change despite ideological attempts to appeal to their immutability.

The goal of *Capital* is to facilitate the radical change of society, a change that Marx claims—echoing his claims about the specter of communism in the *Manifesto*—was already suspected by the ruling class. This critical theory would facilitate revolution by making explicit the way in which capital produces the revolutionary will which will lead to its own destruction, as famously described in chapter 32 of *Capital*: "The expropriators are expropriated."[72]

Marx's critical project is to make manifest, in opposition to the bourgeois economists who defend capitalism, the revolutionary process that is already implicit in capitalism. As capitalism grows, so does the revolutionary will. Although revolutionary political action is the logical outcome of this trajectory, critical theory is its guiding light. The Communist Revolution will not be random violence. Rather it will be the "self-conscious, independent movement of the immense majority, in the interests of the immense majority."[73] This revolution will be a struggle for power: it is not a unanimous social will but a struggle of the vast majority against the powerful minority. For it to be successful it must be guided by theory; it must be self-conscious. Otherwise, the revolutionary will of the people will be unable to see through the ideological mystifications that obscure its already incipient social power. This means that the revolutionary party must be guided by ongoing criticism both of the ideology which it opposes and of its own tendency to succumb to this ideology. As Marx says in the *Eighteenth Brumaire of Louis Bonaparte,* "proletarian revolutions criticize themselves constantly."[74] Such criticism is necessary so that the movement will avoid succumbing to the temptation to worship its chains as cryptic symbols of its emancipation. When the revolutionary class properly understands itself and its relation to the dominant ideology "the situation has been created which makes all turning back impossible, and the conditions themselves cry out: *Hic Rhodus, hic salta*!"[75] In short, for Marx, critical activity is both inspired by the revolutionary conflict implicit in material conditions and contributes to the power with which the revolutionary will will actualize itself.

Marx's Voice

> Hence, nothing prevents us from making criticism of politics, participation in politics, and therefore *real* struggles, the starting point of our criticism and from identifying our criticism with them... We do not say (*sagen*) to the world: Cease your struggles, they are foolish; we will give you the true slogan of struggle. We merely show (*zeigen*) the world what it is really fighting for, and consciousness is something that it *has to* acquire, even if it is does not want to.
>
> —Marx, "Letter to Ruge" in the *Deutsch-Französische Jarhbücher*[76]

Marx claims that the task of the socialist theorist is to put the reality of the proletariat into words. The socialist theorist, to avoid becoming a utopian isolationist or a bourgeois apologist, thus cannot use words that go beyond the reality of proletarian experience to speak of the universality of truth when that universality is nowhere to be found in the concrete experience of the proletariat. If the proletariat is not free, for example, "freedom" cannot be spoken except as an aspiration, the final cause of revolutionary activity. Rather than using language to create a national identity, as Fichte attempted, and rather than speaking for and to the spirit embodied in the bourgeoisie, as Hegel did, Marx asks that the socialist theorist speak for and to the proletariat. In the

Poverty of Philosophy, Marx reaches the following conclusion: "But in the measure that history moves forward, and with it the struggle of the proletariat assumes clearer outlines, they [the socialists] no longer need to seek science in their minds; they have only to take note of what is happening before their eyes and to become its mouthpiece."[77] It is important to notice the connection between this point and the *Communist Manifesto*. I argued that in that text Marx was, in part, speaking for and to the proletariat. Here he explains why this is all he can do: the socialist philosopher is the mouthpiece of the proletariat and its party, the Communists. The socialist philosopher must use language that conflicts with the status quo, thus speaking of the dissolution of capitalism, the alienation of labor, etc. Such language risks being reduced to absurdity, however, unless historical actuality has reached the point where the truth of these words is becoming apparent in the experience of the proletariat. As the mouthpiece of the party of the proletariat, Marx thus brings the proletariat into existence, because linguistic expression is part of the realization of the objective material conditions of society. The social necessity that gives rise to Marx's naming of the proletariat also gives rise to the existence of the proletariat in fact. Of course Marx could be mistaken in his use of language. How would we know? This would be a matter of further political contestation, although Marx thought that the coming political struggle would uphold his claims because his voice was the self-conscious result of the material conditions of that part of society to which it was addressed and for whom it spoke.

In his 1844 "Introduction to the Contribution to the Critique of Hegel's *Philosophy of Right,*" Marx clarifies this further by linking theory and practice to the power of words to both mirror and create actuality. The problem for the socialist revolutionary movement in Germany was that the proletariat (in Germany at least) was only beginning to form itself into a self-conscious class. Thus, although philosophy had already attained the idea of universal freedom in Hegel's thought, this had not been realized in Germany's society and politics. One of Marx's criticisms of Hegel is that his idea of freedom thus had no organic connection to the actuality of German life. Marx demands, as a result, that theory and practice need to move closer together if there is to be a genuine revolution in German social and political life. "Theory can be realized in a people only insofar as it is the realization of the needs of that people."[78] The difference between theory and practice needs to be resolved by both better theory and a transformed political actuality. In what seems to be a response to Hegel's *Doppelsatz*, Marx concludes: "It is not enough for thought to strive for realization, reality must itself strive towards thought."[79] So how will this mediation of reality and theory occur? While Marx clearly is urging practical political activity, this political activity will result from a radicalized use of language that owes much to Hegel's account of expression.

> By proclaiming the dissolution of the hitherto existing world order the proletariat merely states the secret of its own existence, for it is in fact the dissolution of that world order . . . In regard to the world which is coming into being the proletarian then finds himself possessing the same right as the German king in regard to the world which has come into being when he calls the people his people as he calls the horse his horse. By declaring the people his private property, the king simply states (*spricht . . . aus*) that the property owner is king.[80]

This paragraph is pregnant with significance for our consideration of the relation between voice, philosophy, and politics. The proletarian revolution will begin by announcing its theory as the expression of the experience of the proletariat. This is the very activity that Marx undertakes in the *Manifesto*: he makes manifest or announces the fact that the oppression of the proletariat is the real basis of capitalism. This is a process of making explicit the hidden secret of capitalism. However, stating this secret is not a mere representation of the implicit (as in Hegel). Rather, it is a product of material conditions and the struggle for power that occurs in and through language. Marx gives us an idea here of how language and power operate in tandem. The German king has the right to name things as his because he has the power to own these things. Naming and owning are thus linked to political power. Those with the power to own things actually own them; those with the power to name things do the naming. Marx's endeavor, not only in the *Manifesto* but also in his "theoretical" works such as *Capital*, is thus to name the proletariat's experience of capitalism. By announcing the proletariat as the basis of capitalism, Marx's voice begins the movement in which the proletariat will come to own the productive forces that "rightfully" belong to them. Of course the bourgeoisie will disagree, and political struggle will ensue. But this is to be expected because Marx recognizes that he can only address a part of society. Marx's linguistic activity, by making explicit the proletarian experience of capitalism, begins the struggle in which the proletariat will resist ideological claims about its freedom under capitalism. Marx, as the mouthpiece of the proletariat, calls forth the proletariat and names it as historically active and powerful. His theoretical activity thus begins the political movement, which will actualize the proletariat as a political power. In this way Marx locates the philosopher as the voice of a party engaged in concrete political struggle.

CHAPTER 11

Philosophy, Politics, and Voice: The Enduring Struggle

> "Sophistries" (*Sophistereien*) is a slogan that common sense likes to use against educated reason, just as the expression "idle dreaming" (*Träumereien*) sums up what philosophy means to the ignorant.
>
> —Hegel, *Phenomenology of Spirit*[1]

How can we clarify the distinction between philosophical speech and the political rhetoric with which it is often confused? As we've seen, this distinction is to be found in the regulative idea of self-consciousness of this difference and the explication of this difference in speech. We saw this in Kant but it is even more apparent in Hegel. In the Preface to *The Phenomenology,* in response to the Romantic praise for poetic genius, Hegel painstakingly, self-consciously, clarifies the importance of self-consciousness in order to prevent philosophy from slipping back into rhetoric. Philosophical self-consciousness is explicitly contrasted with that sort of high flown rhetoric that masks and popularizes the common sense of a natural philosophy of the heart while entertaining its audience with a "rhetoric of trivial truths (*Rhetorik trivialer Wahrheiten*)."[2] The problem here is that all sorts of contradictory possibilities occur as rhetoric appeals to an inner "truth of the heart." Moreover, as seen in the above epigram, the rhetorical approach accuses philosophy of "sophistry" and "idle dreaming." "When it [consciousness] labors to extricate itself from the bewilderment this sets up, it falls into fresh contradictions, and may very well burst out with the assertion that the question is settled, that so and so is the truth, and that the other views are sophistries."[3] Indeed, this is the irony and dilemma of philosophy since the time of Socrates: philosophy is accused by the sophists of being a form of sophistry. How can the philosopher distinguish his/her voice from the rhetorical voice with which it is confused?

For Hegel, the distinguishing mark of philosophy is its commitment to self-consciousness. He famously claims "everything turns on grasping and expressing (*auszudrücken*) the True, not only as Substance, but equally as Subject."[4] This is a normative demand for self-consciousness about philosophical method with links to Hegel's account of the need for the expression of the implicit. Hegel clarifies this later with the following:

> Science is not that idealism which replaced the dogmatism of assertion with a dogmatism of assurance, or a dogmatism of self-certainty. On the contrary, since [our] knowing sees the content return into its own inwardness, its activity is totally absorbed in the content, for it is the immanent self of the content; yet it has at the same time returned into itself, for it is pure self-identity in otherness.[5]

In other words, what is unique about philosophical knowledge is the fact that, according to the norm of self-consciousness, it makes itself and its method an explicit matter for consideration and is able to articulate the differences and similarities between philosophical speech and nonphilosophical speech. Finally, Hegel indicates that this ideal redounds upon the persuasive, political discourse from which philosophy extricated itself by way of self-consciousness. Self-consciousness is the principle of modern political life, as we saw when we discussed Kant's republican ideal and Hegel's philosophy of right. Persuasive political discourse, since it abjures the norm of self-consciousness, cannot claim to be open for all and thus violates the principles of this republican ideal.

The opposed norm—the norm of political speech—is power, understood as the ability to generate results. It does not matter in political life if the politician is conscious of why his rhetorical strategies work or of their ethical or philosophical significance. It only matters that they do work. In this sense, a successful politician may be completely un-self-conscious, as long as he gets the job done. Political efficacy allows us to understand Machiavelli's amoral Prince, Fichte's overzealous appropriation of rhetoric, and Marx's deliberate politicization of philosophy. Without self-consciousness, however, we are thrown back into a Hobbesian universe. Rhetorical speech reaches an impasse in which, as Hegel explains, subjective opinion is "finished and done with anyone who does not agree; he only has to explain that he has nothing more to say (*nichts zu sagen*) to anyone who does not find and feel the same in himself. In other words, he tramples underfoot the roots of humanity."[6] The philosophical norm of self-consciousness is bound up with the republican ideal of an enlightened humanity engaged in a dialogical process of self-legislation via self-comprehension. Hegel concludes, "for it is the nature of humanity to press onward to agreement with others; human nature only really exists in an achieved community of minds."[7] This achieved community occurs when the philosophical norm of self-consciousness becomes an accepted norm of political life. Only at this point will the truth become "capable of being the property of all self-conscious reason."[8] Unfortunately as we saw in our discussion of Fichte and Marx, Hegel's hopeful rhetoric is undermined by the fact of ignorance and oppression. Thus the philosopher, driven by the norm of self-consciousness, might be tempted to take up political rhetoric and political action—in order to create the conditions for the possibility of self-consciousness.

The task of philosophy is to address itself to political agents, without allowing itself to be confused with political rhetoric, in order to help us to become critically aware of our implicit norms. Philosophers, as living, breathing political agents are intimately concerned with this process of critical enlightenment. The problem is that political and philosophical audiences will continue to disagree about the nature of the philosopher's voice. Philosophy thus continually risks the possibility of being misunderstood as a rhetorical activity, even when it attempts to make its normative presuppositions explicit. Although philosophy has a power to move people, power is not its presiding norm; and of course the politician will fail to understand this. Although philosophy claims to be governed by norms other than power, the political audience will continue to hear this claim as another powerful rhetorical strategy. This culminates in Marx's claim that philosophers suffer from ideological false consciousness in which their appeals to self-consciousness conceal the social class and political power, which they implicitly defend. According to Marx, philosophical claims about objectivity remain rhetorical strategies. And thus, the philosopher is thrown back into political life.

The continuing struggle between philosophy and politics stems from the fact that philosophical speech and political speech each address the same audience and the same set of issues with the intention of changing people's minds, even though this intention is constrained by different norms. The philosopher, although he/she is constrained by respect for truth, is also interested in convincing others about this truth in order to effect social change. At the very least, the philosopher is interested in encouraging individuals to "think for themselves" or, in Kant's words, "to have the courage to use your own understanding."[9] This is both a political and a philosophical goal: it is the republican goal of political progress, conceived as a historically contingent norm of legitimate political practice; it is also the goal of a transformation of human judgment, which Kant saw at the heart of philosophical enlightenment, guided by the universal human norm of truth disclosure. Thus we see that the normative difference between philosophy and politics is not a qualitative difference. Politics and philosophy lie on a continuum. One extreme, the political extreme, is characterized by the norms of subjective certainty (or in Marx's case, class identity), persuasion, and coercion. The other extreme, the philosophical extreme, is characterized by the norms of self-consciousness, dialogue, and truth. These norms have been more or less closely related, during different stages of historical development: despite its condemnation of Socrates, Athenian democracy valued dialogue just as nineteenth century Germany valued systematic philosophical self-consciousness despite the absolutist Prussian bureaucracy and the political tumult of continuing revolution.

The philosophers we have examined were aware that further political and philosophical activity would be necessary if these different norms were ever to coincide. The philosophers who follow Kant came to the conclusion that a resolution of the conflict between philosophy and politics could only occur if political speech and philosophical speech came to share the same norms. This required deliberate attempts to use philosophical speech to influence political life. Kant held this out as a project, a utopian task to be completed: to turn the age of (political) enlightenment into a self-conscious enlightened age. His followers sought to complete this project. Fichte simply postulated a unity of norms in the German language, which he claimed was the living language of spirit. By hypostasizing the synthesis of political and philosophical norms in the German language, Fichte pointed to a political completion of the project of enlightenment: the final attainment of enlightenment required that the philosopher use his voice to transform political life. A similar attempt to complete the project of enlightenment led Hegel self-consciously to constrain philosophy to its task of articulating the norms of political actuality. Marx's insight into the political nature of Hegel's philosophical activity led him to accuse Hegel of ideological duplicity. Marx objected to the notion that there could only be one, necessary synthesis of the norms of political and philosophical speech as long as political life continued to be constituted by class division, oppression, and suffering. Marx's call for revolution can be interpreted as an attempt to open up the possibility of a further project of enlightenment in which different voices, different norms could be heard within an ongoing political process.

It is important to note that claims about a heteronomous difference between philosophy and politics will not resolve the matter. Philosophers attempt to circumvent the homophony, homonymy, homology, and homogeneity that exist between philosophy and politics by claiming that they address their audience with vastly different norms than politicians do. Despite the philosopher's protests, the politician will view the philosopher's claims about truth and self-consciousness as one more rhetorical ploy designed to persuade the audience. "Truth" itself is a homonym with different meanings for politicians and philosophers. For the philosopher, "truth" means some sort of correspondence or disclosive relation with the world; for the politician, "truth" is the ultimate persuasive trump card. When the philosopher claims that he/she appeals to the supposedly "higher" norm of truth, the politician hears this merely as a clever persuasive technique, the deus ex machina of rhetoric: when all else fails, bring in the gods, ego, *Ursprache*, spirit, or "truth." Moreover, self-consciousness itself can be a persuasive technique, as Marx discovered. His goal was to make the proletariat self-conscious so that they could effectively enter into the struggle for power. In this way, Marx's project foreshadows the "identity politics" of the twentieth century. We might thus characterize the politics of the twentieth century as the politics of self-consciousness. The "cult of personality" of twentieth century totalitarianism, for example, is based upon a perverted view of the importance of the "self-consciousness" of the ruler. Moreover, what MacIntyre calls therapeutic self-disclosure is used as a persuasive technique in political campaigns in Western democracies.[10] Thus the imbroglio continues: even the normative differentia of self-consciousness is not as clear as it might have seemed because "self-consciousness" can be used as a persuasive technique. It is possible, then, that there is no way to answer the question that Socrates poses in the *Gorgias* about which is the better life, the life spent conducting politics or the life spent in pursuit of philosophy.[11]

There are two reasons why this question might be irresolvable. First, political life and philosophical life are inextricable tied in practice. Philosophers cannot fully retreat to private life, as Socrates ironically suggests in the *Apology* that they ought. Philosophy and politics are homogeneous: they share a common origin within political life. Philosophy is supported by political life either in the basic sustenance and security provided by political order or in more elaborate institutional settings such as an ancient academy, a medieval monastery, or a modern university. Indeed, philosophers are real individuals whose lives are determined by their bodily needs, their familial relations, their labor, property, and class relations, their national and political identifications. Philosophical reflection cannot occur outside of political life. This is true to the extent that philosophical reflection is understood as a uniquely *human* activity, for as Aristotle tells us, only beasts and gods live outside of the polis, and neither beasts nor gods have need of philosophy. Philosophical speech will always occur within a political context and will use political language, thus risking the problems of homophony and homonymy. Although it does not intend merely to persuade, it will inevitably use political language and will be mistaken for persuasive political rhetoric. This is especially true given the fact that, as we see today in the modern university, philosophy must compete for resources within the political arena. Philosophy then, because it is located within and supported by political life, must continually justify itself politically; it must continually issue apologies for itself, while knowing that these apologies can easily be misinterpreted at the political level. This creates a practical difficulty for philosophy because politicians will understand philosophical speech as just one more rhetorical ploy, one more political mode of speech, one more attempt to persuade. Since the philosopher occupies political space and uses politically allocated time and resources, the politician will only ever understand the philosopher in political terms.

Second, philosophy is political action. At its most extreme, this occurs when the philosopher's self-conscious commitment to the good leads to political intervention in an attempt to actualize the insights of his or her theory, as in Fichte's *Addresses* or Marx's *Manifesto*. Socrates, for example, believes that knowledge of the true, the good, and the just leads the philosopher to remain and continue to act within the polis, even when the polis threatens his very life. Socrates' philosophical insight will not permit him to shut up about political issues; thus Socrates' philosophical commitment to political activity leads him to a political fight to the death. At a less extreme level, the philosopher's concern with theory is itself a form of political action, even when this concern leads the philosopher to give up on direct political intervention: to leave the polis in order to pursue unfettered philosophical contemplation, is still to engage in political action. Thus Socrates recognizes that were he to escape from Athens, his action would be interpreted politically and seen as an admission of guilt; this in turn would sully his supposed claims about philosophical truth. In short, philosophical speech is political action and will be interpreted as such within political life, even when it deliberately attempts to transcend political life. Philosophy cannot escape this imbroglio because philosophical escape is itself political action.

Conclusion

As we have seen, the development from Kant to Marx revolves around the proper definition of the relation between philosophy and politics and is colored by the foundational debate between philosophy and rhetoric. There is basic agreement among these philosophers that philosophy should be brought to bear upon political life and that political life should become more philosophical. However, there is profound disagreement about the meaning of claims about the political nature of philosophy or the philosophical nature of politics. Most of this disagreement focuses upon the meaning of truth. If truth is thoroughly political, then there may well be different truths for different members of the polis, and we may, with Marx, tie philosophical criticism to a definite party within the polis, for philosophical criticism would only speak for and to that party position. On the other hand, if truth is thought to transcend political squabbles and inhabit a philosophical heaven, then philosophy risks being unable to account for the very real diversity of political life and constrains itself to spinning "its own web of scholastic wisdom," an eventuality that even Hegel deplores.[12] Obviously the issue of truth and its relation to the plurality and frailty of political life, to borrow a description from Arendt, is crucial. Kant, Fichte, Hegel, and Marx all agree that truth contains some political element. Even Kant who maintains that the formal definition of truth is the agreement of knowledge with its object, recognized, as we saw, that there is no nondogmatic way of asserting that such agreement obtains and thus appeals to free public communication as the "touchstone" by which we decide whether a belief is true.[13] Kant indicates that since truth-claims must be evaluated publicly by others, truth requires free public communication. The problem that Kant and his followers confront is how to guarantee that the universal agreement of human reason that Kant claims is the touchstone of truth is genuine and has not been produced by persuasive rhetoric.

It is clear that philosophers must continually address members of the polis. It is also clear that philosophy is politically located both with regard to its audience and its concerns: it must make use of a language that it shares in common with political speech. Furthermore, philosophers aim at persuading their audience, in order to obtain the agreement of those educated others who help them toward certainty. Philosophy is a form of speech that, despite its disdain for the coercive techniques of political speech, wants to convince its audience of its truth-claims, wants to enact the good and institute the just. To do this, philosophy must be persuasive. Philosophy overcomes this rhetorical goal, however, to the extent that it is self-conscious of its own political location and the rhetorical strategies it employs, as well as the limits imposed upon these by its own normative methodology. Philosophy comes into its own to the extent that it is able to make its own rhetorical limitations and aspirations explicit. Philosophy is able to distinguish itself from politics by expressing its own limitations as a politically located voice.

As we saw, this self-consciousness of the political location of philosophical speech is an explicit theme for Kant, Fichte, Hegel, and Marx. These philosophers were acutely aware of the rhetorical power of philosophy and of the political location of philosophical speech. Because of the systematic tendency of these philosophers, they each found it necessary to account for their own philosophical activity within the context of political life and within a philosophy of language. Although their precursors—Machiavelli, Locke, and Rousseau—were aware of themselves as political agents, they did not make this an explicit theme for philosophical reflection. This self-consciousness of the political location of philosophical reflection is what makes Kant, Fichte, Hegel, and Marx so significant within the history of the struggle between philosophy and politics: they attempted to account for the rhetorical sound of their own philosophical voices.

Political philosophy ought to be especially conscious of its own voice. In contemporary political life, the issue of voice is, however, quite complicated. Contemporary political life is so diverse that it often appears to be entirely fragmented: a vast mosaic of voices forms our current heterophilic age.[14] Moreover, the very massiveness of contemporary political life, the prevalence of media and marketing, creates serious problems for the institution of any philosophical proposal for improvement.[15] We celebrate difference and view diversity as a good that we ought to cultivate. It might thus seem impossible for us to claim that there is something that could be called *the* philosopher's voice or that the philosopher's voice could be effective as an instrument of progress.

Such problems follow directly from Marx's politicized approach to political philosophy. The politicization of voice is seen clearly today, for example, in contemporary feminism. Catherine MacKinnon, who clearly acknowledges her debt to Marx, states explicitly that epistemology and politics are intertwined. She claims that the very idea of wholeness, the idea that the philosopher's voice could somehow speak for and to all of the members of society, is an illusion used to further disempower women. This is so because the traditional objectivist and universalist model of knowledge that she rejects is a model that has been used by men to oppress women. MacKinnon thus calls for the creation of a "feminist epistemology." This feminist epistemology would understand consciousness within social relations of power and understand knowledge not as an objective representation of the world but as a response to living in the world. MacKinnon links this view directly to Marx's political approach to theory.[16] Feminist epistemology is explicitly political to the extent that it claims to be a theory of women's experience, articulated from the point of view of women, and addressed to women in order to make their experience of oppression self-conscious. MacKinnon's appropriation of Marx thus leads beyond Marx and whatever residual "philosophical" motifs remained for him. For MacKinnon, philosophy and its epistemological project is entirely political. Even the critical space that is opened by theory is conceived by her as "gendered." Thus the philosopher's voice is the voice of a man or a woman, uttered from within a particular social situation. There is no need for mediation between the abstract universality of philosophy and the concrete particularity of political life because the abstract universality of philosophy is reconceived as merely the ideological front for the husky voice of male-dominant society.

This poses a problem, however, both for politics and for philosophy. If we agree that the truths of political philosophy must be understood according to the voice that articulates them, this opens the possibility that there may be a diversity of truths, depending upon whom political philosophy addresses within the polis. Thus philosophers and political agents will continue to talk past one another without ever attaining any sort of synthetic systematic comprehension. Given the diversity we find within our complex, multicultural world and the need for universal norms to govern this diversity, the issue of voice becomes a crucial one. While Fichte turned to linguistic nationalism, while Hegel blithely ignored the political experience of women and the rabble, while Marx had little to say about "the woman question," we cannot so easily ignore those "others" who are excluded from the political arena. Our contemporary problem is to recognize and account for the differences that constitute our political communities. Nonetheless, we must not give up on the philosophical goal of finding unity in difference. Nor must we abandon the political ideal which postulates shared rights that unite us in solidarity. Our own political practice must be founded on the Kantian republican ideal that every human being has the right to be recognized within the political arena, an ideal that Fichte, Hegel, and Marx, despite their differences, share. Political philosophy in the modern era acknowledges that it must address diversity: if we believe that all human beings are equal objects of respect, we must also believe that the concerns of all humans must be properly addressed by political philosophy, including the concerns of those whom the philosopher's voice has excluded in the past. The final task of the philosopher's voice is to become aware of its own inevitable tendency both to reduce the other to the same and to exclude difference from the community of discourse.

In the history I have traced in this book we have seen that it is essential to continue to ask the following questions. To whom does the philosopher address his voice? Is he (or she) explicitly aware of his own language, norms, and method? Who is excluded by this language? And finally, is the philosopher aware of the political location of his/her own voice? In answering these questions, we direct the evaluation of political philosophy toward the crucial question of whether the philosopher's voice can address all members of the political community.

In the movement from Kant to Marx, philosophy became explicitly political. The sorts of questions asked above are questions that can only be asked after the political turn that occurred during this history. In the present work, I have traced this political turn and have shown that the issue of voice is an important issue for each of the philosophers considered. What is significant about these philosophers is that they each take up the issue of voice and make it explicit, thus ushering in a new turn in the history of Western political philosophy, a history within which we are still struggling. One might say, optimistically, that since it is with these philosophers that political philosophy (and indeed philosophy in general) becomes explicitly conscious of its own voice, these philosophers enabled political philosophy to open itself to issues like multiculturalism, racial and gender bias, and even ecology. Or one might conclude, pessimistically, that the issue of voice with which these philosophers struggle leads to Nietzschean perspectivalism, relativism, irrationalism, and the problems that haunt twentieth century postmodernity. Regardless of our evaluation of the result of this historical movement, it is undeniable that the roots of our own struggles are found in this history.

Appendix: Biographical, Bibliographical, and Political Chronology

Date	Personal Events	Publications	Political Events
1700	Leibniz founds the Berlin Academy		
1701			Prussia is founded with crowning of Frederick I in Königsberg
1713–40			Reign of Frederick Wilhelm I
1715–74			Reign of Louis XIV
1724	Kant born		
1740–86			Reign of Frederick II (The Great)
1740		Frederick The Great, *Anti-Machiavelli*	
1744	Herder born		
1755		Rousseau, *Discourses on the Origin of Inequality*	
1756–63			Seven Years War
1762	Fichte born; Herder in Königsberg	Rousseau, *Social Contract;* Rousseau, *Emile*	
1767	Humboldt born		
1770	Hegel born		
1772		Herder, *Essay on the Origin of Language*	
1774–83			Reign of Louis XVI

(continued)

Date	Personal Events	Publications	Political Events
1774		Herder, *Another Philosophy of History Concerning the Development of Mankind*	
1776	Herder in Weimar	Smith, *Wealth of Nations*	
1778	Rousseau dies		
1780		Lessing, *The Education of the Human Race*	
1781		Kant, *Critique of Pure Reason,* 1st edition	
1782		Rousseau, *Confessions* (posthumous); Garve-Feder Review of Kant's *Critique of Pure Reason*	
1783		Kant, *Prolegomena to Any Future Metaphysics*	
1784		Kant, *What is Enlightenment?;* Kant, *Idea for a Universal History with a Cosmopolitan Purpose;* Herder, *Ideas for a Philosophy of the History of Mankind*	
1785		Kant, *Review of Herder's Ideas;* Kant, *Groundwork of the Metaphysics of Morals*	
1786		Kant, *What is Orientation in Thinking;* Kant, *Conjectural Beginning of the History of Mankind*	Death of Frederick the Great
1786–97			Reign of Frederick Wilhelm II
1787		Kant, *Critique of Pure Reason,* 2nd Edition	
1788	Hegel in Tübingen with Hölderlin and Schelling	Kant, *Critique of Practical Reason*	Wöllner's edict censoring unorthodox religion
1789			French Revolution
1790		Kant, *Critique of Judgment*	

(continued)

Date	Personal Events	Publications	Political Events
1791	Fichte meets Kant		
1792	Kant's trouble with the censors in Berlin over his Religion book	Kant, *On the Saying: That May Be True in Theory but not in Practice;* Fichte, *An Attempt at a Critique of all Revelation*	France becomes a republic
1793		Kant, *Religion within the Limits of Reason Alone;* Fichte, *Zurückforderung der Denkfreiheit;* Fichte, *Beitrag zur Berichtigung der Urtheile des Publikums über die französische Revolution*	Louis XVI executed; Robespierre and the Terror
1794	Frederick Wilhelm II admonishes Kant; Kant pledges to remain silent on religious matters; Fichte in Jena; Humboldt in Jena	Fichte, *On the Spirit and the Letter in Philosophy;* Fichte, *Vocation of the Scholar*	Robespierre executed
1795		Kant, *Perpetual Peace*; Fichte, *Foundations of the Science of Knowledge* (*Wissenschaftslehre*); Fichte, *On the Linguistic Capactiy and the Origin of Language*; Schiller, *On the Aesthetic Education of Man in a Series of Letters*	Napoleon Bonaparte begins his conquests; Prussian neutrality
1796		Fichte, *Foundations of Natural Right; Hegel, "System Fragment"*	
1797	Humboldt to Paris	Kant, *Metaphysics of Morals* (includes the *Rechtslehre*);	Death of Frederick Wilhelm II; Wöllner's edict is cancelled: Reign of Friedrich Wilhelm III (1797–1840)
1798	Schelling in Jena	Kant, *The Contest of the Faculties;* Kant, *Anthropology from a Pragmatic Point of View;* Fichte, *Science of Ethics*	
1799	Atheism charges force Fichte to leave Jena	Herder, *Metacritique of the Critique of Pure Reason*	Napoleon becomes First Consul of France

(continued)

Date	Personal Events	Publications	Political Events
1800	Fichte in Berlin	Fichte, *The Vocation of Man*; Fichte, *Die Geschlossene Handelstaat (The Closed Commercial State)*	
1801	Hegel in Jena; Humboldt to Berlin	Hegel, *The Difference between Fichte's and Schelling's Systems of Philosophy;* Fichte, *A Crystal Clear Report to the General Public Concerning the Actual Essence of the Newest Philosophy*	
1802	Hegel and Schelling found the Critical Journal	Hegel, *Natural Law*	Britain declares war on France
1803	Herder dies; Schelling leaves Jena		
1804	Kant dies	1801–1804, F. Schlegel, *Lectures on Fine Art and Literature*	French Civil Code (Napoleonic code) is adopted; Napoleon declared Emperor
1805			Napoleon's victory at Austerlitz
1806	Fichte in Königsberg	Fichte, *Characteristics of the Present Age;* Fichte, *The Way Toward the Blessed Life*	Napoleon defeats Prussia at Jena and occupies Berlin; Frederick Wilhelm III appoints Stein, who begins liberal reforms in Prussia
1807	Fichte in Berlin	Hegel, *Phenomenology of Spirit;* Fichte, *Ueber Machiavelli*	Palm, a Nuremberg bookseller is executed by French authorities for dissent
1808	Hegel in Nuremburg	Fichte, *Addresses to the German Nation*	
1810	Fichte is professor at University of Berlin		Founding of University of Berlin (Friedrich Wilhelm University) under Humboldt
1812		Hegel, *Science of Logic,* vol. 1	

(continued)

Date	Personal Events	Publications	Political Events
1813	Fichte dies	Hegel, *Science of Logic,* vol. 2	Russians invade Berlin; Wilhelm Frederick III, *"Anruf an Mein Volk"*
1814			Napoleon abdicates and goes to Elba
1815			Congress of Vienna; Napoleon returns to France and is defeated at Waterloo; the reactionary Holy Alliance is formed; founding of the German Confederation
1816	Hegel in Heidelberg	Hegel, *Science of Logic,* vol. 3	
1817	Marx born	Hegel, *Encyclopedia of the Philosophical Sciences;* Hegel, *Proceedings of the Estates Assembly in the Kingdom of Würtemburg 1815–1816;* Hegel's first lectures (1817–1818) on the Philosophy of Right	
1818	Hegel to Berlin		
1819		Hegel's second lectures (1818–1819) on Philosophy of Right	Kotzebue assassinated by Karl Sand; Karlsbad decrees of state censorship
1820	Engels born	Hegel, publication of the *Philosophy of Right*	
1824	Hegel writes Prussian authorities defending Victor Cousin		
1827		Hegel, *Encyclopedia* 2nd edition	
1830			July Revolution in France
1831	Hegel dies	Hegel, *On the English Reform Bill*; Hegel, *Encyclopedia,* 3rd edition	

(continued)

Date	Personal Events	Publications	Political Events
1832			First English Reform Bill is passed and other subsequent liberal reforms follow
1835	Humboldt dies		
1836	Marx studies in Berlin	Humboldt, *On the Diversity of Human Language* (posthumous)	
1842	Marx is editor of *Rheinische Zeitung;* Marx and Engels meet in Cologne		
1843	Marx resigns as editor of *Rheinische Zeitung* because of Prussian censorship; Marx founds *Deutsch-Franzosische Jahrbucher* with Ruge in Paris	Marx, *On the Jewish Question;* Marx, *Contribution to the Critique of Hegel's Philosophy of Right;* Feuerbach, *Principles of the Philosophy of the Future*	
1844	Prussians issue arrest warrant for Marx	Marx, *Economic and Philosophical Manuscripts* (Paris Manuscripts of 1844)	
1845	Marx banished from Paris and moves to Brussels; Marx renounces Prussian citizenship	Marx, *Theses on Feuerbach;* Marx and Engels, *The Holy Family;* Engels, *Condition of the Working Class in England*	
1846		Marx and Engels, *The German Ideology*	
1847		Marx, *The Poverty of Philosophy*	Communist League meetings in London with Engels and Marx
1848	Marx and Engels active in revolutions in Germany, found *Neue Rheinische Zeitung*	Marx and Engels, *The Communist Manifesto*	Revolutions throughout Europe; Frankfurt Parliament of German States meets; Louis Napoleon president of 2nd French Republic
1849	Marx in London		Frankfurt Parliament's German constitution; Friedrich Wilhelm IV declines to support liberal constitution

(continued)

Date	Personal Events	Publications	Political Events
1850	Engels in Manchester		
1852–1870			Louis Napoleon becomes Napoleon III and rules as Emperor of 2nd Empire in France
1852		Marx, *Eighteenth Brumaire of Louis Napoleon*	
1857	Marx works on *Grundrisse*		
1859		Marx, *Contribution to the Critique of Political Economy*	
1862–90			Bismarck is minister president of Prussia and then Chancellor of German Empire (in 1871)
1864			Founding of International Working Men's Association in London with Marx and Engels taking an active part
1866			Prussia expands power during Seven Weeks War
1867		Marx, *Capital,* vol.1	Prussia leads North German Confederation
1870			Franco-Prussian War; Napoleon III deposed; Founding of the 3rd Republic in France
1871		Marx, *The Civil War in France*	Founding of the German Empire; Paris Commune (March–May)
1878		Engels, *Anti-Dühring*	
1883	Marx dies		Triple Alliance formed (Germany, Italy, and Austria-Hungary)
1884		Engels, *Origin of the Family, Private Property, and the State*	
1885		Marx (edited by Engels), *Capital*, vol. 2	

(continued)

Date	Personal Events	Publications	Political Events
1886		Engels, *Ludwig Feuerbach and the End of Classical German Philosophy*	
1889			2nd International Founded (with Engels involved) (International Socislist organization that lasted until WW I)
1890			Bismarck resigns
1894		Marx (edited by Engels), *Capital*, vol. 3	
1895	Engels dies		

Notes

Chapter 1

1. Hegel, *Encyclopedia*, § 401, Addition; *Werke* (Hegel-Institut Berlin, from Past Masters, 1999, same edition as the Suhrkamp edition of Hegel's *Werke*), 10: 109.

2. Plato, *Apology* in *Four Texts on Socrates* (trans. Thomas G. West and Grace Starry West, Ithaca, N.Y.: Cornell University Press, 1984), 17 a.

3. The difference between teaching and persuasion is a recurrent theme in Plato's dialogues. The issue becomes even more difficult to resolve if we take Socrates' claims about ignorance seriously. He denies that he uses his voice rhetorically to persuade his audience, and yet he also denies knowing anything that he could teach his audience. One wonders if the problem of Socrates' *elenchos* (examination method) could be resolved by considering his awareness of the ambiguity of voice as politically embodied activity that aims beyond political life. For synoptic discussion of problems with regard to the Socratic *elenchos,* see Thomas C. Brickhouse and Nicolas D. Smith, *The Philosophy of Socrates* (Boulder, Colo.: Westview Press, 2000). For further relevant discussion of Socrates, see Alexander Nehamas, *The Art of Living* (Berkeley: University of California Press, 1998). Nehamas concludes that Socrates actually says nothing to us because he wrote nothing. Rather it is Plato who speaks for Socrates. Such an important point does pose a problem for my subsequent account. I do assume that we can study the voice of the philosophers I consider in the present text by way of their written words. I further try to read their written words back into their historical and rhetorical contexts. Of course, this may be impossible. Indeed the nineteenth century saw a rebirth of irony and a fracturing of the idea of self-identity that seems essential for a consideration of something as unified as "the" philosopher's voice. Kierkegaard and Nietzsche, for example, do not speak with anything like the unified voice I will be ascribing to Kant, Fichte, or Hegel. This is fitting, however, because the content of Kant's, Fichte's, and Hegel's philosophical theories affirm the idea of concrete self-identity. I do, however, take up the issue of multiplicity of voices as well as a consideration of irony of style and presentation in the chapters on Marx. As a result of the content of his own political and philosophical theory, Marx, like Nietzsche and Kierkegaard, opens the possibility that the philosopher has a multiplicity of voices.

4. There are many texts that treat this set of philosophers and this era of philosophical activity. Among these are Joseph M. Schwartz's *The Permanence of the*

Political (Princeton, N.J.: Princeton University Press, 1995), Dick Howard's *From Marx to Kant* (2nd ed., New York: St. Martin's Press, 1993), Bernard Yack's *The Longing for Total Revolution* (Berkeley: University of California Press, 1986), and George Armstrong Kelly's *Idealism, Politics, and History* (Cambridge: Cambridge University Press, 1969). These accounts suffice to show the interpenetration of philosophy and politics in this historical era, however, none of them includes an account of the relation between philosophy, politics, and language that I am arguing lies at the heart of the problematic that instigates the development from Kant to Marx.

5. Wilhelm von Humboldt, *On the Diversity of Human Language Construction and its Influence on the Mental Development of the Human Species* (trans. by Peter Heath, Cambridge: Cambridge University Press, 1999), 41.

6. For a discussion of this see George Steiner, *After Babel* (Oxford: Oxford University Press, 1975), especially chapter 2.

7. Hegel, *Encyclopedia*, § 401, Addition.

8. Hegel, *Encyclopedia*, § 401, Addition.

9. Hegel, *Encyclopedia,* § 459.

10. Kant, *Anthropology from a Pragmatic Point of View* (trans. Victor Lyle Dowdell, Carbondale: Southern Illinois University Press, 1978), 147.

11. Kant, *Anthropology from a Pragmatic Point of View*, 147; *Hauptwerke* [*Akademie Ausgabe* (Immanuel Kant, *Gesammelte Schriften.* Hrsg. von der Königlich-Preussischen Akademie der Wissenschaften zu Berlin. Berlin, 1902-) from Past Masters, 1998), 7: 245.

12. Kant, *Anthropology from a Pragmatic Point of View*, 147; *Hauptwerke*, 7: 245.

13. Kant, *Anthropology*, 23; *Hauptwerke*, 7: 139.

14. Kant, "What is Enlightenment?" in *Kant's Political Writings* (ed. by Hans Reiss, Cambridge University Press, 1991), 54. The contrasting metaphors of maturity, immaturity, tutelage, childishness, and enlightenment are themselves political concepts. As Willi Goetschel interprets this passage: "In fact, the juridical definition of enlightenment suggests with this 'overturn' a crucial point: the concept of legal majority [*Mündigkeit*], the age at which one is competent to use one's understanding without another's guidance, actually serves as a way to redefine enlightenment in terms of self-determination. Instead of treating majority as a legal notion, Kant turns it into an expression of the ability to utilize one's understanding autonomously" [Willi Goetschel, *Constituting Critique* (trans. Eric Schwab, Durham, N.C.: Duke University Press, 1994), 148].

15. The distinction I am making between "hearing" and "listening" may perhaps seem to be an unjustified imposition upon our ordinary usage. However, a convenient distinction between the two modes of reception is needed, and the etymology of the terms suggests such a distinction. The verb "to hear" is linked to the German *hören*

and distantly to *gehören*, to belong to. It thus suggests a more original sense of receptivity: receptivity to the sound of language in which we belong to the sound in such a way as to be swayed by it. The verb "to listen" and especially "to listen to" is related to the English verb "to list," which means to lean toward something; it indicates receptivity with a definite intention. At the very least it is obvious that we can hear something without actually listening to it.

16. Hans Saner, *Kant's Political Thought* (trans. E. B. Ashton, Chicago: The University of Chicago Press, 1973). Also in this line of Kant interpretation is Hannah Arendt and her *Lectures on Kant's Political Philosophy* (ed. Ronald Beiner, Chicago: University of Chicago Press, 1982).

17. Dieter Henrich, "Kant's Notion of a Deduction and the Methodological Background of the First Critique" [in *Kant's Transcendental Deductions*, ed. Eckart Förster, (Stanford University Press, 1989)].

18. "[This is] . . . the core idea that Kant's contemporaries never grasped. In it, Kant's understanding of himself in relation to his philosophical preconceptions, in a simultaneously critical and political sense, is articulated most exactly: the writer's public voice emerges from his private activity, which now takes on a public dimension. And the point of division in this public-private border dispute is occupied by the writer himself" (Goetschel, *Constituting Critique*, 150).

19. Goetschel, *Constituting Critique*, 117. Goetschel is not alone in this assessment of Hegel. Adorno shares this view of Hegel's disdain for language [Theodore Adorno, *Negative Dialectics* (trans. Ashton, New York: Continuum, 1994)]. Others have realized that Hegel is indeed a self-conscious stylist, for example, Jürgen Habermas, *Theory and Practice* [(trans. Viertel, Boston: Beacon, 1974), 179] and Z. A. Pelczynski, "Introductory Essay" to *Hegel: Political Writings* (Garland Publishing Inc.: New York and London, 1984). The concern for language and its impact on critical philosophy was known as the "meta-critique" of critical philosophy and was a theme of most post-Kantian and pre-Hegelian philosophy including the thought of Herder and Fichte. For an excellent account of this, see Frederick C. Beiser *The Fate of Reason* (Cambridge: Harvard University Press, 1993).

20. Marx, "Letter to Ruge" from *Deutsch-Französische Jahrbücher*, September 1843, in *Marx Engels Collected Works* (New York: International Publishers, 1976), 3: 144.

21. Marx, "Letter to Ruge" from *Deutsch-Französische Jahrbücher*, September 1843, in *Collected Works*, 3: 145.

22. Iris Marion Young, *Justice and the Politics of Difference* (Princeton: Princeton University Press, 1990), 14.

23. Ludwig Wittgenstein, *Philosophical Investigations* (trans. G. E. M. Anscombe, New York: Macmillan, 1968), # 110.

24. Hans-Georg Gadamer, *Truth and Method,* 2nd Revised Edition (trans. Joel Weinsheimer and Donald G. Marshall, New York: Continuum, 1993), 458.

25. Carol Gilligan, *In a Different Voice* (Cambridge: Harvard University Press, 1982), 173.

26. Seyla Benhabib, *Critique, Norm, Utopia* (New York: Columbia University Press, 1986), 300.

27. Karl Popper, *The Open Society and Its Enemies* (Princeton, N.J.: Princeton University Press, 1971), II: 9.

28. Popper, *The Open Society and Its Enemies*, II: 21.

29. Popper, *The Open Society and Its Enemies*, II: 266.

30. Jürgen Habermas, "Philosophy as Stand-In and Interpreter" [in *Moral Consciousness and Communicative Action* (trans. Lenhardt and Nicholsen, Cambridge: MIT Press, 1995)], 1.

31. Habermas, *Philosophical Discourses of Modernity* (trans. Lawrence, Cambridge: MIT Press, 1995), 336.

32. Kant, *The Contest of the Faculties* in *Political Writings,* 186; *Hauptwerke*, 7: 89.

33. Habermas provides a detailed history of the way in which "public opinion" and the very concept of "the public sphere" was based upon certain practical social structures. Habermas argues that in Kant's Germany of the late eighteenth century, literary journals and "reading societies" were the basis of what came to be called "public opinion" (Habermas, *Structural Transformation of the Public Sphere* (Cambridge: MIT Press, 1991) pp. 71–73). In the late twentieth century, Habermas argues, the notion of "public opinion" has been co-opted by media sources who themselves control "public opinion" to the extent that they control our ability to address the public critically (Habermas, *Structural Transformation of the Public Sphere*, pp. 247–48).

34. As we shall see, in the chapter on Marx's political philosophy, such a claim is contentious and requires significant qualification for Marx has often been interpreted as one of those utopian theorists whose goal is to transcend politics. Cf. Yack's *The Longing for Total Revolution* and Schwartz's *The Permanence of the Political.*

35. Kant, *Perpetual Peace,* Appendix, in *Political Writings,* 118.

36. An example of this approach can be found in Martha C. Nussbaum, "Four Paradigms of Philosophical Politics" in *The Monist* (vol. 83, no. 4, pp. 465–490).

Chapter 2

1. Marx, *Eighteenth Brumaire of Louis Napoleon,* in *Marx-Engels Reader*, 595.

2. Hegel, "The Constitution of Germany" in *Hegel's Political Writings*, (Cambridge: Cambridge University Press, 1999), 219; *Gesammelte Werke*, 5: 131.

3. Machiavelli, *The Prince*, 4.

4. In this regard it is useful to note that Machiavelli's *Discourses* are also addressed to real individuals in political space, Zanobi Buondelmonte and Cosimo Rucellai. However, the difference between the *Discourses* and *The Prince* is that *The Prince* is addressed explicitly to the prince, its very subject matter, while the *Discourses* are addressed to these individuals as friends who share an interest in the subject matter.

5. Machiavelli, *The Prince*, 96.

6. Hegel, "The Constitution of Germany" in *Hegel's Political Writings*, 233; *Gesammelte Werke*, 5: 136.

7. This is the title of Chapter XXXV of the *Discourses.*

8. Machiavelli, *Discourses*, 514.

9. Machiavelli, *Discourses*, 514.

10. Machiavelli, *Discourses*, 515.

11. Machiavelli, *Discourses*, 515.

12. Kant, "What is Enlightenment?" in *Political Writings*, 59.

13. Cassirer, *The Myth of the State* (New Haven, Conn.: Yale University Press, 1946), 141.

14. Thus Cassirer's interpretation is contentious. Otto Pöggeler indicates that there is a vast amount of misinformation about the Machiavellian roots of Hegel's thought. Pöggeler traces this misinformation to a mistake made by Karl Rosenkranz, in his *Hegel's Leben* (of 1840*)*, in dating Hegel's essay on the "German Constitution." This mistake made it seem that Hegel's discussion of Machiavelli was caught up in the same nationalistic context as Fichte's. Fichte's discussion of Machiavelli in his "*Ueber Machiavelli*" occurs in 1807 in response to the French invasion, as a call for the Prussian king to rise up in defiance of France. Hegel's dissusion of Machiavelli in the "German Constitution" actually occurs in 1799–1801 and is more interested in thinking about the political realities of founding a state in Germany. Cf. Pöggeler, "*Hegel et Machiavel: Renaissance Italienne et Idéalisme Allemand*" *Archives de Philosophie* 41, 1978, 435–467.

15. Hegel, *Philosophy of Right*, Remark to § 279 and Remark to § 281.

16. Friedrich, *Anti-Machiavelli* (trans. Paul Sonnino, Athens, Ohio: Ohio University Press, 1981), 65.

17. Friedrich, *Anti-Machiavelli*, 31.

18. Friedrich, *Anti-Machiavelli*, 100.

19. Herder, "Letters for the Advancement of Humanity," quoted in Pöggeler, *"Hegel et Machiavel,"* p. 439.

20. Kant, *Perpetual Peace,* in *Political Writings*, 125.

21. Hegel, *Constitution of Germany*, in *Hegel's Political Writings*, p. 221; *Gesammelte Werke*, 5: 132.

22. Fichte, *Ueber Machiavelli*, in J.G. Fichte *Gesamtausgabe* I,9.

23. Cf. Hegel, *Philosophy of Right*, §§ 324–329, 350, 351.

24. Strauss, *What is Political Philosophy?* (Chicago: University of Chicago Press, 1988), p. 54.

25. For a criticism of Strauss, see Robert Pippin, "Leo Strauss," in *Idealism as Modernism* (Cambridge: Cambridge University Press, 1997), 213] as well as Victor Gourevitch, "Philosophy and Politics I," *Review of Metaphysics* 22: 58–84 and "Philosophy and Politics II," *Review of Metaphysics* 22: 281–328.

26. Cassirer, *The Myth of the State*, 153.

27. For more on the influence of Machiavelli on nineteenth century German thought, cf. Cassirer, *The Myth of the State* Chapter 10; also Max Lerner's Introduction to Machiavelli's *The Prince and The Discourses.*

28. Pöggeler, "*Hegel et Machiavel*," 455.

29. For more on Machiavelli's alteration of the paradigms of theory and practice, see Habermas, *Theory and Practice*, 59-61; or J. G. A. Pocock, "Custom and Grace, Form and Matter" in *Machiavelli and the Nature of Political Thought* (ed. Martin Fleisher, New York, Atheneum, 1972), 174.

30. Hegel, *History of Philosophy*, 3: 316.

31. Hobbes, *Leviathan*, 407.

32. Hobbes, *Leviathan*, 407.

33. David Johnston, *The Rhetoric of Leviathan: Thomas Hobbes and the Politics of Cultural Transformation* (Princeton, N.J.: Princeton University Press, 1986), 130.

34. Jacques Taminiaux discusses the way in which Hegel's systematic project parallels Hobbes's. He notes that: "In the philosophy of nature, as in political philosophy, the Hobbesian mathesis lets stand a gap between poiesis, the sole source of intelligibility, and its subject matter. It is this gap that Hegel overcomes" [Jacques Taminiaux, "Hegel and Hobbes" in *Dialectic and Difference* [Atlantic Highlands, N.J.: Humanities Press, 1985], 28].

35. "These (pages) which remain, I hope are sufficient to establish the throne of our great restorer, our present King William; to make good his title, in the consent of the people, which being the only one of all lawful governments, he has more fully and clearly, than any prince in Christendom; and to justify to the world the people of England, whose love of their just and natural rights, with their resolution to preserve them, saved the nation when it was on the very brink of slavery and ruin" (Locke, *Second Treatise of Government*, p. 5).

36. Locke, *Second Treatise*, §§ 138–140.

37. C. B. MacPherson makes this argument in his *Political Theory of Possessive Individualism* (Oxford: Clarendon Press, 1962), pp. 232–238.

38. Indeed, in his essay on education Locke admits that his educational ideas are concerned with the education of Young Gentlemen and that they concern "the Gentelman's Calling" John Locke, *Some Thoughts Concerning Education* [in *The Educational Writings of John Locke*, ed. by James L. Axtell (Cambridge: Cambridge University Press, 1968)], "Dedicatory Epistle," p. 112, also p. 197 and p. 325. As Axtell interprets this, "It simply never occurred to Locke that all children should be educated, or that those who should should be educated alike" (Axtell, *The Educational Writings of John Locke*, p. 51). Neal Wood has also argued that Locke's essay is also caught up in a class context: "It is evident, then, that Locke wrote the *Essay* essentially for educated, intelligent men of property—peers and gentry, professionals, civil servants, men of letters, clergy, merchants and manufacturers—who had leisure and inclination for study and participation in public affairs" [Neal Wood, *The Politics of Locke's Philosophy* (Berkeley: University of California Press, 1983), 46].

39. Locke, "Letter Concerning Toleration" in *Classics of Modern Political Philosophy*, 310.

40. Locke, *Second Treatise of Government*, 116.

41. Strauss, *What is Political Philosophy?*, 49.

42. It is important to note that Locke would not agree with this nihilistic conclusion. He maintains, in the "Letter Concerning Toleration," for example, that there is a limit to toleration. We need not tolerate atheists, for example, because atheists have given up on the project of truth and are thus immoral. Thus Locke admits that a stable society must be founded on belief in God, even as he opens up the possibility that political life can be divorced from pursuit of the question of the truth of religious belief.

43. Marx, "On the Jewish Question" in *Marx-Engels Reader*, 34.

44. Marx, "On the Jewish Question" in *Marx-Engels Reader*, 46

45. Kant, "Theory and Practice" in *Political Writings*, 84.

46. Kant, "Theory and Practice" in *Political Writings*, 84.

47. Kant, "Theory and Practice" in *Political Writings*, 85.

48. Kant, "Theory and Practice" in *Political Writings*, 84.

49. Kant, "Theory and Practice," in *Political Writings*, 82.

50. Kant, "Theory and Practice," in *Political Writings*, 84.

51. Locke, *Second Treatise*, §§ 240–243.

52. Locke, *Second Treatise*, § 240.

53. Kant, "Theory and Practice," in *Political Writings*, 87.

54. Rousseau, *Discourses on the Origin of Inequality*, 194.

55. Locke, *An Essay Concerning Human Understanding* (ed. by Alexander Campbell Fraser, New York: Dover Publications, 1959, in 2 volumes), Book 3; Hobbes, *Leviathan*, Part 1, Chapter 4, "Of Speech."

56. Locke, *An Essay Concerning Human Understanding*, vol. 2: 3.

57. Locke, *Some Thoughts Concerning Education*, 300.

58. Cf. Leibniz's discussion of Locke's theory of language in his *New Essays On Human Understanding* (Cambridge: Cambridge University Press, 1981), Book 3. For more on Leibniz's idea of the *Lingua Philosophica,* see Benson Mates, *The Philosophy of Leibniz* (Oxford: Oxford University Press, 1986), 183–188.

59. For a discussion of this see Mates, *The Philosophy of Leibniz*, Chapter 1 or Hegel, *History of Philosophy* III: 325–329. Incidentally, the Berlin Academy was to become a source of consternation for Hegel, as (under the leadership of Hegel's nemesis, Schleiermacher) it refused to ask Hegel to become a member (cf. Pinkard, *Hegel: A Biography* [Cambridge: Cambridge University Press, 2000], 446).

60. Leibniz, "Preface to an Edition of Nizolius" (in Leibniz, *Philosophical Papers and Letters*, trans. and ed. by Leroy E. Loemker (Chicago: University of Chicago Press, 1956), I: 193. Ironically, Hegel goes so far as to reject Leibniz because he wrote in Latin and French and did not utilize his "mother tongue." This is important for Hegel because "it is only when a nation possesses a science in its own language that it can really be said to belong to it..." (Hegel, *History of Philosophy*, III: 351).

61. Rousseau, *Discourse on the Origin of Inequality*, 198.

62. Kant, "Conjectures on the Beginning of Human History, in *Political Writings*, 227; *Hauptwerke*, 8.116.

63. Cassirer, *Rousseau, Kant, Goethe* (Hamden, Conn.: Archon Books, 1961), 6.

64. Rousseau, *Discourse on the Origin of Inequality*, 198.

65. Rousseau, *Social Contract*, 5.

66. Rousseau, *Social Contract*, 111.

67. Rousseau, *Social Contract*, 111.

68. Rousseau, *Social Contract*, 112.

69. Rousseau, *Social Contract*, 44.

70. Rousseau, *Discourse on Inequality*, 158; *Rousseau Oeuvres Politiques* (Paris: Bordas, 1989), p. 11.

71. Rousseau, *Discourse on Inequality*, 160.

72. Rousseau, *Discourse on Inequality*, 175.

73. Rousseau, *Social Contract*, 45.

74. Rousseau, *Discourse on Inequality*, 227.

75. Rousseau, *Émile*, 256.

76. Rousseau, *Émile*, 207.

77. Rousseau, *Émile*, 247.

78. Rousseau, *Émile*, 3.

Chapter 3

1. Kant, *Logic* in *Hauptwerke* [*Akademie Ausgabe* (Immanuel Kant, *Gesammelte Schriften*. Hrsg. von der Königlich-Preussischen Akademie der Wissenschaften zu Berlin. Berlin, 1902) from Past Masters, 1998], 9: 25.

2. This conclusion is shared, in part, by Willi Goetschel, Dick Howard, Hannah Arendt, and Ernst Cassirer. Goetschel argues that Kant's rhetorical style resulted from his awareness of the dialectical nature of philosophical activity [Goetschel, *Constituting Critique* (trans. Eric Schwab, Durham, N.C.: Duke University Press, 1994)]. While Goetschel focuses on Kant's rhetorical style, Howard focuses on the "originary" connection between the critical method and republican politics [Howard, *The Politics of Critique* (Minneapolis: University of Minnessota Press, 1989)]. Howard thus argues that the critical methodology originates together with the republican form of political life. Arendt focuses on the organic nature of Kant's system. She emphasizes the organic connection between Kant's first *Critique*, his third *Critique* and his political writings and the way in which Kant's account of judgment forces us to consider the political location of critical thought [Arendt, *Lectures on Kant's Political Philosophy* (ed. Ronald Beiner, Chicago: University of Chicago Press, 1982)]. Cassirer argues that Kant's style changed drastically in the 1770s in response to the demands of the critical project and that Kant was concerned throughout his critical period with the question of whether or not the critical project could be expressed in a popular form [Cassirer, *Kant's Life and Thought* (New Haven, Conn.: Yale University Press, 1981), especially pp. 139–144]. The method of interpretation which I propose here owes its inspiration to Lukács, whose *History and Class Consciousness* indicates that the "greatness, the paradox, and the tragedy" of classic German philosophy is that its rationalist demand for a complete self-transparent system is based upon a material foundation that makes it impossible to satisfy this demand [Georg Lukács, "Reification and the Proletariat" in *History and Class Consciousness* (trans. Livingstone, Cambridge, Mass.: MIT Press, 1992), 116–117]. This "irrational" element is examined by Lukács further in his *Destruction of Reason* (trans. Peter Palmer, Highlands, N.J.: Humanities Press, 1981). Robert Pippin has more recently called German Idealism, a "metaphysical politics," meaning that it is an attempt to ground both metaphysics and politics in a concept of freedom [Robert J. Pippin, *Idealism as Modernism* (Cambridge: Cambridge University Press, 1997), 8].

3. Kant, *Critique of Pure Reason*, B 766.

4. Kant, *Critique of Pure Reason*, B 356.

5. Kant, *Critique of Pure Reason*, B 21.

6. Kant, *Critique of Pure Reason*, B 22.

7. Heidegger reaches a similar conclusion from a quite different perspective in claiming that Kant "falls back" upon a "philosophical anthropology"—an account of the essence of man—because Kant found himself unable to complete the critical project on its own terms. For Heidegger this falling back upon anthropology indicates a gap within the system, i.e., Kant's failure to follow his questioning through to its logical end [Heidegger, *Kant and the Problem of Metaphysics* (trans. Taft, Bloomington: Indiana University Press, 1990)].

8. This becomes a bit fuzzy if we follow Kant in his discussion of immortality of the soul as a postulate of pure practical reason [Kant, *Critique of Practical Reason* (translated by Lewis White Beck (New York: Macmillan, 1956), 126–28). Although Kant states that good must be achievable, he extends the idea of moral progress beyond the sensible world to the spiritual world of immortality. The problem for Kant is to make sense of the *demand* for the instantiation of goodness or freedom in a world of determination and indifference.

9. Kant, *Foundations of the Metaphysics of Morals* (trans. Lewis White Beck, New York: MacMillan, 1990), p. 50.

10. Kant *Critique of Pure Reason*, B 28.

11. Kant, *Critique of Pure Reason*, B 19.

12. Kant, *Critique of Pure Reason*, B 116.

13. What I am calling a "republican ideal' is called, by Gerald J. Postema, for example, "public practical reason." Postema claims that, following Kant, political legitimacy in modernity amounts to "robust public discourse" and "public deliberation." Postema denies, however, that such a process of *legitimation* amounts to full *justification*—public deliberation may legitimate unjust or immoral practices (Postema, "Public Practical Reason: Political Practice" in *Theory and Practice* (ed. Shapiro and DeCew, New York: New York University Press, 1995). Maria Chiara Pievatolo interprets this distinction as follows: "In its work of legitimating our a priori frameworks, reason attributes to them a conditioned necessity similar to the legal one: it is not an absolute necessity, but a necessity relative to a particular perspective and particular proceedings" (Maria Chiara Pievatolo, "The Juridical Nature of Pure Reason" in *Ratio Juris* 12: 3 (1999), 312). Pievatolo concludes: "Reason can never operate without presupposing itself and its own autonomy" (Pievatolo, 315). The point I want to emphasize is that Kant, in presupposing the autonomy of reason, also presupposes a shared theory and practice of legitimation and justification.

14. For Kant's view of republicanism see *Metaphysical Elements of Justice* (trans. John Ladd, New York: Macmillan, 1965), 112–113.

15. This is Dieter Henrich's interpretation of Kant's Transcendental Deduction, for example. Henrich has also pointed out that Kant's use of the term "deduction" is borrowed from juridical contexts, where the aim of deduction was "to justify controversial legal claims" via perspicuous argumentation (Dieter Henrich, "Kant's Notion of a Deduction and the Methodological Background of the First *Critique*" [in *Kant's Transcendental Deductions*, ed. Eckart Förster, Stanford, Calif.: Stanford University Press, 1989], 32).

16. Kant, *Metaphysical Elements of Justice*, § 41, p. 69.

17. Kant, *Critique of Pure Reason*, B 780.

18. Kant, *Critique of Judgment* (trans. J. H. Bernard, New York: Macmillan, 1951), § 40, p. 136.

19. Kant, "What is Enlightenment?" in *Political Writings*, 55.

20. Kant, *Critique of Pure Reason*, B 19.

21. Kant, *Critique of Pure Reason*, B v.

22. For a discussion of these events, see Greene's introduction to Kant's *Religion within the Limits of Reason Alone* (New York: Harper Torchbook, 1960).

23. Kant, *Critique of Pure Reason,* A xxi.

24. Kant, *Critique of Pure Reason* , A xi–xii.

25. Kant, *Critique of Pure Reason,* B 766–67.

26. Kant, *Metaphysical Elements of Justice*, 78; *Hauptwerke*, 6: 314.

27. Dick Howard describes this problem as the *originary* relation between philosophy and politics: both republican politics and the Kantian critical method originate out of, in Howard's terms, a common space (Howard, *The Politics of Critique*, xxi and xxvii).

28. Kant, *Critique of Pure Reason*, B 848.

29. Kant, *Perpetual Peace* in *Political Writings*, 99.

30. Kant, *Perpetual Peace* in *Political Writings*, 99—footnote.

31. Postema, "Public Practical Reason: Political Practice," 345.

32. Kant, *Perpetual Peace* in *Political Writings*, 99—footnote.

33. Kant, *Critique of Pure Reason*, B 25–26.

34. Kant, *Critique of Pure Reason,* B 708.

35. Kant, *Critique of Pure Reason*, B 848–49.

36. Kant, *Critique of Pure Reason*, B 850.

37. Kant, "What is Enlightenment?" in *Political Writings,* 55.

38. Kant, *Critique of Pure Reason,* B 116–117.

39. Kant, *Critique of Pure Reason,* B 732.

40. Kant, *Critique of Pure Reason*, B 368.

41. Kant, *Prolegomena to Any Future Metaphysics* (translated by Lewis White Beck, New York: Macmillian, 1950), 9.

42. For a discussion of this see Cassirer, *Kant's Life and Thought*, 218–222.

43. Kant, *Critique of Pure Reason*, B xliv.

44. Hamann's metacritique can be found in "*Metakritik uber den Purismus der Vernunft*" in *Hamann, Sämtliche Werke* (Wien: Verlag Herder, 1951), 3: 281–289. Herder's metacritique is articulated in *Verstand und Erfahrung* in *J. G. Herder Werke* (Frankfurt am Main: Deutscher Klassiker Verlag, 1985) vol. 8. The Metacritique of Kant has been the subject of recent discussions by both Fred Beiser (*The Fate of Reason*) and Jere Surber ["German Idealism under Fire" in *Hegel and the Modern World*, Ardis Collins, ed. (Albany: State University of New York Press, 1995) and "The Problems of Language in German Idealism: An Historical and Conceptual Overview," in *Phenomenology on Kant, German Idealism, Hermeneutics, and Logic*, O. K. Wiegand et al., eds. (Dordrecht The Netherlands Kluwer Academic Publishers, 2000), pp. 305–336].

45. Kant's "Review of Herder's *Ideas*" in *Political Writings* 205; *Hauptwerke*, 8.49.

46. Kant, "Conjectures on the Beginnings of Human History," *Political Writings*, 222.

47. For more on this see Surber, "The Problem of Language in German Idealism."

48. Habermas, *Structural Transformation of the Public Sphere*, 104.

49. Kant, *Critique of Judgment*, § 51, p. 165.

50. Kant, *Critique of Judgment*, § 53, p. 171.

51. Kant, "What is Orientation in Thinking?" in *Political Writings*, 247.

52. Dick Howard, for example, sees a shift in Kant's political views from supporting enlightened despotism to a more thoroughgoing republicanism. This shift corresponds to the real historical changes that occurred during the publication of Kant's seminal works. For example, Kant's support for enlightened despotism in "What is Enlightenment?" (1784) becomes more radically republican in the second edition of the first *Critique* (1787) and the *Critique of Judgment* (1790). Cf. Howard, *From Marx to Kant*, Introduction.

53. Kant, *Critique of Pure Reason*, B 117.

54. Kant, *Critique of Pure Reason*, A vii.

55. Hegel confronts this problem in the Introduction to the *Phenomenology of Spirit* (Miller translation, Oxford University Press, 1977) 52; Hegel, *Werke* (Hegel-Institut Berlin, from Past Masters, 1999), 3: 75–76.

Chapter 4

1. Kant, *Perpetual Peace* in *Political Writings*, 115.

2. Cassirer defends Kant by claiming that his old age (he was sixty-two years old when Frederick Wilhelm II took the throne), his personal modesty, and his clear estimate of the power of absolutist Prussia prevented him from more actively protesting the reactionary turn in Prussian policy (Cassirer, *Kant's Life and Thought*, 396–7).

3. Hans Saner presents an interesting theory that reverses this conclusion. He maintains that Kant's entire philosophical edifice can be understood as aimed at the political goal of peace. Saner concludes that "This makes all Kantian metaphysics a propaedeutic for political thinking (though not merely such a propaedeutic), with the result that we can interpret his politics on the one hand as a variant of his metaphysics, and on the other hand as its capstone [Saner, *Kant's Political Thought* (Chicago: The University of Chicago Press, 1973), 312–313].

4. Wolfgang Kersting, for example, interprets Kant's political philosophy as both a metaphysics of right and a "philosophy of compromise and reform" [Kersting, "Politics, Freedom, and Order: Kant's Political Philosophy" in *Cambridge Companion to Kant* (ed. Paul Guyer, Cambridge: Cambridge University Press, 1992), 358]. For a straightforward account of Kant's theory of justice see Kenneth Baynes, *The Normative Grounds of Social Criticism* (Albany: State University of New York Press, 1992).

5. Kant, *Perpetual Peace* in *Political Writings*, 115.

6. Dick Howard discusses this conclusion in his *Politics of Critique*. He claims that it cannot be the philosopher who is the prophet of enlightenment if the philosopher is considered merely to be a "monological, abstract, and formal individual subject" who acts as a führer or, in Howard's terms, as a "vanguard or avant-garde" (Howard, *Politics of Critique*, 185). Thus Howard insists that the guarantor of progress is republican politics (Howard, 185).

7. Kant, *Perpetual Peace* in *Kant's Political Writings*, 115.

8. Ibid., 115.

9. Ibid., 115.

10. Ibid., 115.

11. Ibid., 115.

12. Kant, *Religion within the Limits of Reason Alone*, 39.

13. Kant, *Critique of Pure Reason*, B xxx.

14. Kant, *The Contest of Faculties* in *Political Writings*, 188.

15. Kant, "Perpetual Peace" in *Political Writings*, 122.

16. Kant, *Religion within the Limits of Reason Alone*, 40.

17. Kant, "Idea for a Universal History" in *Political Writings*, 45.

18. Kant, "Idea for a Universal History" in *Political Writings*, 45.

19. Kant, *Perpetual Peace* in *Political Writings,* 114.

20. Kant, *Perpetual Peace* in *Political Writings*, 114.

21. Kant, "Idea for a Universal History" in *Political Writings*, 45.

22. Kant, "Idea for a Universal History" in *Political Writings*, 51.

23. Kant, *Religion within the Limits of Reason Alone*, 29.

24. Kant, *Religion within the Limits of Reason Alone*, 29–30.

25. Kant, *Critique of Judgment*, 324.

26. Kant, *The Contest of Faculties* in *Political Writings*, 188.

27. Kant, *Religion within the Limits of Reason Alone*, 139.

28. Kant, *Religion within the Limits of Reason Alone*, 139.

29. Kant, *Perpetual Peace* in *Political Writings*, 113.

30. Kant, *Perpetual Peace* in *Political Writings*, 113.

31. Kant, *The Contest of the Faculties* in *Political Writings* 186. This idea of educating humanity was a crucial part of the idea of enlightenment in both France and Germany. Lessing's *The Education of the Human Race*, for example, was published in 1780, a year before Kant published the first edition of the first *Critique*.

32. Kant, *Religion within the Limits of Reason Alone*, 113.

33. Kant, *The Contest of Faculties* in *Political Writings*, 177.

34. For example in section 6 of "The Contest of the Faculties" ("An Occurrence In Our Own Times which Proves this Moral Tendency of the Human Race") Kant refers explicitly to the French Revolution and its impact on the movement of history (Kant, *Political Writings*, 182).

35. Kant, *The Contest of Faculties* in *Political Writings*, 185.

36. Kant, *The Contest of Faculties* in *Political Writings*, 185.

37. Kant, "Idea for a Universal History" in *Political Writings*, 51.

38. Kant, "Idea for a Universal History" in *Political Writings*, 50.

39. Kant, *Religion within the Limits of Reason Alone*, 113.

40. Kant, "Conjectures on the Beginning of Human History" in *Political Writings,* 234.

41. Kant, "Conjectures on the Beginning of Human History" in *Political Writings,* 223.

42. The claim about the "system-exploding consequences" of Kant's awareness of history has been elucidated by Habermas in *The Structural Transformation of the Public Sphere*, 116.

43. "The touchstone whereby we decide whether our holding a thing to be true is conviction or mere persuasion is therefore external, namely, the possibility of communicating it and of finding it to be valid for all human reason"(Kant, *Critique of Pure Reason*, B 848). Cf. Habermas, *The Structural Transformation of the Public Sphere*, 107–108.

44. Kant, "What is Enlightenment?" in *Political Writings*, 59. For details on the social and political evolution of the "enlightened" state cf. Habermas, *The Structural Transformation of the Public Sphere* especially section IV.

45. Kant, *The Metaphysical Elements of Justice*, 35.

46. Kant, *Perpetual Peace* in *Political Writings,* 130.

47. Kant, *Perpetual Peace* in *Political Writings,* 93.

48. Kant, *Metaphysical Elements of Justice*, 128–129. Lewis W. Beck makes it clear that Kant's denial of a right to revolution is tenuous insofar as he remains an advocate of evolutionary progress and is sympathetic to the spirit of the French Revolution [Lewis W. Beck, "Kant and the Right of Revolution" in *Journal of the History of Ideas* 1971 (32), 411–422)]. It is thus highly significant that Kant wrote most of his denials of the right to revolt after the French Revolution. Thus, Beck concludes that Kant is really arguing against a right to "restoration" because after the revolution, restoration itself means revolution! Unfortunately this seems to put Kant in the sticky position of maintaining that past revolutions should be permitted to stand, while no future revolution should be viewed as legitimate. Such a conclusion would be, as Beck concludes, a "time-serving dishonesty which one would not willingly attribute to Kant" (Beck, 417). Kant avoids this result by appealing to teleology in history, such that progressive transformations of political life are not really revolutionary in the pernicious sense because they cohere with the implicit moral teleology of history. The problem exposed by the seeming paradox in Kant's discussion of revolution is, of course, the problem of the political force of philosophical pronouncements about political development. Kant does not want his criticism of political life to lead to the dissolution into anarchy of that form of political life in which his critique can reach a public audience.

49. Kant, *Perpetual Peace* in *Political Writings,* 126.

50. Kant, "What is Orientation in Thinking" in *Political Writings,* 249.

51. Kant, *Contest of the Faculties* in *Political Writings,* 189.

52. Kant, "Idea for a Universal History" in *Political Writings,* 50.

53. Kant, *Perpetual Peace* in *Political Writings,* 112.

54. Ibid., 114.

55. Kant, "Theory and Practice" in *Political Writings,* 90.

56. Kant, "Idea for a Universal History" in *Political Writings,* 52.

57. Kant, *Religion within the Limits of Reason Alone*, 62.

58. Cf. *Religion within the Limits of Reason Alone*, pp. 71–2.

59. Cf. *Religion within the Limits of Reason Alone*, 70. Kant admits that grace can only be an object of faith and not an object of knowledge: "The persuasion that we can distinguish the effects of grace from those of nature (virtue) or can actually produce the former within ourselves is fanatacism; for we cannot by any token, recognize a supersensible object in experience, still less can we exert an influence upon it to draw it down to us . . ." (*Religion within the Limits of Reason Alone*, 162).

60. Cf. Kant's description of progress in "Idea for a Universal History" in *Political Writings*, 51.

61. Kant, *Critique of Practical Reason*, 31. Beck interprets this as indicating that Kant offers only an "intuitionist" account of the justification of ethics [cf. Beck, "The Fact of Reason: An Essay on Justification in Ethics," in Beck, *Studies in the Philosophy of Kant*, ed. Lewis W. Beck, Indianapolis: Bobbs-Merrill, 1965), 200–214].

62. Kant, *The Contest of the Faculties* in *Political Writings,* 184.

63. Kant, "Theory and Practice" in *Political Writings*, 81.

64. Kant, *Religion within the Limits of Reason Alone*, 149.

65. Kant, "What is Enlightenment?" in *Political Writings*, 55.

Chapter 5

1. Fichte, "Some Lectures Concerning the Scholar's Vocation" in *Fichte's Early Writings* (trans. and ed. by Daniel Breazeale, Ithaca, N.Y.: Cornell University Press, 1988).

2. Kant, *Perpetual Peace* in *Political Writings*, 115.

3. Fichte, "Scholar's Vocation" in *Fichte's Early Writings*, 173.

4. Numerous critics have argued that Fichte's fiery rhetoric and his educational nationalism seem to lead to a form of nationalistic authoritarianism, if not full blown totalitarianism. Among these we might note Karl Popper [*The Open Society and its Enemies*], John Dewey [*Democracy and Education* (New York: The Free Press, 1966), 95–97], and Isaiah Berlin ("Two Concepts of Liberty" in *Four Essays on Liberty* (Oxford: Oxford University Press, 1969), especially pp. 145–154]. Perhaps Hans Sluga's criticism of Fichte is typical of these. He claims that Fichte is a forerunner of Nazism and understands Fichte's totalitarian tendencies as resulting from an overzealous and un-philosophical faith in philosophy as the savior of political life. He says, "Fichte's

Addresses, in sum rest squarely on the belief that a point of crisis had been reached in German history—a crisis that was at once political and philosophical, a crisis that concerned in particular the German people and the understanding they had of themselves, a crisis of leadership calling for the reestablishment of a true order . . . Joining all these ideas together into a single political-philosophical discourse, he anticipated the full array of themes on which philosophers like Heidegger would draw in their speeches of 1933, and in this sense at least, Fichte can truly be called a forerunner of what happened under the Nazis" (Hans Sluga, *Heidegger's Crisis* (Cambridge: Harvard University Press, 1993) 40–41). More sympathetically, G. A. Kelly, I think, gets it right, however, when he argues that we must be cautious in evaluating Fichte's religious nationalism. He says: "Fichtianity is not embryonic Nazism; it is high metaphysical nineteenth century, pure and simple . . . He believed that mankind, suspect in its natural inclinations, needed to reach the truth through discipline and learning. He carried this conviction far beyond psychology into history, and therein lies the fascination and danger of his message" [Kelly, *Idealism, Politics, and History* (Cambridge: Cambridge University Press, 1969), 188–89]. More recently Ives Radrizzani has articulated a criticism of Fichte whose conclusions I share and develop in what follows: "The philosopher must, like any other man, commit himself to political praxis; but as soon as he does so, he cannot, save by going beyond the limits of a philosophy of finitude, do so in the name of his philosophy—a conclusion which follows from the radical heterogeneity between the philosophical level and the political level." Radrizzani, "Fichte's Transcendental Philosophy and Political Praxis" [trans. by Cristina Bianchi-Murillo and Daniel Breazeale in *New Perspectives on Fichte*, (ed. Daniel Breazeale and Tom Rockmore, Atlantic Highlands, N.J.: Humanities Press, 1996), 209.

5. Tom Rockmore, *Fichte and Marx* (Carbondale: Southern Illinois University, 1980), 77.

6. It is important to note that Fichte's concern with the German spirit is part of his cosmopolitan concern with European spirit. This point is debatable but I believe Martial Gueroult gets it right when he emphasizes that through all of Fichte's discussion of the German language and culture Fichte remains committed to "German-ness" as representing the "aptitude for freedom and the revolutionary mission." Gueroult concludes that "the word German takes on, therefore, an entirely cosmopolitan significance" ("*Fichte et la Revolution Française*" in *Études Sur Fichte* (Hildesheim: Georg Olms Verlag, 1974), 240–241. This is also H. C. Engelbrecht's thesis in *Johann Gottlieb Fichte: A Study of his Political Writings with Special Reference to his Nationalism* (New York: AMS Press, 1968).

7. For discussion of the political side of Fichte's years in Jena cf. Engelbrecht, *Johann Gottlieb Fichte* and Terry Pinkard, *Hegel: A Biography* (Cambridge: Cambridge University Press, 2000), especially pp. 88–105.

8. Fichte, *The Vocation of Man* (trans. by Peter Preuss, Indianapolis: Hackett, 1987), 2.

9. Fichte, *Addresses to the German Nation* (trans. Jones and Turnbull, Chicago: Open Court, 1933), 214; *Fichtes Werke* (ed. I. H. Fichte, Berlin: de Gruyter), 485.

10. Cf. Rockmore, *Fichte and Marx*, 76–80.

11. Freidrich Meinecke, *The Age of German Liberation, 1795–1815*, (trans. by Paret and Fischer, Berkeley: University of California Press, 1977).

12. Engelbrecht, *Johann Gottlieb Fichte*, pp. 124–132 and Chapter 8.

13. Fichte, *Science of Knowledge* (trans. Heath and Lachs, Cambridge: Cambridge University Press, 1982), 16.

14. Fichte, *Science of Knowledge*, 16.

15. Fichte, *Addresses*, 50.

16. Fichte, "A Crystal Clear Report to the General Public Concerning the Actual Essence of the Newest Philosophy" in *Philosophy of German Idealism* (ed. Behler, New York: Continuum, 1987), 106.

17. The phrase "philosophize with spirit" occurs, for example, both in the essay "Concerning the Difference between the Spirit and the Letter in Philosophy" (*Fichte's Early Writings*, 215) and in the *Science of Knowledge*, 250; J. G. Fichte, *Gesamtausgabe* (Stuttgart-Bad Cannstatt: Friedrich Frommann Verlag, 1965), I, 2: 415.

18. Fichte, *Science of Knowledge*, 91; *Gesamtausgabe*, I, 2: 253.

19. Breazeale's introduction to "Concerning the Difference between the Spirit and the Letter within Philosophy" can serve to describe all of Fichte's popular works: "Thus one might say that these lectures provide an essential introduction to philosophy, that they establish the 'subjective conditions' for the possibility of philosophy, and that they accomplish this by describing human freedom and rousing listeners and readers to a new and more lively sense of their own freedom—thereby preparing them for entry into the *Wissenschaftslehre*" (*Fichte's Early Writings*, 191).

20. Fichte, *Science of Knowledge*, 203; *Gesamtausgabe*, I, 2: 370. John Sallis interprets Fichte's discussion of the imagination as follows: "Imagination has no fixed standpoint but is the movement of displacement as such; it posits no fixed limits but circulates among the opposites so as to hold them together, its very displacement delimiting a space of opposition. Imagination hovers in between opposites so as to hold them together in their opposition... Imagination is the power of spacing those oppositions that can be neither dissolved nor eliminated from theoretical knowledge. Imagination is the spacing of truth" [Sallis, *Spacings of Reason and Imagination in Texts of Kant, Fichte, and Hegel* (Chicago: University of Chicago Press, 1987) 64].

21. Fichte, *Science of Knowledge*, 250; *Gesamtausgabe*, I, 2: 415.

22. Fichte, *Science of Knowledge*, 233.

23. Fichte, *Science of Knowledge*, 129. On the importance of "activity" in Fichte's thought and in the transition from ontology to sociology, ethics, and politics, in Fichte cf. Rockmore, *Fichte and Marx*.

24. Fichte, *Science of Knowledge*, 259.

25. "Freedom of thought, if it tries to act independently even of the laws of reason, eventually destroys itself" (Kant, "What is Orientation in Thinking?": in *Kant's Political Writings*, 249). For Fichte cf. *Science of Knowledge*, 27.

26. Fichte, *Science of Knowledge*, 252.

27. Fichte, *Science of Knowledge*, 247.

28. Cf. for example, "On the Extreme Limits of All Practical Philosophy" in *The Metaphysics of Morals*, where Kant explains that freedom is only a postulate that cannot be proved and that thus the moral imperative is itself an unprovable postulate. Or also, the Third Antinomy of the first *Critique,* where freedom is opposed to causality in an antinomy of reason that is only resolved by the move to the practical philosophy in which freedom is a necessary postulate for the existence of good.

29. As Hegel states it in his discussion of Fichte, dogmatism occurs when "the one subjugates the other. The one rules, the other is subservient" [Hegel, *The Difference Between the Fichte's and Schelling's System of Philosophy* (trans. Harris and Cerf, Albany: State University of New York Press, 1977), 115].

30. Fichte, "Some Lectures Concerning the Scholar's Vocation" in *Fichte's Early Writings*, 175.

31. Fichte, *Science of Knowledge*, 78.

32. Fichte, "Crystal Clear Report to the General Public Concerning the Actual Essence of the Newest Philosophy" in *Philosophy of German Idealism*, 100.

33. Fichte, *Science of Knowledge*, 251. In his discussion of history in the *Characteristics of the Present Age* and in the beginning of the *Addresses*, Fichte locates the current era at the midpoint of progress toward enlightenment.

34. Fichte, *Science of Knowledge*, 250–51.

35. Fichte *Science of Knowledge*, 251, footnote, no. 5.

36. Gueroult notes this connection between Fichte's early ethical works and the *Addresses*. It is important to point out that despite the authoritarian tone of Fichte's educational ideal, Fichte's goal of universal education was quite radical and was posited as an antidote to conservative limitations on education. Nonetheless, Gueroult concludes that "in the *Addresses to the German Nation*, Fichte, seeing that education should be given to everyone equally without distinction of birth, rank, or fortune, will be led to give the state a more direct role in the organization of national education; he thus prescribes a monopoly of education" (Gueroult, "*La Doctrine Fichtéenne du Droit*" in *Études Sur Fichte* (Hildesheim: Georgolms Verlag. 1974), 14.

37. Fichte, *Science of Knowledge*, 93.

38. Fichte, *Science of Knowledge*, 93.

39. Fichte, *Science of Knowledge*, 16.

40. Rockmore points out in opposition to my argument here that "Fichte is not so much interested in arriving at agreement regarding this initial fact (of his system), as in utilizing it as an example of the development of his analysis. In this sense, it makes no difference at all from what fact one begins, since the argument in no sense depends upon it" (Rockmore, *Fichte and Marx*, 14). Where I disagree with Rockmore is in the characterization of which principle is the focal point of agreement. While Rockmore focuses on Fichte's claim that "A = A," it seems clear that what is at issue for Fichte is not the proposition "A =A" but the Activity which posits it. Rockmore is correct to point out that agreement about the fact "A = A" is indifferent; what is significant is agreement about the active nature of the consciousness which posits this. Such agreement about this activity can only be attained by an appeal to morality and character.

41. Fichte, *Science of Knowledge*, 90; *Gesamtausgabe*, I, 4: 252.

42. Fichte, *Science of Knowledge*, 91. This despite the fact that the subtitle to the "Crystal Clear Report" is "An Attempt to Force the Reader to Understand."

43. Fichte, *Science of Knowledge*, 76; *Gesamtausgabe*, I, 4: 259.

44. Fichte, *Addresses*, 78; *Werke*, 7: 333.

45. It is important to acknowledge, as Kelly for example does, that Fichte saw German nationalism as merely the vanguard of a greater European cosmopolitan enlightened humanity. "In Fichte's vision, the relation of an ideal Germany to Europe and to history—to all the values comprehended in these terms—was very much like that of the practical, finite ego to the absolute ego of the *Wissenschaftslehre*. German—there was no 'Germany' at the time—ought to be the concrete embodiment of *Humanität*. The German experience was the spiritual aspect of the *Menschenbildung* in microcosm" (Kelly, *Idealism, Politics, and History*, 252). Cf. also Gueroult, "*Fichte et la Révolution Française*."

46. Fichte, *Addresses*, 47; *Werke*, 7: 306.

47. Fichte, *Addresses*, 78; *Werke,* 7: 333.

48. Fichte, *Addresses*, 76; *Werke*, 7: 332.

49. Fichte, *Addresses*, 65; *Werke*, 7: 322. For Fichte's account of the living power of metaphor, Cf. Peter L. Osterreich, "*Politische Philosophie oder Demagogie?*" in *Fichte-Studien* 2 (1990).

50. Fichte, *Addresses*, 86; *Werke*, 7: 339.

51. Fichte, *Addresses*, 86; *Werke*, 7: 339.

52. Fichte, *Addresses*, 46; *Werke*, 7: 306.

53. Fichte, *Addresses*, 46.

54. Fichte, *Addresses*, 78; *Werke* 7: 333.

55. Fichte, *Addresses*, 78; *Werke* 7: 334.

56. Fichte, *Addresses*, 80.

57. Fichte, *Addresses*, 80; *Werke*, 7: 335.

58. Fichte, *Addresses*, 125; *Werke*, 7: 374.

Chapter 6

1. Fichte, *Addresses*, 73; *Werke*, 7: 329.

2. Fichte, *Addresses*, 243; *Werke*, 7: 476.

3. Fichte, *Addresses*, 247; *Werke*, 7: 480.

4. I have borrowed the term "linguistic turn" from Jere Surber who discusses Fichte's early essay on language and its relation to later linguistic philosophy in *Language and German Idealism* (Atlantic Highlands, N.J.: Humanities Press, 1996).

5. Fichte, *Addresses*, 69.

6. Fichte's theory of language and the relation between his 1795 essay and the *Addresses* has been the focus of some new research. *Fichte-Studien* volume 2 is dedicated to this problem. Jere Surber's *Language and German Idealism* (Atlantic Highlands, N.J.: Humanities Press, 1996) develops the linguistic philosophy of the 1795 essay. To my knowledge there has been no attempt in English to discuss the connections between the 1795 essay and the *Addresses*.

7. This is the theme of Jochem Hennigfeld's essay *"Fichte und Humboldt—Zur Frage der Nationalsprache" in Fichte-Studien* 2 (1990), which discusses "*Sprache als Weltansicht*" and links Fichte's account to Humboldt's.

8. Hennigfeld states this nicely: "Language is not only shown as condition for the possibility of actualizing the basic drive toward self-agreement; it is at the same time demonstrated as the condition for the possibility of individual self-consciousness" (Hennigfeld, "*Fichte und Humboldt*," 45).

9. This conclusion is shared by Peter L. Oesterreich. Oesterreich develops an analysis of Fichte's discussion of language and the sensuous imaginative power of the living *Ursprache*. He states, for example, that "symbolic language as absolute unification (*Ineinsbildung*) of the sensible and the intelligible is furthermore not the result of pure rational construction but rather a formation of the productive imagination (*produktiver Einbildungskraft—imaginatio*)" [Oesterreich, "*Politische Philosophie oder Demagogie?*" in *Fichte-Studien* 2 (1990), 78].

10. Fichte says, for example: "Let the original people (*Stammvolke*) who speak this language incorporate as many individuals of other races (*Stammes*) and other languages; if they are not permitted to bring the sphere of their observation up to the point from which, from now on, the language is to develop, then they remain dumb

in the community and without influence on the language, until the time comes when they themselves have entered into the sphere of observation of the original people" (Fichte, *Addresses*, 62; *Werke*, 7: 319–320). Cf. Johannes Heinrichs, "*Nationalsprache und Sprachnation*" in *Fichte-Studien* 2 (1990).

11. "The Science of Knowledge is of a kind that cannot be communicated by the letter merely (*den blossen Buchstaben*), but only through the spirit…" (Fichte, *Science of Knowledge*, 250–51; *Gesamtausgabe*, I, 2: 415).

12. Fichte, *Addresses*, 78; *Werke*, 7: 333.

13. Fichte, *Addresses*, 78; *Werke*, 7: 333.

14. Jere Surber's analysis of Fichte's early essay emphasizes Fichte's sensitivity to the "transcendental-political context" of language [Jere Paul Surber, *Language and German Idealism* (Atlantic Highlands, N.J.: Humanities Press, 1996), 41]. Indeed, Surber claims that according to Fichte, "the development of language, far from appearing as a potential obstacle to political freedom, must be seen as its absolute precondition" (*Language and German Idealism*, 62). Surber concludes by claiming that, with regard to Fichte's early essay, "what is most important to notice is his explicit recognition that linguistic considerations always have political implications and that political questions cannot be adequately treated without an acknowledgment of the centrality of language to the discussion" (*Language and German Idealism*, 64).

15. Fichte "On the Linguistic Capacity and the Origin of Language," in Surber, *Language and German Idealism,* 123. Fichte also writes, for example that "As these [supersensible] ideas now become clearer and clearer to a human being, the drive to acquaint others with what he had discovered would begin to stir in him, for never is the drive to communicate livelier than in the case of new and sublime thoughts" (Fichte, "On the Linguistic Capacity and the Origin of Language," in Surber, *Language and German Idealism,* 132).

16. Fichte, "On the Linguistic Capacity and the Origin of Language," in Surber, *Language and German Idealism*, 124.

17. Ibid., 124.

18. Ibid., 125.

19. Fichte, "On the Linguistic Capacity and the Origin of Language," 144.

20. Ibid., 144.

21. Ibid., 144.

22. Ibid., 144; *Gesamtausgabe*, I, 3: 127. As far as I can tell, this is the first time he uses the word, *Nation*, in this essay.

23. Fichte, *Addresses*, 73; *Werke*, 7: 329.

24. Cf. Fichte, *Addresses*, 46; *Werke*, 7: 306.

25. Fichte, *Addresses*, 46–47; *Werke*, 7: 306.

26. "The difference [between Germans and other Teutonic people] arose at the moment of the separation from the common stock and consists in this, that the German speaks a language which has been alive ever since it first issued from the force of nature (*dass der Deutsche eine bis zu ihrem ersten Ausstromen aus der Naturkraft lebendiges Sprache redet*) . . ." (Fichte, *Addresses*, 68; *Werke,* 7: 325).

27. Fichte, *Addresses*, 55; *Werke*, 7: 314.

28. Fichte, *Addresses*, 55; *Werke*, 7: 314.

29. "But I, by longing and cries and broken accents and various motions of my limbs to express my thoughts, that so I might have my will and yet unable to express all I willed, or to whom I willed, did myself, by the understanding which Thou, my God, gavest me, practice the sounds in my memory. When they named any thing, and as they spoke turned towards it, I saw and remembered that they called what they would point out by the name they uttered. And that they meant this thing and no other was plain from the motion of their body, the natural language, as it were, of all nations..." (Augustine, *Confessions*, (trans. Edward B. Pusey, New York: Collier Books, 1961) Book 1, p. 16).

30. Fichte, *Addresses*, 62; *Werke*, 7: 320.

31. Fichte, *Addresses*, 56; *Werke*, 7: 315.

32. Fichte, *Addresses*, 56; *Werke*, 7: 314–315.

33. Fichte, *Addresses*, 69; *Werke*, 7: 326.

34. Fichte, *Addresses*, 57; *Werke*, 7: 315.

35. Fichte, *Addresses*, 56; *Werke*, 7: 314.

36. This seems to be a new twist in the *Addresses*. The 1795 essay on language emphasized written language at the expense of spoken and indeed interpreted the *Ursprache* in terms of written hieroglyphics. In the *Addresses* Fichte seems more interested in the spoken word. The political and hermeneutical context of the *Addresses* might explain this difference: in the *Addresses*, Fichte is himself speaking German and is acutely aware of the power of his own voice to inspire the German people.

37. Fichte, *Addresses*, 63; *Werke*, 7: 321.

38. Fichte, *Addresses*, 172; *Werke*,, 7: 414.

39. Fichte, *Addresses*, 172; *Werke*, 7: 414.

40. Fichte, *Addresses*, 174; *Werke*, 7: 416.

41. Fichte, *Addresses*, 243; *Werke*, 7: 476.

42. Kant, *The Metaphysical Elements of Justice: Part I of the Metaphysics of Morals* (trans. John Ladd, New York: Macmillan, 1965), 19.

43. As Kelly says, "History is essentially a plan established by the 'highest, truest man' or the philosopher and his task will only be completed when the rational

(or moral) is made actual. That is why the world is a school" (Kelly, *Idealism, Politics, and History*, 276).

44. Hegel (or possibly Schelling or Hölderlin), "Oldest Systematic Program of German Idealism" (trans. Diana Behler, in *Philosophy of German Idealism* ed. Ernst Behler, New York: Continuum, 1987), 162.

45. Fichte, "Some Lectures Concerning the Scholar's Vocation" (in *Fichte's Early Writings*), 172.

46. For example: "Friends of the human race and all that it holds most sacred! Accept whatever seems most credible to you after careful and honest examination, whether it is a matter of facts or of rational arguments; but do not deny reason that prerogative which makes it the greatest good on earth, namely its right to be the ultimate touchstone of truth. If you fail in this respect, you will be unworthy of this freedom and will surely forfeit it; and you will bring the same misfortune down upon those other guiltless souls who would otherwise have been inclined to employ their freedom lawfully and hence in a manner conducive to the world's best interests!" ("What is Orientation in Thinking?" in *Political Writings*, 249).

47. Cf. Gueroult, "*Fichte et la Révolution Française*" in *Etudes sur Fichte*.

48. Fichte *Addresses*, 221; *Werke* 7: 458.

49. Fichte, *Addresses*, 252; *Werke*, 7: 485.

50. Fichte, *Addresses*, 156; *Werke*, 7: 400.

51. Fichte, *Addresses*, 27; *Werke*, 7: 288.

52. Fichte, *Addresses*, 27; *Werke*, 7: 288.

53. Fichte, *Addresses*, 49; *Werke*, 7: 309.

54. Fichte, *Addresses*, 50-51; *Werke*, 7: 309–311.

55. Fichte, *Addresses*, 46; *Werke*, 7: 305.

56. Fichte, *Addresses*, 46; *Werke*, 7: 306.

57. Fichte, *Science of Knowledge*, 77; *Gesamtausgabe*, I, 4: 259–260.

58. Fichte, *Addresses*, 252; *Werke*, 7: 485.

59. Fichte, *Addresses*, 7; *Werke*, 7: 269–70.

60. Fichte, *Addresses*, 76; *Werke*, 7: 332.

61. Fichte, *Addresses*, 61; *Werke*, 7: 319.

62. Fichte, *Addresses*, 62; *Werke*, 7: 320.

63. Fichte, *Science of Knowledge*, 250; *Gesamtausgabe*, I, 2: 415.

64. Fichte, *Science of Knowledge*, 250; *Gesamtausgabe*, I, 2: 415.

65. Fichte, *Addresses*, 50; *Werke*, 7: 309.

66. Fichte, *Addresses*, 50; *Werke*, 7: 309.

67. Sluga, *Heidegger's Crisis*, 35. Again Kelley proposes an antidote to the proto-Nazi reading of Fichte. "Fichte's ideal ruler is, however, the scholar, the philosopher-king, the Brahmin of the *Wissenschaftslehre*. A nation of the spirit should be led by the spirit's chief embodiment" (Kelly, *Idealism, Politics, and History*, 278). The point is truth should matter, even if this truth requires coercion.

Chapter 7

1. Hegel, "Inaugural Lecture at the University of Berlin" (1818), quoted in Pinkard, *Hegel: A Biography*, p. 430; "*Rede zum Antritt des philosophischen Lehramtes an der Universität Berlin" in Hegel, Vorlesungsmanuskripte II (1818-1831), Gesammelte Werke (ed. Rheinish-Westfälische Akademie der Wissenschaften, 1995*), p. 12–13.

2. Hegel, *History of Philosphy*, III: 505.

3. Hegel, *History of Philosophy*, III: 506.

4. Hegel, *Introductory Lectures on Aesthetics*, Bosanquet translation (London: Penguin Books, 1993), 35; *Werke*, 13: 51.

5. "Hence, philosophy can, of course, presuppose some familiarity with its objects; in fact it must presuppose this, as well as an interest in these objects. The reason is that in the order of time (*der Zeit nach*) consciousness produces representations of objects before it produces concepts of them; and that the thinking spirit only advances to thinking cognition and comprehension by going through representation and by converting itself to it (*nur durchs Vorstellen hindurch und auf dasselbe sich wendend)*" (Hegel, *Encyclopedia*, § 1; *Werke*, 8: 41).

6. Hegel, *Lectures on Aesthetics*, Bosanquet translation, 35; *Werke*, 13: 50–51.

7. Hegel, *Lectures on Aesthetics*, Bosanquet translation, 35; *Werke*, 13: 51; also: "The universal need for art is thus the rational one, that man has exalted the inner and outer world into a spiritual consciousness for himself, as an object in which he recognizes his own self. He satisfies the need of this spiritual freedom when he makes all that exists explicit for himself within, and in a corresponding way realizes this his explicit self without, evoking thereby, in this reduplication of himself, what is in him into vision and into knowledge for his own mind and for that of others" (Hegel, *Werke*, 13: 52; Hegel, *Lectures on Aesthetics*, I have altered Bosanquet's translation, p. 36).

8. For further discussion of the way in which Hegel systematically differentiates between art, politics, and philosophy cf. Andrew Fiala, "Aesthetic Education and the Aesthetic State: Hegel's Response to Schiller" in William Maker, ed., *Hegel's Aesthetics* (Albany: State University of New York Press, 2000).

9. *Encyclopedia*, § 15; *Werke*, 8: 60. Also *Philosophy of Right*, § 2, Addition.

10. Hegel, *Science of Logic*, 107; *Werke* 5: 114. It is important to notice that Hegel makes a claim about the connection of philosophical concepts and the German language in which these concepts are expressed: *Aufhebung* has this two-fold meaning (*gedoppelten Sinn*) in the German language itself. The activity of philosophy is the process of leading representational language beyond itself by providing ordinary representations with a higher spiritual concept. Hegel acknowledges that the philosophical character of the German language is merely a contingent occurrence without philosophical significance (Hegel, *Science of Logic*, 107). Hegel clearly distinguishes his praise for German from the Fichtean idea that German is an *Ursprache* capable of exhibiting the primal source of culture. For more on this see John McCumber, *The Company of Words* (Evanston, Ill.: Northwestern University Press, 1983).

11. Hegel claims in the *Differenzschrift* that other than vague pronouncements about the *moral* demand that the system preserve freedom, Fichte did not provide a nondogmatic justification of this moral ideal. Hegel is critical of what he sees as Fichte's negative conception of freedom, a conception that makes it impossible for Fichte to bridge the gap between freedom and nature, between individual and community. Hegel claims that Fichte's negative conception of freedom leads Fichte in both his *System of Ethics* and his *Science of Rights* to the conclusion that the community and the moral law are alien to real empirical individuals and must be imposed upon them from without. According to Hegel, individuals are thus left broken. Hegel says that for Fichte, "absolute dichotomy constitutes the essence of man" (Hegel, *Differenzschrift*, 150). Fichte thus leaves us with eternal striving without hope of final reconciliation with either the ethical community or the moral law because these are both alien forces which the individual will resist. This puts the individual in a troubling relation to morality and political life. Hegel criticizes Fichte's view of the individual as follows: "He must seek for unity; but with absolute non-identity at his very basis only a formal unity remains for him" (Hegel, *Differenzschrift*, 150). Hegel thus rejects Fichte's moral and political theories because they remain dogmatic, despotic, and in Hegel's words, "ugly and hateful" (Hegel, *Differenzschrift*, 154).

12. Cf. "The German Constitution" in *Hegel's Political Writings*, 234–5 or "The English Reform Bill" In *Hegel's Political Writings*, 317–321.

13. Hegel, *Phenomenology*, 14.

14. Hegel, *Philosophy of Right*, 1817–18, § 129, p. 229.

15. McCumber, *The Company of Words*, 328.

16. On the importance of *Bildung* for Hegel's idea of philosophy, cf. Terry Pinkard, *Hegel: A Biography*.

17. Indeed one recent commentary makes it clear that Pietism, the religious context of Hegel's "rational pneumatology," closely linked itself to ethical and political action [Alan M. Olson, *Hegel and the Spirit: Philosophy as Pneumatology* (Princeton, N.J.: Princeton University Press, 1992), 45–46]. Olson does not explicitly locate Hegel's conception of spirit within modern ethical and political life. For this

connection see Joachim Ritter's *Hegel and the French Revolution* [trans. Richard Dien Winfield (Cambridge, Mass.: MIT Press, 1982)] or Jean Hyppolite's account of the young Hegel's use of the term "spirit" in *Introduction to Hegel's Philosophy of History*, trans. Bond Harris and Jacqueline Bouchard Spurlock (Gainesville, Fla.: University Press of Florida, 1996).

18. Hegel, *Phenomenology*, 14.

19. Ibid., 14.

20. Hegel, *Phenomenology*, 14-15; *Werke*, 3: 29.

21. Cf. McCumber's account of the "ladder" passage in *The Company of Words*, 321.

22. Hegel, *The Difference between Fichte's and Schelling's System of Philosophy* (hereafter *Differenzschrift*) (trans. and ed. by H. S. Harris and Walter Cerf, Albany: State University of New York Press, 1977), 89; *Werke* 2: 20.

23. The first of these criticisms has been made most strenuously by Karl Popper in *The Open Society and its Enemies*, vol. 2. Ernst Cassirer also joins in this criticism (Cassirer, *The Myth of the State* (New Haven, Conn.: Yale University Press, 1946, 273). The second criticism was made most famously by Karl Marx, who criticized Hegel as a bourgeois ideologist and apologist for bourgeois morality. The most diligent critics of Hegel recognize that both prongs of the attack on Hegel require a critique of Hegel's logic. This is the thrust of Marx's extended critique of Hegel's *Philosophy of Right,* as we shall see in chapters 9 and 10. For further criticisms of Hegel's "totalizing" tendencies, also see Adorno, *Negative Dialectics,* trans. E. B. Ashton (New York: Continuum, 1994), and Jean-François Lyotard, *Le Differend* (Paris: Les Editions de Minuit, 1983).

24. As Pinkard describes it: "Dialectical philosophy explains the possibility of apparently incompatible categorial beliefs by trying to show that the apparent incompatibility is only apparent, that the contradiction is avoided once one expands one's framework of discourse in the appropriate way" [Terry Pinkard, *Hegel's Dialectic: The Explanation of Possibility* (Philadelphia: Temple University Press, 1988), 19]. John Burbridge's analysis of Hegel's method complicates this a bit. For example, he breaks Hegel's method into five basic stages, although he notes that the text sometimes makes explicit more or fewer stages, depending on the context [John W. Burbridge, *On Hegel's Logic* (Atlantic Highlands, N.J.: Humanities Press, 1981), p. 44].

25. Other commentators who make this point include Herbert Marcuse, *Hegel's Ontology and the Theory of Historicity* (trans. Seyla Benhabib, Cambridge, Mass.: MIT Press, 1987); Tom Rockmore, *Hegel's Circular Epistemology* (Bloomington: Indiana University Press, 1986); and William Maker, *Philosophy Without Foundations* (Albany: State University of New York Press, 1994). For more on this difference and its linguistic connection, cf. John McCumber, *The Company of Words*. The idea of reconciliation has been used to explicate Hegel's political philosophy in, for example, Michael Hardimon's *Hegel's Social Philosophy: The Project of Reconciliation* (Cambridge: Cambridge University Press, 1994).

26. Hegel, *Differenzschrift*, 89; *Werke* 2: 20.

27. Hegel, *Science of Logic*, 54; *Werke*, 5: 50.

28. Hegel, *Science of Logic*, 54–55.

29. Hegel, *Philosophy of Right*, p. 20; *Werke*, 7: 24. The term *Doppelsatz* is used by Hardimon who in turn borrowed it from Dieter Henrich; see Michael Hardimon, *Hegel's Social Philosophy*, Chapter 2. Much has been made recently of the differences between the formulation of this passage as found in the published text of 1821and the formulation that Hegel gives of it in the other versions of his lectures. Ilting suggests that the formulation of the published version was due to the censorship of the Karlsbad decrees: "an analysis of the five available prefaces to the *Rechtsphilosophie* from 1818 to 1831 in their complete circumstances finally allows us to know, the extent to which Hegel left out his own essential unchanging intention under the influence of the Karlsbad decrees" (Ilting's Introduction to Hegel's, *Vorlesungen über Rechtsphilosophie* (Stuttgart: Frommann-Holzboog, 1973), 1: 119). This is significant because it shows us how important the political sound of the philosopher's voice can be. In the present context, I am focusing primarily on the officially published text. For more discussion of this passage from the Preface see Tunick, *Hegel's Political Philosophy* (Princeton, N.J.: Princeton University Press, 1992), 9–10; and Avineri, "The Discovery of Hegel's Early Lectures on the Philosophy of Right" [*Owl of Minerva*, 16, 2 (Spring 1985): 199–208].

30. Hegel, *Science of Logic*, 757–58; *Werke*, 6: 465.

31. Hegel, *Philosophy of Right* (Addition to the Preface), p. 14; *Werke*, 7: 17.

32. Hegel, *History of Philosophy*, 3: 481; *Werke*, 20: 388.

33. Hegel, *History of Philosophy*, 3: 505; *Werke*, 20: 414. The English translation adds the following pregnant phrase: "and hence that Philosophy is quite superfluous." I am unable to find a claim corresponding to this in the German texts. The sentence quoted above reads in the German: "*Das Publikum wurde durch die Kantische und Jacobische Philosophie darin bestärkt, daß das Wissen von Gott ein unmittelbares sei, das man von Haus aus kenne, ohne zu studieren*."

34. Hegel, *History of Philosophy*, 3: 463; *Werke*, 20: 371.

35. Hegel, *History of Philosophy*, 3: 478; *Werke*, 20: 386.

36. Hegel, *Philosophy of Right*, § 273, Addition.

37. Hegel, *Philosophy of Right*, § 343. In the *History of Philosophy*, he states, for example, "the study of the history of philosophy is the study of philosophy itself" (Hegel, *History of Philosophy*, 1: 30). This is what Hegel means when he explains in the Introductory sections to the *Encyclopedia* that philosophy is *Nachdenken* (thinking-over or, literally, thinking-after) that makes the implicit thinking of the determinations of human life explicit (Hegel, *Encyclopedia*, § 2, Remark and § 5).

38. Cf. *Philosophy of Right*, §§ 5–7. The discussion of Fichte occurs in § 6 Remark where "positive" freedom is discussed in terms of Fichte's self-positing "I"

in the *Wissenschaftslehre*: the "I" that sees itself as universal without recognizing its determinate limitations.

39. Hegel, *Phenomenology*, 359.

40. Hegel, *Phenomenology*, 362. For more on the connection between *Phenomenology* and the French Revolution cf. both Kojève's *Introduction to the Reading of Hegel* (New York: Basic Books, 1969) and Ritter's *Hegel and the French Revolution.*

41. Hegel, *Phenomenology*, 358.

42. Hegel, *Philosophy of Right*, § 175, Remark. Fichte does recognize the natural propensity of children toward moral and social development. However, Fichte worries that the child's natural instinct to emulate will inevitably lead to corruption because of the corrupt society that they eagerly emulate; see Fichte, *Addresses to the German Nation* (Tenth Address), 153.

43. Hegel, *Philosophy of Right*, § 151, Addition.

44. "Habit is part of ethics, just as it is part of philosophical thought, since the latter requires that the mind should be trained to resist arbitrary fancies and that these should be destroyed and overcome to clear the way for rational thought" (Hegel, *Philosophy of Right*, § 151, Addition). Habits operate the same way words and names do in Hegel's philosophy of language: as summaries of universal concepts that allow us to achieve greater levels of complexity in thought and action. Thinking consists of habits for connecting names with concepts, which act as shortcuts for achieving greater levels of complexity. In the present context I do not have time to develop the connection between linguistic and ethical habits. Suffice it to say that both forms of habit are necessary for the completion of spiritual education.

45. Although in the *Philosophy of Right* Hegel wants to restrict freedom of speech, he also recognizes that it is almost impossible to prescribe laws that would do this without violating its basis in moral subjectivity (cf. *Philosophy of Right*, §§ 315–320).

46. In the Preface Hegel writes: "The truth concerning right, ethics, and the state is at any rate as old as its exposition and promulgation in public laws and in public morality and religion." The *Philosophy of Right* provides the systematic exposition in which these "old truths" will finally "appear justified" (Hegel, *Philosophy of Right*, p.11; *Werke*, 7: 13–14). I will have more to say about the process of justification of positive law in the next chapter.

47. Robert Pippin nicely articulates the tension in Hegel's view that comes out as he tries to hold rationalism together with the fact of our social and historical facticity (Robert Pippin, "Hegel's Ethical Rationalism" in Pippin, *Idealism as Modernism.*)

48. "In this way ethical substantiality has attained its right, and the latter has attained validity"(Hegel, *Philosophy of Right*, §152).

49. Cf. Hegel, *Encyclopedia*, § 67.

50. Hegel, *Phenomenology of Spirit*, 43; *Werke*, 3: 65.

51. Hegel, *Philosophy of Right*, Preface, p. 17; *Werke*, 7: 21.

52. Hegel, *Philosophy of Right,* Preface, p. 23.

53. Hegel, *Philosophy of Right*, Preface, p. 17; *Werke*, 7: 21.

54. Hegel, *Philosophy of Right*, Preface, p. 18; *Werke*, 7: 21.

55. Hegel, *Philosophy of Right*, Preface, p. 18; *Werke*, 7: 21.

56. "The state is the actuality of the ethical Idea—the ethical spirit as substantial will, manifest and clear to itself, which thinks and knows itself and implements what it knows in so far as it knows it" (Hegel, *Philosophy of Right*, § 257).

57. Hegel, *Encyclopedia*, § 574. Cf. *Philosophy of Right*, § 157.

58. Hegel, *Philosophy of History* (trans. J. Sibree, New York: Dover, 1956), 446.

59. Charles Taylor has gone so far as to suggest that there are three frameworks in which we should interpret Hegel's political philosophy: the political, the ontological, and the historical [Taylor, *Hegel* (Cambridge: Cambridge University Press, 1975), 365]. For my purposes, history may be reduced to politics. The problem with Taylor's insightful analysis is his failure to consider the methodological problems involved in trying to synthesize these frameworks.

60. Michael Hardimon uses the term "social theodicy" in *Hegel's Social Philosophy: The Project of Reconciliation*, 19–21; Georg Lukács uses the term "social ontology" in his *The Ontology of Social Being* (trans. Fernbach, London: Merlin Press, 1982), especially "Volume 1: Hegel."

61. These political writings are published as *Political Writings* (trans. T. M. Knox, New York: Garland Publishing Inc., 1984). These political essays seem to indicate that, despite what Hegel says in the Preface to the *Philosophy of Right*, he thought that philosophers should intervene in political life. If one emphasizes the practical strategy of the "political writings," one may surmise that the *Philosophy of Right* is merely another example of this political practice, and we may dismiss the ontological reading of the text. Such an interpretation remains unsatisfying, however, because it must ignore most of what Hegel says about the absolute nature of philosophy in both the Preface to the *Philosophy of Right* and in the *Encyclopedia.* This strategy is employed by Tunick in his *Hegel's Political Philosophy.* Following Ilting, Tunick sees the philosophical withdrawal advocated in the Preface to the published text as resulting from the censorship pressures of the Karlsbad decrees. Tunick and Ilting both appeal to the unpublished lecture notes from other years in order to establish the fact that at certain times, Hegel was more politically minded than he appears to be in the published text.

62. Habermas, *Theory and Practice* (trans. Viertel, Boston: Beacon, 1974), 191.

63. Mark Tunick uses the term "legal interpretivism" in *Hegel's Political Philosophy*, 17–20; the charge that Hegel is an apologist for the bourgeoisie is found, for

example, in Marx's *The German Ideology* [in *Marx-Engels Collected Works,* vol. 5 (New York: International Publishers, 1976)]. Hegel is seen as a defender of the bourgeois family structure in, for example, Max Horkheimer's "Authority and Family" [in *Critical Theory: Selected Essays* (New York: Continuum, 1995)].

64. Stephen Houlgate, for example, claims that the whole of Hegel's system is "a prolonged meditation on and determination of the proper meaning of freedom itself" [Stephen Houlgate, *Freedom, Truth and History* (New York: Routledge, 1991), 79].

65. Habermas, *Theory and Practice* (trans. Viertel, Boston: Beacon, 1974), 179. Z. A. Pelczynski also recognizes that there are two voices at work in Hegel's political thought: "the thorny path of the publicist . . . and the approach of a philosopher which proved to be a royal highway to success and fame" (Hegel, *Political Writings*, Introductory Essay, 17).

66. Habermas, *Theory and Practice*, 191.

67. Hegel, *Science of Logic*, Preface to the Second Edition, 40.

68. Hegel, *Philosophy of Right*, Preface, p. 9; *Werke*, 7: 11.

69. Cf. Ilting's Introduction to Hegel's *Vorlesungen über Rechtsphilosophie: 1818–1831.*

70. Some examples: In connection with Karl Sand's assassination of Kotzebue, Hegel's student, Asverus, (who was also the son of one of his friends) was arrested. In conjunction with this and the government's crackdown on the *Burschenschaften*, Hegel's student assistant, Carové, was denounced. Hegel's intervention with the political authorities on behalf of Victor Cousin brought unwanted political attention. Several times Hegel's "reformist" political philosophy was brought to the attention of the political authorities. Hegel had to reply to charges of atheism. Toward the end of his life the crown prince complained to Hegel about the reformist views being taught by his disciple Gans. For details see Pinkard, *Hegel: A Biography*, chapters 10–14.

71. Cf. Pinkard, *Hegel: A Biography*, pp. 632–34.

72. For information about "Hegel as Celebrity" cf. *Hegel: The Letters* (trans. Butler and Seiler, Bloomington: Indiana University Press, 1984), 401–405. Also see Pinkard, *Hegel: A Biography*, chapters 13–15.

73. *Hegel: The Letters*, 450.

74. Hegel, *Philosophy of Right*, § 270, Addition.

75. Hegel, *Philosophy of Right*, § 244, Addition. The section concerning the rabble from the 1819–1820 lectures quoted in Wood's note to this section makes it clear that the problem with poverty is its tendency to stifle freedom and self-consciousness because of the arbitrary nature of the bad luck that causes their poverty (p. 453).

76. Hegel, *Philosophy of Right*, § 187 and Remark and Addition; also *Philosophy of Right* § 268 and Remark.

77. Hegel, *Philosophy of Right* § 166, Addition.

78. Cf. Marx, *German Ideology*; Jean Bethke Elshtain, *Public Man, Private Woman* (Princeton: Princeton University Press, 1981); also Horkheimer's "Authority and the Family."

79. Hegel states in a letter to von Altenstein (April 16, 1822) that "students tend to come to the university without the requisite preparation for the study of philosophy" (*Hegel: The Letters*, 390).

80. Hegel, *Philosophy of Right*, § 257.

81. Hegel, *Philosophy of Right*, Preface, p. 9; *Werke*, 7: 11.

82. Letter to von Altenstein (October 10, 1820), in *Hegel: The Letters*, 458.

83. Letter to von Hardenberg (mid-October 1820), in *Hegel: The Letters*, 459.

84. Ilting's Introduction to Hegel's *Vorlesungen über Rechtsphilosophie*, 1: 100–102.

85. Cassirer, *The Myth of the State*.

86. Hegel, *Philosophy of Right*, § 280, Addition. In the second edition it was added that the formal character of the monarch's decision "was a natural bulwark (*Festigkeit*) against passion. One is unjust (*unrecht*), therefore, to demand objective characteristics in the monarch."

87. Hegel, *Philosophy of Right*, § 284.

88. For a discussion of the modern division of labor, cf. Hegel, *Philosophy of Right*, §198. Hegel admits the necessity of the division of labor within the state itself in § 290, although here he indicates that the division of labor needs to be organized rationally again indicating the need for philosophical comprehension of the system of the whole.

89. Hegel, *Philosophy of Right*, Preface, p. 20.

90. Hegel, *History of Philosophy*, 1: 95.

91. Cf. Wood's note (# 4) on p. 394 of *Philosophy of Right*.

92. Hegel, *Philosophy of Right*, Preface, p. 15.

93. Hegel, *Philosophy of Right*, § 187, Remark.

Chapter 8

1. Hegel, *Phenomenology of Spirit*, 60; *Werke*, 3: 85—I have modified the Miller translation substantially.

2. For a discussion of different interpretations of the opening sections of the Phenomenology, cf. Terry Pinkard, *Hegel's Phenomenology: The Sociality of Reason* (Cambridge: Cambridge University Press, 1996), pp. 350–51. Pinkard says, "Hegel's

point here seems to be: If you can't say it or show it, you don't know it" (*Hegel's Phenomenology*, 27).

3. Hegel, *Jena System Entwürfe* I, in *Hegel Gesammelte Werke* 6: 280.

4. Pinkard discusses the Lessing connection in *Hegel: A Biography*, pp. 15–16, including the idea that Lessing had to *create* his public by educating them—an idea we saw in Fichte. This idea of creating the public will be rejected by Hegel, as he takes up the task of *expressing* the implicit truths of political life.

5. Hegel, *History of Philosophy*, 3: 553; *Werke*, 20: 461.

6. Hegel, *History of Philosophy*, 3: 553; *Werke*, 20: 462.

7. Habermas, *Theory and Practice*, 152; Pinkard, *Hegel's Phenomenology: The Sociality of Reason*, 265–66.

8. Hegel, "The Oldest Systematic Program of German Idealism" trans. Diana I. Behler in *Philosophy of German Idealism*, 162; *Werke*, 1: 235–36.

9. Hegel, "Aphorisms from the Wastebook" (trans. Klein, Roochnik, and Tucker in *Independent Journal of Philosophy*, 3 (1979), 4. This is a translation of portions of the *Jenaer Schriften 1801–1807*, vol. 2 of the Suhrkamp edition of Hegel's *Werke*.

10. Hegel, "Aphorisms from the Wastebook," p. 4. Pinkard points out that Hegel's development in Jena was influenced by Hölderlin's goal of fashioning a new language for the modern age (Pinkard, *Hegel: A Biography*, 82). Indeed the goal of Romantic poetry was postulated at around the same time as, in Novalis's words, "to estrange art in a pleasant way, to make an object strange and yet known and attractive" [quoted in Marianne Thalmann, *The Literary Sign Language of German Romanticism* (Detroit: Wayne State University Press, 1972), p. 6]. In the similar fashion, Hegel is interested in estranging us from our ordinary way of speaking and thinking.

11. Hegel, *Jena System Entwürfe* I, in *Gesammelte Werke* 6: 318.

12. For a discussion of Hegel's Jena Philosophy of Mind and the importance of language and its connection with labor and property, see Habermas, *Theory and Practice*, chapter 4 or Marcuse, *Reason and Revolution* (Atlantic Highlands, N.J.: Humanities Press, 1983), chapter 3.

13. Hegel, *Phenomenology*, 35.

14. For a discussion of the "monological" element in the Kantian system of ethics and Hegel's critique of this, cf. Benhabib, *Critique, Norm, Utopia*, chapter 3 and chapter 8, part 2; or Habermas, *Theory and Practice*, pp. 149–152. Despite the advance of Hegel's social interpretation of spirit over Kant's monological transcendentalism, Benhabib admits that Hegel remains authoritarian to the extent that Hegel "substitutes ethical integration for political participation" (Benhabib, 101).

15. Whether or not Hegel deliberately cultivated this dialogical result of his own poor lecturing ability remains debatable. Pinkard suggests that what had been a liability to Hegel in terms of his teaching—a slight speech impediment, a Swabian accent, an inability to express himself succinctly—became in his Berlin years an asset both

in terms of his status as a genius/celebrity and in terms of the burdens his style placed upon his audience to actively engage with Hegel in a dialogical fashion (cf. Pinkard, p. 612).

16. Hegel, *Philosophy of Right*, p. 11.

17. Hegel, "Authority and Freedom" in Quentin Lauer's *Hegel's Idea of Philosophy* (New York: Fordham University Press, 1971), 148. (This is a translation of some student lecture notes to the *History of Philosophy* lectures of 1827–1828).

18. Hegel, *Philosophy of Right*, § 224 and *Philosophy of Right*, § 228, Remark.

19. Hegel, *Philosophy of Right*, § 228, Remark.

20. Hegel, *Philosophy of Right*, § 212.

21. Both of these last points are discussed in *Philosophy of Right*, § 212, Remark.

22. Hegel, *Philosophy of Right*, p. 11; *Werke*, 7: 13–14.

23. Hegel, *Philosophy of Right*, § 269. Cf. *Logic*'s remarks on spiritual life (*Logic*, 762–763; *Werke*, 6: 470–471). Cf. Marcuse's discussion of life throughout his *Hegel's Ontology and the Theory of Historicity*.

24. Hegel, *Philosophy of Right*, § 270.

25. Hegel, *Philosophy of Right*, § 263.

26. Hegel, *Philosophy of Right*, § 264.

27. Hegel, *Encyclopedia*, § 12.

28. All of the quotations in the present paragraph are from Remark to *Philosophy of Right* § 270.

29. Hegel, *Philosophy of History*, 36.

30. Ibid., 36.

31. Hegel, *Philosophy of Right*, § 270, Remark. Hegel states this more strongly in 1819/20: "In order to comprehend (*begreifen*) the state one must undertake to conquer one's opinions through the work of study, the work of thinking (*Nachdenken*)" (*Philosophy of Right*, p. 219).

32. Hegel, *Philosophy of Right*, § 360. In the Nisbett translation Wood provides a note to this section that suggests that Hegel has the French Revolution in mind, citing paragraph 581 of *Phenomenology* (Miller trans., p. 355).

33. Hegel, *Philosophy of Right*, § 360.

34. Hegel, *Philosophy of Right*, § 270.

35. Hegel, *Encyclopedia*, §§ 571–573.

36. Hegel's note is found on p. 292 of the Nisbett translation and on p. 417 of the *Werke* edition.

37. Hegel's discussion of free speech is relevant here. Cf. Hegel, *Philosophy of Right*, § 315. The crucial distinction for Hegel is that public opinion consists of educated, rational thought. (*Philosophy of Right*, § 219, Remark). Science is the paradigm for educated opinion. Thus science should not be subject to censorship.

38. Hegel does note a limit to freedom of thought in the Remark to § 270—the state's right to self-defense against subversive opinion. Hegel says that the state, religion, and science are all in conflict and that each has the right to defend itself against the others. This adversarial relationship seems to open the space for critique that many commentators feel is missing in Hegel.

39. Hegel, *Philosophy of Right*, §§ 173–175.

40. Hegel, *Philosophy of Right*, § 296.

41. Hegel, *Philosophy of Right*, § 295, Remark.

42. Hegel, *Encyclopedia*, § 462, Addition.

43. Hegel does not develop the connection between language and objective spirit in any detail. This is an obvious failure on Hegel's part, because language is obviously part of the objectivity of spirit—its inherited culture and history. In the Jena System, Hegel makes this link more explicit, as noted at the outset of the present chapter.

44. Hegel, *Encyclopedia*, § 462 and Addition.

45. Hegel, *Encyclopedia*, § 401, Addition; *Werke* 10: 109.

46. Hegel, *Encyclopedia*, § 401, Addition; *Werke* 10: 109.

47. Hegel, *Encyclopedia*, § 401, Addition; *Werke*, 10: 115–16.

48. Hegel, *Encyclopedia*, § 401, Addition; *Werke*, 10: 113.

49. Hegel, *Encyclopedia*, § 401, Addition; *Werke*, 10: 116.

50. Hegel, *Encyclopedia*, § 457, Addition.

51. John McCumber organizes this dispute nicely throughout his *The Company of Words*. The dispute breaks down along Right vs. Left Hegelian lines. McCumber's conclusion is that for Hegel, philosophy must continually express the difference between historical/representational language and its philosophical development.

52. Hegel, *Encyclopedia*, § 459; *Werke*, 10: 271.

53. Hegel, *Science of Logic*, 708.

54. Hegel, *Encyclopedia*, § 573; *Werke*, 10: 378.

55. Hegel, *Encyclopedia* § 459, Addition.

56. Hegel, *Encyclopedia* § 459, Addition; *Werke*, 10: 277.

57. Hegel, *Encyclopedia* § 459, Addition; *Werke*, 10: 277.

58. As an example of the contemporary emphasis on the written word, see Gadamer, *Truth and Method*, 391. For Gadamer, who ironically adopts his perspective

from Hegel, mere oral transmission of history is not sufficient for true historical self-consciousness or progress (cf. Introduction to the *Philosophy of History*, pp. 60–63). For historical consciousness, we need historical documents. Nonetheless, Hegel says, "Speech (*Die Sprache*) is the act of theoretical intelligence in a special sense; it is its external expression (*sie ist die äußerliche Äußerung derselben*)" (*Philosophy of History*, 63; *Werke*, 12: 85). For a discussion of the way in which Hegel privileges spoken over written language, the connection of this with Hegel's account of memory, the privilege of temporality over spatiality, and connections with the history of metaphysics, cf. Derrida's "Speech and Writing According to Hegel" in *Hegel: Critical Assessments* (ed. Robert Stern, New York: Routledge, 1993).

59. Hegel, *Encyclopedia*, § 459.

60. Hegel, *Philosophy of Right*, § 281, Remark.

61. Hegel, *Philosophy of Right*, § 270, Remark.

62. Hegel, *Philosophy of Right*, § 343.

Chapter 9

1. Marx, *German Ideology*, in *Marx-Engels Collected Works* (New York: International Publishers, 1976), 5: 446; *Marx Engels Werke* [*MEW*] (Berlin: Dietz Verlag, 1962), 3: 432.

2. This conservatism became apparent in Hegel's lack of enthusiasm for the July Revolution of 1830 and in his essay on the "English Reform Bill" (1831), where he criticized the liberal democratic reforms being proposed for England because they could easily "introduce not reform but revolution." Hegel, "The English Reform Bill" in *Hegel's Political Writings*, 330, cf. Pinkard's discussion of reaction against Hegel's conservative tendencies in Chapter 15 of *Hegel: A Biography*.

3. Wilhelm von Humboldt, *On Language: On the Diversity of Human Language Construction and its Influence on the Mental Development of the Human Species*, trans. Peter Heath (Cambridge: Cambridge University Press, 1999), § 22.

4. Ludwig Feuerbach, *Principles of the Philosophy of the Future,* trans. Manfred H. Vogel (Indianapolis: Hackett Publishing, 1986), § 1.

5. Karl Löwith indicates that all of the Young Hegelians and anti-Hegelians struggled outside of the political establishment. These "excluded" philosophers include Schopenhauer, Feuerbach, Kierkegaard, Ruge, Bauer, Stirner, Dühring, Nietzsche, and Marx. Because of their political and philosophical views, none of the Young Hegelians became state-sponsored philosophers in the way that Kant, Fichte, and Hegel had. Karl Löwith, *From Hegel to Nietzsche,* trans. David E. Green (New York: Columbia University Press, 1964), 69–70.

6. Marx, *Economic and Philosophical Manuscripts of 1844*, in *Collected Works*, 3: 333.

7. I am using the term "political" at this point in a sense that includes economics. Marx emphasizes economic class interests. But these classes are themselves involved in political struggles for power.

8. Marx, Contribution to the Critique of Hegel's *Philosophy of Law,* in *Collected Works*, 3: 7.

9. Ibid., 18.

10. Ibid., 9.

11. Marx, Contribution to the Critique of Hegel's *Philosophy of Law*, in *Collected Works*, 3: 17-18.

12. Ibid., 47, 61, 101.

13. Ibid., 29.

14. Ibid., 30.

15. Althusser, *For Marx* (trans. Ben Brewster, London: Verso, 1996), 227.

16. Ibid., 229.

17. Marx, "Estranged Labor" in *Economic and Philosophical Manuscripts of 1844*, in *Collected Works*, 3: 270–282.

18. Marx, "Theses on Feuerbach," in *Collected Works*, 5: 3; *MEW*, 3: 5.

19. Marx, "Estranged Labor" in *Economic and Philosophical Manuscripts of 1844*, in *Collected Works*, 3: 270.

20. Marx, *The German Ideology* in *Collected Works*, 5: 59.

21. Ibid., 59; *MEW*, 3: 46.

22. Marx, "Estranged Labor" in *Economic and Philosophical Manuscripts of 1844*, in *Collected Works*, 3: 304; *Marx Engels Gesamtausgabe* (Berlin: Dietz Verlag, 1982) (*MEGA*), I, 2: 272.

23. Marx, Contribution to the Critique of Hegel's *Philosophy of Law*, in *Collected Works*, 3: 28.

24. Justin Schwartz, "The Paradox of Ideology" [*Canadian Journal of Philosophy* 23 (4), December 1993].

25. Allen Wood, *Karl Marx* (London: Routledge and Kegan Paul, 1981), Chapter 12.

26. As Elster says, "the central task of the theory of ideology must be to explain how ideas arise or take root in the minds of persons holding them" Elster, *Making Sense of Marx* (Cambridge: Cambridge University Press, 1985), 476. As Althusser explains, "ideology, as a system of representations, is distinguished from science in that in it the practico-social functions is more important than the theoretical function (function as knowledge)" (Althusser, *For Marx*, 231).

27. Elster, *Making Sense of Marx*, 485.

28. Marx, *The German Ideology* in *Collected Works*, 5: 60.

29. Terrell Carver, *The Postmodern Marx* (State College Penn. State: Pennsylvania University Press, 1998), 168, and 104–107.

30. Carver summarizes this in part in *The Postmodern Marx*, 171.

31. Ulrich Erckenbrecht, *Marx' Materialistische Sprachtheorie* (Kronberg: Scriptor, 1973), 1.

32. Erckenbrecht explains this methodology in *Marx' Materialistische Sprach theorie*, 2.

33. Wood, *Karl Marx*, 174.

34. Ibid., 163.

35. Marx, *Grundrisse*, in *Collected Works*, 28: 414; *MEW*, 42: 398.

36. Marx, *Grundrisse*, in *Collected Works*, 28: 416; *MEW*, 42: 400.

37. Marx, *German Ideology*, in *Collected Works*, 5: 43–44; *MEW*, 3: 30.

38. Marx, *Economic and Philosophical Manuscripts of 1844*, in *Collected Works*, 3: 304; *MEGA*, I, 2: 272.

39. Marx, *German Ideology*, in *Collected Works*, 5: 44.

40. Marx, *Rheinische Zeitung*, July 14, 1842, in *Collected Works*, 1: 195.

41. Ibid., 195.

42. Marx, *German Ideology*, in *Collected Works*, 5: 446.

43. Ibid., 447.

44. Marx, *German Ideology*, in *Collected Works*, 5: 447; *MEW*, 3: 432–33.

45. Cf. for example, Marx's praise of philosophy in *Rheinische Zeitung*, July 12, 1842, in *Collected Works*, 1: 191–92.

46. Marx, "Contribution to the Critique of Hegel's *Philosophy of Right:* Introduction," in *Collected Works*, 3: 187.

47. Marx, *Rheinische Zeitung*, July 14, 1842, in *Collected Works*, 1: 195.

48. Marx, *Economic and Philosophical Manuscripts of 1844*, in *Collected Works*, 3: 298; *MEGA*, I, 2: 267.

49. Marx, *Rheinische Zeitung*, July 14, 1842, in *Marx-Engels Collected Works*, 1: 195.

50. Ibid. 197.

51. Marx continues ironically: "If society wants to 'eliminate all the drawbacks' that assail it, well, let it eliminate all the ill-sounding terms, change the language; and

to this end it has only to apply to the Academy for a new edition of its dictionary" [Marx, *The Poverty of Philosophy* (Moscow: Foreign Languages Publishing House, 1936), 63].

52. Marx, *The Poverty of Philosophy*, 118.

53. Marx, *The German Ideology*, in *Marx-Engels Collected Works*, 5: 231.

54. Marx, *Grundrisse*, in *Collected Works*, 28: 18; *MEW*, 42: 20.

55. Elie Kedourie claims, for example, that "we would not be exaggerating if we thought that Marx looked upon himself as another—and better—Hegel whose life work would be characterized by the same all-embracing universality, but would be free from the mystification which infected Hegel's philosophy" [Elie Kedourie, *Hegel and Marx* (Oxford: Blackwell, 1995), 168].

56. As Marcuse describes it, Marx's categories refer to the negation of the existing order just as they aim at the negation of traditional (Hegelian) philosophy's defense of this order. "They aim at a new form of society even when describing its current form. Essentially they address themselves to a truth to be had only through the abolition of civil society. Marx's theory is a 'critique' in the sense that all concepts are an indictment of the totality of the existing order" (Marcuse, *Reason and Revolution*, 258).

57. Thus I only agree in part with Dick Howard when he states, "When he fell back to criticism as a theory *for* revolution, as when he leaped forward to dialectics as a theory *of* revolution, Marx closed to himself the political dimension [of capitalism—which Howard explains as ultimately democratic] which only the critique theory could open up. At the same time, and for the same theoretical reason, he misunderstood the *political* question carried by democratic modern societies" (Dick Howard, *The Politics of Critique*, 24).

58. Marx, *German Ideology*, in *Collected Works*, 5: 193.

59. Marx, *German Ideology*, in *Collected Works*, 5: 195; *MEW*, 3: 178.

60. Marx, *Communist Manifesto*, in *Marx-Engels Reader*, 2nd Edition (ed. Robert C. Tucker, New York: Norton, 1978), 484; *MEW*, 4: 475.

61. Marx, "Letter to Ruge" in *Deutsche-Französische Jahrbücher*, September 1843, in *Collected Works*, 3: 142.

62. Marx, "Contribution to the Critique of Hegel's *Philosophy of Right:* Introduction," in *Collected Works*, 3: 176; *MEGA*, I, 2: 171.

63. Cf. Marx, "Letter to Ruge" in *Deutsche-Französische Jahrbücher*, Sept. 1843, in *Collected Works*, 3: 14–145.

64. Cf. Allen Wood, "The Marxian Critique of Justice" in Cohen, Nagel, Scanlon, eds., *Marx, Justice, and History* (Princeton, N.J.: Princeton University Press, 1980), 26.

65. Richard Miller, *Analyzing Marx* (Princeton, N.J.: Princeton University Press, 1984), 96. This criticism as a general indictment of (Rawlsian) liberalism has been

posed, for example by Michael Sandel in his *Liberalism and the Limits of Justice*. Also see Michael Walzer, *Spheres of Justice* (New York: Basic Books, 1983), 28–29.

66. Marx, "Contribution to the Critique of Hegel: Introduction" in *Collected Works*, 3: 182.

67. Ibid., 182.

68. Ibid., 183.

69. Marx, "Critique of the Gotha Program" in *Marx-Engels Reader*, 531.

70. Ibid., 531.

71. Ibid., 531.

72. Marx, *The German Ideology*, in *Collected Works*, 5: 78.

73. Ibid., 80.

74. Wood, "The Marxian Critique of Justice" in *Marx, Justice, and History,* 28.

75. Wood attempts to make Marx consistent by claiming that "Marx falls into no inconsistency if he morally condemns an attitude of complacency in the face of massive and remediable nonmoral evil, while refusing to condemn morally the non-moral evil itself" [Allen Wood, *Karl Marx* (London: Routledge and Kegan Paul, 1981), 153].

76. Ibid., 139.

77. I thus agree with Miller's critique of Wood and with Miller's conclusion that "When people speak of the justice or injustice of important, large-scale institutions, a main motivation, indeed the main one, is an interest in choosing how to act as agents in a political process. The motivating question is whether to defend or oppose one's institutions" (Miller, *Analyzing Marx*, 84).

78. *Neue Rheinische Zeitung*, May 19, 1849, *Collected Works,* 9: 452.

79. This is not to say that the revolution must be violent, although Marx seems to have supposed that it would be, at least in certain countries (although in other countries the revolution might be more gradual). Consistent with my emphasis on the situatedness of theory and practice, the nature of the revolution will depend upon the social and historical circumstances in which it is to take place. Thus Marx admits in 1872 that even though "Someday the workers must seize political power in order to build up the new organization of labor," "we have not yet asserted that the ways to achieve that goal are everywhere the same" (Marx, "September 8, 1872 Speech to the First International in Amsterdam," in *Marx-Engels Reader*, 523). Marx concludes that in England, America, and Holland, the revolution might very well be peaceful. Shlomo Avineri explains this in his discussion of Marx's theory of revolution by emphasizing that the question of the means of revolution is itself tied up with the question of the legitimation of social change within the context of conflict: different classes will view the question of violence differently. "The question of violent versus peaceful revolu-

tion thus resolves itself into the question whether the recourse to violence will occur prior to its legitimization by majority decision or after such legitimization. For Marx, this question is trivial, since it emphasizes the accepted bourgeois modes of legitimization and divorces legitimacy from social praxis" [Shlomo Avineri, *The Social and Political Thought of Karl Marx* (Cambridge: Cambridge University Press, 1968), 218].

80. Habermas, *Theory and Practice*, 249.

81. Lukács, "Reification and the Consciousness of the Proletariat," in *History and Class Consciousness.*

82. Habermas, *Theory and Practice*, 238; Wood, *Karl Marx*, Chapter 12.

83. I thus agree with Robert Meister's conclusion that Marx is not practicing either a liberal/moral critique or a skeptical critique. Rather, he is engaged in what Meister calls the process of creating political identity [Robert Meister, *Political Identity: Thinking Through Marx* (Cambridge, Mass.: Basil Blackwell, 1990), 93].

Chapter 10

1. Marx, *The German Ideology*, in *Marx-Engels Collected Works*, 5: 150; *MEW*, 3: 133.

2. Seyla Benhabib, *Critique, Norm, Utopia*, 135.

3. Ibid., 140.

4. Marx's connection to the rest of German Idealism has been extensively chronicled by the likes of Lukacs, Marcuse, and Habermas. The connection with Fichte deserves to be further emphasized. Tom Rockmore has begun this discussion in his *Fichte, Marx, and the German Philosophical Tradition.* Rockmore indicates that explicit connections between Fichte and Marx are few. Marx does not quote Fichte, for example, despite the fact that he names him on a number of occasions. Nonetheless, Rockmore concludes "available evidence points strongly to an early and perhaps enduring Marxian interest in Fichte's position. There seems little doubt that Marx was aware of Fichte's position" (Rockmore, *Fichte, Marx, and the German Philosophical Tradition,* 126). The point is that, although Marx does not make Fichte an explicit matter for consideration, Fichte's thinking was in the air at the time that Marx was educated. I would argue in addition to Rockmore's discussion of Fichte's "theory of man," Marx was more than likely aware of Fichte's political activity in his *Addresses to the German Nation.*

5. Feuerbach, *Principles of the Philosophy of the Future* [trans. Vogel (Indianapolis: Hackett, 1986)], § 41, pp. 58–59.

6. Ibid., § 62, p. 72.

7. Marx, *Doctoral Dissertation*, in *Collected Works*, 1: 85.

8. Ibid., 1: 85.

9. Marx, *Contribution to the Critique of Political Economy* in *Marx-Engels Reader*, 4.

10. Cf. Marx, *German Ideology*, in *Collected Works*, 5: 322.

11. Marx, *German Ideology*, in *Collected Works*, 5: 329; *MEW*, 3: 311.

12. Feuerbach, *Principles of the Philosophy of the Future*, Preface of 1843, p. 3.

13. Ibid., p. 3.

14. Marx, *Communist Manifesto*, in *Marx-Engels Reader*, 490.

15. This caveat seems to be an ubiquitous feature of discussions of Marx and the *Manifesto*. For a concise discussion cf. Wal Suchting, "What is Living and What is Dead in the Communist Manifesto?" in *The Communist Manifesto: New Interpretations* (ed. Mark Cowling, New York: NYU Press, 1998).

16. Marx, *Communist Manifesto*, in *Marx-Engels Reader*, 489.

17. Ibid., 489.

18. Ibid., 483.

19. For a discussion of the problem of eschatology in Marx cf. Avineri, *The Social and Political Thought of Karl Marx*, 250–52. This problem leads to the question of literal vs. nonliteral readings of Marx's texts (as seen in the debate between Miller and Moore in *Marx, Justice, and History*, 211–263). In what follows I maintain, following Carver, that there are multiple levels on which to read Marx, the literal, the prophetic, the bombastic, and the sarcastic.

20. Stuart Wilks-Heeg, "The Communist Manifesto and Working-Class Parties in Western Europe" in *The Communist Manifesto: New Interpretations* (ed. Mark Cowling, New York: New York University Press, 1998), 129.

21. Marx, *Communist Manifesto*, in *Marx-Engels Reader*, 489.

22. Ibid., 490.

23. "The executive of the modern State is but a committee for managing the common affairs of the whole bourgeoisie" (Ibid., 475).

24. Karl Marx, *German Ideology* in *Marx-Engels Reader*, 149.

25. For example: Michael Bakunin, *Statism and Anarchy* (trans. and ed. Marshal S. Shatz, Cambridge: Cambridge University Press, 1990); Rosa Luxemburg, "Marxism or Leninism," in *The Russian Revolution and Leninism or Marxism* (Ann Arbor: University of Michigan Press, 1961); Lenin, *Two Tactics of Social Democracy in the Democratic Revolution* (New York: International Publishers, 1935), Chapter 6.

26. Paul Wetherly, "A Capitalist State? Marx's Ambiguous Legacy" in *The Communist Manifesto: New Interpretations*, 174.

27. Karl Popper, *The Open Society and its Enemies*, Vol.2, Chapter 17, especially pp. 118–120. Marcuse claims that "According to Marx, the correct theory is the consciousness of a practice that aims at changing the world. Marx's concept of truth, however, is far from relativism" (Marcuse, *Reason and Revolution*, 321).

28. Robert Tucker, "Marx as a Political Theorist," in *Marx's Socialism* (ed. Shlomo Avineri, New York: Lieber-Atherton, 1972), 149.

29. Schwartz, *The Permanence of the Political*, 104.

30. Marx, *Communist Manifesto*, in *Marx-Engels Reader*, 500.

31. Marx, *Communist Manifesto*, in *Marx-Engels Reader*, 478.

32. For a brief discussion of the historical context of the *Manifesto* see Michael Levin, "'The Hungry Forties': The Socio-Economic Context of the Communist Manifesto" in *The Communist Manifesto: New Interpretations.*

33. For a discussion of Marx's prophetic voice cf. Neal Riemer, *Karl Marx and Prophetic Politics* (New York: Praeger, 1987).

34. Engels, "The Tactics of Social Democracy," in *Marx-Engels Reader*, 562.

35. Marx, *Communist Manifesto*, in *Marx-Engels Reader*, 482 (my italics).

36. Felix, *Marx as Politician* (Carbondale: Southern Illinois Press, 1983), 75.

37. Jacques Derrida focuses on Marx's "conjuring trick" throughout *Specters of Marx* (trans. Peggy Kamuf, New York: Routledge, 1994). For a criticism of Derrida's reading, see Carver, *The Postmodern Marx*, Chapter 1.

38. Marx, *Communist Manifesto*, in *Marx-Engels Reader*, 483.

39. Marx, "Alienation and Social Classes" in *Marx-Engels Reader*, 134–35.

40. Marx, *Communist Manifesto*, in *Marx-Engels Reader*, 500; *MEW*, 4: 493.

41. Marx, *Communist Manifesto*, in *Marx-Engels Reader*, 484.

42. Marx, Preface to the 1872 edition of the *Communist Manifesto*, in *Marx-Engels Reader*, 469.

43. Marx, *Communist Manifesto*, in *Marx-Engels Reader*, 481.

44. Ibid., 481.

45. Ibid., 484.

46. Ibid., 484.

47. Cf. the debate about "opportunism" between Luxembourg and Lenin in Luxembourg, "Leninism or Marxism" in *The Russian Revolution and Leninism or Marxism* (Ann Arbor: University of Michigan Press, 1961) and Lenin, *What is to be Done?* (New York: International Publishers, 1961).

48. Marx, *Communist Manifesto*, in *Marx-Engels Reader*, 500.

49. This is Yack's criticism of Marx, *The Longing for Total Revolution*, Chapter 7.

50. Marx, *The German Ideology*, in *Marx-Engels Collected Works*, 5: 37; *MEW*, 3: 27

51. Marx, "Contribution to the Critique of Hegel's *Philosophy of Right*" in *Marx-Engels Reader*, 60.

52. Marx, *Communist Manifesto*, in *Marx-Engels Reader*, 492; *MEW*, 4: 483.

53. Marx, *Communist Manifesto*, in *Marx-Engels Reader*, 495.

54. Marx, *Communist Manifesto*, in *Marx-Engels Reader*, 497; *MEW*, 4: 489

55. Marx, *Communist Manifesto*, in *Marx-Engels Reader*, 497.

56. Marx, *Communist Manifesto*, in *Marx-Engels Reader*, 498; *MEW*, 4: 490.

57. Marx, *Communist Manifesto*, in *Marx-Engels Reader*, 498.

58. Marx, *Capital* (trans. Ben Fowkes, New York: Vintage, 1977), 1: 929.

59. David Felix, *Marx as Politician* (Carbondale: Southern Illinois Press, 1983), 154. This conclusion concurs with Felix's thesis that "Marx was primarily a politician and not a thinker . . . as great as Marx was a thinker, he was a greater politician" (Felix, ix).

60. Marx, *Capital*, 1: 169.

61. Ibid., 169.

62. Marx, *Capital*, 1: 167 ; *MEW*, 23 : 88.

63. Marx, *Capital*, 1: 187.

64. Marx, *Capital*, 1: 181. Marx quotes both *Revelation* 13: 17 and 17:13.

65. Marx, *Capital*, 1: 168–69.

66. I am ignoring arguments for and against Marx's critique of political economy and his labor theory of value because I am not so much interested in the accuracy of his critique as in its relation to Marx's practical political activity. For discussions of the labor theory of value cf. G. A. Cohen, "The Labor Theory of Value and the Concept of Exploitation," in Cohen, Nagel, and Scanlon, eds., *Marx, Justice, and History*. Carver interprets Marx's economics ironically: he may have been exposing the assumptions of political economy rather than simply affirming them. The difficulty that Carver notes for such an interpretation is what he calls the "parody/satire/reality" problem: Marx did such a good job of representing the assumptions of bourgeois political economy that it is difficult to detect any critical distance or irony in his presentation [Carver, *The Postmodern Marx*, Chapter 4].

67. My interpretation here runs counter to the one offered by Jon Elster. Elster states in a footnote that one may find in Marx a connection between the process of

reification in language and the fetishism of commodities and money. However, he concludes by ambivalently stating that he is "not at all certain that these are issues worth looking into, but then again they might be" (Elster, *Making Sense of Marx*, p. 97, note 6).

68. Marx, *Grundrisse*, in *Collected Works*, 28: 23; *MEW*, 42: 20–21.

69. Marx, *Capital*, 1: 92–93.

70. Ibid., 520.

71. This supposed freedom of labor is glossed by Marx as a market "where children under 13 years are compelled to work like adults, and for that reason can be sold at a higher price" (Marx, *Capital*, 1: 520).

72. Ibid., 929.

73. Marx, *Communist Manifesto*, in *Marx-Engels Reader*, 482.

74. Marx, *Eighteenth Brumaire of Louis Bonaparte*, in *Marx-Engels Reader*, 597.

75. Marx, *Eighteenth Brumaire of Louis Bonaparte*, in *Marx-Engels Reader*, 598.

76. Marx, "Letter to Ruge," September 1843, in the *Deutsch-Französische Jarhbücher* in *Marx-Engels Collected Works,* 3: 144; *MEW*, 1: 345.

77. Marx, *The Poverty of Philosophy*, 140.

78. Marx, "Contribution to the Critique of Hegel's Philosophy of Right: Introduction" in *Collected Works*, 3: 183.

79. Ibid., 183.

80. Marx, "Contribution to the Critique of Hegel's *Philosophy of Right:* Introduction" in *Collected Works*, 3: 187; *MEGA*, I, 2: 182.

Chapter 11

1. Hegel, *Phenomenology of Spirit*, 43; *Werke*, 3: 64.

2. Hegel, *Phenomenology of Spirit*, 42; *Werke*, 3: 64. Hegel probably has Schelling in mind here, although the charges could apply to Fichte, Fries, or to Schlegel and the Romantics.

3. Hegel, *Phenomenology of Spirit*, 43; *Werke*, 3: 64.

4. Hegel, *Phenomenology of Spirit*, 10; *Werke*, 3: 23.

5. Hegel, *Phenomenology of Spirit*, 33.

6. Hegel, *Phenomenology of Spirit*, 43; *Werke*, 3: 64.

7. Hegel, *Phenomenology of Spirit*, 43; *Werke*, 3: 65.

8. Hegel, *Phenomenology of Spirit*, 43.

9. "What is Enlightenment?" in *Kant's Political Writings*, 54

10. MacIntyre claims, for example, that in our therapeutic culture, "truth has been displaced as a value and replaced by psychological effectiveness" [Alisdair MacIntyre, *After Virtue* (Notre Dame: Notre Dame University Press, 1984) 30].

11. Plato, *Gorgias* (trans. Terence Irwin, Oxford: Clarendon Press, 1979), 500 c.

12. Hegel, *Philosophy of Right*, Preface, p. 19.

13. Kant, *Critique of Pure Reason*, B 84 and B 848.

14. The idea of our "heterophilic age" is borrowed from Zygmunt Bauman, *Post-Modernity and its Discontents* (New York: New York University Press, 1997), 30.

15. I develop this in Fiala, "The Irony of Political Philosophy" [*Philosophy in the Contemporary World*, 5:1 (Fall), 1999].

16. She claims: "In its account of itself, women's point of view contains a duality analogous to that of the Marxist proletariat: determined by the reality the theory explodes, it thereby claims special access to that reality. Feminism does not see its view as subjective, partial, or undetermined but as a critique of the purported generality, disinterestedness, and universality of previous accounts" [Catherine MacKinnon, *Toward a Feminist Theory of the State* (Cambridge: Harvard University Press, 1989), 121].

Bibliography

Primary Sources

Fichte

"Concerning the Difference between the Spirit and the Letter in Philosophy." In *Fichte's Early Writings*, trans. and ed. by Daniel Breazeale. Ithaca, N.Y.: Cornell University Press, 1988.

"A Crystal Clear Report to the General Public Concerning the Actual Essence of the Newest Philosophy." In *Philosophy of German Idealism*, trans. and ed. Behler. New York: Continuum, 1987.

"On the Linguistic Capacity and the Origin of Language." In *Language and German Idealism*, trans. and ed. by Jere Paul Surber. Atlantic Highlands, N.J.: Humanities Press, 1996. *J. G. Fichte Gesamtausgabe*, I, 3. Stuttgart-Bad Cannstatt: Friedrich Frommann Verlag, 1965.

"Some Lectures Concerning the Scholar's Vocation." In *Fichte's Early Writings*, trans. and ed. by Daniel Breazeale. Ithaca, N.Y.: Cornell University Press, 1988.

Addresses to the German Nation. Trans. Jones and Turnbull. Chicago: Open Court, 1923. *Fichtes Werke,* vol. 7. Ed. I. H. Fichte, Berlin: de Gruyter, 1965.

Grundlage des Naturrechts. In *Fichtes Werke*, vol. 3. Ed. I. H. Fichte, Berlin: de Gruyter, 1965.

Science of Knowledge. Trans. Heath and Lachs. Cambridge: Cambridge University Press, 1982. *J. G. Fichte Gesamtausgabe*. I, 2. Stuttgart-Bad Cannstatt: Friedrich Frommann Verlag, 1965.

Ueber Machiavelli. In *J. G. Fichte Gesamtausgabe I,* 9. Stuttgart-Bad Cannstatt: Friedrich Frommann Verlag, 1965.

The Vocation of Man. Trans. by Peter Preuss. Indianapolis: Hackett, 1987.

Hegel

"Aphorisms from the Wastebook." Trans. Klein, Roochnik, and Tucker in *Independent Journal of Philosophy*, 3 (1979). This is a translation of portions of the *Jenaer Schriften 1801–1807*, vol. 2 of the Suhrkamp edition of Hegel's *Werke*.

"Authority and Freedom." In Quentin Lauer's *Hegel's Idea of Philosophy*. New York: Fordham University Press, 1971.

"The Constitution of Germany" in *Hegel's Political Writings*. Ed. by Dickey, Cambridge: Cambridge University Press, 1999; *Gesammelte Werke*, vol. 5. Hamburg: Meiner Verlag, 1968.

"Oldest Systematic Program of German Idealism." In *Philosophy of German Idealism* Trans. Diana Behler, ed. Ernst Behler, New York: Continuum, 1987. *Werke*, vol. 1. Hegel-Institut Berlin, 1999 Electronic text from Past Masters (same pagination as the Suhrkamp edition).

The Difference between Fichte's and Schelling's System of Philosophy (*Differenzschrift*). Trans. and ed. by H. S. Harris and Walter Cerf, Albany: State University of New York Press, 1977. *Werke,* vol. 2. Hegel-Institut Berlin, 1999 Electronic text from Past Masters (same pagination as the Suhrkamp edition).

Encyclopedia of Philosophical Sciences in Outline. *Encyclopedia Logic*, Trans. Geraets, Suchting, and Harris, Indianapolis: Hackett Publishing, 1991. Hegel's *Philosophy of Mind*, trans. J. N. Findlay, Oxford: Oxford University Press, 1971. *Werke*, vol. 8–10. Hegel-Institut Berlin, 1999 Electronic text from Past Masters (same pagination as the Suhrkamp edition).

Hegel: Political Writings. Trans. T. M. Knox, New York: Garland Publishing Inc.

Hegel: The Letters. Trans. Butler and Seiler, Bloomington: Indiana University Press, 1984.

History of Philosophy, 3 volumes. Trans. Haldane and Simson, Lincoln: University of Nebraska Press, 1995. *Werke*, vol. 18–20. Hegel-Institut Berlin, 1999 Electronic text from Past Masters (same pagination as the Suhrkamp edition).

Jena System Entwürfe I. In *Gesammelte Werke,* vol. 6. Hamburg : Meiner Verlag, 1968

Introductory Lectures on Aesthetics. Trans. Bosanquet, London: Penguin, 1993. *Werke*, vol. 13. Hegel-Institut Berlin, 1999 Electronic text from Past Masters (same pagination as the Suhrkamp edition).

Lectures on Natural Right and Political Science: The First Philosophy of Right (1817–1818). Trans. J. Michael Stewart and Peter C. Hodgson, Berkeley: University of California Press, 1995.

Phenomenology of Spirit. Trans. Miller, Oxford: Oxford University Press,1977. *Werke*, vol. 3. Hegel-Institut Berlin, 1999 Electronic text from Past Masters (same pagination as the Suhrkamp edition).

Philosophie des Rechts: Die Vorlesung von 1819/20. Ed. Dieter Henrich, Frankfurt am Main: Suhrkamp Verlag, 1983.

Philosophy of Right. Trans. Nisbett, ed. Wood, Cambridge: Cambridge University Press, 1991. *Werke,* vol. 7. Hegel-Institut Berlin, 1999 Electronic text from Past Masters (same pagination as the Suhrkamp edition).

"Rede zum Antritt des philosophischen Lehramtes an der Universität Berlin." In *Vorlesnngsmannskripte II (1818–1831), Gesammelte Werke.* Ed. Rheihish-West Fälische Akademie der Wissenschaften, 1995.

Science of Logic. Trans. Miller, Atlantic Highlands, NJ: Humanities Press, 1993. *Werke*, vol. 5. Hegel-Institut Berlin, 1999 Electronic text from Past Masters (same pagination as the Suhrkamp edition).

Vorlesungen über Rechtsphilosophie: 1818–1831, in 4 volumes. Ed. Karl-Heinz Ilting, Stuttgart: Frommann-Holzboog, 1973.

Kant

Anthropology from a Pragmatic Point of View. Trans. Victor Lyle Dowdell, Carbondale: Southern Illinois University Press, 1978. *Hauptwerke*, vol. 7. *Akademie Ausgabe* (Immanuel Kant, *Gesammelte Schriften.* Hrsg. von der Königlich-Preussischen Akademie der Wissenschaften zu Berlin. Berlin, 1902). Electronic text from Past Masters, 1998.

Critique of Judgment. Trans. J. H. Bernard, New York: MacMillan, 1951. *Hauptwerke*, vol. 5–6. *Akademie Ausgabe* (Immanuel Kant, *Gesammelte Schriften.* Hrsg. von der Königlich- Preussischen Akademie der Wissenschaften zu Berlin. Berlin, 1902). Electronic text from Past Masters, 1998.

Critique of Practical Reason. Trans. Lewis White Beck, New York: MacMillan, 1956. *Hauptwerke*, vol. 5. *Akademie Ausgabe* (Immanuel Kant, *Gesammelte Schriften.* Hrsg. von der Königlich-Preussischen Akademie der Wissenschaften zu Berlin. Berlin, 1902). Electronic text from Past Masters, 1998.

Critique of Pure Reason. Trans. Kemp-Smith, New York: St. Martin's Press, 1956. *Hauptwerke*, vol. 2. *Akademie Ausgabe* (Immanuel Kant, *Gesammelte Schriften.* Hrsg. von der Königlich-Preussischen Akademie der Wissenschaften zu Berlin. Berlin, 1902). Electronic text from Past Masters, 1998. Distinctions between the first and second editions of this text are indicated by the convention 'A', for first edition, and 'B' for second edition.

Foundations of the Metaphysics of Morals. Trans. Lewis White Beck, New York: MacMillan, 1990. *Hauptwerke*, vol. 4. *Akademie Ausgabe* (Immanuel Kant, *Gesammelte Schriften.* Hrsg. von der Königlich-Preussischen Akademie der Wissenschaften zu Berlin. Berlin, 1902). Electronic text from Past Masters, 1998.

Logic. Hauptwerke, vol. 9. *Akademie Ausgabe* (Immanuel Kant, *Gesammelte Schriften.* Hrsg. von der Königlich-Preussischen Akademie der Wissenschaften zu Berlin. Berlin, 1902). Electronic text from Past Masters, 1998.

The Metaphysical Elements of Justice: Part I of the Metaphysics of Morals (*Rechtslehre*). Trans. John Ladd, New York: Macmillan, 1965. *Hauptwerke*, vol. 6. *Akademie Ausgabe* (Immanuel Kant, *Gesammelte Schriften.* Hrsg. von der Königlich-Preussischen Akademie der Wissenschaften zu Berlin. Berlin, 1902). Electronic text from Past Masters, 1998.

Political Writings. Ed. by Hans Reiss, Cambridge: Cambridge University Press, 1991. *Hauptwerke*, vol. 8. *Akademie Ausgabe* (Immanuel Kant, *Gesammelte Schriften*. Hrsg. von der Königlich-Preussischen Akademie der Wissenschaften zu Berlin. Berlin, 1902). Electronic text from Past Masters, 1998.

Prolegomena to Any Future Metaphysics. Trans. Lewis White Beck, New York: Macmillan, 1950.

Religion Within the Limits of Reason Alone. Trans. T. H. Greene, New York: Harper Torchbooks, 1960.

Marx

"Alienation and Social Classes." In *Marx-Engels Reader,* 2nd Edition. Ed. Robert C. Tucker, New York: Norton, 1978.

"Contribution to the Critique of Hegel's *Philosophy of Right:* Introduction." In *Collected Works*, vol. 3. New York: International Publishers, 1976. *Marx Engels Gesamtausgabe* (MEGA), I, 2. Berlin: Dietz Verlag, 1982.

"Critique of the Gotha Program." In *Marx-Engels Reader,* 2nd Edition. Ed. Robert C. Tucker, New York: Norton, 1978.

"Letter to Ruge" from the *Deutsche-Französische Jahrbücher*. In *Collected Works*, vol. 3. New York: International Publishers, 1976.

"On the Jewish Question." In *Marx-Engels Reader,* 2nd Edition. Ed. Robert C. Tucker, New York: Norton, 1978.

"Speech to the First International in Amsterdam, September 8, 1872." In *Marx-Engels Reader,* 2nd Edition. Ed. Robert C. Tucker, New York: Norton, 1978.

"Theses on Feuerbach." In *Collected Works*, vol. 5. New York: International Publishers, 1976.

Articles from the *Rheinische Zeitung*. In *Collected Works*, vol. 1. New York: International Publishers, 1976.

Capital. Vol. 1. Trans. Ben Fowkes, New York: Vintage, 1977. *Marx Engels Werke (MEW)*. Vol. 23. Berlin: Dietz Verlag, 1962.

Communist Manifesto. In *Marx-Engels Reader,* 2nd Edition. Ed. Robert C. Tucker, New York: Norton, 1978.

Contribution to the Critique of Hegel's Philosophy of Law. In *Collected Works*, vol. 3. New York: International Publishers, 1976.

Contribution to the Critique of Political Economy. In *Marx-Engels Reader,* 2nd Edition. Ed. Robert C. Tucker, New York: Norton, 1978.

Doctoral Dissertation. In *Collected Works*, vol. 1. New York: International Publishers, 1976.

Economic and Philosophical Manuscripts of 1844. In *Collected Works*, vol 3. New York: International Publishers, 1976. *Marx Engels Gesamtausgabe (MEGA),* I, 2. Berlin: Dietz Verlag, 1982.

Eighteenth Brumaire of Louis Napoleon. In *Marx-Engels Reader,* 2nd Edition. Ed. Robert C. Tucker, New York: Norton, 1978.

The German Ideology. In *Marx-Engels Collected Works*, vol. 5. New York: International Publishers, 1976. *Marx Engels Werke (MEW),* vol. 3. Berlin: Dietz Verlag, 1962.

Grundrisse. In *Collected Works*, vol. 28. New York: International Publishers, 1976. *MEW*, vol. 42. Berlin: Dietz Verlag, 1962.

The Poverty of Philosophy. Moscow: Foreign Languages Publishing House, 1936.

Secondary Sources

Adorno, Theodore. *Negative Dialectics*. Trans. E. B. Ashton, New York: Continuum, 1994.

Althusser, Louis. *For Marx*. Trans. Ben Brewster, London: Verso, 1996.

Arendt, Hannah. *The Human Condition*. Chicago: University of Chicago Press, 1958.

Arendt, Hannah. *Lectures on Kant's Political Philosophy*. Ed. Ronald Beiner, Chicago: University of Chicago Press, 1982.

Arendt, Hannah. *The Life of the Mind*. San Diego: Harcourt Brace Jovanovich, 1978.

Arendt, Hannah. *On Violence*. San Diego: Harcourt Brace and Co., 1970.

Aristotle. *Politics*. Trans. Carnes Lord. Chicago: University of Chicago Press, 1984.

Augustine. *Confessions*. Trans. Edward B. Pusey, New York: Collier Books, 1961.

Avineri, Shlomo. "The Discovery of Hegel's Early Lectures on the Philosophy of Right." *Owl of Minerva*, 16: 2 (Spring 1985).

Avineri, Schlomo. *The Social and Political Thought of Karl Marx*. Cambridge: Cambridge University Press, 1968.

Bakunin, Michael. *Statism and Anarchy*. Trans. and ed. Marshal S. Shatz, Cambridge: Cambridge University Press, 1990.

Bauman, Zygmunt. *Post-Modernity and its Discontents*. New York: New York University Press, 1997.

Baynes, Kenneth. *The Normative Grounds of Social Criticism*. Albany : State University of New York Press, 1992.

Beck, Lewis W. "The Fact of Reason: An Essay on Justification in Ethics." In *Studies in the Philosophy of Kant*. Ed. Lewis W. Beck, Indianapolis: Bobbs-Merrill, 1965.

Beck, Lewis W. "Kant and the Right of Revolution." In *Journal of the History of Ideas* 32 (1971): 411–422.

Beiser, Frederick C. *The Fate of Reason*. Cambridge: Harvard University Press, 1993.

Benhabib, Seyla. *Critique, Norm, Utopia*. New York: Columbia University Press, 1986.

Benjamin, Walter. "Critique of Violence." In *Reflections*. Trans. Jephcott, New York: Schocken Books, 1986.

Berlin, Isaiah. "Two Concepts of Liberty." In *Four Essays on Liberty*. Oxford: Oxford University Press, 1969.

Breazeale, Daniel. Introduction to "Concerning the Difference between the Spirit and the Letter within Philosophy." In *Fichte's Early Writings*. Trans. and ed. by Daniel Breazeale. Ithaca, NY: Cornell University Press, 1988

Brickhouse, Thomas C., and Nicolas D. Smith. *The Philosophy of Socrates*. Boulder, Colo.: Westview Press, 2000.

Burbridge, John W. *On Hegel's Logic*. Atlantic Highlands, N.J.: Humanities Press, 1981.

Carver, Terrell. *The Postmodern Marx*. State College, Penn.: Pennsylvania State University Press, 1998.

Cassirer, Ernst. *Kant's Life and Thought*. New Haven, Conn.: Yale University Press, 1981.

Cassirer, Ernst. *The Myth of the State*. New Haven, Conn.: Yale University Press, 1946.

Cassirer, Ernst. *Rousseau, Kant, Goethe*. Hamden, Conn.: Archon Books, 1961.

Cohen, G. A. "Karl Marx and the Withering Away of Social Science." In *Marx, Justice, and History*. Ed. Cohen, Nagel, and Scanlon, Princeton, N.J.: Princeton University Press, 1980.

Cohen, G. A. "The Labor Theory of Value and the Concept of Exploitation." In *Marx, Justice, and History*. Ed. Cohen, Nagel, and Scanlon, Princeton, N.J.: Princeton University Press, 1980.

Derrida, Jacques. "Force of Law." In *Deconstruction and the Possibility of Justice*. Ed. Cornell, Rosenfeld, and Carlson, New York: Routledge, 1992.

Derrida, Jacques. *Specters of Marx*. Trans. Peggy Kamuf. New York: Routledge, 1994.

Derrida, Jacques. "Speech and Writing According to Hegel." In *Hegel: Critical Assessments*. Ed. Robert Stern, New York: Routledge, 1993.

Dewey, John. *Democracy and Education*. New York: The Free Press, 1966.

Elshtain, Jean Bethke. *Public Man, Private Woman*. Princeton, N.J.: Princeton University Press, 1981.

Elster, Jon. *Making Sense of Marx*. Cambridge: Cambridge University Press, 1985.

Engelbrecht, H. C. *Johann Gottlieb Fichte: A Study of his Political Writings with Special Reference to his Nationalism*. New York: AMS Press, 1968.

Engels, Friedrich. *Herr Eugen Duhring's Revolution in Science*. Moscow: Co-operative Publishing Society of Foreign Workers in the U.S.S.R., 1934.

Engels, Friedrich. "The Tactics of Social Democracy." In *Marx-Engels Reader*, 2nd edition. Ed. Robert C. Tucker, New York: Norton, 1978.

Erckenbrecht, Ulrich. *Marx' Materialistische Sprachtheorie*. Kronberg: Scriptor, 1973.

Felix, David. *Marx as Politician*. Carbondale: Southern Illinois Press, 1983.

Feuerbach, Ludwig. *Principles of the Philosophy of the Future*. Trans. Vogel. Indianapolis: Hackett Publishing, 1986.

Fiala, Andrew. "Aesthetic Education and the Aesthetic State: Hegel's Response to Schiller." In *Hegel's Aesthetics*. Ed. William Maker, Albany: State University of New York Press, 2000.

Fiala, Andrew. "The Irony of Political Philosophy." *Philosophy in the Contemporary World* 5:1 (Fall, 1999).

Friedrich the Great of Prussia. *Anti-Machiavelli*. Trans. Paul Sonnino, Athens, Ohio: Ohio University Press, 1981.

Gadamer, Hans-Georg. *Truth and Method* 2nd Revised Edition. Trans. Joel Weinsheimer and Donald G. Marshall, New York: Continuum, 1993.

Gilligan, Carol. *In a Different Voice*. Cambridge: Harvard University Press, 1982.

Goetschals, Willi. *Constituting Critique*. Trans. Eric Schwab, Durham, N.C.: Duke University Press, 1994).

Gourevitch, Victor. "Philosophy and Politics I." *Review of Metaphysics* 22: 58–84.

Gourevitch, Victor. "Philosophy and Politics II." *Review of Metaphysics* 22: 281–328.

Gueroult, Michel. "*La Doctrine Fichtéenne du Droit.*" In *Études Sur Fichte*. Hildesheim: Georg Olms Verlag, 1974.

Gueroult, Michel. "*Fichte et la Revolution Française.*" In *Études Sur Fichte*. Hildesheim: Georg Olms Verlag, 1974.

Habermas, Jürgen. *Philosophical Discourses of Modernity*. Trans. Lawrence, Cambridge: MIT Press, 1995.

Habermas, Jürgen. "Philosophy as Stand-In and Interpreter." In *Moral Consciousness and Communicative Action*. Trans. Lenhardt and Nicholsen, Cambridge: MIT Press, 1995.

Habermas, Jürgen. *Structural Transformation of the Public Sphere*. Trans. Burger, Cambridge: MIT Press, 1991.

Habermas, Jürgen. *Theory and Practice*. Trans. Viertel, Boston: Beacon, 1974.

Haman, Johann Georg "*Metakritik uber den Purismus der Vernunft.*" In *Hamann Sämtliche Werke* 3: 281–289. Wien: Herder Verlag, 1951.

Hardimon, Michael. *Hegel's Social Philosophy: The Project of Reconciliation*. Cambridge: Cambridge University Press, 1994.

Heidegger, Martin. *Kant and the Problem of Metaphysics*. Trans. Taft, Bloomington: Indiana University Press, 1990.

Heinrichs, Johannes. "*Nationalsprache und Sprachnation.*" In *Fichte-Studien* 2 (1990).

Hennigfeld, Jochem. "*Fichte und Humboldt—Zur Frage der Nationalsprache.*" In *Fichte-Studien* 2 (1990).

Henrich, Dieter. "Kant's Notion of a Deduction and the Methodological Background of the First Critique." In *Kant's Transcendental Deductions*. Ed. Eckart Förster, Stanford, Calif.: Stanford University Press, 1989.

Herder, Johann Gottfried. "Letters for the Advancement of Humanity." *Herders Samtliche Werke* vol. 17. Berlin: Weidmann, 1877–1913.

Herder, Johann Gottfried. *Verstandund Erfahrmy* in J. G. Merder Werke, volume 8. Frankfurt am Main: Deutscher Klassiker Verlag, 1985.

Hobbes, Thomas. *Leviathan*. Ed. C. B. Macpherson, London: Penguin Classics, 1985.

Horkheimer, Max. "Authority and Family." In *Critical Theory: Selected Essays*. New York: Continuum, 1995.

Houlgate, Stephen. *Freedom, Truth and History*. New York: Routledge, 1991.

Howard, Dick. *From Marx to Kant*. 2nd ed. New York: St. Martin's Press, 1993.

Howard, Dick. *The Politics of Critique*. Minneapolis: University of Minnesota Press, 1989.

Humboldt, Wilhelm von. *On Language: On the Diversity of Human Language Construction and its Influence on the Mental Development of the Human Species*. Trans. by Peter Heath, Cambridge: Cambridge University Press, 1999.

Hyppolite, Jean. *Introduction to Hegel's Philosophy of History*. Trans. Bond Harris and Jacqueline Bouchard Spurlock. Gainesville: University Press of Florida, 1996.

Johnston, David. *The Rhetoric of Leviathan: Thomas Hobbes and the Politics of Cultural Transformation*. Princeton, N.J.: Princeton University Press, 1986.

Kedourie, Elie. *Hegel and Marx*. Oxford: Blackwell, 1995.

Kelley, George Armstrong. *Idealism, Politics, and History*. Cambridge: Cambridge University Press, 1969.

Kersting, Wolfgang. "Politics, Freedom, and Order: Kant's Political Philosophy." In *Cambridge Companion to Kant*. Ed. Paul Guyer, Cambridge: Cambridge University Press, 1992.

Kojève, Alexandre. *Introduction to the Reading of Hegel*. New York: Basic Books, 1969.

Lauer, Quentin. *Hegel's Idea of Philosophy*. New York: Fordham University Press, 1971.

Leibniz, G. W. *New Essays On Human Understanding*. Trans. and ed. Peter Remnant and Jonathan Bennett, Cambridge: Cambridge University Press, 1981.

Leibniz, G. W. von *Philosophical Papers and Letters*. 2 vols. Trans. and ed. by Leroy E. Loemker, Chicago: University of Chicago Press, 1956.

Lemos, Ramon M. *Rousseau's Political Philosophy*. Athens : University of Georgia Press, 1977.

Lenin, Vladimir. *What Is To Be Done?* New York: International Publishers, 1961.

Lerner, Max. Introduction to Machiavelli's *The Prince and The Discourses*. New York Modern Library, 1950

Levin, Michael. "'The Hungry Forties': The Socio-Economic Context of the Communist Manifesto." In *The Communist Manifesto: New Interpretations*. Ed. Mark Cowling, New York: New York University Press, 1998.

Locke, John. *An Essay Concerning Human Understanding*. 2 vols. Ed. by Alexander Campbell Fraser, New York: Dover Publications, 1959.

Locke, John. "Letter Concerning Toleration." In *Classics of Modern Political Philosophy*. Ed. Steven M. Cahn, Oxford: Oxford University Press, 1997.

Locke, John. *Second Treatise of Government*. Ed. C. B. Macpherson, Indianapolis: Hackett Publishing, 1980.

Locke, John. *Some Thoughts Concerning Education*. In *The Educational Writings of John Locke*. Ed. by James L. Axtell, Cambridge: Cambridge University Press, 1968.

Löwith, Karl. *From Hegel to Nietzsche*. Trans. David E. Green, New York: Columbia University Press, 1964.

Lukács, Georg. *Destruction of Reason*. Trans. Peter Palmer, Atlantic Highlands, N.J.: Humanities Press, 1981.

Lukács, Georg. *History and Class Consciousness*. Trans. Livingstone, Cambridge, Mass.: MIT Press, 1992.

Lukács, Georg. *The Ontology of Social Being*. Trans. Fernbach, London: Merlin Press, 1982.

Luxemburg, Rosa. "Marxism or Leninism." In *The Russian Revolution and Leninism or Marxism*. Ann Arbor: University of Michigan Press, 1961.

Lyotard, Jean-Francois. *Le Differend*. Paris: *Les Editions de Minuit*, 1983.

Machiavelli, Nicolo. *The Prince and the Discourses*. New York: Modern Library, 1950.

MacIntyre, Alisdair. *After Virtue*. Notre Dame: Notre Dame University Press, 1984.

MacKinnon, Catherine. *Toward a Feminist Theory of the State*. Cambridge: Harvard University Press, 1989.

MacPherson, C. B. Editor's Introduction to John Locke's *Second Treatise of Government*. Indianapolis: Hackett Publishing, 1980.

MacPherson, C. B. *Political Theory of Possessive Individualism*. Oxford: Clarendon Press, 1962.

Maker, William. *Philosophy Without Foundations*. Albany: State University of New York Press, 1994.

Marcuse, Herbert. *Hegel's Ontology and the Theory of Historicity*. Trans. Seyla Benhabib, Cambridge, Mass.: MIT Press, 1987.

Marcuse, Herbert. *One-Dimensional Man*. Boston: Beacon Press, 1964.

Marcuse, Herbert. *Reason and Revolution*. Atlantic Highlands, N.J.: Humanities Press, 1983.

Mates, Benson. *The Philosophy of Leibniz*. Oxford: Oxford University Press, 1986.

McCumber, John. *The Company of Words*. Evanston, Ill.: Northwestern University Press, 1983.

Meinecke, Freidrich. *The Age of German Liberation, 1795–1815*. Trans. Paret and Fischer, Berkeley: University of California Press, 1977.

Meinecke, Friedrich. *Die Idee der Staatsräson in der neueren Geschicht*. München: R. Oldenbourg, 1925.

Meister, Robert. *Political Identity: Thinking Through Marx*. Cambridge, Mass.: Basil Blackwell, 1990.

Miller, Richard. *Analyzing Marx*. Princeton, N.J.: Princeton University Press, 1984.

Miller, Richard. "The Consistency of Historical Materialism." In Cohen et al., *Marx, Justice, and History*. Princeton, N.J.: Princeton University Press, 1980.

Moore, Stanley. "A Consistency Proof for Historical Materialism." In Cohen et al., *Marx, Justice, and History*. Princeton, N.J.: Princeton University Press, 1980.

Moore, Stanley. "Marx and Lenin as Historical Materialists." In Cohen et al., *Marx, Justice, and History*. Princeton, N.J.: Princeton University Press, 1980.

Nehamas, Alexander. *The Art of Living*. Berkeley: University of California Press, 1998.

Neuhauser, Frederick. "Fichte and the Relationship between Right and Morality." In *Fichte: Historical Contexts/Contemporary Controversies*. Ed. Daniel Breazeale and Tom Rockmore. Atlantic Highlands, N.J.: Humanities Press, 1994.

Nussbaum, Martha. "Four Paradigms of Philosophical Politics." *The Monist* 83: 4 (2000).

Nussbaum, Martha. *The Fragility of Goodness*. Cambridge: Cambridge University Press, 1986.

Olson, Alan M. *Hegel and the Spirit: Philosophy as Pneumatology*. Princeton, N.J.: Princeton University Press, 1992.

Osterreich, Peter L. "*Politische Philosophie oder Demagogie*?" in *Fichte-Studien* 2 (1990).

Peivatolo, Maria Chiara. "The Juridical Nature of Pure Reason." In *Ratio Juris* 12: 3 (1999).

Pelczynski, Z. A. "Introductory Essay" to *Hegel: Political Writings*. New York: Garland Publishing Inc., 1984.

Pinkard, Terry. *Hegel: A Biography*. Cambridge: Cambridge University Press, 2000.

Pinkard, Terry. *Hegel's Dialectic: The Explanation of Possibility*. Philadelphia: Temple University Press, 1988.

Pinkard, Terry. *Hegel's Phenomenology: The Sociality of Reason*. Cambridge: Cambridge University Press, 1996.

Pippin, Robert J. *Idealism as Modernism*. Cambridge: Cambridge University Press, 1997.

Plato. *Apology*. In *Four Texts on Socrates*. Trans. Thomas G. West and Grace Starry West. Ithaca, N.Y.: Cornell University Press, 1984.

Plato, *Gorgias*. Trans. Terence Irwin. Oxford: Clarendon Press, 1979.

Pocock, J. G. A. "Custom and Grace, Form and Matter." In *Machiavelli and the Nature of Political Thought*. Ed. Martin Fleisher, New York: Atheneum, 1972.

Pöggeler, Otto. Editorial Introduction to Hegel, *Lectures on Natural Right and Political Science: The First Philosophy of Right (1817–18)*. Trans. J. Michael Stewart and Peter C. Hodgson, Berkeley: University of California Press, 1995.

Pöggeler, Otto. "*Hegel et Machiavel: Renaissance Italienne et Idéalisme Allemand.*" *Archives de Philosophie* 41 (1978): 435–467.

Popper, Karl. *The Open Society and Its Enemies*. 2 vols. Princeton, N.J.: Princeton University Press, 1971.

Postema, Gerald J. "Public Practical Reason: Political Practice." In *Theory and Practice*. Ed. Shapiro and DeCew, New York: New York University Press, 1995.

Radrizzani, Ives. "Fichte's Transcendental Philosophy and Political Praxis." Trans. Cristina Bianchi-Murillo and Daniel Breazeale. In *New Perspectives on Fichte*. Ed. Daniel Breazeale and Tom Rockmore, Atlantic Highlands, N.J.: Humanities Press, 1996.

Riemer, Neal. *Karl Marx and Prophetic Politics.* New York: Praeger, 1987.

Ritter, Joachim. *Hegel and the French Revolution.* Trans. Richard Dien Winfield. Cambridge, Mass.: MIT Press, 1982.

Rockmore, Tom. *Fichte and Marx*. Carbondale: Southern Illinois University, 1980.

Rockmore, Tom. *Hegel's Circular Epistemology*. Bloomington: Indiana University Press, 1986.

Rousseau, Jean-Jacques. *Discourse on the Origin of Inequality,* in *The Social Contract Discourse on the Origin of Inequality.* Ed. by Lester G. Crocker, New York: Washington Square Press, 1967.

Rousseau, Jean-Jacques. *Émile*. Trans. Barbara Foxley, London: Everyman, 1993.

Rousseau, Jean-Jacques. *Rousseau Oeuvres Politiques*. Paris: Bordas, 1989.

Rousseau, Jean-Jacques. *The Social Contract in The Social Contract and Discourse on the Origin of Inequality.* Ed. by Lester G. Crocker, New York: Washington Square Press, 1967.

Sallis, John. *Spacings of Reason and Imagination in Texts of Kant, Fichte, and Hegel*. Chicago: University of Chicago Press, 1987.

Sandel, Michael. *Liberalism and the Limits of Justice*. Cambridge: Cambridge University Press, 1982.

Saner, Hans. *Kant's Political Thought*. Trans. E. B. Ashton, Chicago: The University of Chicago Press, 1973.

Schwartz, Joseph M. *The Permanence of the Political*. Princeton, N.J.: Princeton University Press, 1995.

Schwartz, Justin. "The Paradox of Ideology." *Canadian Journal of Philosophy* 23, no. 4, (December 1993).

Sluga, Hans. *Heidegger's Crisis*. Cambridge: Harvard University Press, 1993.

Soll, Ivan. *Introduction to Hegel's Metaphysics*. Chicago: University of Chicago Press, 1969.

Sophocles. *Antigone.* Trans. Robert Fagles. New York: Penguin, 1982.

Steiner, George. *After Babel.* Oxford: Oxford University Press, 1975.

Strauss, Leo. *What is Political Philosophy?* Chicago: University of Chicago Press, 1988.

Suchting, Wal. "What is Living and What is Dead in the Communist Manifesto?" In *The Communist Manifesto: New Interpretations*. Ed. Mark Cowling, New York: New York University Press, 1998.

Surber, Jere Paul. "German Idealism under Fire." In *Hegel and the Modern World.* Ardis Collins, ed. Albany: State University of New York Press, 1995.

Surber, Jere Paul. *Language and German Idealism*. Atlantic Highlands, N.J.: Humanities Press, 1996.

Surber, Jere Paul. "The Problems of Language in German Idealism: An Historical and Conceptual Overview." In O. K. Wiegand et al., eds. *Phenomenology on Kant, German Idealism, Hermeneutics, and Logic*. Dordrecht, The Netherlands: Kluwer Academic Publishers, 2000.

Taminiaux, Jacques. "Hegel and Hobbes." In Jacques Taminiaux, *Dialectic and Difference*. Atlantic Highlands, N.J.: Humanities Press, 1985.

Taylor, Charles. *Hegel*. Cambridge: Cambridge University Press, 1975.

Taylor, Charles. "The Opening Arguments of the *Phenomenology*." In *Hegel: A Collection of Critical Essays*. Ed. Alasdair MacIntyre, Garden City, N.J.: Doubleday, 1972.

Thalmann, Marianne. *The Literary Sign Language of German Romanticism*. Detroit: Wayne State University Press, 1972.

Tucker, Robert. "Marx as a Political Theorist." In *Marx's Socialism*. Ed. Shlomo Avineri, New York: Lieber-Atherton, 1972.

Tunick, Mark. *Hegel's Political Philosophy*. Princeton, N.J.: Princeton University Press, 1992.

Walzer, Michael. *Spheres of Justice*. New York: Basic Books, 1983.

Wetherly, Paul. "A Capitalist State? Marx's Ambiguous Legacy" In *The Communist Manifesto: New Interpretations*. Ed. Mark Cowling, New York: New York University Press, 1998.

Wilks-Heeg, Stuart. "The Communist Manifesto and Working-Class Parties in Western Europe." In *The Communist Manifesto: New Interpretations*. Ed. Mark Cowling, New York: New York University Press, 1998.

Wittgenstein, Ludwig. *Philosophical Investigations*. Trans. G. E. M. Anscombe, New York: Macmillan, 1968.

Wood, Allen. *Karl Marx*. London: Routledge and Kegan Paul, 1981.

Wood, Allen. "The Marxian Critique of Justice." In *Marx, Justice, and History* . Ed. Cohen, Nagel, Scanlon, Princeton, N.J.: Princeton University Press, 1980.

Wood, Neal. *The Politics of Locke's Philosophy*. Berkeley: University of California Press, 1983.

Yack, Bernard. *The Longing for Total Revolution.* Berkeley: University of California Press, 1986.

Young, Iris Marion. *Justice and the Politics of Difference*. Princeton, N.J.: Princeton University Press, 1990.

General Index

Citation Index